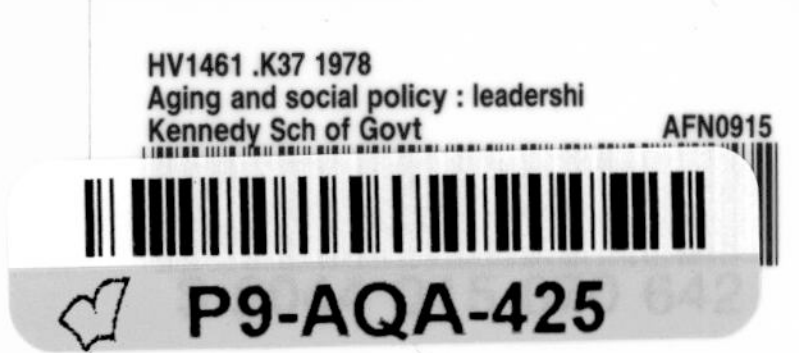

Aging and Social Policy

Aging and Social Policy

Leadership Planning

Patricia L. Kasschau

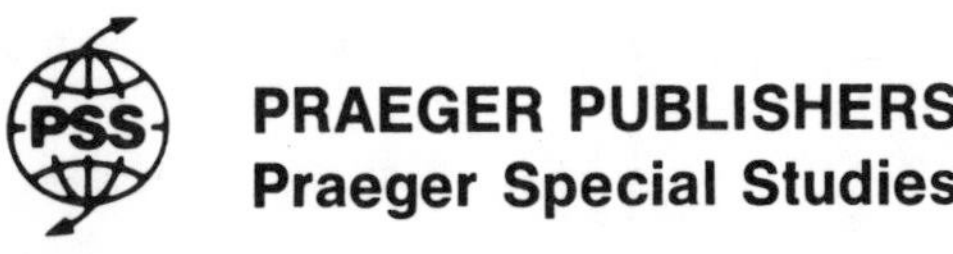

New York • London • Sydney • Toronto

Library of Congress Cataloging in Publication Data

Kasschau, Patricia.
Aging and social policy.

Includes bibliographical references.
1. Aged--United States. 2. Aged--United States--Economic conditions. 3. United States--Social policy. I. Title.
HB1461.K37 1978 362.6'0973 78-15481

ISBN 0-03-046411-0

This material was prepared with the support of the National Science Foundation Grant No. APR75-21178. However, any opinions, finding, conclusions, and/or recommendations expressed herein are those of the author and do not necessarily reflect the views of NSF.

PRAEGER PUBLISHERS
PRAEGER SPECIAL STUDIES
383 Madison Avenue, New York, N.Y. 10017, U.S.A.

Published in the United States of America in 1978
by Praeger Publishers,
A Division of Holt, Rinehart and Winston, CBS, Inc.

89 038 987654321

Printed in the United States of America

To John Bullaro, age 81

PREFACE

Starting from the premise that social problems exist by virtue of the way they are collectively defined in a particular society, this book undertakes to survey the way in which a cross section of the decision-making community responsible for developing and implementing programs to assist the elderly collectively define the problems of growing old and assess the parameters for social policy intervention. Structured interviews averaging nearly two hours were conducted with legislators, agency administrators and program heads, supervisory service delivery personnel, corporate directors of personnel, union local presidents, and advocates for the aged. The subject matter of those interviews ranged through income maintenance, health care, housing, transportation, employment, and retirement.

Analysis of the interview data focuses upon the way in which a decision-maker's perspectives on aging and social policy are influenced first and foremost by his position in the policy process, which would structure his contact with elderly people and hence his perceptions of their needs and problems; and secondarily by his biographical characteristics, including age, sex, ethnicity, and educational background, which could be expected to mold contrasting personal life experiences that might also influence his perceptions of the problems people face as they grow old. Additionally, the decision-makers' perspectives on aging and social policy are compared with the perceptions and policy recommendations offered by the elderly themselves.

The results of this five-year survey reveal a striking lack of congruence between reported needs and perceived needs in many areas of planning and program development in the field of aging. Many decision-makers operate on the basis of considerable misinformation about the needs and problems of elderly people, and existing programs and policies intended to assist the elderly frequently seem to reflect planning based on these misperceptions. The decision-makers' planning orientations are often influenced by their position in the policy process and the degree or nature of their involvement with elderly people structured by that professional role. The decision-makers' personal characteristics, on the other hand, generally have a less dramatic and less consistent impact on their analyses of the policy issues.

The role of decision-makers' planning orientations in a policy process frequently dominated by political bargaining, institutional imperatives, economic constraints, and the like is difficult to analyze. For this reason, in lieu of evaluating the import of these decision-makers' planning orientations within any single theoretical framework that the author might choose to describe the operation of the policy process, the decision-makers' perceptions of the elderly's problems together with their recommendations for social policy redress are interpreted within a number of contrasting and sometimes complementary models of the policy process. Thus, policies and programs are variously considered as the outcome of rational problem-solving, interest-group activity, elite preferences, institutional activity, and incremental policy-making.

Each of these models focuses upon different aspects of the climate of decision-making that shapes aging program outcomes. Hence, each of these models is used to explore different research questions with the decision-maker data. For example, from the rational perspective, the book is concerned with how accurately the decision-makers perceive the elderly's pressing problems; from an interest-group perspective, the volume explores whether advocates for the aged accurately reflect their constituents' demands or needs; and from the incremental model, the text monitors whether decision-makers prefer to make minor modifications in existing programs in lieu of major overhauls in program design or operation.

Americans persist in their goal to develop more enlightened social policies to redress the nation's enduring social problems. Policy-makers, policy analysts, and the general public alike are concerned about how to get more and better information into the policy-making process. Only in relatively recent history, however, have the advances in social science research methodologies and the establishment of computerized national data banks provided even the rudimentary capabilities to plan assistance programs on the basis of accurate information about needs in the population and the relative effectiveness of alternative intervention strategies.

Although even the most optimistic supporters of efforts to institutionalize rational planning mechanisms in the policy process would have to admit those efforts have been only marginally effective to date, occasions nevertheless do occur when rational planning contributes significantly to program outcomes. For instance, in times of a perceived crisis requiring immediate policy action, or when public opinion is aroused by an issue, decision-makers are considerably more likely to plan program responses on the basis of available empirical information that documents the problem and suggests the most effective means of intervention. In such circumstances, it becomes relevant to understand how decision-makers propose to solve the problems confronting the nation's elderly. These data thus offer the opportunity to see how a cross section of the decision-making community suggests handling the fiscal crisis confronting the social security retirement trust fund or the mobility crisis confronting millions of handicapped elderly.

Information regarding the knowledge gaps or apparent misperceptions of the decision-makers can inform advocates, service providers, professional groups, researchers, and other interested persons as to where and when to intervene in the policy process in order to educate decision-makers about the needs and problems of elderly people or about the best strategies for social intervention. The data on decision-makers' attitudes and perceptions detailed in this volume can inform advocates working on behalf of the elderly about where in the decision-making community they are likely to find support for their proposals and where they are likely to find strong opposition. With that knowledge, these advocates should emerge more effective brokers on behalf of the elderly within the policy process.

Students of the policy process should be interested to learn what these data suggest about program implementation in bureaucratic settings. From the standpoint of obtaining program outcomes consistent with legislatively enacted guidelines, the congruence of perceptions among legislators, agency administrators and program heads, and service delivery personnel is certainly an important consideration. Where lacking, there could be serious implications for program implementation in the community. Similarly, in the private sector, where labor and management concur in their assessment of the problems confronting older workers and retirees, it bodes well for the development of new programs that can help these older workers to make adjustments on the job or ease their transition into retirement. These data highlight areas in the public and private sectors where program development may be stymied by dissension in the decision-making community.

Hopefully this book will stimulate further research on the attitudes, perceptions, and policy preferences of public officials and decision-makers in the private sector. The opinions and beliefs of those in positions to affect the development or implementation of programs and policies to assist various target groups in the population have heretofore received far too little attention in research efforts devoted to gaining a better understanding of the climate of decision-making that shapes program outcomes.

As the product of a five-year research project, this book is published by the efforts of many in addition to the author. Their contributions are recognized here, and I express my deepest appreciation to them: to my colleagues on the project, Lamar Empey, Vern Bengtson, Pauline Ragan, Sally Moore, Barbara Myerhoff, Andrei Simic, Stephen McConnell, Bill Davis, Fernando Torres-Gil, Deborah Newquist, Mary Simonin, Mel Henry, and James Dowd; to the staff of the UCLA Institute for Social Research who were responsible for data collection and data reduction, but especially to Eve Fielder and Vy Dorfman, who supervised those tasks; to the team of typists, Alex Pinkston, Edna Bell, Mayda Vera, and Joanne Maize; and to the two administrative assistants on the project, Elaine Correy and Jan Wolverton. A special debt is owed to Robert Binstock, who offered useful comments on earlier drafts of the book. Finally, appreciation must be expressed to the National Science Foundation, which funded this project generously for five years under its RANN (Research Applied to National Needs) program. The opinions expressed in this book are those of the author alone, however, and do not necessarily reflect the view of the National Science Foundation.

CONTENTS

Chapter | Page

Chapter | Page

Chapter | Page

Chapter | Page

LIST OF TABLES AND FIGURES

Table		Page

Table		Page

1 The Role of Policy Leadership Planning in Structuring Social Policy on Aging

This study of policy leadership planning in the field of aging explores how decision-makers who have some formal responsibility in the development of aging programs and policies view the problems of the elderly and assess the potential for social policy intervention. In-depth interviews were conducted with a cross section of the decision-making community in metropolitan Los Angeles County in order to examine the diverse perspectives on aging and social policy entertained by policy-makers, policy administrators, service providers, advocates for the aged, and business and union management officials. The data analysis is intended to identify the values and beliefs, attitudes and opinions, and perceptions and predilections of these decision-makers and thereby contribute to a better understanding of the "climate of decision-making" in which programs and policies for the aged are currently fashioned.

Implicit in the survey design and data analysis of this research are certain assumptions about the nature of social problems and social policy intervention that merit some discussion in order to understand more fully how the decision-makers' planning orientations outlined in this report may ultimately affect real-world program outcomes in the field of aging. The major assumptions are two. First, social problems do not exist in the objective arrangement of social institutions and processes in society but rather in the way in which individuals in the society collectively define the social problem. Second, participants in the policy process are not, for the most part, engaged in rationally solving the nation's social problems but rather must make policy decisions within the constraints imposed by the political bargaining process, existing institutional arrangements, budgetary limitations, and other restricting influences in the policy-making environment. Elaboration of these perspectives on social problems and social policy, particularly as they set the stage for the present investigation of decision-makers' orientations toward aging as a social problem, is the central concern of this introductory chapter.

AGING AS A SOCIAL PROBLEM IN U.S. SOCIETY

Social problems have often been analyzed as if they existed as an objective condition in the institutions and other social arrangements of the society. An alternative perspective that has guided the design of this research suggests that a social problem is the product of a highly selective process of collective definition within a society and that the social problem exists primarily as a function of the way in which it is defined in that society.[1] According to this conceptualization of the nature of social problems, not every harmful social condition in a society constitutes a social problem. Indeed, history provides numerous examples of dire social conditions gone unnoticed or unattended in societies with disastrous consequences. More accurately, then, many problems compete for societal recognition, but few emerge as full-blown, legitimated social problems within any one society at any one point in time. Societal recognition necessarily entails a collective definition of the social problem. It is this societal definition that structures the social problem in reality. It gives the social problem its nature, lays out how it is to be approached, and shapes what is to be done about it. In the process of arriving at this collective definition, every social problem is the focal point for the engagement of divergent and often conflicting interests, intentions, and objectives of different collectivities within the society, and it is the interplay of these interests and objectives that constitutes the way in which the society deals with the social problem.

Aging has achieved recognition as a serious social problem in U.S. society, although only in relatively recent time. As late as the 1930s, when the elderly in nearly all Western European nations were guaranteed at least some economic security in their postemployment years by virtue of government-operated old-age social insurance systems, Americans persisted in the belief that care of the indigent elderly rested with the individual's own family, private charity, or state and local public welfare agencies. Even as the rolls of these private and public welfare organizations swelled to the point of bankruptcy with the ballooning size of the elderly population throughout the first third of the twentieth century, considerable resistance endured to organizing those "charity" functions in formal structures at the federal level of government. Subsequent passage of the Social

Security Act in 1935, which established an old-age insurance system in the United States, was viewed with suspicion by many Americans who perceived the program as institutionalized welfare indistinguishable from the other New Deal programs they adamantly opposed. Today, however, the overwhelming majority of the public, young and old alike, believes the government should assume the primary responsibility in providing care for the aged. Only a small minority still maintains that the primary responsibility rests with the individual and/or his family.[2] Even among the ethnic subcultures where extended family contact and assistance persist as the promoted norm, government is still held most accountable for care of the elderly.[3]

The government's participation in solving the multiple problems confronting the nation's elderly, beyond guaranteeing a small replacement income to those no longer working in their later years, materialized very slowly at first but has escalated rapidly in the past few decades. Throughout the 1950s, 1960s, and 1970s, the federal government has become involved in the provision of a range of essential services to the aged population. The National Housing Act of 1956 authorized the first large-scale construction of nonprofit housing for the aged. A decade later, the 1965 amendments to the Social Security Act established medicare, a national health insurance system of sorts for the aged. And today, a diverse number of smaller programs exist to serve other identified needs in the elderly population: homemaker services, hot meals in congregate or home settings, special transportation services, multipurpose senior citizen centers, community service employment and volunteer programs, and multiphasic health screening clinics for senior citizens. In total, the federal government in 1976 supported more than 50 programs housed in nearly half as many different agencies that provided significant services to the elderly population. The majority of those programs had been in operation only a decade or less. A similar, if somewhat slower, proliferation of aging programs has occurred at the state and local levels of government over the same period of time.

But the problems of the aging are not easily redressed by social policy intervention. In spite of social security, more than one in six elderly persons continue to live on incomes that are below the official poverty guideline. A decade after the enactment of national health insurance for the aged, the elderly pay more out-of-pocket medical expenses annually than they did the year preceding the enactment of medicare. Following a full two decades of housing construction programs designed specifically for the elderly, less than 3 percent of the elderly population has been rehoused, although an estimated one in five continue to live in substandard housing.[4] This is strong evidence that effective problem-solving is not the probable outcome of social policy deliberations, a discussion to be revisited in the latter part of this chapter. The persistence of such problems despite public policy action means additionally that aging must continually be relegitimated as a pressing social problem in U.S. society. Only if the elderly and their advocates are successful in publicizing the elderly's ongoing problems will aging programs continue to receive attention in public policy deliberations and thus be assured of receiving some share of the national resources distributed annually by this complex decision-making process. Hence, agencies and organizations that operate aging programs annually scramble to increase their budget allocation on the premise that expanded staff and programs are required to address the elderly's pressing needs. The definition of aging as a social problem is thus an ongoing process of "renewed claims-making" within the policy process.[5]

DECISION-MAKERS VIEW AGING AS A SOCIAL PROBLEM: AN EMPIRICAL INVESTIGATION

To the extent that the aging social problem is fashioned by the process of collective definition in the U.S. context, the contrasting perceptions of the elderly's problems and the alternative policy preferences that are entertained by the various decision-makers who are instrumental in shaping policies and programs for the aged must certainly constitute an important contribution to the continuing relegitimation of aging as a social problem. From their disparate roles within the policy process, decision-makers undoubtedly operate with preexisting value orientations, attitude sets, and policy preferences that will inevitably influence how they handle any specific policy issue.

Specifically, decision-makers' preexisting values and attitudes may be expected to mediate their recognition of the existence of a social problem, influence whether the identified problem is considered appropriate or amenable to social policy intervention, structure the definition of a problem so as to identify those aspects that are amenable to external modification through policy intervention, and, finally, restrict the range of alternative policy intervention strategies that are evaluated to redress the identified problem. To be sure, other political, social, and economic aspects of the policy process--institutional arrangements, idiosyncrasies of political actors, and budgetary constraints, for instance--structure the way in which social problems are identified and addressed by various social programs. Nonetheless, the decision-makers' own preexisting policy orientations remain an important component of the climate of decision-making that affects specific policy outcomes. A discussion of how decision-makers' perspectives on social problems and social policy may influence policy outcomes, given other, often more important determinants of decision-making in the political process such as those enumerated above, is reserved for later analysis in this chapter.

Despite the vastly increasing redistribution of society's resources to the aged mandated by decision-makers in the United States,[6] very little is known about how these decision-makers perceive the elderly population and the problems of growing old. Still less is known about the strategies of program intervention that these decision-makers prefer or the limits that they place on such policy interventions in the lives of older Americans. To illustrate, what do these decision-makers consider the appropriate role for public policy versus private sector responses to the identified needs of the elderly? To what extent do they believe that providing for the later years is still the responsibility of the individual and/or his family? Where public social programs seem required to guarantee the elderly a reasonable quality of life, do these decision-makers believe the needs of the aged can be satisfied through generic assistance programs that serve the general public or do they believe categoric programs must be designed that will serve the elderly exclusively? Do the decision-makers prefer income subsidy or benefits-in-kind program assistance for the elderly? Do decision-makers prescribe a life of engagement and social participation for the elderly or do they idealize a life of retirement and reduced community involvement? Questions such as these are to be addressed in this volume with data collected from in-depth structured interviews with 316 decision-makers in federal, state, and local positions who make policy decisions that impact directly on elderly persons residing in Los Angeles County.

As suggested earlier, widespread recognition that aging is a serious social problem in U.S. society in no way implies that there is collective agreement regarding how to solve the most pressing problems confronting the elderly. The impetus for this research was a limited number of articles appearing in professional journals that suggested decision-makers do not always possess accurate information about the needs or problems of the elderly population, decision-makers often hold negative attitudes toward the elderly, the decision-makers' attitudes affect the decisions they make in their professional capacity relating to the elderly, and decision-makers' perspectives concerning the problems of aging and the appropriate modes of policy intervention vary according to their formal position in the policy process.[7]

This study of decision-makers' attitudes regarding aging and social policy thus made a special effort to sample the diverse views on the problems and solutions that potentially exist in the policy process. Many policy analysts consider existing social policy as merely the prevailing compromise between the various points of view represented in the policy process. In order to gain an accurate understanding of the policy-making climate in which aging programs are developed, representative decision-makers were sampled from a variety of positions in the policy process to ensure eliciting multiple perspectives on the issues in aging social policy. The sample of decision-makers in this study was designed in application of a systems model of the policy process outlined by Leonard Goodwin in his work at the Brookings Institution. His schematic conceptualization of the policy process detailing the operation of a single national public program proved particularly appropriate in application to the range of public programs in aging that were the focus of this study. (See Figure 1.1 for a diagram of his model, slightly modified for the purposes of this study.)

The sample of 316 decision-makers interviewed in this study was composed of six separate subsamples representing the various strata in the Goodwin systems model of the policy process.

Legislators--The Role of Policy Enactment

This subsample in Goodwin's description is composed of "persons who, through legislation and appropriations, define and provide resources for meeting the problem." The legislative decision-makers interviewed in this study included, from the local level, individuals from the Los Angeles County Board of Supervisors and the mayors and city councilmen from the five largest cities in Los Angeles County (Los Angeles, Long Beach, Torrance, Glendale, and Pasadena); from the state level, Senate and Assembly representatives elected from Los Angeles County, members of the Joint Legislative Committee on Aging, and the chairing legislator of other selected committees in the state legislature (among them Employment, Retirement, Transportation, Taxation, Health, and Urban Development and Housing Committees); and from the national level, U.S. senators and representatives elected from Los Angeles County. Seventy-one legislators were interviewed.

Agency Administrators--The Role of Policy Elaboration

In the administrative system, Goodwin located "persons charged with overall responsibility for administering the various programs that will presumably solve the problem." Directors of

FIGURE 1.1

Model of the Systems Involved in the Operation of a National Public Program

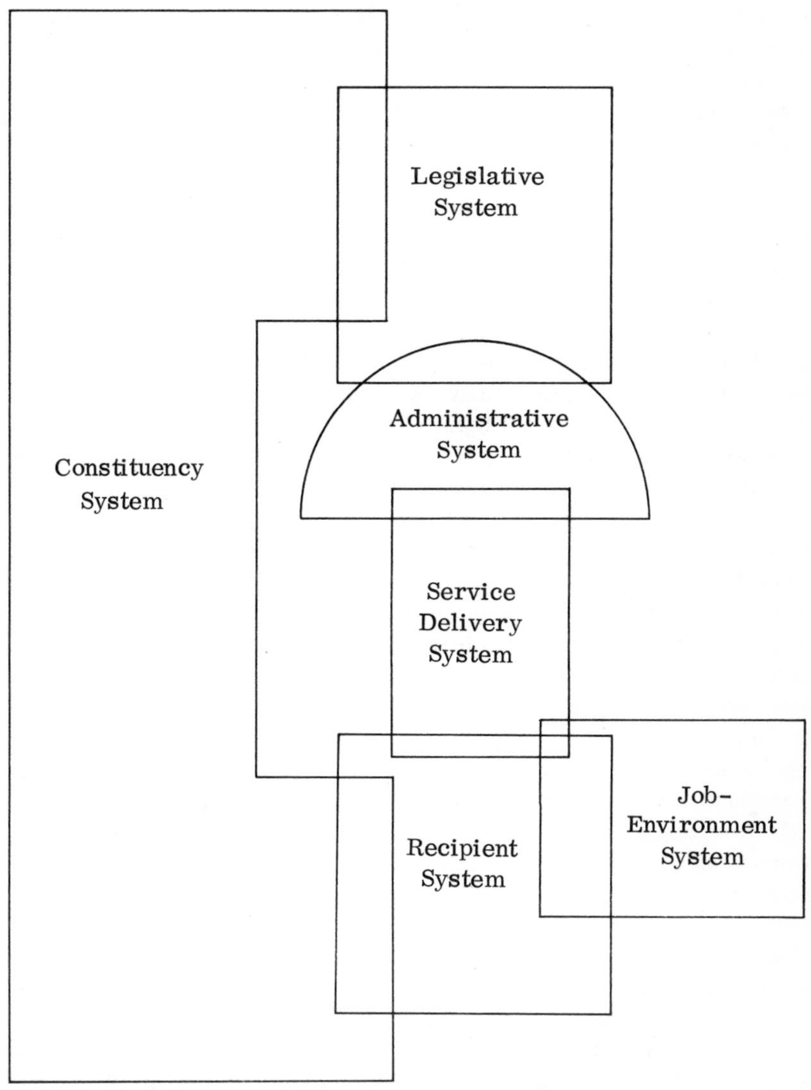

Source: Reproduced by special permission from Leonard Goodwin, "Bridging the Gap between Social Research and Public Policy: Welfare, a Case in Point," Journal of Applied Behavioral Science 9, no. 1 (January/February 1973): 89. Copyright 1973 NTL Institute for Applied Behavioral Science.

categoric assistance programs that exclusively or primarily served the elderly, directors of generic assistance programs that served the elderly as one of many constituencies, and top-level agency administrators in local, state, and federal positions who typically bore responsibilities extending beyond aging programs to other programs and other constituencies were interviewed in each of the following public social service hierarchies: health services, nursing homes and protective services, housing and urban development, transportation, income maintenance, employment, recreation, and senior citizens affairs. Seventy such administrators were sampled.

Service Delivery Personnel--The Role of Program Implementation

The service delivery system in Goodwin's model includes "the people who interact with recipients and actually provide, under the guidelines of the administrative system, the services mandated by the [legislators]." To enhance interpretation of the similarities or differences that might emerge in the decision-makers' perceptions regarding aging and social policy dependent on their role or position in the policy process, every effort was made to trace the natural linkages between the subsample of service delivery personnel and the subsample of administrative agency heads and program directors. Thus, service delivery personnel were interviewed from the same programs in the same agencies identified in the subsample of administrative agency heads and included physicians, nurses, and social workers in the health care and nursing home systems, housing program aides or counselors, transit program operators, financial or retirement consultants, employment counselors, recreation center directors, and staff workers in senior citizens affairs offices. In all, 70 professionals engaged in delivering services to the elderly were interviewed.

Corporate Directors of Personnel--Corporate Decision-Making in the Private Sector

Decision-makers were sampled from the private sector as well as from the public sector. Business and labor management certainly fashion policies concerning employment, retirement, and income maintenance that impact very directly on the life circumstances of older Americans. The corporate directors of personnel in 35 of the largest California corporations headquartered in Los Angeles County were interviewed. The following industries were among those represented: utilities, financial institutions, aerospace firms, food manufacturing and drug chains, media and entertainment industries, medical and insurance organizations, basic metal and chemical manufacturing businesses, computer and electronics firms, and construction and oil companies. The corporate director of personnel was interviewed because he was typically the single person ultimately responsible for hiring, firing, and promotion procedures, on the one hand, and the administration of employee benefits, such as pensions and insurance, on the other.

Union Local Presidents--The Complement to Corporate Decision-Making in the Private Sector

The subsample of 35 union representatives was constructed so as to maintain the natural parallelism with the corporate subsample. Thus the unions included in this sample were those most likely to be representing employees at the corporations identified in the corporate subsample. Among those unions selected were public employees' unions, construction unions, chemical and metalworkers' unions, food and merchandising unions, media unions, and clothing workers' unions. In each organization, the chief ranking officer was interviewed.

Advocates for the Aged--Middlemen for the Aged in the Policy Process

Yet another important contribution to the policy process is made by the advocate groups that seek to influence policy outcomes in directions favorable to the elderly (such advocate groups are not directly specified in the Goodwin model, though perhaps they are subsumed under his "constituency system"). In Los Angeles County, there exists a countywide network of advocacy on behalf of the elderly that is based on the grass-roots work of nearly 50 local committees on aging. The president of each of these committees was included in the advocate subsample. Additionally, a number of independent organizations are actively engaged in lobbying for better programs for the elderly in the county and the state, and the president of each of these organizations was included in the advocate subsample. In total, 35 advocates for the elderly were interviewed.

The sample description suggests the complexity and richness of the data on decision-makers' perceptions of aging social policy that are to be presented in this volume. Moreover, these data are to be supplemented with data from a companion survey of Los Angeles County residents aged 45 to 74, which was conducted concurrently with the study of decision-makers. (See the appendix for an expanded description of the conceptual framework integrating the decision-maker study with the companion community survey.) Although the data from the community survey have been analyzed independently and are presented in a separate volume of research findings, occasional reference will be made to the findings of the community survey for the purpose of comparing constituent, client, or recipient perspectives on aging and social policy with those of the decision-makers in this sample.

In-depth structured interviews were conducted with the sample of 316 decision-makers in 1974. The interviews averaged 1 hour and 40 minutes and covered a wide range of current topics concerning aging social policy, which each decision-maker was asked to discuss from his own perspective. They were queried about what they considered to be the most pressing problems confronting elderly persons in obtaining good health care, achieving a decent income, finding adequate housing, getting around in the city, securing a job or staying employed, and so on. The decision-makers were then asked to recommend feasible policy solutions for the problems thus identified. They were requested to evaluate some existing policies and programs providing aid to the elderly; where the decision-makers perceived that programs failed to reach the goals of intervention, they were encouraged to recommend modifications in those programs or to suggest new programs that might better accomplish the desired intervention. The decision-makers further speculated about long-range planning to meet the needs of future generations of the elderly in the United States.

The interview also probed the decision-makers' perceptions regarding various facets of the policy process itself. For example, the decision-makers enumerated the sources of information on which they rely to obtain information about the needs and problems of the aging population. They offered their own evaluations regarding the adequacy of the information base on which they must rely to construct effective intervention strategies to assist the elderly. The success of the elderly as an emerging interest group in the political bargaining process proved a popular topic with these decision-makers. They reflected, too, on their own opportunities for input into structuring aging program outcomes within the policy process. Such was the substance of the structured interview administered to all 316 decision-makers.

One assumption of this study, as discussed earlier, is that decision-makers approach the deliberations over specific policy or program issues in the field of aging with preexisting notions about the nature of aging as a social problem and the appropriate modes of social policy assistance. Anticipating that a decision-maker's perceptions of the elderly's problems and his predilection to elect one or another mode of policy intervention are influenced by, among other things, his position in the policy process, the sample for this study was designed to interview decision-makers from multiple locations within the policy process. The rationale for this study suggests that the perceptions and predilections of these decision-makers are often in opposition or conflict with one another and that the temporal resolution of these conflicting perspectives constitutes the way in which the social system manages the aging social problem. It thus becomes important to understand how a cross section of the decision-making community defines the problems of growing old and assesses the parameters of social policy intervention intended to ameliorate the life circumstances of the elderly.

THE POLICY PROCESS AND SOLVING THE NATION'S SOCIAL PROBLEMS: THE AGING PROBLEM

What role do decision-makers' values, attitudes, perceptions, and policy preferences actually play in shaping program outcomes in the policy process? Despite the focus of this study on decision-makers' planning orientations, one should not assume that these or any decision-makers necessarily seek first and foremost to solve the problems confronting elderly people. To adopt such a perspective would ignore that social policy proposals are typically brokered many times over, initially in the adoption stage by the trade-off for votes to ensure enactment and later in the implementation stage by the vested interests of administering agencies.[8] Hence, the second assumption underlying this survey of decision-makers in the field of aging is that these participants in the policy process do not make their decisions or govern their actions by what would maximize benefits to the elderly; rather, other motives--career ambitions, budgetary trade-offs, agency survival needs, and so on--contribute to and often dominate the decision-maker's thoughts and actions in circumstances where the decision outcome may directly and significantly affect the welfare of senior citizens.

The brief history of aging legislation is replete with examples of programs developed far less in response to the documented needs of the elderly than in response to political exigencies, organizational imperatives, economic constraints, social or philosophical dictates, and other considerations. Old-age social insurance was enacted in the United States more in response to the needs of the depressed economy than the needs of older workers.[9] Medicare began as a movement to revolutionize health care services in this country in order to provide national health insurance coverage to all Americans, but as a result of the compromises in consecutive legislative proposals exacted by the health professions, medicare was reduced to a plan of limited hospital coverage for social security recipients.[10] Even advocates for the aged, by the competition among their respective aging organizations to gain the coveted middleman role in the administration of certain aging programs, have inadvertently killed legislative proposals benefiting the elderly.[11]

The fundamental economic, biomedical, and social problems confronting the elderly remain unchanged by the several decades of public policy activity devoted to improving the life circumstances of the elderly. In 1968, the Task Force on Older Americans concluded that most programs for the aged, "while promising in direction, are too fragmented and limited in scale to reverse the trends that bar aging persons from opportunities to participate in the benefits and responsibilities of American life."[12] The indictment is no less true in the mid-1970s.

It is difficult to say how much of the failure of public policy to redress adequately the problems of the aging is due to the magnitude and complexity of the problems and how much to inefficient intervention strategies. But the belief persists that programs designed on the basis of documented needs and efficiently implemented with minimal bureaucratic machinery would go considerably farther toward eliminating the elderly's problems than the programs currently in existence, which have been diluted in goals by political compromises and fragmented in service delivery by vested agency interests. Despite the repeated appeals from all sectors of the policy environment to adopt more rational modes of decision-making that would focus more exclusively on solving the nation's social problems (among them, aging), history confirms that policies and programs for older Americans will continue to be enacted and implemented in a decision-making context that can only produce brokered program solutions to the elderly's problems in the tradition of social security, medicare, or the Older Americans Act.

The climate of decision-making refers to the aggregate of contextual variables and environmental forces that shape the content of social policy outcomes. All too often, when policy outcomes are adjudged to fall short of rational solutions to perceived problems, the policy process itself is condemned as completely political and arbitrary. Actually, most policies are established through some combination of rational planning, incrementalism, interest-group activity, elite preferences, competition, systemic or environmental forces, and institutional or organizational imperatives.[13] Understanding how decision-makers' planning orientations specifically relate to aging social policy and program outcomes requires an appreciation of the complex external forces and constraints that are part of the decision-making context.

The climate of decision-making is so complex in terms of the numbers and kinds of decisions being made that ultimately shape policy outcomes that observers can typically isolate only a small sector or facet of the policy process for analysis at any one time. Accordingly, there exist a number of conceptually distinct models of the policy process, each focusing on different aspects of decision-making and each proposing different explanations for the causes and consequences of social policy outcomes. Though policy analysts and observers may personally prefer one perspective, each of these models contributes to understanding the policy process and program outcomes.

Several contrasting models are outlined briefly here, including examples of the kinds of questions proponents of each perspective might seek to answer with these data on decision-makers' perceptions.

Policy as the Outcome of Rational Problem-Solving

Here the decision-maker is a rational actor who assesses needs and goals, evaluates policy alternatives, and then opts for the policy that will most efficiently attain the desired goal. Policy outcomes are expected to be relevant to expressed needs and efficient in implementation. Though this model persists as an ideal, the barriers to rational planning and problem-solving are so pervasive as to preclude the appearance of this mode of decision-making in pure form in the real-world policy process.[14] Nevertheless, it is useful for those who desire to locate barriers to rational problem-solving in existing policy arrangements.

Proponents of this perspective should be interested in learning from the results of this study how accurately the sample of decision-makers perceives the needs and problems of the elderly population. While rational problem-solving would not be guaranteed even if the decision-makers did possess accurate information about the problems, rational solutions would be impossible without it. As a corollary, proponents of this model of the policy process would undoubtedly be interested in ascertaining the decision-makers' awareness of the existing information base in the field of aging. To what extent do the decision-makers rely upon the available empirical data base as opposed to obtaining information about aging problems from other "accurate" sources, such as family and friends, occasional chats with elderly constituents or clients, mass media reports, and the like?

Policy as the Outcome of Interest-Group Activity

According to this much-used model, individual citizens who share common interests band together to press their demands on the government.[15] Politics is characterized by the constant struggle among these advocate groups to influence policy allocation decisions in their favor, and policy outcomes reflect the temporary equilibrium achieved among the competing demands of these groups. Decision-makers are depicted as endlessly responding to group pressures and attempting to balance competing bids from multiple constituencies.

Examining the decision-maker data from this perspective, the reader would probably inquire whether the advocates for the aged, purporting as they do to represent the elderly's best interests, more accurately articulate their expressed needs than do other decision-maker groups. Similarly, are the legislators, who as elected officials are the usual targets of influence attempts by advocates or the elderly themselves, more sensitive than other segments of the decision-making community to the expressed needs of elderly residents? Finally, are advocates and legislators especially sensitive to the emergence of "senior power"? Are they more likely than the other decision-makers to assert that the elderly will obtain their fair share in the distribution of society's resources only if they organize politically and lobby on their own behalf in the policy process?

Policy as the Outcome of Elite Preferences

In this third model, policy is viewed as reflecting the preferences and values of the governing elite in the political system. In direct contrast to the interest-group model of the policy process, which emphasizes popular activism, the public or the masses in the elite preference model are depicted as relatively silent or passive generally because they are viewed as ill-informed and/or apathetic. Elite values and preferences shape the prevailing public opinion, not vice versa. Thus, whereas influence flows upward in the interest-group model, policies flow downward in the elite model. This is not to say that elite values run counter to the public's "best interest"; indeed, elites may show considerable regard for the welfare of the masses in their enacted policies and programs. Finally, the elite model suggests that the elites tend to exhibit considerable consensus concerning the fundamental values in society and the broad goals of social policy intervention. Though elites may disagree from time to time on implementation of goals in policy, the range of disagreement is quite restricted; elites agree on more matters than they disagree.[16]

The data at hand provide the elite model proponents with several issues to explore. Is the decision-making community as a whole in agreement about certain basic issues regarding care of the elderly, for example, the role of the family and the concept of relative responsibility, the reliance on income subsidies versus services-in-kind to assist the aged, and the appropriate division of labor between private sector and public sector responsibility in meeting the needs of the elderly? A second line of inquiry focuses upon whether the elite decision-makers impose their own perceptions of the elderly's problems on policy outcomes, albeit in the spirit of doing only what appears to be required for the elderly's own "best" interests, but nevertheless in complete disregard of the elderly's expressed needs and desires? Do decision-makers' perceptions of the problems confronting the elderly agree or conflict with the perceptions of elderly residents themselves; and, if conflicting, which point of view, elite or consumer, do existing policies and programs reflect?

Policy as the Outcome of Institutional Activity

The fourth perspective suggests that policy outcomes are largely influenced by institutional arrangements in the public and private sectors. Institutions are structured patterns of behavior among individuals or groups. Because they persist over time with relatively little change, these institutional arrangements may exercise considerable influence over policy outcomes. For example, institutional arrangements may facilitate adoption of some policies and programs and impede the implementation of others. Institutional arrangements may structure access of groups and/or individuals to the arena of decision-making, giving greater access to some groups than to others.

A clear illustration of this perspective on policy-making is the considerable debate that has waged for years over the best location for the Administration on Aging in the federal government. Many have argued that placing it higher within the Department of Health, Education and Welfare (HEW) bureaucracy, or giving it independent status outside of HEW, or, even better, placing an Office on Aging at the cabinet level in the White House would each give aging advocates greater access to top-level decision-makers, thereby creating greater visibility for the problems of the aging, which should result in greater allocation of resources to aging programs. This model enjoys considerable popularity, if one can judge by the number of bureaucratic reorganizations that are undertaken in the spirit of effecting subsequent changes in policy outcomes.[17]

With the data collected from the sample of decision-makers, the institutional perspective of policy-making would frame yet another set of questions. Agencies and organizations have survival needs, for without the continuation of their existing programs, they may be reduced in size or phased out. Similarly, individuals have survival needs in their own jobs; if their program is cut back or eliminated, their jobs could be jeopardized. Thus proponents of this model might inquire whether categoric decision-makers (for example, officials in senior citizens affairs), as well as individuals working in categoric positions within generic agencies (for example, older worker specialists in state employment offices), specifically emphasize the unique aspects of the elderly's problems and the need for categoric programs to solve these problems. In contrast, individuals in generic positions or agencies might be expected to emphasize the commonalities of the elderly's problems with other groups in the population and hence recommend serving the elderly as one of many client groups in their agency's generic programs.

To pursue a slightly different slant on the same theme, do the data reveal that legislators prefer income solutions because money is a resource that these decision-makers can manipulate directly themselves through established income-maintenance systems? In contrast, do agency administrators and service providers prefer to redress those same problems through service programs precisely because these decision-makers would be in line to manage such programs themselves?

Policy as the Outcome of Incremental Changes

A fifth and final model assesses policy outcomes as minor changes in preexisting policies and programs. Decision-makers agree on the utility of existing programs and agree to continue in the same direction, with perhaps only an increase or decrease in budget allocation or minor modifications in the program itself. Many programs are cast in this mode of decision-making. Typically, a full investigation of program alternatives is not possible or feasible, and so the decision-makers endorse what's already in operation. Moreover, existing programs probably have already gained a measure of legitimacy by having been in operation a number of years, whereas any new program would be a political risk in terms not only of substantive outcome but also of public acceptance. Finally, in a pluralist political economy such as that of the United States, it is far easier to agree to continue the existing mesh of programs that provide something for nearly everyone than it is to engage in overall social planning. In other words, incrementalism is politically feasible. Agreement is far more easily achieved over budget increments or modifications in existing programs than it is over major redirections in policy or radical program modifications.[18]

From the decision-maker data, proponents of the incremental model would inquire to what extent the decision-makers recommend minor modifications as opposed to radical revisions in existing policies and programs. The data, for example, reveal the extent these decision-makers think in terms of changing benefit levels as opposed to revamping the coordination between the social security and private pension systems in order to provide more adequate income maintenance to the elderly, or the extent decision-makers concern themselves with minor additions to medicare coverage rather than considering a fully comprehensive national health insurance plan for the elderly?

These five models are merely conceptual tools that focus on different aspects of decision-making in the policy system. Though one mode of decision-making may appear dominant from time to time, in reality all are operative to some extent. Rarely, if ever, do policies reflect the exclusive influence of one mode of decision-making. Policies typically are a combination of rational planning, incrementalism, elite preferences, interest-group activity, institutional constraints, and other social forces. The various conceptual models have been outlined here in order to suggest the kinds of questions that can be examined with these data on the decision-makers' perspectives on aging and social policy in the mid-1970s.

NOTES

1. Elaboration on this perspective may be found in the following books and articles: Howard S. Becker, Social Problems: A Modern Approach (New York: Wiley, 1966); Herbert Blumer, "Social Problems as Collective Behavior," Social Problems 18, no. 3 (Winter 1971): 298-306; John I. Kituse and Malcolm Spector, "Toward a Sociology of Social Problems: Social Conditions, Value-Judgments, and Social Problems," Social Problems 20, no. 4 (Spring 1973): 407-19; Malcolm Spector and John I. Kituse, "Social Problems: A Reformulation," Social Problems 21, no. 2 (Fall 1973): 145-59.

2. Louis Harris and Associates, The Myth and Reality of Aging in America (Washington, D.C.: National Council on the Aging, 1975).

3. Ben M. Crouch, "Age and Institutional Support: Perceptions of Older Mexican Americans," Journal of Gerontology 27, no. 4 (October 1972): 524-29; Pauline K. Ragan and J. Eugene Grigsby, "Responsibility for Meeting the Needs of the Elderly for Health Care,

Housing and Transportation: Opinions Reported in a Survey of Blacks, Mexican Americans and Whites" (Paper presented at the Annual Meeting of the Western Gerontological Association, San Diego, March 29, 1976).

4. U.S. Department of Health, Education and Welfare, Facts about Older Americans 1975, DHEW Publication No. OHD 75-20006, 1975.

5. Spector and Kituse, "Social Problems."

6. For an informative discussion of the expanding allocation of federal budget expenditures to aging programs, consult Edward R. Fried et al., Setting National Priorities: The 1974 Budget (Washington, D.C.: Brookings Institution, 1973).

7. A limited review of the literature in gerontology since 1960 uncovered a number of relevant empirical studies that had investigated service providers' and professionals' attitudes toward elderly clients. Some of the published findings, readily available to the interested reader, are cited here: Pat M. Keith, "Evaluation of Services for the Aged by Professionals and the Elderly," Social Services Review 49, no. 2 (June 1975): 271-78; Mark J. Riesenfeld et al., "Perceptions of Public Service Needs: The Urban Elderly and the Public Agency," Pt. I, Gerontologist 12, no. 2 (Summer 1972): 185-90; John Colombotos, "Physicians and Medicare: A Before-After Study of the Effect of Legislation on Attitudes," American Sociological Review 34, no. 3 (June 1969): 318-34; Tom Hickey et al., "Attitudes toward Aging as a Function of In-Service Training and Practitioner Age," Journal of Gerontology 31, no. 6 (November 1976): 681-86; Rodney M. Coe, "Professional Perspectives on the Aged," Pt. I, Gerontologist 7, no. 2 (June 1967): 114-19; Catherine Cyrus-Lutz and Charles M. Gaitz, "Psychiatrists' Attitudes toward the Aged and Aging," Pt. I, Gerontologist 12, no. 2 (Summer 1972): 163-67; Phyllis Mutschler, "Factors Affecting Choice of and Perseveration in Social Work with the Aged," Pt. I, Gerontologist 11, no. 3 (Autumn 1971): 231-41; Louis Lowy, "Roadblocks in Group Work Practice with Older People," Pt. I, Gerontologist 7, no. 2 (June 1967): 109-14; Margaret E. Campbell, "Study of the Attitudes of Nursing Personnel toward the Geriatric Patient," Nursing Research 20, no. 2 (March-April 1971): 147-51; Donald L. Spence and Elliott M. Feigenbaum, "Medical Student Attitudes toward the Geriatric Patient," Journal of the American Geriatrics Society 16, no. 9 (September 1968): 976-83; Jordan I. Kosberg, "Opinions and Expectations of Nursing Home Administrators," Journal of Sociology and Social Welfare 2, no. 1 (Fall 1974): 73-80; Harold Wilensky and Joseph E. Barmack, "Interests of Doctoral Students in Clinical Psychology in Work with Older Adults," Journal of Gerontology 21, no. 3 (July 1966): 410-14; Jordan I. Kosberg and Johanna F. Gorman, "Perceptions toward the Re-

habilitation Potential of Institutionalized Aged," Gerontologist 15, no. 5 (October 1975): 398-403; David M. Levine, "Staffing Patterns and Professional Profiles of the Health Care Manpower," Gerontologist 15, no. 4 (August 1975): 314-17; Marie T. Latz, Study of Decision-Making on Public Welfare Programs for the Aged, 2 vols. (Harrisburg, Pa.: Office for the Aging, Department of Public Welfare, 1965); Jordan I. Kosberg et al., "Comparison of Supervisors' Attitudes in a Home for the Aged," Pt. I, Gerontologist 12, no. 3 (Autumn 1972): 241-45.

8. For a good discussion of the political dilemmas attendant to social intervention strategies, consult Robert H. Binstock and Martin A. Levin, "The Political Dilemmas of Intervention Policies," in The Handbook of Aging and the Social Sciences, ed. Robert H. Binstock and Ethel Shanas (New York: Van Nostrand-Reinhold, 1976), pp. 511-35.

9. Leonard D. Cain, "The Growing Importance of Legal Age in Determining the Status of the Elderly," Gerontologist 14, no. 2 (April 1974): 167-74.

10. Theodore R. Marmor, The Politics of Medicare (Chicago: Aldine, 1973).

11. Robert H. Binstock, "Interest-Group Liberalism and the Politics of Aging," Pt. I, Gerontologist 12, no. 3 (Autumn 1972): 265-80.

12. Reported in Robert H. Binstock, Planning--Background and Issues, 1971 White House Conference on Aging (Washington, D.C.: U.S. Government Printing Office, 1971), p. 10.

13. An excellent introduction to policy analysis is to be found in Thomas R. Dye, Understanding Public Policy, 2nd ed. (Englewood Cliffs, N.J.: Prentice-Hall, 1975).

14. For penetrating criticisms of the rational decision-making model of the policy process, see Graham T. Allison, Essence of Decision: Explaining the Cuban Missile Crisis (Boston: Little, Brown, 1971); and Raymond A. Bauer and Kenneth Gergen, The Study of Policy Formation (New York: Free Press, 1968). There have, nevertheless, been efforts to salvage the model and give it limited application. See Dye, Understanding Public Policy; Alfred J. Kahn, Theory and Practice of Social Planning (New York: Russell Sage Foundation, 1969).

15. See Dye, Understanding Public Policy; Theodore J. Lowi, The End of Liberalism (New York: Norton, 1969); David B. Truman, The Governmental Process: Political Interests and Public Opinion (New York: Knopf, 1951).

16. Dye, Understanding Public Policy; Heinz Eulau and Robert Eyestone, "Policy Maps of City Councils and Policy Outcomes: A Developmental Analysis," American Political Science Review 62,

no. 1 (March 1968): 124-43; Harold D. Lasswell, "Agenda for the Study of Political Elites," in Political Decision-Makers, ed. Dwayne Marvick (New York: Free Press, 1961), pp. 264-87.

17. Dye, Understanding Public Policy; A. Lee Fritschler, Smoking and Politics: Policymaking and the Federal Bureaucracy, 2nd ed. (Englewood Cliffs, N.J.: Prentice-Hall, 1975); Harold Seidman, Politics, Position and Power: The Dynamics of Federal Organization (New York: Oxford University Press, 1970).

18. See Binstock and Levin, "The Political Dilemmas of Interventive Policies"; Dye, Understanding Public Policy; David Mechanic, "Sociological Critics versus Institutional Elites in the Politics of Research Application: Examples from Medical Care," in Social Policy and Sociology, ed. N. J. Demerath III et al. (New York: Academic Press, 1970), pp. 99-108; Charles E. Lindblom, "The Science of Muddling Through," Public Administration Review 19, no. 2 (Spring 1959): 79-88.

2 The Climate of Decision-Making in the Field of Aging: A Select Overview

Chapter 1 discussed how decision-makers' planning orientations (consisting of their general attitude sets, their basic value system, their selective perceptions, and their global policy preferences) might affect their policy decisions and thereby program outcomes, despite numerous constraints inherent in the policy process itself (including budgetary constraints, institutional barriers, and political impasses) that also operate continuously upon the decision-makers in the execution of their professional responsibilities. The focus now narrows to the substance of those planning orientations and the ways in which it affects social provision for the elderly.

Of central importance to understanding decision-makers' planning orientations is learning how they see elderly people in general. That is, how do decision-makers see the elderly in terms of their income resources, health status, social integrations, and competence or capacity for independent living? Such perceptions would naturally constitute the operating assumptions and preconceptions about the elderly upon which these decision-makers would be seeking to design and implement various social assistance programs. Most revealing then, would be an overlay of the decision-makers' views with empirical data describing the elderly's actual life circumstances.

Closely related to the decision-makers' general image of the elderly population is their assessment of the problems that they believe elderly people typically encounter as they grow old. Based upon their selective perceptions of the elderly's personal resources and life circumstances, the decision-makers conceivably would tend to focus their attention on selected problems facing the elderly and overlook other perhaps equally pressing problems afflicting many elderly residents. Hence, it is important to learn whether the decision-makers' assessments of the elderly's problems agree with those reported by the elderly themselves.

Decision-makers' selective perceptions of the elderly's problems, together with their basic value orientations, would predictably structure their choices among alternative modes of social intervention to assist the elderly, for example, supplying additional money as opposed to providing in-kind service delivery programs. Further, the decision-makers' evaluations of the ability of most elderly to manage competently on their own with little or no assistance from outside sources may be expected to influence how the decision-makers assess the desirability and effectiveness of long-term planning to meet the needs of future generations of the elderly in the United States. In short, planning for the needs of today's elderly can be expected to structure the way in which the decision-makers seek to prepare for providing services to future generations of elderly.

The present chapter focuses upon each of these issues, but only in a general overview, the purpose of which is to provide basic background information on the way decision-makers typically view the elderly and their problems and by the way they assess the broad parameters of social intervention. Subsequent chapters will explore in far greater detail the decision-makers' perceptions of the problems and solutions in numerous specific policy-making contexts: income maintenance, health care, housing, transportation, and employment/retirement.

In addition simply to describing the decision-makers' planning orientations, this and subsequent chapters attempt to explain why decision-makers may hold certain opinions, attitudes, or perceptions. As was explained in Chapter 1, an assumption was made in designing the sample that a decision-maker's planning orientations would reasonably be expected to vary according to the kind of contact he has with elderly people, which in turn would be significantly structured by his professional position within the policy process. Specifically, subsequent analyses of the decision-makers' perceptions will examine whether they vary systematically according to the kind of position which the decision-maker occupies in the policy process (for example, legislator versus advocate), the extent of contact he has with elderly people in the performance of his job (for example, working with elderly people is a major versus a minor part of his job), and also the decision-maker's primary area of substantive expertise (for example, income maintenance versus housing).

Additionally, however, it seems reasonable to posit that a decision-maker's personal biographical characteristics, such as his age, education, sex, or ethnicity,[1] might also shape his attitudes toward the aging social problem independent of the perceptions he might entertain on the basis of the position he holds in the policy process. The data reveal that the decision-maker's position often influences his perceptions about aging and social policy, whereas his personal or biographical characteristics exhibit far less dramatic and consistent influence on his perceptions. Nevertheless, this and the following chapters analyze the decision-makers' attitudes toward the aging problem and attempt to explain whatever differences of opinion found to exist among the decision-makers in terms of either the position occupied by the individual in the policy process or, where pertinent, in terms of his personal biographical characteristics. Preliminary to analyzing the decision-makers' perceptions of the aged, then, we take a closer look at the demographic characteristics of the sample of 316 decision-makers in order to learn more about the individuals whose observations on aging and social policy compose the substance of this book.

SELECTED DEMOGRAPHIC CHARACTERISTICS OF THE 316 DECISION-MAKERS

Not surprisingly, the sample of 316 decision-makers interviewed in this survey turned out to be mostly white, middle-aged males with at least a college education, if not also a professional degree (see Table 2.1). One half of the sample was 50 years of age or younger, although relatively few were under the age of 35. Three quarters of the decision-makers interviewed were men, and the minority of women in the sample was disproportionately represented in the service delivery subsample. The position of minorities in this sample bore a striking resemblance to that of women, namely, the minority decision-makers were outnumbered by their white counterparts three to one and the minority respondents were also disproportionately represented among the service provider group. Women and minorities in this broad cross section of the decision-making community held very few of the positions that wield relatively great amounts of authority or discretionary decision-making power. For the most part, the role of women and minorities in the policy-making arena still appears relegated to the level of service provider, where they are responsible for implementing programs designed by others.

As expected in a sample of elites, these decision-makers were highly educated. Two thirds had completed college and more than one third had completed professional degree programs beyond the college diploma. Five of six agency administrators had at least completed college compared to only one out of six union local presidents. The advocates for the aged were the only other subsample in which significantly less than two out of three (only 40 percent) had completed college.

TABLE 2.1

Selected Demographic Characteristics of the Final Sample of Decision-Makers (sample size = 316)

Age	Percent	Education	Percent
24-34	11	Some high school	2
35-44	20	High school graduate	12
45-54	31	Some college	20
55-64	28	College graduate	31
65 and over	10	Predoctoral graduate work (MA, MS, MSW, RN, and so on)	23
Sex			
Male	73		
Female	27	Doctoral degree or equivalent (PhD, MD, JD, DDS, and so on)	14
Ethnicity			
White	74		
Black	13		
Mexican American	9	Major	
Other	4	Business	16
Tenure in present position		Social science	13
		Law	8
Less than one year	14	Social work	5
One or two years	26	Humanities	4
Three or four years	23	Life science	4
Five to nine years	21	Medicine	4
Ten to fourteen years	10	Education	4
Fifteen years or more	5	Nursing	4
No response	1	Engineering	3
		Public health	2
		Miscellaneous	9
		No response	23

Source: Compiled by the author.

The turnover of occupants in the policy process is rather substantial, if this sample represents a fair cross section of the decision-making community. Half had been in their respective positions three years or less and nearly two out of three for under five years. Nearly two thirds of the agency administrators (62 percent) had been in their present position two years or less. The union local presidents, on the average, enjoyed the longest tenure in their present position--well over one quarter of them (29 percent) had been head of their local for ten years or more.

The sample was designed to include both categoric and generic decision-makers, that is, those who were primarily or exclusively concerned with aging programs in their position and those who had responsibilities for programs that served the general public with the elderly, thus composing only one of their constituencies. Implicit was the belief that those who work more closely with aged persons might view the elderly's problems differently from those who work with the aged only in a more distant capacity.

Table 2.2 reflects the spread in the final sample among generic and categoric decision-makers. One in four claimed aging programs were the primary or exclusive focus of their position; five out of six of the advocates, for example, reported lobbying exclusively for elderly constituencies. Another quarter of the decision-maker sample reported that aging programs were an important but not central part of their job responsibilities; a majority of the legislators in the sample, for instance, defined their association with the elderly in this light.

TABLE 2.2

The Centrality of Working with Aging Persons to the Decision-Maker's Position in the Policy Process*

Decision-Maker's Position in the Policy Process (percent)	The Major Focus	An Important Part	A Minor Part	Total
Legislators	7	54	39	71
Agency administrators	37	31	32	70
Service delivery personnel	34	20	46	70
Corporate directors of personnel	0	17	83	35
Union local presidents	3	14	83	35
Advocates for the aged	83	9	9	35
Total				
Percent	27	28	44	99
Number	85	88	143	316

*As defined by the respondent himself.

Source: Compiled by the author.

Finally, a little less than one half of the sample of 316 decision-makers asserted that aging programs played only a minor role in their job functions. Fully five out of six of the corporate personnel directors and the union local presidents claimed they had little to do with the problems of the aging. It should be remembered, however, that personnel directors can facilitate or obstruct hiring and promotion of older workers, while union leaders are responsible for representing the best interests of older and retired workers in the collective bargaining process. Thus, whether or not these officials recognize and assume their responsibilities for promoting the welfare of older and retired workers, their professional obligations to do so persist, and for that reason they have been included in the sample.

DECISION-MAKERS' IMAGE OF THE AGED

Collectively, the decision-makers in this sample make innumerable decisions that directly or indirectly affect the well-being of many elderly people; indeed, many of these decisions purportedly are promulgated specifically in the interest of improving the life circumstances of the elderly. It is thus germane to inquire into the decision-makers' perceptions of the elderly's life circumstances together with the decision-makers' evaluations of the elderly's ability to manage their daily affairs competently and in an independent manner. It is important to understand to what extent these decision-makers depict the elderly in welfare-dependent terms--impoverished, in frail health, lonely and isolated, unable to keep pace with younger generations and the changes in society.

Apart from their own personal observations about old age, these decision-makers generally concurred that old age is viewed negatively in contemporary U.S. society (see Table 2.3). Advocates for the aged proved the most sensitive to the unfavorable cultural image of aging, although the administrative and professional staff in government agencies also subscribed to this opinion relatively more often than the rest of the decision-making community. Senior citizens affairs specialists and mental health counselors in particular were very concerned about the elderly's negative image. In general, the more involved the decision-maker was with programs for the elderly, the more likely he was to believe that old age is negatively viewed in the United States. This attitude has been directly reflected in the delivery of services to the elderly population in the past.

The prestige of professionals derives in no small measure from the prestige of the clientele they serve. Because the elderly command relatively little prestige in this society (in contrast to

TABLE 2.3

"Do You Feel That Old Age Is Negatively Viewed in Contemporary American Society?"
(percent responding "yes")

Positional Characteristics of the Decision-Makers	
Position in the Policy Process	
Legislators (N = 71)	62
Agency administrators (N = 70)	73
Service delivery personnel (N = 70)	77
Corporate directors of personnel (N = 35)	60
Union local presidents (N= 35)	63
Advocates for the aged (N = 35)	83
Responsibility for Aging Programs	
Primary function (N = 85)	78
Important but not central function (N = 88)	73
Minor function (N = 143)	64
Area of Program Expertise	
Health (N = 37)	73
Mental health (N = 23)	91
Housing (N = 29)	76
Employment (N = 92)	63
Income maintenance (N = 26)	62
Recreation/leisure (N = 18)	67
Senior citizens affairs (N = 49)	82
Generalists (N = 42)	60
Personal Characteristics of the Decision-Makers	
Age of the Respondent	
Under 45 (N = 98)	76
45-54 (N = 98)	65
55-64 (N = 90)	66
65 and over (N = 30)	80
Sex of the Respondent	
Male (N = 230)	65
Female (N = 86)	84
Ethnicity of the Respondent	
White (N = 235)	71
Minority (N = 81)	67
Educational Level of the Respondent	
High school graduate or less (N = 42)	52
Some college (N = 64)	73
College graduate (N = 99)	73
Postcollege professional education (N = 111)	71
Total (N = 316)	70

Source: Compiled by the author.

children, for instance), old people in need do not easily gain the attention of professionals. It is well documented that generic agencies frequently neglect serving the aged even when the elderly compose a sizable segment of the target groups these practitioners purport to serve, for example, inner-city residents, the poor, the sick, and the ill-housed.

The decision-makers' own impressions about aging and the aged were generally none too positive, and in some cases, none too accurate. Many stereotyped the elderly in welfare-dependent terms that went far beyond what available statistics would warrant. A brief survey will suffice to sketch the broad outlines of the decision-makers' operating assumptions and preconceptions about the elderly as a target population for social assistance.

Probably the single best indicator of the decision-makers' assessment of the well-being of the aged in the United States is their evaluation of the elderly's income status. Adequate income to procure food, housing, clothing, medical care, transportation, and so on is crucial to maintaining a decent quality of life at any age. It is all the more critical in old age because, in the event of physical disability and limited mobility, money can mean the difference between securing appropriate in-home support services and thus maintaining a relatively independent lifestyle in the community or being forced to move into an institutional or congregate setting for those remaining years. Adequate income is essential to maintaining a lifestyle of independence in old age.

At the time of this survey, 1974, approximately one out of every six older Americans (16 percent of 3.4 million of the elderly nationwide) lived on incomes equal to or less than the government-designated poverty income line.[2] A Los Angeles County survey conducted by the Community Analyses Bureau, an agency sponsored jointly by the city of Los Angeles and Los Angeles County, in that year found 20 percent of the county's elderly residents living on incomes at or below poverty income guidelines established by the federal government's Office of Equal Opportunity (OEO). But a single figure is a deceptive way to describe poverty in the elderly age group. For one thing, there are clearly marked pockets of poverty within the aged population; among single, female, and minority subgroups in the elderly population, the percentage of elderly poor is several times higher than it is in the total elderly population.[3] Equally important to consider, too, are the many elderly who live only marginally above the official poverty income line. When the near-poor are included with the poor, the percentage of elderly persons living under serious income constraints rises to one in four.[4]

In light of these statistics, the sample of decision-makers interviewed in this study collectively far overestimated the incidence of severe poverty in the elderly population. When asked, "What percentage of elderly people in Los Angeles would you estimate are living at or below the poverty level (based on OEO figures of $2,330 per person or $3,070 per couple per year)?" the decision-makers' estimates ranged from 0 to more than 95 percent, and one in ten felt unable to provide any estimate whatsover (see Figure 2.1). Less than 5 percent of the decision-makers markedly underestimated the incidence of extreme poverty among the aged by placing the figure of elderly poor at under 10 percent. A mere quarter of the sample of decision-makers (28 percent) provided reasonably accurate estimates of the number of elderly living in poverty, judging the elderly poor between 10 and 25 percent of the total elderly population. In sharp contrast are the number of decision-makers who vastly distorted the size of the elderly poor populations. Roughly half of the sample of 316 decision-makers (43 percent) believed that the majority of the elderly (50 percent or more) lived in dire poverty. One in eight decision-makers even maintained that the elderly poor was 70 percent or more of the total aged population.

The decision-making community thus generally viewed the elderly as contributing disproportionately to the ranks of the very poor; roughly half of the decision-makers, however, dramatized the problem out of all reasonable proportions. Drawing upon such perceptions of the elderly's income status; the decision-makers might logically be expected to stress the cost barriers to the elderly's securing needed goods and services. This thesis is borne out repeatedly in the specific policy-making contexts examined in subsequent chapters of this volume.

While the decision-makers' emphasis on the income problems of the elderly is undoubtedly not misplaced, their misperception of the numbers living in abject poverty could easily prove to be a kind of double-edged sword. Alarmed by the numbers of elderly they perceive living in dire poverty, decision-makers have pushed for the development of a wide range of social and financial assistance programs, but then restricted participation in those programs to only those elderly who live on incomes equal to or less than the official poverty guidelines. Many elderly living on incomes only marginally above the official poverty line are thereby denied services that they need and would use if available to them.[5] Ironically, these are elderly whom the decision-makers probably intended to help by establishing the program in the first place, elderly whom they thought would be eligible to participate in the program under its "low-income" requirement for entitlement. The decision-makers' inaccurate perceptions regarding the income status of the elderly thus may have far-ranging impact on their perceptions of the unmet need in the elderly population as well as on the development of suitable social assistance

FIGURE 2.1

Decision-Makers' Perceptions of the Extent of Poverty in the Aged Population

Percentage of the Aged Population Estimated to Be Living in Poverty	Percentage of the 316 Decision-Makers Supplying Estimates within Each Decile	
	Relative Percentage	Cumulative Percentage
0-9	3.5	3.5
10-19	10.1	13.6
20-29	15.2	28.8
30-39	13.9	42.7
40-49	3.8	46.5
50-59	16.8	63.3
60-69	13.6	76.9
70-79	7.6	84.5
80-89	2.2	86.7
90 and over	3.2	89.9
No estimate provided	10.1	100.0

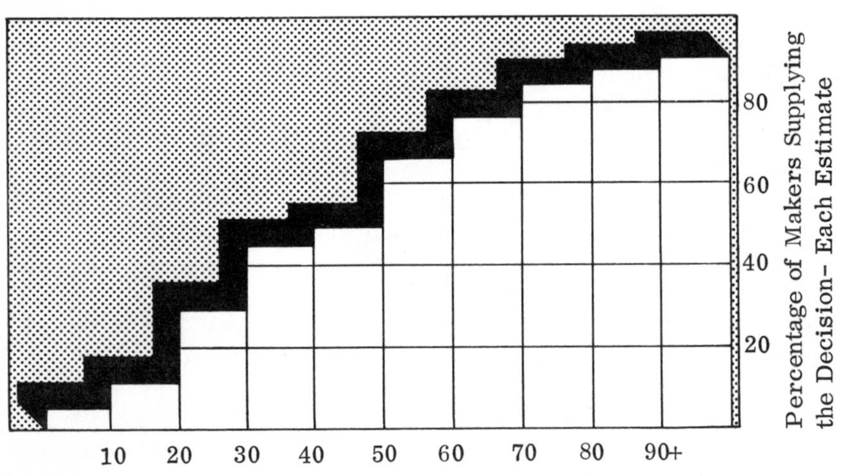

Percentage of Aged Population Estimated to Be Living in Poverty

Source: Compiled by the author.

programs to redress those needs. This hypothesis is monitored throughout the remaining chapters.

Good health, along with adequate income, is crucial to maintaining a lifestyle of independence during the later years. It is certainly true that the later years bring greater vulnerability to acute and chronic illnesses, but it is by no means accurate to depict the elderly as decrepit and incapacitated to the point of requiring institutional care. Seven in eight older persons suffer from chronic ailments, but only 18 percent report any major interference in their mobility due to those conditions. At the same time, more than twice that number (38 percent) do report some limitation of their major work activity because of their chronic conditions.[6] Nevertheless, the vast majority of the elderly are sufficiently healthy to live independently in the community and assume full responsibility for the management of their daily affairs.

This sample of decision-makers was far from confident that most elderly enjoy good health and are able to manage for themselves within the community. Only a little more than one quarter of the 316 decision-makers (28 percent) expressed any agreement with the statement, "Most older people in this country are in good health." In contrast, more than one third of the decision-makers (38 percent) mildly disagreed with that evaluation of the elderly's state of health and another third of the sample strongly disagreed with that assessment. In all, nearly three quarters (72 percent) of the decision-makers interviewed believed that most older people do not enjoy good health.

It is not surprising, then, to learn that the decision-makers also vastly overestimated the percentage of elderly persons who are currently institutionalized. National statistics locate less than 5 percent of the 65 and older population in custodial institutional settings of all kinds. The median estimate supplied by this sample of decision-makers, however, was 20 percent (see Figure 2.2). To underscore the magnitude of the disortion in the decision-makers' perceptions, not even 20 percent of the oldest segments of the elderly population, those over 85 years of age, are institutionalized.[7] One in five of the decision-makers (19 percent) correctly placed the percentage of institutionalized elderly at under 10 percent. An identical percentage of the decision-makers, however, far overestimated the number of institutionalized elderly at one in every three or even higher. Thus, not only did the decision-makers underestimate the moderately good health status that elderly people typically enjoy but most of the decision-makers assumed that sizable segments of the elderly population had been forced by their poor health to give up independent living in the community and move into custodial institutions.

FIGURE 2.2

Decision-Makers' Estimates of the Percentage of the Aged Who Are Institutionalized

Percentage of the Aged Population Estimated to Be Institutionalized	Percentage of the 316 Decision-Makers Supplying Estimates within Each Decile	
	Relative Percentage	Cumulative Percentage
0-9	15.1	15.1
10-19	22.2	37.3
20-29	18.4	55.7
30-39	11.1	66.8
40-49	4.1	70.9
50-59	4.4	75.3
60-69	1.9	77.2
70-79	1.9	79.1
80-89	0.3	79.4
90 and over	0.0	79.4
No estimate provided	20.6	100.0

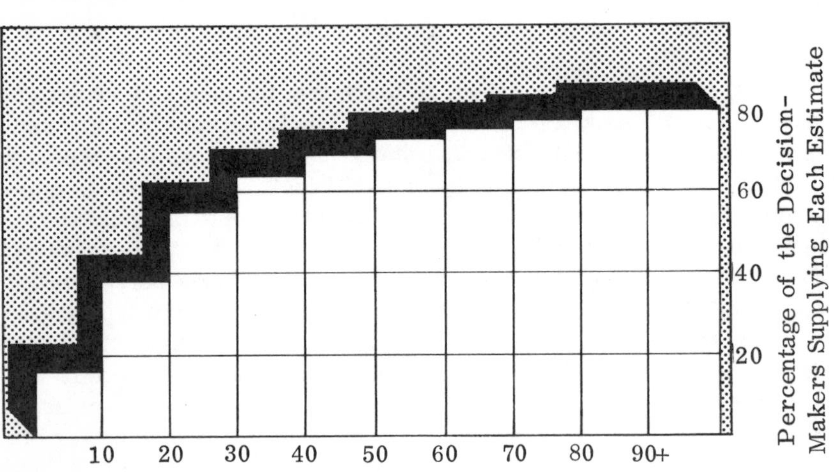

Percentage of Aged Population Estimated to Be Institutionalized

Source: Compiled by the author.

The majority of the decision-makers entertained impressions about the income and health status of the older population in general that would constitute an exaggeration of the demographic profile of even the oldest and most disadvantaged segments of the elderly population. Such perceptions can only be characterized as unrealistic distortions, then, when applied to the entire population 65 years of age or older. Taken as a whole, the sample of decision-makers clearly stereotyped the elderly in welfare-dependent terms; only a minority of the decision-making community appeared to hold reasonably accurate assessments of the income and health resources that elderly people possess.

The effect of decision-makers' undue emphasis on welfare-dependent characteristics in the elderly population, particularly as those perceptions might influence their assessment of the elderly's most pressing problems and their choice for the best means of social intervention, is a theme carried throughout the next five chapters, which focus on different facets of current social policy for the aging. For example, do these decision-makers focus primarily on income and/or health-related barriers to the elderly's utilization of existing social assistance programs and services? To what extent do the decision-makers believe that the elderly's current unmet needs can be solved simply by providing additional income; or alternatively, to what extent do the decision-makers believe that an extensive network of supplementary social service programs will be required to deal effectively with the elderly's special needs and problems? Finally, are decision-makers who perceive the need for home-based care and door-to-door transport programs to keep frail elderly at home and in their communities prepared to underwrite the development of these programs to stem the growing transfer of these aged into congregate settings of one kind or another?

Decision-makers who believe that many or most elderly are too poor to purchase needed goods and services in the community and/or too ill to get around in the community as required to tend to their personal needs might logically conclude that these elderly would be lonely and isolated; and indeed, more than three out of four (76 percent) of the sample of decision-makers interviewed in this study did assert that most older people are isolated and lonely (see Table 2.4, line A). Service providers, who have frequent contact with needy elderly recipients in various social assistance programs, most often attested to the elderly's experience of loneliness and isolation. The operations supervisor of a district Social Security office (I.D. 348) observed, "Loneliness is one of the biggest problems. I worked in a downtown Social Security office and older people came in day after day, just to talk--they really didn't need office help." A local legislator (I.D. 125) confirmed this belief based on his similar experiences

TABLE 2.4

Decision-Makers' Perceptions of Aging and the Aged (percentage agreeing with the statement in the margin)

Decision-Makers' Perceptions of the Aged	Legislators (N = 71)	Agency Administrators (N = 72)
A. Most older people are isolated and lonely.	70	74
B. Older people are apt to complain.	69	56
C. The secret to successful old age is to stay as active as ever.	90	91
D. The secret to successful old age is to take life easy and relax.	30	26
E. Older people are not very useful to themselves or others.	2	3
F. Older people are valuable because of their experience.	96	96
G. People become wiser with the coming of old age.	70	59
H. Older people can learn new things just as well as younger people.	70	70
I. In most jobs, older people can perform as well as younger people.	56	66
J. Most older people cannot find a job even though they are able and willing to work.	89	94
K. There should be no mandatory retirement age.	69	76
L. Most older people are set in their ways and unable to change.	68	40
M. Older people are often against needed reforms in our society because they want to hang on to the past.	54	44
N. Older people are often treated more like children than adults who can make their own decisions.	72	79

Source: Compiled by the author.

Decision-Makers' Position in the Policy Process				
Service Delivery Personnel (N = 70)	Corporate Directors of Personnel (N = 35)	Union Local Presidents (N = 35)	Advocates for the Aged (N = 35)	Total Sample (N = 316)
86	80	72	72	76
67	71	63	69	65
96	94	89	97	93
34	11	57	31	31
9	0	20	8	6
97	100	97	97	97
57	83	63	83	75
86	74	63	83	75
63	69	71	74	65
99	100	97	92	95
81	54	74	83	74
53	57	63	57	55
53	71	69	51	55
91	83	71	86	80

with elderly people: "Look at the elderly man who shows up at my Emergency Department at 3 a.m. with a sore knee just because he is really lonely or the fact that elderly people really go to County Hospital because they can sit in the halls and congregate with a lot of other old people who are lonely."

Very few elderly people will actually admit to any such loneliness or isolation in their own experience, although these very same elderly will assert that they know many other old people who are lonely.[8] Is the elderly woman who chatters away with the nurses and physician during her office visit, however, so very different from the elderly man who goes down to County Hospital just to sit in the waiting rooms and talk to the other people? The truth is that many elderly people are probably lonely from time to time, and undoubtedly more often than they would like to admit; but, at the same time, loneliness is not the ongoing experience for all or even most of these older people. The elderly appear to lead lives as happy as other adults in the population.[9] The decision-makers in this sample, however, did not perceive the elderly as basically happy or content. Rather, two out of three decision-makers (65 percent) alleged that older people are apt to complain about things (see Table 2.4, line B). But this is understandable in the eyes of these decision-makers. The elderly have a great deal about which they could justifiably complain--not enough money, too few friends, poor health, and so forth.

The decision-makers' perceptions of the realities of aging hardly squared with their prescriptions for a successful old age. In a rare display of near unanimity, the decision-makers wholeheartedly embraced the activity theory of aging. Ninety-three percent of the sample of 316 decision-makers agreed that the secret to successful old age is to stay as active as ever (see Table 2.4, line C). But for those elderly who live a lonely and isolated existence in the community because of the constraints imposed on their lifestyle by poor health and/or poverty-level incomes--the vast majority of the elderly in the view of these decision-makers--what chance do those elderly have to "stay as active as ever" in their old age?

In contrast to the decision-makers' perceptions, available empirical studies confirm that most elderly do seek to continue lifestyles they created in middle age and that the decline in the elderly's activities and associations in old age is neither so sudden nor so dramatic as these decision-makers would seem to envision. In middle age, individuals typically experiment to find new leisure and avocational interests that can be pursued into retirement. At retirement, these pursuits expand to fill the time available; only activities and associations that were occupation related show significant decline. In their late 60s or early 70s, individuals begin to modify their activities, usually in response to changes in their health status or changes in their life circumstances (for example, becoming widowed). Individuals in their 70s and 80s inevitably venture out into the community less and less and confine their activities to home and neighborhood more and more; and the activities they choose to pursue are less strenuous in keeping with their declining energy levels.

Hence another theme to be monitored throughout the chapters that follow is the extent to which these decision-makers fashion specific programs to assist the elderly based on the activity theory of aging to which they subscribe. Committed as they are to the belief that long life and happiness in old age are a function of continued participation in community life and meaningful involvement in worthwhile activities, to what extent are the decision-makers dedicated to reversing this tendency of the elderly to become homebound and sedentary in old age by mandating the development of community programs that would give senior citizens more opportunities to get out and participate in their communities? Quite clearly, the decision-makers here opposed the alternative, namely, that the elderly might relax and take life easy in old age (see Table 2.4, line D). The union local presidents were the only strong dissenting voice in the decision-making community. The majority of the union leadership endorsed the elderly's adopting a lifestyle of reduced activity and involvement in old age--after 40-odd years of hard and/or tedious physical labor on the job, a lifestyle of leisure and lots of rest undoubtedly sounds inviting. But for much of the rest of the decision-making community, the elderly should maintain as full and active a lifestyle as their health and income resources will permit.

How did the decision-makers interviewed in this study evaluate the elderly's role as contributing members in society today? At the same time that the decision-makers emphasized the elderly's health decrements, they somewhat contradictorily averred that the elderly continue to be useful, contributing members in the society. They virtually unanimously rejected the proposition that "older people are not very useful to themselves or others," asserting instead that "older people are valuable because of their experiences" (see Table 2.4, lines E and F). Nearly two thirds of the sample urged that "people become wiser with the coming of old age," and three quarters of the decision-makers insisted that "older people can learn new things just as well as younger people can" (see Table 2.4, lines G and H). The decision-makers' confidence in the elderly's ability to continue making valuable contributions to society is reflected in the fact that between half and three quarters of all the subsamples maintained that "in most jobs, older people can perform as well as younger people" (see Table 2.4, line I).

Despite beliefs that the elderly could still make substantial contributions to their own community or the broader society, the decision-makers acknowledged that the elderly are frequently shut out of meaningful social roles and relationships and all too often are simply ignored by society. The 316 decision-makers all agreed that "most older people cannot find a job even though they are able and willing to work" (see Table 2.4, line J). It is hardly surprising that the overwhelming majority (74 percent) of the decision-makers were thus in favor of abolishing mandatory retirement policies (see Table 2.4, line K). Only the corporate directors of personnel, who administer these mandatory retirement provisions, were not strongly in favor of eliminating them. Their lack of support, however, considerably diminishes the prospects for abolishing the mandatory retirement programs at least in the foreseeable future (see Chapter 7).

The decision-makers' evaluations of the elderly's potential role in community life were not entirely positive and laudatory. More than half (55 percent) of the decision-makers asserted that "most older people are set in their ways and unable to change" (see Table 2.4, line L). An identical percentage of the total sample (55 percent) alleged that "older people are often against needed reforms in our society because they want to hang on to the past" (see Table 2.4, line M). Corporate directors of personnel and union local presidents were far more likely than the rest of the decision-makers to believe that old people oppose reform, that they are more comfortable staying with the way things have been done in the past. The prevalence of this belief in the business world no doubt supports the persistence of early and forced retirement policies under the rationale that those policies are necessary in order to get younger, more aggressive, and more innovative thinkers into upper management positions.

If the majority of decision-makers characterize most elderly as psychologically rigid and unwilling to experiment with anything new, these data also suggest that most advocates for the aged are not likely to be effective in reeducating other decision-makers to see the elderly as adaptable and open-minded. The reason is that the majority of the advocates in this sample agreed that most older people are set in their ways, unable to change, and likely to resist reforms because they want to hang on to the past. Before the reader reaches the conclusion that these advocates have unfairly betrayed the elderly whom they purport to represent in the policy process, he should take note of the findings of a recent nationwide survey that found that nearly two thirds (63 percent) of the elderly considered themselves to be "very open-minded and adaptable," but only one third of the elderly respondents were prepared to say that such adaptability was characteristic of most elderly people.[10] Neither the elderly nor their advocates appear likely in the near future to change decision-makers' beliefs regarding the adaptability of older persons.

If the majority of these decision-makers perceive the elderly in welfare-dependent terms, isolated from the broader social community and individually often unable to adapt well to changing life circumstances in old age, the decision-makers conceivably would believe that other people would increasingly have to be called upon to do things for the elderly person. It is thus essentially consistent with some of these other perceptions of the aged population that these decision-makers overwhelmingly agreed that "older people are often treated more like children than adults who can make their own decisions" (see Table 2.4, line N). All too often, concerned relatives and professionals, motivated by desires to do what is best for the aged person who seems unable to manage reasonably competently for himself, make decisions concerning his welfare that impinge on the elderly's autonomy to think and act for himself. It remains to be seen in chapters to follow whether these decision-makers think in terms of programs that will allow the elderly person to retain his personal autonomy, or whether by contrast, these decision-makers themselves express patronizing attitudes and adopt paternalistic postures when dealing with the elderly. The display of such attitudes or behaviors by public sector officials or service providers could easily offend the elderly and turn many in need away from programs offering assistance that they might otherwise accept.

To summarize with a very broad overview of the decision-makers' perceptions on aging, this sample conceded that old age is negatively viewed in U.S. society. Of greater concern, however, is the finding that the majority of these decision-makers themselves revealed negative attitudes, reflected commonplace negative stereotypes, and conveyed considerable misinformation about aging and the aged. The decision-makers' perspectives on aging emerged little more informed than those of the general public.

DECISION-MAKERS ASSESS THE PROBLEMS THAT OLDER PEOPLE TYPICALLY EXPERIENCE

These decision-makers disparage old age because they perceive the elderly almost exclusively as being assaulted by various insurmountable problems that interfere with the older person's enjoyment of life: inadequate retirement income, declining health, retirement from the job, loss of spouse, giving up driving, selling the house, and so on. The decision-makers were asked to identify what they considered to be the three major problems facing elderly people who live in Los Angeles County; their responses are presented in Table 2.5, along with the responses to a similar question (Table 2.6) asked of 335 elderly residents living in the county.

TABLE 2.5

Decision-Makers' Perceptions of the Most Pressing Problems Facing Older People (problems rank ordered by subsamples with percent citing each problem)

Decision-Maker's Position in the Policy Process													
Legislators (N = 71)		Agency Administrators (N = 70)		Service Delivery Personnel (N = 70)		Corporate Directors of Personnel (N = 35)		Union Local Presidents (N = 35)		Advocates for the Aged (N = 35)		Total Sample (N = 316)	
Finances	(86)	Finances	(85)	Finances	(82)	Finances	(83)	Finances	(97)	Finances	(74)	Finances	(84)
Health	(56)	Health	(54)	Health	(59)	Mental health	(57)	Health	(40)	Transportation	(63)	Health	(52)
Transportation	(35)	Mental health	(43)	Mental health	(56)	Health	(23)	Housing	(37)	Health	(60)	Mental health	(43)
Mental health	(33)	Transportation	(27)	Transportation	(24)	Transportation	(23)	Mental health	(31)	Housing	(43)	Transportation	(32)
Housing	(24)	Housing	(26)	Housing	(21)	Employment	(20)	Transportation	(29)	Mental health	(37)	Housing	(28)
Leisure	(9)	Employment	(6)	Employment	(4)	Leisure	(20)	Employment	(14)	Employment	(3)	Employment	(8)
Employment	(6)	Leisure	(4)	Leisure	(1)	Housing	(14)	Leisure	(6)	Crime	(3)	Leisure	(6)
Crime	(2)	Crime	(1)	Crime	(0)	Crime	(0)	Crime	(3)	Leisure	(0)	Crime	(2)

Source: Compiled by the author.

The decision-makers by and large seemed to have accurately identified the elderly's major problem areas. The decision-makers' enumeration of the elderly's problems rank ordered in approximately the same way as the elderly's self-reported problems, the only major oversight being the salience of the crime problem for elderly residents in the community.

It should be noted, however, that in specific problem-solving contexts (health care services, housing programs, transportation services, and so on), the decision-makers often inaccurately assessed the elderly's needs and preferences. They analyzed the elderly's transportation problems primarily in terms of the availability of public transportation, but only 8 percent of the elderly residents interviewed in the companion community survey reported relying on the bus as their primary means of transportation (see Chapter 6). As regards the barriers preventing old people from getting adequate medical care, the decision-makers were most concerned about the costs and accessibility of existing services, whereas the elderly themselves were more concerned about the quality of health care services they received at the facilities (see Chapter 4). In the same way, decision-makers focused on the costs of housing, while the elderly residents of the community were more worried about crime in their neighborhood (see Chapter 5).

These discrepancies in perceptions between the decision-makers and their elderly constituents will be highlighted in subsequent chapters that explore aging programs and policies in more limited problem-solving contexts. These few illustrations are presented here simply to underscore the point that the decision-makers' overview of the elderly's major problem areas may be relatively on target, while their closer analyses of specific problems may be considerably less accurate.

Some interesting differences surfaced among various subgroups in the decision-making community in relation to defining the elderly's most pressing problem areas. The advocates for the aged did not give quite the same emphasis to the elderly's financial problems that the other subsamples did, the result being that the advocates tended to stress other problems of the elderly (health, transportation, housing, and so forth).

Advocates for the aged can perform a very useful function in the policy process by continually reminding other decision-makers of some of the elderly's less visible or less publicized problems. For example, note the way the advocates stressed the elderly's transportation problems far more than any other subsample. Until delegates to the 1971 White House Conference on Aging documented transportation as one of the elderly's most pressing problems, decision-makers, except for advocates, were substantially ignorant about the serious problems many elderly people encountered trying to get around their own communities.

The advocates for the aged were also nearly twice as likely as other subsamples to believe that finding suitable housing posed a serious problem for many elderly. Only the union local presidents similarly stressed the elderly's housing problems. Unions already sponsor many nonprofit housing projects for senior citizens and thus are responding to what union leaders interviewed here perceived to be one of the elderly's pressing needs.

The corporate directors of personnel, who are probably the most intimately involved with helping workers make the retirement transition, were unusually concerned about the adaptation that individuals make to retirement and old age. Service delivery personnel, who have contact with elderly persons seeking assistance from various social service programs, were the only other subsample in the majority to stress the problems that their aged clients seemed to have making basic psychosocial adjustments to old age. Decision-makers need to be aware of some of these psychosocial problems in adaptation to old age in order to design programs fully sensitive to the elderly's needs. The elderly's income or physical health problems inevitably have mental health implications for the life satisfaction or morale of the elderly person. Professionals who are aware of these mental health ramifications can more sensitively attend to the tangible problems of the elderly person whom they are trying to help.

The corporate directors of personnel and the union local presidents were the only subsamples to stress the elderly's employment problems. They, of course, would be the most acutely aware of the problems created by forced and premature retirements or age discrimination. Despite greater media coverage of age discrimination and mandatory retirement issues in recent years, these potential problems were overlooked here in the responses volunteered by the rest of the decision-making community. Similarly, only the corporate personnel directors in any number believed that the use of leisure time in retirement posed a serious problem for older people. The concern expressed by these few personnel managers undoubtedly derived from watching scores of older workers approach retirement without making appropriate plans to use the leisure time they would soon have on their hands.

Before leaving this discussion of the decision-makers' general observations on the problems confronting elderly people, one final observation is proffered. Decision-makers may identify more problems affecting the elderly than elderly persons themselves would ever admit to personally experiencing. Many elderly understandably would be reticent to admit to an interviewer who is a perfect stranger that they don't have adequate income, that they feel afraid to walk the streets alone, or that they have trouble climbing the stairs. Thus decision-makers must often assume the role of predicting latent or unexpressed needs in the elderly population, and this may indeed be the role the decision-makers have adopted in planning transportation programs or housing projects for the elderly. (Note in Tables 2.5 and 2.6 the sizable discrepancy between the number of decision-makers citing transportation or housing as a major problem for the elderly and the number of elderly who declared transportation or housing a major problem.) Obviously, housing projects, once built, do not go unoccupied and transportation services for the elderly, once initiated, are used by the elderly to get around the community. So decision-makers' perceptions need not always mirror manifest demand. It is better, in fact, if they predict latent need.

TABLE 2.6

Major Problems Reported by the Aged, 65 to 74 Years Old Living in Los Angeles County (problems rank ordered by mentioning the problem)

	Sample of Los Angeles County Community Residents Aged 65-74 (N = 335)
Finances	69
Health	35
Mental Health	18
Crime	8
Transportation	7
Housing	7
Employment	6
Leisure	3

DECISION-MAKERS' PREFERENCES AMONG ALTERNATIVE STRATEGIES OF SOCIAL INTERVENTION TO HELP THE AGED

The foregoing discussion is intended as only a broad overview of the major problems that decision-makers believe people typically experience in old age. Similarly, this section delineates the broad parameters of social intervention defined by this cross section of the decision-making community. Without regard to specific problems or policy issues, to what extent do these decision-makers believe the elderly's problems can be solved simply by giving them additional income that would allow the elderly to buy the goods and services they need? What role do these decision-makers assign to family support or corporate and union provisions to assist older people throughout their retirement years? After sketching the broad outlines of the decision-makers' presentiments here, subsequent chapters will explore the consistency with which decision-makers recommend these various modes of social intervention to solve the elderly's various problems related to income, health, housing, employment, and transportation.

Additional Income as the Solution to the Aged's Most Pressing Problems

To date, social provision for the aged as well as other needy persons in U.S. society has been rendered primarily in the form of monetary assistance and not services-in-kind.[11] For one thing, direct income transfers can be accomplished with a minimum of bureaucratic machinery compared to the level of institutionalization that would be required to deliver a range of services-in-kind to the elderly in the community; the result is that more benefits per budget dollar allocation reach the elderly in income transfer as opposed to social service programs. This single advantage more than any other probably accounts for the growing popularity of the direct income transfer as the primary mode of assistance provided to elderly persons.

On the other hand, some attention to the elderly's unique characteristics as a recipient subgroup in government assistance programs raises questions about whether direct income supplements can adequately redress the elderly's pressing problems.[12] For example, even if the aged individual received a supplemental housing allotment in his income, could he find housing on the market that was architecturally designed to accommodate his needs for a barrier-free environment? The answer is probably not, and so the government subsidizes construction of housing projects that are architecturally designed to meet the elderly's special housing needs. Although many elderly people receive food stamps to supplement their income, the stamps do not necessarily guarantee these elderly an improved diet if they are physically unable to get to a market that will accept the food stamps. Many gerontologists and advocates for the aged thus prefer using the services-in-kind approach to solve many of the elderly's problems, despite the added burdens and inefficiencies that derive from the implementation of middleman programs.

The decision-makers in this sample also tended to reject sole reliance on income supplements to solve the elderly's problems. When asked, "Would an adequate income alone resolve most of the problems that older people face?" six out of ten replied in the negative. They typically insisted that additional income could not solve many of the elderly's problems related to poor health, loneliness, or feelings of uselessness. Many of them did add, however, that additional income would certainly help to alleviate many of the elderly's other pressing problems. The union local presidents, who had stressed the elderly's financial problems far more than their other problems (see Table 2.5) were the most likely to maintain that added income alone would resolve most of the other problems that older people face; nearly six out of ten of these union local presidents favored the income supplements. (The data are presented and discussed in greater detail in Chapter 3, see especially Table 3.3.)

Decision-Makers' Prescriptions for Familial Support of Aging Parents

Notwithstanding recent changes in the law abolishing mandatory contributions from children with dependent elderly parents, considerable ambivalence appears to exist in the decision-making community over the obligation of grown children to take care of their aged parents (see Table 2.7). A slight majority of the 316 decision-makers (57 percent) insisted that grown children do have an obligation to care for their aging parents. The legislators and the corporate directors of personnel were the strongest advocates of familial support for the aging.

Men were much more likely than women to endorse the idea that children should look after the needs of their elderly parents. This must be considered something of a surprise, because statistics confirm that women are far more likely to arrive at old age without any source of income, which means these women must rely on assistance from their families or survive on the minimal levels of monetary assistance they will receive from SSI (Supplemental Security Income, a financial assistance program sponsored by the Social Security Administration for low-income elderly). Without family assistance, the lives of elderly women are likely to be very much more destitute than the lives of elderly men.

Minority decision-makers were also considerably more opposed to the idea of children providing for their elderly parents than were the white decision-makers. And this, too, is an unexpected finding, because the ethnic subcultures ostensibly promote the norm of extended family relations, which give the elderly parent a meaningful

TABLE 2.7

"It Is the Obligation of Grown Children to Take Care of Their Parents"
(percentage in agreement)

Positional Characteristics of the Decision-Makers	
Position in the Policy Process	
Legislators (N = 71)	73
Agency administrators (N = 70)	50
Service delivery personnel (N = 70)	43
Corporate directors of personnel (N = 35)	71
Union local presidents (N = 35)	57
Advocates for the aged (N = 35)	51
Responsibility for Aging Programs	
Primary function (N = 85)	51
Important but not central function (N = 88)	64
Minor function (N = 143)	57
Area of Program Expertise	
Health (N = 37)	49
Mental health (N = 23)	43
Housing (N = 29)	69
Employment (N = 92)	61
Income maintenance (N = 26)	62
Recreation/leisure (N = 18)	39
Senior citizens affairs (N = 49)	49
Generalists (N = 42)	69
Personal Characteristics of the Decision-Makers	
Age of the Respondent	
Under 45 (N = 98)	59
45-54 (N = 98)	53
55-64 (N = 90)	58
65 and over (N = 30)	60
Sex of the Respondent	
Male (N = 230)	61
Female (N = 86)	45
Ethnicity of the Respondent	
White (N = 235)	60
Minority (N = 81)	49
Educational Level of the Respondent	
High school graduate or less (N = 42)	52
Some college (N = 64)	59
College graduate (N = 99)	55
Postcollege professional education (N = 111)	59
Total (N = 316)	57

Source: Compiled by the author.

role and position within the family unit. The finding is nevertheless consistent with other studies in those ethnic communities that have reported an erosion in the point of view that families must assume the primary responsibility in caring for their elderly members and that it is a shameful admission of the family's inability to make adequate provision to let their elders accept public assistance in any form.[13]

Table 2.8 further illustrates the decision-makers' ambivalence about the family's role in caring for the aged. Four out of five decision-makers asserted that "older people ought to be more independent of their families." Union local presidents and advocates for the aged believed the most ardently in the elderly's remaining independent of their families. Those who worked closely with the elderly in other professional capacities were similarly more in favor of the elderly's developing more independence from their families. Only the youngest decision-makers in the sample of 316, those under 45 years of age, were relatively less committed to encouraging the elderly's independence from their families.

It is clear that many of the decision-makers interviewed here (43 percent) jointly held both of these beliefs; thus they believed that the elderly ought to be more independent of their families at the same time that they maintained that grown children have an obligation to take care of their aging parents. The two attitudes seem to be somewhat inconsistent when held together. Perhaps the only way to interpret these decision-makers' perspectives on family assistance is to assume that first and foremost they believe that the elderly should live independent of any support from their families, but that should the elderly need additional support to make ends meet, then their grown children should provide whatever assistance is required to the extent that they can.

These data suggest that the attribution of responsibility for care of the aged to their grown children is indeed a norm undergoing considerable revision in the mid-1970s. Many lament that the geographic mobility of U.S. families has eroded the extended family networks that once ensconced the aged within the family unit. Although it is true that the number of multigeneration households has declined in recent decades, such living arrangements were never particularly common in this country. The nuclear family unit as it is seen today has always been the modal family structure, and the elderly have always tended to live independently in their own households.[14]

The concept of family assistance is not inconsistent with the elderly's maintaining an independent household apart from their children's nuclear family so long as the elderly have some regular contact with their adult children. The decision-makers in this sample apparently were not particularly confident, however, about the extent

TABLE 2.8

"Older People Ought to Be More Independent of Their Families"
(percentage responding in agreement)

Positional Characteristics of the Decision-Makers	
Position in the Policy Process	
Legislators (N = 71)	70
Agency administrators (N = 70)	79
Service delivery personnel (N = 70)	79
Corporate directors of personnel (N = 35)	74
Union local presidents (N = 35)	91
Advocates for the aged (N = 35)	89
Responsibility for Aging Programs	
Primary function (N = 85)	88
Important but not central function (N = 88)	73
Minor function (N = 143)	77
Area of Program Expertise	
Health (N = 37)	84
Mental health (N = 23)	70
Housing (N = 29)	72
Employment (N = 92)	80
Income maintenance (N = 26)	81
Recreation/leisure (N = 18)	83
Senior citizens affairs (N = 49)	84
Generalists (N = 42)	71
Personal Characteristics of the Decision-Makers	
Age of the Respondent	
Under 45 (N = 98)	62
45-54 (N = 98)	82
55-64 (N = 90)	92
65 and over (N = 30)	83
Sex of the Respondent	
Male (N = 230)	78
Female (N = 86)	80
Ethnicity of the Respondent	
White (N = 235)	79
Minority (N = 81)	78
Educational Level of the Respondent	
High school graduate or less (N = 42)	90
Some college (N = 64)	80
College graduate (N = 99)	80
Postcollege professional education (N = 111)	73
Total (N = 316)	79

Source: Compiled by the author.

to which the elderly living alone could rely on assistance from their families. Half of the decision-makers estimated that the majority of elderly did not have even weekly contact with their adult children. Empirical studies, however, confirm that more than three quarters of the elderly in this country live within a half-hour drive of one of their children, and in one nationwide study two thirds of the elderly reported seeing at least one of their children within the 24-hour period preceding the interview.[15] This evidence strongly suggests that the elderly have remained integrated within a larger family unit whether or not they actually live with their adult children. These and other studies document that a considerable amount of assistance already does flow between the households of middle-aged children and the aged parents. Despite the decision-makers' doubts, older Americans continue to receive considerable support from their grown children. Subsequent chapters will afford the opportunity to see what role these decision-makers believe family assistance should play in underwriting a decent quality of life for older Americans.

Decision-Makers' Assessments of Corporate Responsibility toward Retirees

The decision-makers were queried about employers' responsibilities for their retirees: "When an employee retires, he is pretty much on his own. What could employers do, within reason, to help make their retirees' lives more meaningful and comfortable?" (see Table 2.9). The decision-makers' responses centered on four suggestions: develop preretirement counseling programs to assist older workers in making the transition to retirement living, reemploy retirees on a part-time basis whenever possible, establish retiree organizations to sponsor social activities for retired workers, and develop better pension plans for retiring workers. Interesting differences emerged among the six subsamples in where they were relatively more likely to assign employers responsibility in making better provision for their retiring workers.

One third of the decision-makers recommended that employers develop preretirement counseling programs for employees that would give those about to retire a more realistic appraisal of what life in retirement would be like. Nearly half of the advocates for the aged, agency administrators, and corporate directors of personnel identified preretirement counseling as a responsibility employers should assume on behalf of their older workers. Legislators and union local presidents, on the other hand, infrequently cited preretirement counseling programs as an obligation on employers. Because the legislators apparently do not assign to employers any specific obligation to

TABLE 2.9

Decision-Makers' Assessments of Employers' Responsibilities to Their Retiring Workers (percentage agreeing with the statement in the margin)

"What Could Employers Do, within Reason, to Help Make Their Retirees' Lives More Meaningful and Comfortable?"	Legislators (N = 71)	Agency Administrators (N = 70)
Develop preretirement counseling programs.	15	46
Employ retirees on a part-time basis.	30	36
Establish retiree organizations to sponsor various social activities for the retirees.	32	27
Develop better pension plans for retiring workers.	23	24
Develop phased or gradual retirement options for older workers in the company.	8	13
Allow retirees to remain eligible for company benefits after retirement.	4	9
Encourage older workers and retirees to get involved in community projects and activities.	10	6
Provide career retraining for employees who are approaching retirement.	1	7
Encourage older workers and retirees to develop hobbies and avocations.	7	1
Miscellaneous other responses.	6	4
It is not the employers' responsibility to make any provisions for their retirees.	21	7

Source: Compiled by the author.

Decision-Maker's Position in the Policy Process				
Service Delivery Personnel (N = 70)	Corporate Directors of Personnel (N = 35)	Union Local Presidents (N = 35)	Advocates for the Aged (N = 35)	Total Sample (N = 316)
33	40	14	49	32
40	34	20	20	32
37	49	17	20	30
13	26	37	17	17
9	0	6	6	8
6	9	11	6	7
9	6	3	3	7
6	3	6	6	5
1	3	0	0	3
6	3	0	3	4
4	9	14	6	10

conduct preretirement counseling programs for older workers, it is unlikely that any legislature will soon try to mandate the development of such programs within business and industry. Similarly, it appears unlikely that unions will press employers to develop such programs for retirees as part of their collective bargaining package. Unfortunately, as long as the development of preretirement counseling programs is left solely to the discretion of the employer, the development of new programs is likely to be slow and those programs that do exist are likely to remain only marginally effective in preparing older workers for retirement. (See Chapter 7 for a further discussion of these issues.)

One third of the decision-makers also urged employers to rehire retired employees on a part-time, consultant, adjunct, or temporary basis as business conditions permitted or required. They believed such arrangements would benefit industry by allowing them to take advantage of the skills and experience these older workers had amassed during their many years on the job, while also benefiting the retiree by giving him a continuing role in the organization to which he belonged for so many years. Some suggested that retired workers be used to train novice employees. Others recommended that retirees be employed as consultants in the organization or hired on special assignment to undertake special projects for the company. The service providers were the most in favor of rehiring retired workers. They were concerned about the alternative--"So many executives retire and die within a year" (a continuing education teacher, I.D. 362). Union local presidents and advocates for the aged, on the other hand, were relatively less enthusiastic about the desirability and/or feasibility of rehiring retirees.

The interesting question is why more of the decision-makers did not press for employers rehiring their retirees when these same decision-makers insisted that the elderly are valuable because of their experience, that the elderly can learn new things and perform on most jobs as well as younger people can, and that many elderly would like to work but they simply cannot find jobs (recall the data presented in Table 2.4). Three quarters of the decision-makers asserted that there should be no mandatory retirement age, yet only one third of the decision-makers suggested skirting existing mandatory retirement policies by rehiring retirees.

Many decision-makers urged employers to sponsor retirement clubs and host social activities at the company for their retirees; in other words, give the employees something to do with their free time after they have been retired by the company. Nearly half of the corporate directors of personnel believed this to be a reasonable commitment that employers should make on behalf of their retiring employees. Union local presidents did not perceive retirement clubs as an employer's responsibility primarily because they envisioned union-sponsored clubs in their stead. Unfortunately, at the present time few companies have any kind of regular follow-up contact with their retired employees, let alone sponsor special programs and activities for them.[16] Impetus for establishing such company-sponsored retiree organizations or programs would probably come from the personnel division of the company. The fact that many of the corporate personnel directors in this sample were in favor of developing such retiree groups under company supervision may bode well for the future growth of retiree organizations in the business world.

Only one in six of the decision-makers in this sample asserted that employers would substantially meet their obligations to retiring workers if they merely guaranteed those retiring workers adequate pensions at the time they retired from the company. Union local presidents were the most vocal about employers needing to develop better pension plans to cover retiring workers. Pensions are one of the many items in the collective bargaining package negotiated between the unions and business management. Union officials thus should be acutely sensitive to the pension obligations employers show their retirees. On the other side of the bargaining table, however, only one quarter of the corporate personnel directors similarly urged the development of improved company-sponsored pension plans. As these are the corporate officers in charge of administering these company plans, is it appropriate to conclude that the other personnel directors in this sample were satisfied with the operation of the private pension system in general or at least the operation of their own company plan? The subject is explored further in Chapter 3.

A number of additional observations by the decision-makers concerning employers' responsibilities toward retiring workers are also detailed in Table 2.9 for the interested reader. It is important to note that a substantial minority of these decision-makers (one in ten) believed that employers had no obligations toward their retirees. One California assemblyman (I.D. 158) expressed the opinion, "When you leave government or any service, you just leave. Why should an employer have to do anything?" Similar attitudes were voiced by one in five legislators and one in seven union local presidents. With a substantial minority of these subsamples in particular reluctant to assign employers any responsibilities toward retiring workers, it reduces the likelihood that employers will be pressured from outside the organization to assume greater responsibility for the quality of life of their retirees.

Decision-Makers' Assessments of Unions' Responsibility toward Retired Workers

The decision-makers were also asked about what they perceived to be the role of unions in guaranteeing retirees a reasonable quality of life (see Table 2.10). In many ways, the decision-makers' assessment of the unions' responsibilities paralleled their assignment of responsibilities to the employers. The most common suggestions included establishing retiree clubs for retired members of the union, developing union-sponsored preretirement counseling programs for retiring union members, negotiating better pension plans for union members, including retirees in collective bargaining with employers, helping retired union members who want to continue working after retirement find work, and providing supplemental insurance benefits to retired union members.

Unions were most often urged to establish retiree clubs that would sponsor various social activities specifically for retired members in their organizations. Nearly half of the union local presidents interviewed believed this was a good idea, and a number of them asserted that their own union local was already engaged in planning social programs for their retirees. Their emphasis on developing recreational programs for retired members was completely consistent with the unique point of view expressed by the majority of these union local presidents that old people ought to relax and take life easy (recall Table 2.4, line D). Many of the other decision-makers, however, disliked the idea of organized social activities. The comments of a health center director (I.D. 212) adequately summarize their points of view: "I personally can't stand organized activity. A lot of people don't fit into such groups. The majority of people just don't want to be part of a frenetic group. This bothers me. What is left for them ?"

Many decision-makers cited the unions' responsibility for developing preretirement counseling programs that would adequately prepare older workers for life in retirement. A plurality of the advocates for the aged considered this the number one obligation of the unions toward their older members. The union local presidents, however, typically did not identify preretirement counseling as a proper function of the unions' internal activities and organization. This being the case, it is unlikely that these union locals will soon assume the responsibility for developing such programs to assist their members in preparing for retirement.

Only one in five of the decision-makers specifically said that it was the unions' responsibility to assume an active role in developing better pension plans for retiring workers. But another one in five suggested that the unions ought to represent retired members' needs in collective bargaining and certainly primary among their retirees' needs would be pension benefits. Representation of the retirees' interests in collective bargaining is presently a controversial issue. A recent federal court ruling held that unions are not required to bargain with employers on behalf of retirees. The court's rationale was that to require the unions to serve as legal representatives for retirees in collective bargaining would bring into unhealthy conflict the retirees' interests in higher pension benefits and the younger union members' interests in higher wages.[17] At the present time there is no union where retired members are accorded all the voting privileges that accompany active union membership. In unions where retirees are eligible to vote, they still cannot vote on the ratification of collective bargaining agreements. Of some encouragement, however, is the fact that the union local presidents in this sample of decision-makers were the most in favor of reversing precedent and including retired members in the collective bargaining process. More than one third of these union officials supported the idea.

Advocates for the aged could find strong allies in labor management if retirees' needs were thus represented in collective bargaining. It is disappointing that advocates in this sample did not appear more sensitive to the union's potential role in representing the interests of older and retired workers in collective bargaining. Advocates for the aged cannot afford to ignore or overlook opportunities that exist to strengthen the elderly's political and economic bargaining position. More than one union leader in these interviews boasted that, "Labor has been one of the elderly's best friends" (president of a multiple union membership association, I.D. 506). While everyone may not agree with that assessment of the union's performance in the past, it is certainly true that labor could be one of the elderly's best friends. Perhaps in the future, advocates for the aged will be able to work more effectively with the union leadership, building strong coalitions to help the nation's elderly. The feasibility of such coalitions is explored in greater detail in Chapter 9.

Overview of Decision-Makers' Allocation of Responsibilities in Providing for the Aged

The response of this cross section of the decision-making community reveals that only a minority of the decision-makers assigns major responsibilities in providing for the aged to employers or unions or even the elderly's own families. Although the decision-makers virtually unanimously agreed about the elderly's pressing financial problems, only a small minority underscored the employers' and unions' responsibilities for improving private pension

TABLE 2.10

Decision-Makers' Assessments of Unions' Responsibilities to Their Retiring Members (percentage agreeing with the statement in the margin)

"What Could Unions Do, within Reason, to Help Make Their Retirees' Lives More Meaningful and More Comfortable?"	Legislators (N = 71)	Agency Administrators (N = 70)
Establish retiree clubs and organizations to sponsor social activities for retirees.	25	27
Develop preretirement counseling programs.	11	27
Develop better pension plans for retiring members.	21	27
Include retirees' needs and concerns in collective bargaining agreements.	18	14
Find employment for retired members who want to continue working.	16	17
Provide supplemental benefits (health and life insurance) to retired members.	3	11
Maintain regular contact with retired members through newsletters and other publications.	3	13
Provide career retraining for older union members who desire to continue working.	1	7
Invite retired union members to union meetings and allow them to participate in decision-making.	4	7
Build or sponsor senior citizen housing projects and retirement communities.	9	9
Encourage older and retired union members to get involved in community projects and activities.	10	4
Develop phased or gradual retirement options for older union members.	3	3
Encourage older and retired union members to develop hobbies and avocations.	4	1
Miscellaneous other responses.	4	1
It is not the unions' responsibility to make any provisions for their retired members.	7	6

Source: Compiled by the author.

Decision-Maker's Position in the Policy Process				
Service Delivery Personnel (N = 70)	Corporate Directors of Personnel (N = 35)	Union Local Presidents (N = 35)	Advocates for the Aged (N = 35)	Total Sample (N = 316)
33	26	43	29	30
33	26	17	40	25
21	23	17	11	21
11	20	34	20	18
14	11	14	11	15
11	6	23	20	11
4	20	6	0	7
6	3	6	6	5
6	0	3	6	5
1	0	3	3	5
6	3	3	3	5
1	0	3	3	2
0	3	0	0	2
7	6	0	6	4
4	6	0	0	4

benefits. The decision-makers more commonly considered the employers' and unions' responsibilities to retirees in terms of establishing special retiree organizations that would provide them a variety of social and recreational opportunities. While it is undoubtedly important to give retirees something to do with their leisure time in retirement, that is clearly a secondary concern for retirees who are hard-pressed to secure adequate food, decent housing, and quality medical care.

Aside from improved pension support, unions and employers might significantly contribute to the material well-being and security of their retirees by guaranteeing their continued coverage under the various insurance and fringe benefits plans provided for the currently employed. Few companies now make such arrangements for their retirees and few decision-makers here seemed to recognize the bonus that such coverage could be to retiring workers. Also, relatively few decision-makers urged expanding employment opportunities for retirees, even though many of the decision-makers in the sample insisted that there are many retirees who are willing and able to work but simply unable to find suitable jobs. In sum, only a minority of the decision-makers pressed for modes of corporate and union assistance that would significantly improve the material well-being of their retirees.

At the same time, the decision-makers viewed as a group were not deeply committed to familial assistance as a primary mode of support for the elderly in need. The vast majority of all subgroups in the decision-making community, except for the very youngest decision-makers, strongly urged that the elderly should be more independent of their families. Moreover, only a bare majority of the decision-makers believed that the family should provide assistance to their aged parents, even as a last resort, if their parents are unable to provide adequately for themselves. The family does not emerge as a major source of assistance for the elderly in the eyes of the decision-makers who were interviewed here.

As a result, individuals will have to make adequate provision for their own old age or government will need to assume the major burden in providing for the aged throughout the postemployment years of their life. As will become clear in the chapters to follow, decision-makers anticipate more and more that the elderly's needs can be met only through the continued growth of government programs and services.

DECISION-MAKERS' PROJECTIONS FOR THE FUTURE

The decision-makers in this sample foresee a growing burden on government as future generations arrive at old age, even though

TABLE 2.11

"In the Next 30 Years, Do You Foresee Major Breakthroughs in Medical Research That Will Significantly Increase Life Expectancy?"
(percentage responding "yes")

Positional Characteristics of the Decision-Makers	
Position in the Policy Process	
Legislators (N = 71)	82
Agency administrators (N = 70)	82
Service delivery personnel (N = 70)	83
Corporate directors of personnel (N = 35)	86
Union local presidents (N = 35)	89
Advocates for the aged (N = 35)	86
Responsibility for Aging Programs	
Primary function (N = 85)	91
Important but not central function (N = 88)	78
Minor function (N = 143)	83
Area of Program Expertise	
Health (N = 37)	70
Mental health (N = 23)	74
Housing (N = 29)	83
Employment (N = 92)	88
Income maintenance (N = 26)	85
Recreation/leisure (N = 18)	89
Senior citizens affairs (N = 49)	88
Generalists (N = 42)	86
Personal Characteristics of the Decision-Makers	
Age of the Respondent	
Under 45 (N = 98)	87
45-54 (N = 98)	80
55-64 (N = 90)	88
65 and over (N = 30)	83
Sex of the Respondent	
Male (N = 230)	85
Female (N = 86)	81
Ethnicity of the Respondent	
White (N = 235)	83
Minority (N = 81)	89
Educational Level of the Respondent	
High school graduate or less (N = 42)	95
Some college (N = 64)	87
College graduate (N = 99)	84
Postcollege professional education (N = 111)	80
Total (N = 316)	84

Source: Compiled by the author.

TABLE 2.12

Decision-Makers' Perceptions Regarding the Impact That a Greatly Enlarged Aged Population Would Have on U.S. Society

Areas of Perceived Stresses and Strains in the Social System	Legislators (N = 71)	Agency Administrators (N = 70)
Income maintenance programs	62	54
Leisure and recreation problems	24	17
Employment market	11	19
Health care systems	44	11
Housing market	11	9
Morale and mental health problems	3	3
Transportation services	3	3
Family problems	0	0
No problems	13	4

Source: Compiled by the author.

these future cohorts are expected to be better prepared to cope with the problems of old age because they will enjoy better incomes and better health and they will be better educated and have more familiarity in dealing with government bureaucracies.

The decision-makers interviewed in this study anticipate a burgeoning elderly population in future decades. Five out of six of the decision-makers said that they expected major medical breakthroughs within the next 30 years that will significantly increase the life expectancy of Americans (see Table 2.11). The prospects are not necessarily remote. If major cardiovascular diseases were eliminated, for example, it is estimated that those who reach age 65 in the future would enjoy an additional life expectancy of ten years or more beyond what they do today.[18] Solving the cancer riddle might add as much as five to seven years to the life expectancy of older Americans. Projecting on the basis of current demographic processes, the percentage of elderly in the population is not likely to increase dramatically until around the year 2010 when the post-World War II babies arrive at age 65. Major medical breakthroughs

Decision-Maker's Position in the Social Policy Process (percent)					
Service Delivery Personnel (N = 70)	Corporate Directors of Personnel (N = 35)	Union Local Presidents (N = 35)	Advocates of the Aged (N = 35)	Total Percent	Total No.
47	69	46	54	50	157
16	20	9	17	18	56
21	11	14	6	16	51
20	11	14	20	13	41
14	6	14	14	11	36
6	3	0	3	3	10
1	3	0	3	2	7
3	0	0	0	1	2
3	9	14	14	8	27

conceivably could alter these projections, but how soon such medical breakthroughs will come and how soon their impact will be felt is a matter of quite some conjecture. The point is, however, that the decision-makers believe such medical breakthroughs are virtually a certainty within the next 30 years, and they appeared quite worried about how the social system is going to be able to support such a large dependent aged population.

The decision-makers envisioned multiple stresses and strains in the social system that would result from trying to support this rapidly expanding aged population (see Table 2.12). The majority of the decision-makers were concerned first and foremost about the strain that would be placed on existing income-maintenance programs to provide adequate income support for these aged throughout their lengthened postemployment lifetime. The decision-makers' concern about the strain on income-maintenance programs was undoubtedly heightened by their perceptions of the trend toward early retirement, which they projected was likely to continue in the foreseeable future. The trend toward early retirement coupled with the expected increase in life expectancy in the latter part of the life cycle would mean that more people would have to be supported in retirement for a longer period of time. Many decision-makers wondered where the resources would come from to finance the retirement income programs that would be required. As might be expected, the corporate directors of personnel, followed by the legislators, were the most sensitive to the problems of financing retirement for a greatly expanded elderly population.

Evoking considerable less concern among the decision-makers were a number of other stresses and strains that they perceived would be created if life expectancy suddenly increased dramatically. One in five worried about what the elderly would find to do to occupy the time in those extra years of their life. They urged the development of new, more meaningful roles in the community for elderly residents. One in six predicted that older workers would seek to stay in the labor market longer, thereby creating severe competition for jobs between older and younger workers. One in eight worried that the years added at the end of the life cycle would be plagued with illness and disease, which would make the elderly population an even greater burden on existing health care facilities. One in ten suggested that the existing housing supply would be inadequate to meet the increased demand for retirement housing and barrier-free living environments.

The problems explored with these decision-makers in the chapters to follow are thus problems that they foresee having long-range implications well into the twenty-first century. The broad overview of the climate of decision-making in the field of aging presented in this chapter should provide a useful frame of reference for the exploration of many issues in aging and social policy that will be discussed from the decision-makers' perspectives in the remaining chapters of this volume.

NOTES

1. A number of studies have found that a professional's age has significant influence on his attitudes toward aging. See David M. Levine, "Staffing Patterns and Professional Profiles of the Health Care Manpower," Gerontologist 15, no. 4 (August 1975): 314-17; Tom Hickey et al., "Attitudes toward Aging as a Function of In-Service Training and Practitioner Age," Journal of Gerontology 31, no. 6 (November 1976) : 681-86; Catherine Cyrus-Lutz and Charles M. Gaitz, "Psychiatrists' Attitudes towards the Aged and Aging," Pt. I, Gerontologist 12, no. 2 (Summer 1972): 163-67; Phyllis Mutschler, "Factors Affecting Choice of and Perseveration in Social

Work with the Aged," Pt. I, Gerontologist 11, no. 3 (Autumn 1971): 231-41. A minority of studies has found that the age of the professional or practitioner is a relatively unimportant determinant of his attitudes toward aging and the aged. See Jordan I. Kosberg and Joanna F. Gorman," Perceptions toward the Rehabilitation Potential of Institutionalized Age," Gerontologist 15, no. 5 (October 1975): 398-403; Jordan I. Kosberg et al., "Comparison of Supervisors' Attitudes in a Home for the Aged," Pt. I, Gerontologist 12, no. 3 (Autumn 1972): 241-45. Some studies have found that negative attitudes toward aging and negative stereotyping of the elderly increase among decision-makers who have extensive or recent education. See Kosberg and Gorman, "Perceptions toward the Rehabilitation Potential of Institutionalized Aged"; Levine, "Staffing Patterns and Professional Profiles of the Health Care Manpower." A few studies, however, have also found the reverse relationship, that is, where extensive education leads to reduced stereotyping of the aged. See Margaret E. Campbell, "Study of the Attitudes of Nursing Personnel toward the Geriatric Patient," Nursing Research 20, no. 2 (March-April 1971): 147-51.

2. U.S. Department of Health, Education and Welfare, Facts about Older Americans: 1975, DHEW Publication No. OHD 75-20006, 1975.

3. Herman B. Brotman, "Income and Poverty in the Older Population in 1975," Gerontologist 17, no. 1 (February 1977): 23-26.

4. U.S. Department of Health, Education and Welfare, Statistical Reports on Older Americans. No. 2. Income and Poverty among the Elderly: 1975, DHEW Publication No. OHD 77-20286, 1975.

5. Byron D. Gold, "The Role of the Federal Government in the Provision of Social Services to Older Persons," Annals of the American Academy of Political and Social Science 415 (September 1974): 55-69.

6. U.S. Department of Health, Education and Welfare, Facts about Older Americans: 1975.

7. Robert C. Atchley, The Social Forces in Later Life (Belmont, Calif.: Wadsworth, 1972), p. 123.

8. Louis Harris and Associates, The Myth and Reality of Aging in America (Washington, D.C.: National Council on the Aging, 1975), p. 36.

9. Ibid., p. 154; Gerald Gurin, Joseph Verloff, and Sheila Feld, Americans View Their Mental Health (New York: Basic Books, 1960).

10. Harris, The Myth and Reality of Aging in America, pp. 48, 53.

11. Merlin Taber and Marilyn Flynn, "Social Policy and Social Provision for the Elderly in the 1970's," Pt. II, Gerontologist 11, no. 4 (Winter 1971): 51-54; Gold, "The Role of the Federal Government in the Provision of Social Services to Older Persons"; Byron Gold, Elizabeth Kutza, and Theodore Marmor, "United States Social Policy on Old Age: Present Patterns and Prediction" (Paper presented at the Tenth International Congress of Gerontology, Jerusalem, Israel, June 1975).

12. Stephen R. McConnell and Patricia L. Kasschau, "Income versus In-Kind Services for the Elderly: Correlates of Decision-Makers' Preferences," Social Service Review 51, no. 2 (June 1977).

13. See, for example, Ben M. Crouch, "Age and Institutional Support: Perceptions of Older Mexican Americans," Journal of Gerontology 27, no. 4 (October 1972): 524-29.

14. Stephen M. Golant, "Residential Concentrations of the Future Elderly," Pt. II, Gerontologist 15, no. 1 (February 1975): 16-23; Judith Treas, "Aging and the Family," in Aging: Scientific Perspectives and Social Issues, ed. Diana S. Woodruff and James E. Birren (New York: Van Nostrand, 1975), pp. 92-108.

15. Ethel Shanas, "Living Arrangements and Housing Old People," in Behavior and Adaptation in Later Life, ed. Ewald W. Busse and Eric F. Pfeiffer (Boston: Little, Brown, 1969), pp. 129-49.

16. National Survey of Fortune's "500" Pre-retirement Plans and Policies (Ann Arbor: University of Michigan-Wayne State University, Institute of Labor and Industrial Relations, 1976); Roger O'Meara, "Retirement--The Eighth Age of Man," Conference Board Record 11, no. 10 (October 1974): 59-64.

17. Allied Chemical and Alkali Workers of America, Local Union No. 1 v. Pittsburgh Plate Glass Co., Chemical Division, 404 U.S. 157, 1971.

18. Herman Brotman, "Who Are the Aged?" A Demographic View," Useful Facts No. 42 (Washington, D.C.: Administration on Aging, August 1968).

3 Income Maintenance for the Aged: The Foundation of U.S. Social Policy on Aging

Income-maintenance programs constitute the foundation of social provision for older Americans. Whenever gerontologists or social planners, practitioners or policy-makers, gather to discuss the problems of the aged, essentially the same theme emerges from their discussions: Provision of an adequate income for older persons must be the area of highest priority. Without a decent income, most proposals for programs to assist the elderly turn out to be lip service or wishful thinking. The concept of independent living so fundamental to the design of these social programs is rendered void and meaningless if the elderly lack sufficient income to purchase the bare essentials in food, housing, medical care, and other requisites of daily living. The decision-makers' evaluation of the adequacy of current income-maintenance programs would thus seem an appropriate place to begin this topical survey that will analyze their perspectives on a broad range of social policies and programs.

This chapter focuses on a number of basic questions that are important for understanding the climate of decision-making that is shaping policy deliberations and program reforms on matters pertaining to income maintenance for the aged. For example, how does the cross section of the decision-making community interviewed in this study evaluate the income status of the elderly population in general, or phrased alternatively, how widespread do they believe poverty is in the elderly age group? To what extent do these decision-makers believe lack of money is the cause of most or all of the other problems that elderly people commonly face? How would the decision-makers recommend improving the level of income support for elderly persons no longer actively employed? More specifically, how do the decision-makers assess the respective contributions of social security and private pension benefits to the elderly's aggregate retirement income so as to guarantee retirees and their dependents an income that is adequate to cover at least their basic needs? And, finally, how adequately do these decision-makers believe existing income-maintenance programs will serve the needs of future generations of retirees? Before exploring decision-makers' perspectives on these issues, however, it would be useful to have an overview of the retirement income system for general background information.

INCOME MAINTENANCE FOR THE AGED: CONCEPTUAL DESIGN AND REALITY

The level of retirement income support and consequently the quality of life that the majority of older Americans will enjoy after a lifetime of hard work are determined not so much by their individual and independent initiative as by the collective policy decisions made by this sample of decision-makers and others similarly situated who control the various public and private sector income-maintenance programs on which retirees rely for their income after they are no longer active in the labor force. Making adequate provision for the post-employment years of life is typically not a do-it-yourself affair. Few Americans earn enough money throughout their work lifetime to pay for current expenses of living and raising a family and still have money to set aside for their retirement.[1] More typically, they have at most five or ten years to save for their retirement after the major expenses of raising the family have diminished, and those five or ten years are rarely enough to accumulate an income base that will see them through a retirement period lasting ten, fifteen years, or even longer.[2] Most of the elderly in this country are thus dependent on the income that they receive from public and/or private pensions, and their standard of living is governed for the most part by the size of those pension benefits, which, in turn, are determined largely by the discretion of the decision-makers in charge of managing the pension programs.

Retirement income for the elderly is supposed to derive from a tripartite system of income maintenance, including social security, private pensions, and individual savings or earnings. The linchpin of this tripartite system is the social security retirement income program, which pays retirement benefits to employees who have, for all practical purposes, withdrawn from the labor force.[3] Today, more than 90 percent of the U.S. labor force is covered by the social security retirement program. In August 1974 (the month preceding the commencement of interviewing in this survey), the average social security benefit paid to a retired worker was approximately $2,200 per year, and the average spouse benefit was about $1,100 per year.[4]

Social security, however, was never meant to represent the retiree's sole source of income during the postemployment years of his life. Social security retirement benefits were intended to provide only a partial replacement of lost earnings when the employee retired from the labor force. The individual's social security retirement benefits were presumed to be supplemented by individual savings and financial assets, on the one hand, and private pension benefits, on the other. The reality is, however, that the majority of retirees rely on social security retirement benefits as their primary and oftentimes only source of retirement income.

More than two thirds of all elderly couples and nearly 80 percent of single elderly persons reported financial assets of less than $5,000 in the 1968 Social Security Survey of the Aged; 43 and 61 percent, respectively, held less than $1,000 in assets and 26 and 42 percent, respectively, reported having no assets.[5] Many elderly do, however, have some equity in their homes; four fifths of the elderly homeowners even own their homes free of any mortgage.[6] Put simply, the elderly's savings are for the most part tied up in the equity of their home and not available to use in meeting monthly living expenses.

Like individual savings and financial assets, private pension benefits are a far smaller share of the elderly's aggregate retirement income than is generally presumed or reasonably could be expected at this stage of their development.[7] Based on a survey of households conducted by the Bureau of Census in April 1972, the Social Security Administration estimated that only 44 percent of all wage and salary workers in private industry were covered by private pensions in 1972.[8] But many workers who are "covered" by private pension plans because they work for a company or a union that sponsors such a plan are not covered by that plan when it really counts--at the time of their retirement--because they have failed to complete the requisite term of service to qualify for a prorated or fully vested pension benefit. The Social Security Administration surveyed the 1.2 million persons who were newly entitled to retiree benefits under social security between July 1969 and June 1970. According to that survey, only 25 percent had achieved vested rights in a private pension plan; the median annual private pension benefit among those retirees was $2,080 for men and a mere $970 for women.[9]

Throughout the past decade, many sectors of the decision-making community have expressed growing concern over the adequacy of existing income-maintenance systems in this country. In fact, there has not been so much serious discussion of matters pertaining to income maintenance for the aged since the spirited debates of the early 1930s that produced the original blueprint for an old-age social insurance plan to cover U.S. workers enacted into law by the Social Security Act of 1935. Among the issues most frequently highlighted in these current debates are the prevalence, and worse, the persistence, of poverty in the aged population; the proper role of social security in alleviating poverty among the nation's senior citizens; the suitable contribution that individuals' earnings, on the one hand, and union and corporate pension benefits, on the other, might make to the elderly's aggregate retirement income; the adequacy of the present replacement ratio in public and private retirement income programs; the appropriate mechanisms for ensuring that retirees continue to benefit directly from economic growth in the country; and the fiduciary or actuarial soundness of existing retirement income systems, which are confronted with increasing demands for payment of retirement benefits that outstrip the accumulation of assets.

Beginning in the late 1960s and continuing to the present day, popular and political support has been coalescing in favor of a major overhaul of the income-maintenance system in its various parts. By the time of this survey in 1974, the studies and debates had already forged several significant pieces of reform legislation. Confronting the fact that more than one out of every three elderly persons in the country lived on poverty incomes in 1965, Congress voted successive increases in social security retirement benefit levels between 1969 and 1972, which increased by more than half the benefits received by most retirees and cut by more than half the number of elderly living in extreme poverty. In order to guarantee that the elderly would never again lag so far behind the prosperity enjoyed by the rest of the population, Congress provided that social security retirement benefit levels would automatically increase to keep pace with the consumer price index beginning in the year 1975. To supplement the social security retirement program, Congress established the new Supplemental Security Income (SSI) program, which, beginning in January 1974, provided a guaranteed minimum annual income to more than three million elderly poor. Bold reform legislation to curb the abuses in corporate and union pension plans that were previously woefully inadequate to the needs of retiring workers was effected with the Employee Retirement Income Security Act (ERISA) passed by Congress in 1974. Also by 1974, discussions concerning the future directions of social security were well under way. Thus, even at the present time, the prospect remains of additional major reforms still to come in the social security system and other income-maintenance programs for the aged.

Among the most critical of the problems remaining to be solved in this century concerns the fiduciary or actuarial soundness of the various income-maintenance programs. The incremental expansions of these systems over the past several decades to support an ever-increasing dependent aged population have inched these income-support programs closer and closer to economic collapse. Because of increases in longevity, more people have survived to retirement age, and coupled with the trend toward earlier retirements, more retirees are being supported outside the labor force for long periods of time--15 and 20 years instead of only two or three. The drain on the assets of existing income-maintenance systems to support this burgeoning retiree population has been staggering.

Perhaps the single most important question of the day is, To what extent will reform of these income-maintenance systems match the magnitude of the existing problems? Will the reforms be innovative and involve significant revamping of the programs, or will the outlines of grand reform be reduced by compromises to mere tinkerings and peripheral modifications in the systems? The recent legislative reforms discussed earlier suggest that decision-makers today may indeed be more receptive to making major modifications in existing income-maintenance systems than they have been at any time since the 1930s. The data reported in this chapter seem to confirm that speculation. Sizable segments of the decision-making community interviewed in this study appeared cognizant of the need to reform the income-maintenance system in order to provide better income support for elderly persons during their postemployment years, and many of the decision-makers proved not at all bashful in recommending major reforms in existing income-maintenance programs.

DECISION-MAKERS' PERSPECTIVES ON POVERTY IN THE AGED POPULATION

All segments of the decision-making community sampled in this survey emphasized the elderly's financial problems far more than any other problem. (Table 3.1 summarizes the decision-makers' responses by subgroups.) Advocates for the aged and other persons who work closely with the aged were the least likely rather than the most likely to cite "finances" as a major problem for the elderly, although three quarters of these decision-makers did also cite the problems created by the lack of enough money. The union local presidents, on the other hand, nearly unanimously focused upon the elderly's financial problems.

The apparent reason for the decision-makers' concern about the elderly's financial problems is the common perception in the decision-making community that many elderly are forced to live on poverty-level incomes. As observed in the overview provided in the preceding chapter, many of the decision-makers interviewed in this study overemphasized the prevalence of poverty in the elderly population.*

*See Figure 2.1 and the accompanying discussion in Chapter 2.

TABLE 3.1

Decision-Makers Who Identified "Finances" as One of the Three Major Problems Commonly Facing Older People

	Percent	Rank
Positional Characteristics of the Decision-Makers		
Position in the Policy Process		
Legislators (N = 71)	86	1
Agency administrators (N = 70)	86	1
Service delivery personnel (N = 70)	81	1
Corporate directors of personnel (N = 35)	83	1
Union local presidents (N = 35)	97	1
Advocates for the aged (N = 35)	74	1
Responsibility for Aging Programs		
Primary function (N = 85)	78	1
Important but not central function (N = 88)	88	1
Minor function (N = 143)	87	1
Area of Program Expertise		
Income-maintenance specialists (N = 61)	89	1
Specialists in other program areas (N = 255)	84	1
Personal Characteristics of the Decision-Makers		
Age of the Respondent		
Under 45 (N = 98)	84	1
45-54 (N = 98)	86	1
55-64 (N = 90)	86	1
65 and over (N = 30)	80	1
Sex of the Respondent		
Male (N = 230)	83	1
Female (N = 86)	85	1
Ethnicity of the Respondent		
White (N = 235)	85	1
Minority (N = 81)	82	1
Educational Level of the Respondent		
High school graduate or less (N = 42)	81	1
Some college (N = 64)	92	1
College graduate (N = 99)	85	1
Postcollege professional education (N = 111)	81	1
Total (N = 316)	84	1

Source: Compiled by the author.

Only one quarter of the sample of decision-makers (28 percent) entertained a reasonably accurate impression of the incidence of poverty among the aged. In contrast, nearly half of the decision-makers (43 percent) asserted that at least one half of the elderly population live on poverty incomes. (It will be recalled from those earlier discussions that about 16 percent of the elderly throughout the country live on incomes at or below official poverty income guidelines, with the figure rising to 20 percent in Los Angeles County, the site of this study.) These latter decision-makers are clearly misinformed about the income status of the elderly population. Closer examination of the data is required to determine which subgroups in the decision-making community are more disposed to overestimate the extent of poverty in the aged population; these data are presented in Table 3.2.

Substantial numbers of decision-makers within each of the six subsamples distinguished by different positions in the policy process overestimated the extent of poverty in the aged population. Nevertheless, among those six subsamples, the corporate directors of personnel were significantly less likely than all the others to misjudge the income status of the elderly. Nearly one third of these corporate officials correctly estimated that 10 to 20 percent of Los Angeles County elderly lived in poverty, whereas less than one in eight of any of the other subsamples estimated the figure within that range. Although one third of the corporate subsample (31 percent) placed the percentage of elderly poor in the county at half or more, the percentage of corporate personnel directors thus miscalculating the number of elderly poor was still significantly lower than the percentage of decision-makers in the other five subsamples making similar miscalculations. For example, the majority of the service delivery personnel and union local presidents incorrectly believed that at least half of the elderly residents in the county lived in dire poverty.

The contrasting perceptions of the corporate directors of personnel and the union local presidents are readily explained in terms of their contrasting positions in the business world. The union local presidents are the advocates for the rank-and-file blue-collar and perhaps lower level white-collar workers in the corporate structure. Many of these union management officials have been the chief ranking officers of their union locals for ten years or more, and during that time they have undoubtedly observed many union members forced to retire on inadequate pensions and insufficient savings after a lifetime of hard work. The corporate directors of personnel, in contrast, deal mostly with the nonunion personnel in the corporate structure, which, not coincidentally, are the higher salaried mid- and top-level white-collar managers of the company. The corporate personnel directors are thus more concerned with monitoring the retire-

TABLE 3.2

"What Percentage of Elderly People in Los Angeles Would You Estimate Are Living at or below the Poverty Level (Based on OEO Figures $2,330 per Person or $3,070 per Couple, per Year)?"
(percentage estimating 50 percent of the elderly or more)

Positional Characteristics of the Decision-Makers	
Position in the Policy Process	
Legislators (N = 71)	41
Agency administrators (N = 70)	40
Service delivery personnel (N = 70)	51
Corporate directors of personnel (N = 35)	31
Union local presidents (N = 35)	54
Advocates for the aged (N = 35)	40
Responsibility for Aging Programs	
Primary function (N = 85)	41
Important but not central function (N = 88)	43
Minor function (N = 143)	45
Area of Program Expertise	
Income-maintenance specialists (N = 61)	30
Specialists in other program areas (N = 255)	47
Personal Characteristics of the Decision-Makers	
Age of the Respondent	
Under 45 (N = 98)	42
45-54 (N = 98)	48
55-64 (N = 90)	37
65 and over (N = 30)	43
Sex of the Respondent	
Male (N = 230)	39
Female (N = 86)	55
Ethnicity of the Respondent	
White (N = 235)	37
Minority (N = 81)	62
Educational Level of the Respondent	
High school graduate or less (N = 42)	45
Some college (N = 64)	45
College graduate (N = 99)	42
Postcollege professional education (N = 111)	43
Total (N = 316)	43

Source: Compiled by the author.

ment transition of those employees in the company who are relatively more likely to receive adequate pensions and to have accumulated sizable savings out of their salary over their work lifetime (see note 1).

Female decision-makers were far more likely to overestimate the incidence of poverty among the elderly than were men. Nearly four out of ten (39 percent) of the male decision-makers believed that fewer than one in three older persons lived in dire poverty, but only one in seven (15 percent) female decision-makers believed the incidence of poverty among the elderly was so limited. Rather, the majority of the women (55 percent) asserted that poverty confronted half or more of the elderly residents in the county. There were similar and even more marked contrasts in perceptions between the minority and the white decision-makers. White decision-makers (34 percent) were more than twice as likely as minority decision-makers (15 percent) to place the figure of elderly poor under 30 percent; but minority decision-makers (62 percent) were almost twice as likely as white decision-makers (37 percent) to believe that half or more of the elderly were poor. These contrasting perceptions between white and minority, men and women, decision-makers mirror differences in the real world. The burden of poverty in the aged population falls heaviest on single women and the minority aged.[10] Thus the female and the minority decision-makers may only reflect their respective constituencies when they emphasize the income disadvantage that many elderly suffer.

To summarize briefly, substantial segments of the decision-making community emphasized poverty and welfare dependency among the elderly. Union officials and female and minority decision-makers were the most likely to distort the incidence of poverty in the elderly age group, but it is conceivable that these decision-makers were simply reflecting the incidence of poverty in their respective constituencies--the blue-collar workers, women, and the minority aged--where the incidence of poverty does approach the level of half or more. If so, it would be a strong argument for encouraging a divesting of decision-making responsibilities to provide for greater representation of minority points of view (that is, ethnic, sex, and socioeconomic minority viewpoints) in the decision-making processes. On the other hand, union, female, and minority decision-makers may simply be misinformed in greater numbers. The data did show that those decision-makers who reported working most closely with the elderly, regardless of the decision-makers' positional or personal characteristics, registered more accurate impressions concerning poverty in the elderly age group.

The data do not allow for a more refined analysis that could be resolved in favor of one hypothesis or the other concerning the union, women, and minority decision-makers' perceptions. It is an interesting question that deserves further empirical exploration given the rather obvious implications it might have for public policy-making under either an interest-group model focusing on constituency representation in the policy process or a rational problem-solving model concerned with developing adequate program responses based on accurate perceptions of fundamental aspects of the problem under consideration. These data can only suggest the need for more research on this issue.

SOLVING THE AGED'S PROBLEMS BY INCREASING THEIR INCOME

Given the income deprivation that these decision-makers generally believed the elderly age group experiences, it is not surprising that nearly 40 percent believed that most of the elderly's problems could be solved if they were given an adequate income (see Table 3.3). An additional quarter of the sample of decision-makers (23 percent) suggested that more income probably would not solve all the elderly's other problems, "but it would help like hell" (the head of a manufacturing union local, I.D. 511A). The union local presidents, who most distorted the incidence of poverty among the aged, were more likely than decision-makers in all other positions in the policy process to maintain that an adequate income alone would resolve most of the problems facing older people.* At the same time,

---

*The educational level of these union local presidents is undoubtedly a relevant factor in patterning their perceptions here. In the sample generally, there was a strong relationship between the decision-maker's level of education and his belief that income alone could solve most of the elderly's problems. Table 3.3 shows that those with only a high school education were more than twice as likely as those with professional degrees or training to believe that income was a panacea for the elderly's various problems. The major contrast in perceptions developed between those with some college education and those with none. The union local presidents, as a group, averaged the least education among the six subsamples (nearly 60 percent of the union leaders had never attended college). Those union leaders who had attended college were far less likely than those who had only completed high school to believe that income alone could solve the elderly's other major problems. Whereas four out of every five of the lesser educated union officials believed

TABLE 3.3

"Would an Adequate Income Alone Resolve Most of the Problems Older People Face?" (percentage responding "yes")

Positional Characteristics of the Decision-Makers	
Position in the Policy Process	
Legislators (N = 71)	48
Agency administrators (N = 70)	30
Service delivery personnel (N = 70)	39
Corporate directors of personnel (N = 35)	26
Union local presidents (N = 35)	57
Advocates for the aged (N = 35)	37
Responsibility for Aging Programs	
Primary function (N = 85)	32
Important but not central function (N = 88)	41
Minor function (N = 143)	43
Area of Program Expertise	
Income-maintenance specialists (N = 61)	26
Specialists in other program areas (N = 255)	42
Personal Characteristics of the Decision-Makers	
Age of the Respondent	
Under 45 (N = 98)	40
45-54 (N = 98)	43
55-64 (N = 90)	34
65 and over (N = 30)	40
Sex of the Respondent	
Male (N = 230)	42
Female (N = 86)	33
Ethnicity of the Respondent	
White (N = 235)	38
Minority (N = 81)	42
Educational Level of the Respondent	
High school graduate or less (N = 42)	64
Some college (N = 64)	41
College graduate (N = 99)	38
Postcollege professional education (N = 111)	30
Total (N = 316)	39

Source: Compiled by the author.

the corporate directors of personnel, who least distorted the number of elderly poor, were the least likely to believe that additional income would solve the elderly's other problems.

The legislators were another subsample that substantially supported the proposition that added income alone would solve most of the elderly's other problems. Their opinions in this regard are important because they are in the position to vote increases in the level of benefits available to the elderly through various public retirement income programs. If the legislators act consistently with this belief, they should prefer direct income transfers, or alternatively, income substitutes such as vouchers, stamps and coupons, benefits-in-kind assistance for solving the elderly's various problems related to health care, housing, transportation, and so forth. Subsequent chapters in this volume will afford repeated opportunities to examine this proposition.

It should not be forgotten that the majority of the decision-making community, however, was not convinced that additional income would solve most of the problems that elderly people typically face on account of their advanced age. Among the frequent rejoinders were "You can't buy your friends or your health" (a local legislator, I.D. 344B); "Money wouldn't solve their transportation problems, because buses don't run in some of the areas, especially near senior citizen housing units" (head of a local committee on aging, I.D. 634); "Money alone definitely will not solve most of the elderly's problems. The most critical thing in a person's life is having something worthwhile to do" (personnel director of a utility company, I.D. 435D); "Money can't buy friends. It won't resolve loneliness or give one self-satisfaction" (a local legislator, I.D. 125); "It wouldn't solve the crime situation" (a state assemblyman, I.D. 152A). None of these decision-makers, however, wanted to be interpreted as saying that additional income would not help to solve some of these other problems typically confronting older people. They only sought to underscore the fact that money alone could not take care of these problems.

SOLVING THE AGED'S INCOME PROBLEMS

The decision-makers were asked during the interview, "Many people are poor for the first time in their lives when they retire on

---

additional income was the panacea for the elderly's problems, only one in four of the college-educated believed so. The education variable is thus a crucial determinant of a union official's attitude toward solving the elderly's problems with added income.

inadequate income. What do you think can be done to change this situation?" The majority of the sample (56 percent) suggested improving the private pension system in order to enhance the contribution that private pension benefits add to the elderly's retirement income (see Table 3.4). In contrast, only one in three of the decision-makers (34 percent) mentioned improvements in the social security system. These findings were the reverse of what this researcher expected to find. Since the retirement benefit program was established in 1935, social security benefits have been the primary source of retirees' income support during the postemployment years of their lives. Apparently, however, more and more decision-makers in the 1970s are diverting their attention from social security to private pensions as they look for ways to bolster the elderly's retirement income support. Many of the decision-makers interviewed here seem to be returning to the original concept of a tripartite system of income maintenance for these elderly in which social security retirement benefits would be substantially supplemented by private pension benefits and personal savings and, in some cases, earnings from employment.

In Table 3.4 the data confirm that many decision-makers are thinking in just such terms. One in five of the decision-makers (19 percent) insisted that older people had a responsibility to make suitable provision for their own old age. For example, a national legislator (I.D. 168) admonished, "People are relying too much on government to take care of them. They must realize that they will get old. It is partly <u>their</u> responsibility." A like percentage (17 percent) of the decision-makers suggested that schools, government, and employers should help employees plan for retirement more effectively by sponsoring retirement preparation seminars or providing individual retirement counseling sessions: "Companies and individuals have to share the load. Companies should help but individuals should direct their own retirement planning" (president of a service union local, I.D. 534).

Only one in ten of the decision-makers suggested earnings from employment as a viable means to improve the income status of retired people.[11] About half of these decision-makers recommended abolishing the so-called "retirement means" test, which provides for a one-dollar reduction in social security benefits for every two dollars earned by the retiree in excess of $3,000 per year. They felt that many impoverished retirees were deterred from seeking part- or full-time jobs because they feared losing their social security benefits.[12] Gerontologists and advocates for the aged have repeatedly launched crusades to get the social security retirement means test abolished, but to date no such movement has been successful.[13] The reason why is clear from these data. Only a very small minority

TABLE 3.4

Decision-Makers' Recommendations for Improving the Income Status of the Aged

Decision-Makers' Positional and Personal Characteristics	Improve Private Pension System (percent)	Improve Social Security Program (percent)
Positional Characteristics		
Position in the Policy Process		
Legislators (N = 71)	52	28
Agency administrators (N = 70)	60	29
Service delivery personnel (N = 70)	54	30
Corporate directors of personnel (N = 35)	57	37
Union local presidents (N = 35)	74	57
Advocates for the aged (N = 35)	40	34
Responsibility for Aging Programs		
Primary function (N = 85)	44	40
Important, not central function (N = 88)	68	28
Minor function (N = 143)	56	33
Area of Program Expertise		
Income-maintenance specialists (N = 61)	55	28
Specialists in other program areas (N = 255)	56	35
Personal Characteristics		
Age of the Respondent		
Under 45 (N = 98)	59	38
45-54 (N = 98)	57	24
55-64 (N = 90)	57	36
65 and over (N = 30)	40	40
Sex of the Respondent		
Male (N = 230)	56	35
Female (N = 86)	56	29
Ethnicity of the Respondent		
White (N = 235)	57	34
Minority (N = 81)	54	33
Educational Level of the Respondent		
High school graduate or less (N = 42)	57	38
Some college (N = 64)	58	28
College graduate (N = 99)	55	38
Postcollege education (N = 111)	56	31
Total (N = 316)	56	34

Source: Compiled by the author.

"Many People Are Poor for the First Time in Their Lives When They Retire on Inadequate Income. What Do You Think Can Be Done to Change This Situation?"				
Provide More Government-Subsidized Social Services (percent)	Provide More Employment Opportunities for Seniors (percent)	Provide More Retirement Preparation Programs (percent)	Individual's Responsibility to Save for Retirement (percent)	Nothing Can Be Done (percent)
39	6	9	28	0
29	10	24	16	0
20	13	17	17	1
20	11	26	20	3
29	6	9	11	0
43	14	23	17	3
32	15	21	18	2
32	7	11	14	0
27	9	19	23	1
13	10	21	20	0
19	10	17	18	1
31	10	20	16	0
30	9	16	21	1
26	6	17	21	2
37	23	13	13	0
33	11	15	20	1
21	7	23	16	2
29	10	17	21	1
31	10	17	12	1
38	12	12	17	2
33	8	20	13	3
25	13	17	23	0
29	7	18	20	0
30	10	17	19	1

of the decision-making community seems to consider elimination of the retirement means test a priority policy question at this point in time.

Nearly one third of the sample of decision-makers (30 percent) preferred subsidized social services to provide for all the elderly's basic needs--housing, food, medical care, transportation--as opposed to hiking the level of direct income payments received by the elderly from the various public and private retirement benefit programs. One state legislator (I.D. 143B), affirming that the government has to find a way to provide adequate housing, food, and medical care for the elderly, reached the ultimate conclusion, "I really don't know what can be done except plan state-owned senior citizens communities."

Most of these decision-makers, however, seemed to envision a coupon book filled with food stamps, housing discounts, transportation vouchers, and free recreation passes that would be sent to each social security pensioner along with his benefit check each month. Only a very few of the decision-makers actually opposed the idea of providing such subsidies to enable the elderly to purchase necessary goods and services. The director of a moderately expensive retirement home (I.D. 319A) insisted, "Food stamps are really a terrible disgrace. Not only have they been badly abused, but it hurts the dignity of the elderly to have to use stamps to pay for their food. A financial increase is the answer." His observation inevitably applies to the other coupons in the book just as well. A state legislator (I.D. 153A) opposed subsidized social services for a different reason: "I am not in favor of increasing retirement benefits with government supplements, because of the psychological effect it has on many people to do less and less to take care of their own problems." Many decision-makers, however, perceive government subsidy of basic social services for the elderly as a viable alternative to increasing retirement benefits directly.

The data reveal some very interesting differences among various subgroups in the decision-making community. A few of these differences will be highlighted here, but the reader is encouraged to scan Table 3.4 for additional contrasts in perceptions. Union local presidents were far and away the most supportive of expanding the role of private pension contributions to the elderly's aggregate retirement income. They were also the most likely to recommend increases in social security benefit levels. Their responses were thus entirely consistent with their common belief that poverty is widespread in the elderly population and that improving the income status of the elderly would alleviate most of the problems that the aged commonly confront. The important question now is whether these unions will assume an active role negotiating better pension plans for employees through collective bargaining.[14] Only two of the union officials interviewed in this study (I.D. 517, president of a public employees union, and I.D. 506, the head of an overview union association) specifically affirmed this role for the union leadership.

The advocates for the aged and legislators were most in favor of helping the elderly by providing a range of subsidized social services to cover their basic needs.* Perhaps the legislators believed that additional increases in social security retirement benefits are not politically feasible at the present time, given the pending fiscal crisis in the system. Rather, the legislators may feel that they have considerably more freedom to develop a variety of social service programs to supplement social security benefits because those programs would be subsidized wholly from general revenues and would not rely on the overworked payroll tax on workers and employers that finance the social security system. A sizable minority of the legislators (28 percent), however, believed not that government should provide more social services to the elderly, but that individuals should assume more responsibility for making adequate provision for their own retirement.

Nevertheless, given the agreement between many of the legislators and advocates for the aged regarding the desirability of providing a range of social service programs to assist the elderly, and given the possible advantage to the legislators that derives from being able to finance these social programs out of general revenues, it is possible that this service-in-kind mode of assistance to help needy elderly people may expand, at least so long as the fiscal crisis in the social security system renders unfeasible any substantial increases in the elderly's social security retirement benefits.

As informative as are the decision-makers' recommendations for solving the elderly's income problems, what they did not say is equally interesting. For example, only one of the entire sample of 316 decision-makers volunteered the elderly person's family as a source of assistance. A nursing supervisor in a large hospital (I.D. 329) recommended that "the family should be able to help where

---

*This finding does not ostensibly support the hypothesis suggested earlier in this chapter that legislators, because they believe at least in a plurality that income alone will solve the elderly's major problems, should favor direct income transfers over benefits-in-kind as the appropriate means for solving the elderly's various problems. A plausible reason for the legislators' retreat from that position is discussed in the text however.

there is need and receive some type of tax exemption." It is an eminently sensible proposition, and it is surprising that more decision-makers did not similarly identify the family as a source of assistance for needy elderly people, especially when 57 percent of these decision-makers, queried directly on the point in the interview, responded that grown children have an obligation to take care of their aged parents (see Chapter 2). The concept of relative responsibility does not appear to be as strongly rooted in the decision-makers' thinking about the problems of the aged as they verbalize it to be.

Curiously, too, not one of the decision-makers suggested as a possible solution to the elderly's existing impoverished status political organization by the elderly to effect changes in the income needs. The Townsend and the Ham-and-Eggs movements, both of the 1930s, were the only two major age-based social movements seen in the United States, and they were both mounted by elderly people who were discontented with being relegated to a life of abject poverty after a lifetime of hard work. The decision-makers interviewed here quite obviously do not anticipate a similar age-based movement sparked by the aged's feelings of income deprivation in the 1970s. Later in the interview, when talking about the political activism of this and future generations of elderly, however, 73 percent of the decision-makers asserted that income-maintenance issues would stimulate elderly persons to organize politically in order to affect programs and policies that directly impinge on their well-being and social status in the United States.

Here, then, are two examples where decision-makers expressed strong convictions in a general or abstract context that were not similarly reflected in their responses to problem-solving in specific contexts. Possibly the decision-makers volunteered what they perceived to be the most socially acceptable response to some of the questions in the interview. Possibly the decision-makers hold certain beliefs that they sacrifice to political or economic exigencies in specific problem-solving contexts. Whatever the explanation, it is a caveat to both reader and researcher to examine the decision-makers' verbalizations with care and to look wherever possible for additional data that might confirm whether the decision-maker is consistent in the ideas he expresses in the abstract and in the specific.

To recap briefly, the decision-makers, confronting the problem of improving the income status of the elderly population, generally preferred direct improvements in pension levels over subsidizing services to them or encouraging them back into the labor force. As regards putting more money in the elderly's pocket, the decision-makers agreed in the majority that the burden rests more with corporate and union pension plans than with the social security retirement program. The 316 decision-makers were unanimously agreed, however, that something has to be done to improve the income status of older Americans. Their recommendations for strengthening the private pension system and social security retirement program are now considered.

THE DECISION-MAKERS' RECOMMENDATIONS FOR REFORM OF THE PRIVATE PENSION SYSTEM

On Labor Day, 1974, just prior to commencement of interviewing in this survey, the Employee Retirement Income Security Act (or the pension reform law as it is also often called) was signed into law. Its major provisions are outlined in Figure 3.1.[15] ERISA greatly tightened federal government supervision over the operation of corporate and union pension plans. It established minimum vesting requirements to guarantee employee participation in the plans, and it established a federal insurance program that would provide beneficiaries with payments up to $750 per month in the event that their pension plans terminated with insufficient funds. To guard against such collapse, however, ERISA established new funding and fiduciary requirements for the pension plans. ERISA provided for the voluntary transfer of an employee's pension credits when he changed jobs, but only if his old and new employer approved of the transfer of those accumulated credits. The absence of any required portability provision in the enacted law has been broadly criticized. Earlier versions of the reform legislation did include mandatory portability allowances for transferring workers. Many congressmen, however, were concerned that no appropriate administrative arrangement existed to oversee the transfer of credits among thousands of disparate pension plans, and so portability in the private pension system was set aside for reconsideration at some future time.

ERISA also fails to make a number of other provisions. For example, it does not include the stiff investment controls over pension fund assets sought by some congressmen who were concerned that these pension funds account for approximately one third of the nation's investable wealth (at $186.3 billion), which monies are also virtually exempt from taxation by the government. ERISA also does not mandate minimum pension benefit levels or provide for automatic cost of living increases in those pension levels. ERISA does not even require an employer or union to sponsor a retirement plan for its employees. Nevertheless, ERISA is considered a good beginning on regulating the operation of the private pension system for the benefit of its contributors. Additional controls on the operation

FIGURE 3.1

Major Provisions of the Employee Retirement Income Security Act of 1974

---

1. Plans must minimally vest benefits using one of three alternatives:
   a. Vesting of 25 percent after five years of service, going up by 5 percent each year of the next five years and by 10 percent thereafter until 100 percent vesting after 15 years.
   b. Vesting of 100 percent after 10 years of service.
   c. Vesting of 50 percent when age and service add up to 45 years, with 100 percent vesting five years thereafter--subject to the constraint that employees must be 50 percent vested after ten years service and 100 percent vested after 15 years.
2. Plan termination insurance is established, up to $750 monthly for employees whose plans terminate without sufficient funds.
3. Funding and fiduciary standards are strengthened.
4. Individual retirement accounts (exempt from federal income taxation) may be established by workers without private or public employee pension coverage, investing up to $1,500 annually or 15 percent of annual compensation (whichever is less).
5. New disclosure regulations permit participants to request once each year a statement from the plan administrator of total benefits, both vested and non-vested, which have accrued and the earliest date on which unvested benefits will become nonforfeitable.
6. The Social Security Administration receives reports (through the Treasury Department) from employers of vested benefits held by separated workers; Social Security notifies employees of all vested pension rights at the time of Social Security entitlement.
7. With the consent and cooperation of their employers, employees may transfer upon separation vested pension rights on a tax-free basis from one employer to another; or, the employee may transfer the funds to an "individual retirement account."

Source: James H. Schultz, "Income Distribution and the Aging," in Handbook of Aging and the Social Sciences, ed. Robert H. Binstock and Ethel Shanas (New York: Van Nostrand-Reinhold, 1976), p. 582. A more comprehensive summary of the law is available in Alfred M. Skolnick, "Pension Reform Legislation of 1974," Social Security Bulletin 37, no. 12 (December 1974): 35-42.

of these private pension plans will undoubtedly follow in time if the sentiment of the decision-making community in general is reflected accurately in the sample of 316 interviewed in this study.

This sample of 316 decision-makers expressed strong support for stricter supervision of the private pension system by the federal government. Most of them even preferred to see government controls extending beyond those already instituted by ERISA. The decision-makers were virtually unanimous in their support for ERISA's minimum vesting standards to protect employees' pension rights (see Table 3.5). Although ERISA provided for only voluntary transfers of pension credits when an employee changes jobs, more than five out of six (85 percent) of the decision-makers in this sample also overwhelmingly supported establishing mandatory portability provisions in the private pension system. A like percentage (86 percent) endorsed ERISA's new funding requirements for the pension plans to ensure solvency of the plans. Three out of four of the decision-makers also supported developing regulations that would govern the type of investments managers of pension funds could make, something that ERISA does not now do. Finally, three out of four (74 percent) of the decision-makers approved of ERISA's new federally sponsored insurance system that guarantees some continued coverage of beneficiaries in the event that their corporate or union pension plan collapses for lack of sufficient funds.

Not all segments of the decision-making community emerged equally supportive of these changes in the private pension system, however. The corporate directors of personnel, for example, were not strongly in favor of mandating portability in the private pension system. A sizable minority of the legislators (18 percent) was similarly wary of requiring portability provisions in all pension plans. The union local presidents, on the other hand, almost unanimously recommended providing for the transfer of a worker's accumulated pension credits when he changes jobs; the union leadership must have seen too many union employees lose out on pension benefits when they were laid off from one job because their employer lost the bid on the next big contract.* Even if the union officials choose to

---

*The union local presidents were, similarly, the most concerned about the employees' loss of pension benefits in the event that the pension plan collapses because of insufficient funds to meet its current pension obligations. They were thus nearly unanimous in their support for the federal government mandating new funding requirements for the pension plans in the private sector to ensure that they could meet their funding obligations to present and future beneficiaries.

TABLE 3.5

Decision-Makers' Recommendations Concerning Private Pension Plan Reforms

Decision-Makers' Positional and Personal Characteristics	Vesting Standards (percent)	Portability Provisions (percent)
Positional Characteristics		
Position in the Policy Process		
Legislators (N = 71)	93	82
Agency administrators (N = 70)	96	90
Service delivery personnel (N = 70)	97	94
Corporate directors of personnel (N = 35)	94	46
Union local presidents (N = 35)	97	97
Advocates for the aged (N = 35)	97	94
Responsibility for Aging Programs		
Primary function (N = 85)	96	92
Important but not central function (N = 88)	94	88
Minor function (N = 143)	96	80
Area of Expertise		
Specialists on income maintenance (N = 61)	97	54
Specialists in other program areas (N = 256)	95	93
Personal Characteristics		
Age of the Respondent		
Under 45 (N = 98)	98	84
45-54 (N = 98)	94	80
55-64 (N = 90)	96	91
65 and over (N = 30)	93	93
Sex of the Respondent		
Male (N = 230)	95	82
Female (N = 86)	97	93
Ethnicity of the Respondent		
White (N = 235)	95	85
Minority (N = 81)	96	93
Educational Level of the Respondent		
High school graduate or less (N = 42)	93	93
Some college (N = 64)	94	84
College graduate (N = 99)	97	78
Postcollege professional education (N = 111)	96	90
Total (N = 316)	96	85

Source: Compiled by the author.

Should Pension Reform Legislation Include the Following Reforms?		
Fiduciary (Solvency) Standards (percent)	Investment Standards (percent)	Benefit Insurance Provisions (percent)
85	77	63
86	83	79
80	67	70
89	57	71
97	86	86
89	77	89
85	80	84
89	77	73
85	71	70
84	64	66
87	78	76
83	63	69
84	75	63
89	84	87
97	87	90
89	75	72
78	71	81
87	75	76
84	77	70
93	71	81
86	83	73
93	67	80
85	79	74
86	75	74

make pension portability a collective bargaining issue,* these data suggest it is unlikely that they will win sufficient support and cooperation from corporate management to establish a widespread system of pension portability in the private sector. If established, a system of pension portability will more likely be mandated by legislation than by collective bargaining negotiations, but the prospects for any legislative solution are necessarily reduced when one in five legislators and one of every two personnel directors are openly unsupportive of the proposal.

As can well be imagined, people who work closely with the aged were more supportive of establishing portability mechanisms in the private pension system than were those less closely involved with the elderly's problems. At the same time, individuals who manage or supervise the various retirement income-support programs were far less often in favor of mandating portability requirements. Once again, it appears that any attempt to mandate portability in private pension plans will encounter some significant opposition.

The segments of the decision-making community most opposed to implementing portability provisions in private pension plans--the corporate directors of personnel and the pension plan managers in particular--were also most displeased about any proposal to increase federal government supervision over the investment activities of these private pension funds. Nevertheless, more than half of the corporate personnel directors and two in three of the other decision-makers in the sample who supervised the operation of various income-support programs did maintain the necessity of developing stringent investment standards in order to protect the existing assets of these pension funds.

Borrowing from the idea of the Federal Deposit Insurance Corporation (FDIC), which protects individual bank accounts up to $40,000 in the event of a bank collapse, ERISA established a federally sponsored insurance system to guarantee retired employees a monthly benefit up to $750 should his private pension plan become bankrupt or otherwise terminate with outstanding liabilities. The advocates for the aged and the other decision-makers working closely with the elderly recorded the highest level of approval for this provision of ERISA. Curiously, the legislators as a group were the least enthusiastic about the federal insurance plan. Perhaps they envision an economic doomsday, another depression, when one pen-

---

*As noted in note 14, the likelihood that portability will become a major collective bargaining issue is slight, at least in the foreseeable future.

sion plan after another might collapse and leave the federal government to pay the pension checks of millions of workers across the country. If these data had been available before passage of ERISA, the future of the mandatory insurance system would certainly have seemed in doubt. Fortunately for older and retired workers, the insurance proposal survived the extended debates over ERISA's various components much intact, and now the insurance system exists as law.

The decision-makers' widespread support for these various pension system reforms proved consistent with their frequent observations that improving the income status of the elderly population in general would rest primarily upon strengthening the existing private pension system and not on extending social security even further. The union local presidents spoke most often about improving the existing private pension system as the best means of helping the elderly achieve a better quality of life, and across the board these union leaders were also the most supportive of each of the various specific proposals for reforms in the private pension system. Most of the decision-making community supported each one of ERISA's individual reforms of the pension system, and the vast majority of the decision-making community was prepared to support additional reforms that would tighten the federal government's control over the operation of these private pension plans even more. Specifically, many segments of the decision-making community stand ready to consider mandatory portability provisions and minimum investment standards, although some resistance to these proposals would undoubtedly be forthcoming from corporate management and pension fund supervisors, as well as from some of the legislators asked to consider the reform measures. In all probability, pension reform will again emerge as a viable policy issue in the not too distant future.

THE DECISION-MAKERS' RECOMMENDATIONS FOR RESOLVING THE FISCAL CRISIS FACING THE SOCIAL SECURITY SYSTEM

In recent decades, the social security retirement benefit program has been expanded to cover more and more U.S. workers and their dependents. At the same time, the benefit levels have increased more or less steadily, and an escalator clause has operated since 1975 to hike social security retirement benefit levels automatically by the same percentage as rises in the consumer price index. The result has been an astronomical growth in the size of the social security retirement system since its establishment in 1935. Cash transfer programs, the largest being social security, but including as well civil service and veterans' pensions and the new SSI program, today comprise the second largest category of expenditures in the federal budget, exceeded only by expenditures related to the country's defense.[16] More than 25 million beneficiaries receive retiree or survivors benefits totaling more than $85 billion each year from the social security retirement benefit program alone.[17]

The problem has been to finance these expansions of the social security retirement program. Because social security was designed to pay current beneficiaries from monies contributed in payroll taxes by currently employed workers and their employers, the increased obligations to beneficiaries have been managed in the past by increases in the payroll tax levied on employees and employers. Thus, in 1937, a payroll tax of 1 percent was paid by both the employee and his employer on the worker's first $3,000 of earnings. In 1977, the payroll tax was 5.85 percent on the first $16,500, paid by both the covered employee and his employer. Although more workers are contributing to the system with considerably heftier payroll taxes than in 1937, the payroll hikes have not kept pace with the increasing obligations to an expanding number of beneficiaries. The result is that the social security system is operating with a large annual deficit that is expected to deplete trust fund reserves in the system by the early to mid-1980s unless major modifications in the funding and/or benefit structure of the retirement program are undertaken, and undertaken quickly. Because decision-makers are understandably reluctant to reduce benefits to retirees and their dependents, the only remaining alternative is to bolster the trust fund's sagging reserves.

Many, many recommendations have been proffered from all corners of the decision-making community regarding a solution to the fiscal crisis now confronting the social security system. Some believe it is important to maintain the concept of social security as a system of social insurance for old age in which each individual saves for his own old age by making regular payroll tax contributions to the retirement system. They would solve the fiscal crisis by hiking payroll taxes until the income thus generated matched the payment obligations of the system.

The problem with this solution is that for the first time since the inception of the retirement program in the 1930s, payroll taxes simply cannot keep pace with the growth in beneficiary obligations. The reason is that certain assumptions regarding the continued growth of the economy and the population that supported the original design of the social security system no longer endure. For example, the growth of the retired population was to be matched by the continued growth of the working population, who would finance the former's retirement with payroll taxes on increased earnings. Instead, the United States is approaching zero population growth, and the economy has experienced slow growth with inflation eroding the incomes of many workers; and all the while, the trend toward early retirement has swelled the ranks of newly entitled beneficiaries.[18]

Even if Congress did not act to raise social security benefits beyond the automatic increases already mandated by law, and assuming an extremely modest inflation rate of 2.75 percent and increases in wage levels averaging 5 percent per year, the maximum retirement benefit would top $30,000 in the year 2010, when the postwar babies arrive at age 65. The maximum payroll tax contribution per worker to finance these retirement benefits would be $8,288 on the first $66,300 of the covered worker's earnings.[19] While it is true that workers' earnings would have increased as well, many analysts still find reason for alarm in these projected costs of the retirement system several decades into the future, and many predict a worker revolt against paying the ever-higher payroll taxes to finance the system.

For this reason many decision-makers appear to be searching for other alternatives to solve the fiscal crisis, and they seem willing to sacrifice something of the social insurance concept of social security in order to put the system on a sounder financial base.[20] These decision-makers suggest refinancing social security wholly or partially from general revenues, which, of course, derive from personal and corporate income taxes, not payroll taxes. The proponents of the social insurance concept of social security argue that financing the program out of general revenues will render the social security program indistinguishable from SSI and a plethora of other social welfare programs designed to help the poor and dependent population of the country.

A very few of the analysts surveying the fiscal crisis have recommended an altogether different solution--not reducing benefits to retirees and not increasing revenues, but rather reducing the number of beneficiaries eligible to receive social security retirement benefits. Most of these recommendations focus on eliminating or raising the age of eligibility for early retirements under the retirement program. (Currently, women may begin drawing social security benefits at age 60 and men at age 62, although they do receive reduced benefits for retiring before the normal age of 65.) A very small minority, however, has even advocated moving the primary age of eligibility for retirement benefits upward to 67, 68, or 70. These last proposals have not had much support to date, but it is possible that the closer the decision-making community gets to studying the problem and seeking a solution, the more desirable this alternative may seem. After all, what is magical about age 65 for entitlement to social security retirement benefits other than it is the age that Congress selected in 1935.

How did age 65 get chosen? Wilbur Cohen, a key figure in the development of the original social security legislation in the mid-1930s, provides an illuminating answer.

> The simple fact is that at no time in 1934 did the staff or members of the Committee on Economic Security deem feasible any other age than 65 as the eligible age for the receipt of old age insurance benefits. There is, therefore, very little material available to analyze the economic, social, gerontological or other reasons for the selection of this particular age. . . .
>
> The Committee made no detailed studies of alternative ages or of any proposals for voluntary retirement or of any flexible retirement program in relation to the disability of an individual. . . . It was understood that a reduction in the age below 65 would substantially increase costs and, therefore, might impair the possibility . . . of acceptance of the plan by Congress. A higher retirement age, of say 68 or 70, was never considered because of the belief that the public and Congressional opposition would develop against such a provision in view of the widespread unemployment that existed.[21]

The decision-makers interviewed in this study clearly seemed to believe that the social security system is stretched nearly to its limits, and that, at least for now, it is crucial that the private pension system contribute more substantially to the retirement income support of the dependent aged population. But considerably less agreement existed in this cross section of the decision-making community concerning how to reform the social security retirement system as opposed to the private pension system. As this survey was conducted just after ERISA was signed into law, it is conceivable that the decision-makers' strong consensus regarding pension reform priorities was created by the process of political debate on reform alternatives and enactment of an agreeable compromise. At the time of this survey, the issues surrounding the growing fiscal crisis in the social security system were just being articulated and drawing closer scrutiny. A considerable diversity of opinion regarding solving social security's fiscal crisis thus existed in this sample of decision-makers (see Table 3.6).

One quarter (24 percent) of the sample of decision-makers wished to retain the concept of social security as social insurance for old age in pristine form; they lobbied for raising payroll taxes in the future as much as necessary to cover the growing payment obligations in the system. In contrast, more than one half (54 percent) of the 316 decision-makers were prepared to sacrifice the social insurance concept and finance the social security program partially or wholly out of general revenues. Among this latter group, however, the preferred alternative by a margin of more than two to one was to finance social security only partially from general revenues; in other words, these decision-makers were urging retention of the social insurance concept and the payroll tax and at the same time pragmatically conceding that these revenues should be supplemented as necessary to keep the retirement program abreast of its current obligations. Hence, the data may also be read as saying that 62 percent of the decision-makers urged retention of the payroll tax to finance the social security retirement program. Finally, and as to be expected, only one in 15 (6 percent) of the decision-makers entertained a proposal not for refinancing the system but for changing the structure of entitlements, suggesting a change in the age eligibility for social security, especially directed toward disallowing early retirements.

There were important differences among specific subgroups in the decision-making community regarding their level of support for each of these reform proposals. The advocates for the aged and the service delivery personnel were the most committed to the idea of refinancing the social security system wholly or partially out of general revenues, although the majority of the service providers still preferred to retain the payroll tax and merely supplement program revenues where necessary with general revenues. Only among the advocates and the union local presidents was a sizable minority in favor of refinancing social security wholly from general revenues and eliminating the payroll tax entirely.

Looking at the decision-making community as a whole, the data reveal that those individuals charged with the various responsibilities for the operation of the income-maintenance system in its component parts were far less receptive to proposals for refinancing the social security retirement program wholly or partially from general revenues than were decision-makers who had different program responsibilities vis-a-vis the aged. Thus those most intimately involved with the income-maintenance system appeared to be those most captivated by the social insurance concept of the social security retirement program, and they are the ones most interested in maintaining a clear distinction between the social security retirement benefit program and such social welfare programs as SSI. Any discussions focused on resolving the fiscal crisis now confronting the social security system will undoubtedly reflect the opinions of those charged with managing the nation's income-maintenance system in its various parts, and to the extent that this is so, it is likely that

TABLE 3.6

Decision-Makers' Recommended Solutions for the Fiscal Crisis Confronting the Social Security System

Decision-Makers' Positional and Personal Characteristics	Raise Payroll Taxes as Necessary (percent)	Partially Refinance from General Revenues (percent)
Positional Characteristics		
Position in the Policy Process		
Legislators (N = 71)	15	37
Agency administrators (N = 70)	37	36
Service delivery personnel (N = 70)	19	53
Corporate directors of personnel (N = 35)	23	31
Union local presidents (N = 35)	37	17
Advocates for the aged (N = 35)	14	43
Responsibility for Aging Programs		
Primary function (N = 85)	22	45
Important but not central function (N = 88)	22	38
Minor function (N = 143)	27	34
Area of Expertise		
Specialists on income maintenance (N = 61)	33	30
Specialists in other program areas (N = 255)	22	40
Personal Characteristics		
Age of the Respondent		
Under 45 (N = 98)	20	45
45-54 (N = 98)	18	37
55-64 (N = 98)	33	32
65 and over (N = 30)	27	37
Sex of the Respondent		
Male (N = 230)	26	34
Female (N = 86)	19	49
Ethnicity of the Respondent		
White (N = 235)	25	37
Minority (N = 81)	21	40
Educational Level of the Respondent		
High school graduate or less (N = 42)	26	29
Some college (N = 64)	20	33
College graduate (N = 99)	27	39
Postcollege professional education (N = 111)	23	43
Total (N = 316)	24	38

Source: Compiled by the author.

Preferred Means of Dealing with the Fiscal Crisis in the Social Security Retirement System

Wholly Refinance from General Revenues (percent)	Disallow Early Retirements (percent)	Miscellaneous Solutions (percent)	No Recommended Solution for the Problem (percent)
7	11	24	6
13	1	10	3
16	7	1	4
9	11	23	3
34	6	6	0
31	0	11	0
21	2	8	1
19	6	15	1
11	9	13	6
7	10	18	3
18	6	11	3
14	9	9	2
18	5	13	8
14	6	14	0
20	3	13	0
17	7	14	3
15	6	7	5
14	6	14	3
21	7	9	2
29	2	14	0
20	8	17	2
10	8	12	3
14	5	9	5
16	6	12	3

the payroll tax will be retained as the central financing mechanism of the social security program.

Recently enacted legislation aimed at ending the fiscal crisis confronting the social security retirement benefit program confirms the continued viability of the social insurance concept on which the old-age retirement system was constructed. Despite President Jimmy Carter's proposal to refinance the retirement program partially from general revenues, the new law provides for financing the increasing beneficiary obligations of the social security system exclusively through raises in the payroll taxes of those currently employed and their employers. After a decade of debates, the new legislation finally did little more than change the numbers in the existing formula used to compute the level of payroll tax contributions. The taxation rate is now set to rise from the present 5.85 percent to 7.15 percent in 1987 and the maximum annual income taxed will rise from the present $16,500 to $42,600 in 1987. The formula modifications are expected to yield between $225 and $250 billion additional revenues for the ailing social security system, which it is hoped will eliminate fiscal deficits in the trust fund at least well into the next century.

Although incremental program reform ultimately prevailed, it is nevertheless significant that debates over the past decade regarding the "future directions of social security" have generated numerous proposals for a more radical restructuring of the entire retirement system. Not too long ago, proposals for financing social security even in part out of general revenues were labeled radical and heretical because they were inimical to the concept of social security as an old-age social insurance system. The data presented in this chapter suggest that the climate of decision-making may be very different today. The decision-makers in this sample seem to recognize the need to shore up the social security retirement program, and they are prepared to consider a wide range of reform proposals, many of which would never have received consideration in earlier decades.

The depression in the 1930s converted Americans of all faiths and philosophies into pragmatists, and in response to the ailing economy they fashioned an old-age social insurance system that would provide for older workers outside of the labor force. Now, social and economic forces in the country's present stage of development--a slow growth economy and zero population growth in particular--are forcing a reevaluation of the original plans for the social security retirement system. Economic conditions once again may be turning Americans of all faiths and philosophies into pragmatists who will seek to solve the recurrent fiscal crises confronting social security in the most rational manner possible. Further incremental expansion of the income system to ease this burden or that strain may not be feasible. More radical reforms may soon be required. According to these data, however, the decision-making community appears ready to respond to the challenge of reform.

THE DECISION-MAKERS' PERSPECTIVES ON INCOME MAINTENANCE FOR THE AGED IN FUTURE DECADES

One reason that the decision-makers in this sample urged major reform of the income-maintenance system in its various parts is that they envision a growing strain on that income-maintenance system in future decades. More than six out of seven (84 percent) of the decision-makers interviewed here asserted that the trend toward early retirement was going to continue in the foreseeable future in the United States. A like percentage (87 percent) of the decision-makers anticipated increased longevity, which would mean even more workers surviving to retirement and living well into old age. These jointly held beliefs have led half of the decision-makers to give serious thought to the strain that providing for these future generations of retirees will place on existing income-maintenance systems. (The data are reported in Table 2.12.) Nearly one in three (29 percent) of the decision-makers, for example, cited the added tax burden on the working population to support this growing dependent aged population in the country. Not a few decision-makers predicted a worker revolt against rising payroll taxes in the not too distant future.

Legislators and corporate directors of personnel, as could be expected, were the most concerned about the ability of existing retirement income programs to provide adequately for the growing number of retired beneficiaries who are expected in future decades. Curiously, however, the corporate personnel directors were far more dire in their predictions of an actual revolt by workers against payroll taxes than were the legislators, who enact those tax increases. If such sentiment is strong among the currently employed, it is the legislators who could least afford to ignore it, because they need labor's votes to get reelected.

The willingness of those employed to share the economic and social returns from production and growth in the economy with those no longer actively engaged in the labor market is an important determinant of the quality of life the dependent aged will be allowed to enjoy, for it is the workers' payroll taxes and pension fund contributions that finance the retirement income support provided to today's retirees. Herman Brotman, formerly with the Administration on Aging, very aptly described the posture of the aged in this regard:

> When someone retires, he does not have a basement stuffed with goods and services he will need for the rest of his life. For him, as for everyone else, practically everything consumed comes out of the current production of goods and services. The owners, the managers and the members of the labor force exercise first claim. The non-producers, including the aged, get a share based mostly on the producers' willingness to share. The size of the aged's share is determined by how much purchasing power is transferred to them. Methods of financing and the like are important, but incidental. It comes down to the younger group's willingness to share--in other words, on the ordering of our national priorities.[22]

Income maintenance for the aged is thus a social decision that affects the entire social order. Decision-makers can ill-afford to make decisions about income support for the aged without considering the impact of those retirement programs on other sectors of the population and on future generations of retirees. Planning for the income support of the dependent aged population requires long-term planning, not short-term reaction to immediate stresses and strains in the existing systems. The decision-makers' awareness of the long-term implications of developing income-maintenance programs for the elderly that will serve future generations will clearly emerge from this survey, and give hope that the climate of decision-making may facilitate rational solutions to some of the serious problems created by trying to support an ever-increasing aged population on inadequately funded retirement income programs.

SUMMARY

The decision-makers interviewed in this study expressed considerable concern over the adequacy of existing programs of income support for the dependent aged population in the United States. For one thing, they perceive large numbers of the elderly living in abject poverty, far more, in fact, than really do. The decision-makers have concluded on the basis of that observation that existing public and private pension benefits are inadequate to guarantee the vast majority of elderly a reasonable quality of life in their later years (on that score, many of the elderly's protagonists would agree). For this reason, the vast majority of the decision-makers urged reform of the income-maintenance system in its various parts to underwrite a better quality of life for older Americans.

The decision-makers for the most part acknowledged that major reforms of both private and public pension systems are required in order to improve the level of income support provided to retirees. At the same time, decision-makers have evidenced a readiness to give radical reform proposals serious consideration. Income maintenance for the aged is a political issue pressing for major public policy response within the next five to ten years.

A number of major reforms may be forecast on the basis of this limited analysis of the current climate of decision-making. First is the greater coordination of private pension plans with public pension systems in order to develop a more broad-based system of retirement income support for the elderly. Second is the tightening of federal government controls over the operation of corporate and union pension plans beyond that provided in ERISA. Third is the refinancing of the social security retirement program partially from general revenues to see the program through this period when trust fund reserves are depressed, with a possible effort to institutionalize similar emergency actions in the future whenever unemployment or inflation is high and normal payroll revenues are insufficient to meet current payment obligations in the program. The reform of income-maintenance systems that began in the early 1970s is certainly going to continue well into the 1980s.

NOTES

1. Only among the self-employed and professional workers do incomes exceed expenditures by a sufficient margin to make saving for retirement across a work lifetime a viable alternative. For all other occupational groups, income does not exceed expenditures by a margin sufficient to support significant savings for retirement until well into the workers' 50s; and for the semiskilled, unskilled, and marginally employed workers, income may never exceed expenditures by a margin sufficient to allow saving for retirement. Juanita M. Kreps, "Aging and Financial Management," in Aging and Society, Volume II: Aging and the Professions, ed. Matilda White Riley, John W. Riley, Jr., and Marilyn E. Johnson (New York: Russell Sage Foundation, 1969), pp. 201-28.

2. In 1970, a male retiring at 65 years of age had an additional life expectancy of approximately 13 years, while his wife at age 65 had an additional life expectancy of nearly 17 years. Herman B. Brotman, "Life Expectancy: Comparison of National Levels in 1900 and 1974 and Variations in State Levels, 1969-1971," Gerontologist 17, no. 1 (February 1977): 19.

3. Retirees may continue to work on a limited basis and still collect retirement benefits from social security. But their retirement benefits are reduced by one dollar for every two dollars that they earn in excess of $3,000 per year on the theory that they are not fully retired and hence they do not require the social security benefits to replace lost earnings. The term "retirement means test" or "earnings test" is often used to describe this one-for-two formula that establishes eligibility for social security benefits among those elderly who continue to work past age 65. For those unfamiliar with the social security system, consult Robinson Hollister, "Social Mythology and Reform: Income Maintenance for the Aged," Annals of the American Academy of Political and Social Science 415 (September 1974): 19-40. The article discusses complex issues in a highly informative and interesting survey of the problems inherent in the existing system of income maintenance for the elderly.

4. Up-to-date figures are reported in issues of the Social Security Bulletin, published monthly by the Social Security Administration.

5. Janet Murray, "Houseownership and Financial Assets: Findings from the 1968 Survey of the Aged," Social Security Bulletin 35, no. 8 (August 1972): 3-23.

6. One in four (23 percent) of the elderly couples and one in six (17 percent) of the elderly singles who are homeowners hold equity in their homes worth $20,000 or more; four in ten of the home-owning elderly enjoy a home equity valued at between $10,000 and $19,999; 37 percent of the couples and 44 percent of the singles have less than $10,000 equity in their homes. Ibid.

7. Walter W. Kolodrubetz and Donald M. Landay, "Coverage and Vesting of Full-Time Employees under Private Retirement Plans," Social Security Bulletin 36, no. 11 (November 1973): 20-36.

8. Walter W. Kolodrubetz, "Employee-Benefit Plans, 1972," Social Security Bulletin 37, no. 5 (May 1974): 15-21.

9. Walter W. Kolodrubetz, "Private Retirement Benefits and Relationship to Earnings: Survey of New Beneficiaries," Social Security Bulletin 36, no. 5 (May 1973): 16-36.

10. Among the elderly who lived on poverty incomes in 1971, 60 percent are unrelated individuals, and of these, 83 percent are women. Single and widowed women thus bear the major burden of poverty within the elderly population. Neal E. Cutler and Robert A. Harootyan, "Demography of the Aged," in Aging: Scientific Perspectives and Social Issues, ed. Diana S. Woodruff and James E. Birren (New York: Van Nostrand, 1975), p. 62. Similarly, in 1973, one in seven (14 percent) of the white elderly lived on poverty-level incomes compared to more than one in three (36 percent) of the minority elderly in the country. Robin Jane Walther, "Economics

and the Older Population," in Aging: Scientific Perspectives and Social Issues, ed. Diana S. Woodruff and James E. Birren (New York: Van Nostrand, 1975), p. 341.

11. A recent nationwide survey conducted in 1974 by Harris poll researchers found 12 percent of the 65 and older population in the country employed. Another three in ten (31 percent) of those who were retired or unemployed indicated that they would like to find some work. Thus more than one third of the elderly population is discontented with the idea of complete withdrawal from the labor force. Louis Harris and Associates, The Myth and Reality of Aging in America (Washington, D.C.: National Council on the Aging, 1975), pp. 87-88.

12. The Harris survey in 1974, however, found that very few (4 percent) of the retired and unemployed elderly who desired to return to work cited loss of their pension benefits as the reason why they had not found other employment. The majority of the elderly cited their poor health (57 percent) or their age (28 percent). One in seven (15 percent), however, did blame the lack of available job opportunities. Ibid., p. 89.

13. The estimated cost of removing the retirement means test would be about $4 billion annually, which, if financed by the payroll tax, would require adding about one fourth of a percentage point to both the employee and employer contributions. The major resistance to abolishing the retirement means test is the persistence of the belief that social security benefits are intended as a partial replacement of earnings from work and the fear that this concept will be diluted or lost completely if elderly persons are permitted to work full time and still collect their entire social security pension. Many view the retirement means test as an archaic holdover from the 1930s when social security was enacted as a response to the economic crisis created by the worldwide depression. Social security was initially perceived as a way to entice older workers out of the labor force by offering them a modest monthly income contingent on their not working. The purpose of social security would obviously have been defeated during the 1930s if workers had retired from their jobs, begun collecting social security retirement benefits, and then subsequently reentered the labor force on a full- or part-time basis to supplement their retirement benefits with additional earnings. Consequently, the architects of the social security retirement system conditioned payment of benefits on withdrawal from the labor force. Today, it is argued, the economic situation of the country does not require this forced choice between employment and retirement, between work and leisure, and hence the retirement means test ought to be abolished. See Hollister, "Social Mythology and Reform"; and Daniel A. Quirk, "The Retirement Test: The Debate Continues," Industrial Gerontology 2, no. 1 (Winter 1975): 76-80.

14. The U.S. Supreme Court decided in 1949 that retirees' pensions were a proper subject of collective bargaining negotiations between unions and employers (Inland Steel Co. v. National Labor Relations Board, 170 F.2d 247, 1949). In 1971, however, the U.S. Supreme Court affirmed a lower court decision that held unions were not required to negotiate alterations in pension benefit levels for retired employees (Allied Chemical and Alkali Workers of America v. Pittsburgh Plate Glass Co., 404 U.S. 157). In 1974, only one in ten private pension plans were subject to collective bargaining. Theodor Schuchat, "Pension Reform: Limits and Accomplishments," Industrial Gerontology 1, no. 2 (Spring 1974): 31.

15. For an excellent elementary introduction to concepts and issues in the study of private pension plans, consult Merton C. Bernstein, The Future of Private Pensions (New York: Free Press, 1964).

16. Edward R. Fried, Alice M. Rivlin, Charles L. Schultze, and Nancy H. Teeters, Setting National Priorities: The 1974 Budget (Washington, D.C.: Brookings Institution, 1973), p. 5.

17. Current figures are available in monthly issues of the Social Security Bulletin published by the Social Security Administration.

18. As of 1972, more than half of all new beneficiaries drawing social security retirement benefits had retired before the age of 65. Julian Abbott, "Covered Employment and the Age Men Claim Retirement Benefits," Social Security Bulletin 37, no. 4 (April 1974): 3-16.

19. See Hollister, "Social Mythology and Reform," p. 32.

20. Ibid.

21. Leonard D. Cain, "The Growing Importance of Legal Age in Determining the Status of the Elderly," Gerontologist 14, no. 2 (April 1974): 169-70.

22. Herman B. Brotman, "The Aging: Who and Where," Perspectives on Aging 2, no. 1 (January-February 1973): 1.

4 Health Care Planning for the Aged: Ensuring the Aged's Access to the Best Possible Medical Care

Americans of all ages, but the elderly in particular, cite poor health as the major drawback to being old.[1] Their fears about poor health far overshadow their other concerns about loneliness, poverty, growing dependence, neglect, and boredom. They worry about having to give up favorite activities or possibly an entire lifestyle on account of declining health status. They dread the prospect of not being able to care for themselves throughout the last years of their life. They uncomfortably contemplate the possibility of catastrophic illness that could strike and leave them infirmed and destitute after a lifetime of hard work in which they tried to make adequate provision for their old age. They recoil from thoughts of the pain and suffering that could color the last days, months, or even years of their lives. These are the discomforting thoughts with which most Americans apparently face old age, and they seem little solaced by living in a country that is able to provide the best health care that medical science can make available.

While access to good medical care is crucial to maintaining good health at any stage of the life cycle, it is particularly important for the individual during the later years of his life when he is likely to show greater vulnerability to common infectious diseases and to suffer as well from one or more of the degenerative diseases that typically strike in later life. National health statistics confirm that the probabilities of illness and impairment do increase with age; older people experience many more days of restricted activity and bed disability in a year than younger people do.[2] As would be suggested by these data, the elderly must spend considerably more on health maintenance in any given year than younger people do; in fact, the elderly's expenditures in nearly all health care categories are between two and three times more than those of younger people.[3]

The elderly's access to good quality medical care is more and more becoming a political question.[4] In the United States, health maintenance and health care costs traditionally have been viewed as the individual's private responsibility. But this assessment is changing. Soaring medical care costs in the years following World War II prompted serious discussions about the federal government's role in guaranteeing Americans access to available medical care through a program of national health insurance.[5] The enactment of medicare in 1965, a federally administered medical insurance program to help cover the elderly's extraordinary health care costs, and the continued discussions concerning a national health insurance plan that would extend some kind of insurance coverage to all Americans, are evidence of the changing perspectives in the United States on the matter of health maintenance as a private versus a public concern.

But the political issues in health care for the aged extend far beyond making the medical care currently available in the community affordable for the elderly via the medicare insurance program. The very level of medical technology available from advances in medical science can be limited by the political decisions that determine the amount of money to be allocated for research in the diseases of late life. Even when the medical technology is available, political decisions determine its proper role within the total framework of health services to be delivered to the elderly population. For instance, is it worthwhile to support 200,000 cardiac transplants a year at a cost several times that of the current appropriation for the nutrition program that benefits far more people? Or consider the willingness of the government to support a $7 billion a year nursing home care program, while home health care programs continue to be resisted as a legitimate health care expense. Ultimately, these are political decisions broadly grounded in the values of the culture. They are decisions made by decision-makers similar to those interviewed in the present study.

This chapter affords an opportunity to examine the climate of decision-making in the area of health care policy for the aging during the mid-1970s. A decade after the enactment of medicare, how do decision-makers generally evaluate the elderly's access to good medical care? How do they assess the elderly's need for medical care, and how do they evaluate the quality of health care the elderly receive from the health services delivery system?

In anticipation of evaluating the climate of decision-making in the area of health care policy for the aged in the mid-1970s, it may be useful to review briefly the origins of health care policy for the elderly, in particular, the politics of medicare, which is relatively recent history. Many believe that the political climate of decision-making in which medicare was enacted a little over a decade ago is still very much part of the climate of decision-making in the field of health care policy today.[6] A brief understanding of the historic context of health care policy for the aged should make the evaluation of the present climate of decision-making more meaningful.

U.S. HEALTH CARE POLICY FOR THE AGED: MEDICARE'S ORIGINS AND OPERATION

Although medical science breakthroughs in the first part of the twentieth century meant more Americans surviving to and even well into old age, the availability of new medical technology sparked increased demands for medical services that sent the costs of health care services skyrocketing by mid-century. Concern over the barrier that rising costs erected to Americans utilizing available health care services generated political support for consideration of various health insurance proposals to underwrite affordable medical care for all Americans.

Opponents of national health insurance staunchly maintained that the proposed plans were unrestricted "give-away" programs, which did not distinguish between those in need and those not in need, between the needy deserving of help and the needy not deserving of help. They blasted national health insurance as creeping socialism, and for well over three decades, their view effectively dominated the politics of health care in the United States, stalling legislative action on any national health insurance proposal.

But the special plight of the elderly in securing adequate medical care could not be ignored. Through no fault of their own, they suffered more illness and required more medical care, but most of them simply could not afford to pay the spiraling costs to obtain the medical care they required. Proponents and opponents of national health insurance could at least agree that the elderly would be deserving recipients of a federally administered health insurance program. The feasibility of financing this health insurance plan for the aged as an adjunct to the already well-established and highly respected social security retirement program made the proposal seem all the more legitimate and ensured the political support required for enactment. Medicare, a national health insurance system for the aged, was enacted as Title 18 of the 1965 amendments to the Social Security Act.[7]

But medicare hardly proved to be a comprehensive health insurance plan. The opponents of the national health insurance concept, particularly the health professions, had exacted numerous compromises in the original plan in exchange for their support of the final compromise solution. Some policy analysts maintain that the substance of national health insurance for the aged was so compromised by these negotiations that the version of medicare finally enacted does little to modify either the mode or the nature of health services actually delivered to the elderly population, but merely changes the way health services for the aged are financed. Some charge that medicare was designed more to serve the institutional needs of the health professions than the health care needs of the elderly population.

The deficiencies of medicare as an insurance plan to cover the health care needs of the elderly population have been demonstrated repeatedly in legislative hearings, in the gerontological literature, and occasionally in the mass media.[8] Medicare is accused of causing unnecessary hospitalization of many elderly who could just as effectively be treated in medical outpatient clinics. The insurance covers medical services provided in the hospital, but not when medical services are administered in an outpatient setting; the elderly thus choose to enter the hospital simply to obtain the reimbursable medical care, even though hospitalization itself may not be medically required.

Medicare also has been criticized for providing inadequately for long periods of hospitalization when it is required by the nature of the illness (for example, as in the case of chronic conditions or illnesses that entail a long recuperative period, such as strokes). The 60-day limitation on medicare reimbursement has precipitated the premature reassignment of many elderly patients out of the hospital and into extended care facilities. The problem is that many of these convalescent care facilities are not equipped to provide the skilled medical care and treatment these elderly need and should most appropriately be receiving in the hospital setting from where they were removed.

Many other oversights in the medicare insurance plan have been noted: no reimbursement for outpatient drug prescription costs; no reimbursement for eyeglasses, hearing aids, or dentures; no reimbursement for routine physical examinations and other preventive health care costs; and unreasonable limitations on home health care services and rehabilitation therapy. Many believe any so-called national health insurance program for the aged should cover these and other health care costs fundamental to effect the elderly's health maintenance. They prefer a health insurance plan that would offer a more balanced reliance on outpatient and home health care along with institutional medical care. They would prefer a program that focused more on health maintenance and preventive health care than on aleviative treatment of illness and disease.

Policy analysts have documented, and legislators and health professionals have acknowledged, the serious deficiencies in medicare, but the program has yet to be revised to provide a better match for the elderly's unique health care needs. In the decade following enactment, the politics of incremental expansion and modification changed the medicare program remarkably little. The trend under succeeding Republican administrations was not even to expand but rather to restrict reimbursement of the elderly's health care costs under medicare. Rising health care costs and raised deductibles had the elderly paying on the average $42 more out of his own pocket for medical care in 1972 than he did in 1964, the year before medicare was enacted to improve the elderly's access to affordable medical care.[9]

But, with U.S. health care policy for the aging virtually wrapped up in the medical insurance program, cost may not be the only barrier that elderly people face in obtaining good medical care. For many elderly, transportation to a nearby medical facility may be a more pressing problem.[10] Other elderly may not know where to go to get medical attention for their particular health problem, and still others may not even know that they have a health problem.[11] Gerontologists worry too that health professionals are rarely specialized to treat the elderly patient, and perhaps of greater concern is that gerontologists have found that health providers avoid treating elderly patients because they dislike aging and/or the aged.[12]

These and other barriers to the elderly's acquiring the best health care that medical science can make available have largely been overlooked in the consuming quest for solutions to the problems of affordable health care. Practically speaking, health care policy for the aging in the United States has been limited to the medicare insurance program in the past, and it is probably a safe bet that medical insurance will continue to be the mainstay of the government's provision for the health care needs of the elderly.

This chapter affords an opportunity to reexamine the climate of decision-making in the health care policy area a brief decade after the enactment of medicare. Illustrated by the responses from this sample of 316 decision-makers, does the climate of decision-making appear conducive to a serious reexamination of issues involved in health care planning for the elderly? How do the decision-makers evaluate the health status of the elderly population generally? What barriers do these decision-makers believe prevent the elderly from obtaining good medical care? In particular, how do the decision-makers assess the adequacy of the health insurance coverage that medicare presently affords the elderly? Are they cognizant of the limitations in its coverage? Is there growing sentiment in favor of expanding medicare so that the plan will provide comprehensive insurance coverage for its elderly beneficiaries?

Of special interest will be whether legislators and/or the health-related professions are crusading for reforms in health care policy for the elderly or whether they remain relatively more satisfied with the existing health care system and the health care services that are currently being delivered to the elderly population. The lesson of medicare is that these two subgroups in the decision-making community will have the determinative input in any policy decisions relating to public health care planning for the elderly.

DECISION-MAKERS' PERCEPTIONS OF THE HEALTH STATUS OF THE AGED

From the outset of the interview, many of the decision-makers reflected a concern about the elderly's health status that carried throughout the remainder of their interview. In the leadoff question of the interview, a majority of the decision-makers (51 percent) cited health as one of the three major problems typically facing elderly residents in the community (see Table 4.1). Only the elderly's financial problems were mentioned more often. Some segments of the decision-making community were relatively more likely than others to focus on the elderly's health problems. As might be expected, for example, health professionals were more likely than specialists in other program areas to stress health as one of the elderly's major problems. On the other hand, the corporate directors of personnel rarely cited health as a major problem for the elderly; the reason, as will soon be seen, is that the personnel directors generally believed that most elderly enjoy good health.

Old age is typically associated with poor or rapidly deteriorating health, but this image is not altogether accurate. While seven out of eight older persons do suffer from one or more chronic diseases, only 18 percent report that those chronic disabilities interfere with their personal mobility. A greater percentage, however, report some limitation on their major activities due to their chronic conditions.[13] Nevertheless, the majority of older Americans enjoys relatively good health, at least up to the age of 75.[14] As would be expected, the health status of the very old (those 75 years of age and older) is considerably more impaired than that of the young-old (those between 65 and 74 years of age). Whereas 40 percent of those between 65 and 74 years of age suffer some impairment, half again as many of those 75 years of age and older do, with nearly one in four of the very old being totally disabled. Only 5 percent (or approximately 1 million) of the total elderly population in the United States resided in institutions of any kind in 1974. This aggregate figure, however, broke down to less than 1 percent of the population

TABLE 4.1

"What Would You Say Are the Three Greatest Problems Facing People in Los Angeles Who Are 65 and Over?"
(percent mentioning "health" as a problem and problem's rank based on number of mentions)

	Percent	Rank
Positional Characteristics of the Decision-Makers		
Position in the Policy Process		
Legislators (N = 71)	56	2
Agency administrators (N = 70)	54	2
Service delivery personnel (N = 70)	59	2
Corporate directors of personnel (N = 35)	23	3
Union local presidents (N = 35)	40	2
Advocates for the aged (N = 35)	60	3
Responsibility for Aging Programs		
Primary function (N = 85)	51	2
Important but not central function (N = 88)	57	2
Minor function (N = 143)	48	2
Area of Expertise		
Health-related professions (N = 60)	70	2
Specialists in other program areas (N = 256)	44	2
Personal Characteristics of the Decision-Makers		
Age of the Respondent		
Under 45 (N = 98)	54	2
45-54 (N = 98)	50	2
55-64 (N = 90)	49	2
65 and over (N = 30)	53	2
Sex of the Respondent		
Male (N = 230)	53	2.5
Female (N = 86)	48	2
Ethnicity of the Respondent		
White (N = 235)	52	2
Minority (N = 81)	48	2
Educational Level of the Respondent		
High school graduate or less (N = 42)	45	2
Some college (N = 64)	42	3
College graduate (N = 99)	50	2
Postcollege education (N = 111)	59	2
Total (N = 316)	51	2

Source: Compiled by the author.

age 65 to 74 compared to nearly 14 percent of the population age 85 and older.[15]

By reference to these statistics, the decision-makers in this sample substantially overstated the health decrements and the extent of dependency to be found in the elderly population. The vast majority (more than 70 percent) of the decision-making community did not believe that most older Americans enjoy good health (see Table 4.2). The majority of the decision-makers (54 percent) acknowledged that most older people suffer from some kind of chronic illness (see Table 4.3). Although national health statistics confirm that the presence of one or more chronic conditions does not necessarily interfere with the elderly's mobility or major activities, these decision-makers nevertheless concluded that poor health is a major limiting factor in the elderly's getting around in the community and in their looking after personal needs. For example, nearly half of the decision-makers in the sample believed that poor health prevented most elderly from getting around freely in their own communities (see Chapter 6), and nearly one third of the decision-makers identified poor health as a major factor mitigating against continued employment past age 65 (see Chapter 7).

In the context of these perceptions regarding the health status of the elderly population in general, it is not surprising that this sample of decision-makers vastly overestimated the number of elderly persons who were confined to institutions because they could no longer manage their own affairs on a day-to-day basis. Only 10 percent of the entire sample of 316 decision-makers accurately located between 4 and 5 percent of the elderly population in institutions, and only 15 percent of the decision-makers limited their estimates of the institutionalized elderly to less than 10 percent of the aged population (see Table 4.4). In contrast, one fifth of the sample could not even guess what percentage of the elderly were living in institutions, and another quarter of the sample of 316 decision-makers estimated the institutionalized elderly to be 30 percent or more of the total elderly population. The estimates on institutionalization provided by the majority of these decision-makers substantially exceeded even the percentage of very old (those 85 years of age and older) who live in institutions; these estimates are thus quite distorted when applied to the total elderly population aged 65 and older.

To understand possible impacts on aging policy, it would be useful to consider which segments of the decision-making community are most likely to emphasize the elderly's incapacity and dependency rather than their competence and independence. One of the more interesting comparisons is between the corporate directors of personnel and the union local presidents. The corporate directors of

TABLE 4.2

"Most Older People in This Country Are in Good Health"
(percent responding in agreement)

Positional Characteristics of the Decision-Makers	
Position in the Policy Process	
Legislators (N = 71)	23
Agency administrators (N = 70)	24
Service delivery personnel (N = 70)	29
Corporate directors of personnel (N = 35)	54
Union local presidents (N = 35)	17
Advocates for the aged (N = 35)	26
Responsibility for Aging Programs	
Primary function (N = 85)	31
Important but not central function (N = 88)	25
Minor function (N = 143)	27
Area of Expertise	
Health-related professions (N = 60)	17
Specialists in other program areas (N = 256)	30
Personal Characteristics of the Decision-Makers	
Age of the Respondent	
Under 45 (N = 98)	30
45-54 (N = 98)	19
55-64 (N = 90)	32
65 and over (N = 30)	33
Sex of the Respondent	
Male (N = 230)	26
Female (N = 86)	31
Ethnicity of the Respondent	
White (N = 235)	29
Minority (N = 81)	25
Educational Level of the Respondent	
High school graduate or less (N = 42)	26
Some college (N = 64)	30
College graduate (N = 99)	30
Postcollege professional education (N = 111)	25
Total (N = 316)	28

Source: Compiled by the author.

TABLE 4.3

"Most Older People Suffer from Some Kind of Chronic Illness"
(percent responding in agreement)

Positional Characteristics of the Decision-Makers	
Position in the Policy Process	
Legislators (N = 71)	42
Agency administrators (N = 70)	54
Service delivery personnel (N = 70)	63
Corporate directors of personnel (N = 35)	34
Union local presidents (N = 35)	69
Advocates for the aged (N = 35)	63
Responsibility for Aging Programs	
Primary function (N = 85)	68
Important but not central function (N = 88)	40
Minor function (N = 143)	54
Area of Expertise	
Health-related professions (N = 60)	62
Specialists in other program areas (N = 256)	52
Personal Characteristics of the Decision-Makers	
Age of the Respondent	
Under 45 (N = 98)	48
45-54 (N = 98)	48
55-64 (N = 90)	66
65 and over (N = 30)	57
Sex of the Respondent	
Male (N = 230)	54
Female (N = 86)	53
Ethnicity of the Respondent	
White (N = 235)	55
Minority (N = 81)	49
Educational Level of the Respondent	
High school graduate or less (N = 42)	69
Some college (N = 64)	50
College graduate (N = 99)	48
Postcollege professional education (N = 111)	54
Total (N = 316)	54

Source: Compiled by the author.

TABLE 4.4

"What Percentage of All People 65 and Older Would You Estimate Are in Institutions?"
(percent correctly estimating under 10 percent of the aged)

Positional Characteristics of the Decision-Makers	
Position in the Policy Process	
Legislators (N = 71)	6
Agency administrators (N = 70)	20
Service delivery personnel (N = 70)	17
Corporate directors of personnel (N = 35)	14
Union local presidents (N = 35)	9
Advocates for the aged (N = 35)	29
Responsibility for Aging Programs	
Primary function (N = 85)	27
Important but not central function (N = 88)	9
Minor function (N = 143)	12
Area of Expertise	
Health-related professions (N = 60)	13
Specialists in other program areas (N = 256)	16
Personal Characteristics of the Deoision-Makers	
Age of the Respondent	
Under 45 (N = 98)	14
45-54 (N = 98)	15
55-64 (N = 90)	14
65 and over (N = 30)	20
Sex of the Respondent	
Male (N = 230)	13
Female (N = 86)	20
Ethnicity of the Respondent	
White (N = 235)	17
Minority (N = 81)	9
Educational Level of the Respondent	
High school graduate or less (N = 42)	7
Some college (N = 64)	14
College graduate (N = 99)	17
Postcollege professional education (N = 111)	17
Total (N = 316)	15

Source: Compiled by the author.

personnel were the only subsample to believe in the majority that elderly people generally experience good health (see Table 4.2). In contrast, the majority (63 percent) of the union local presidents strongly disagreed with the assertion that "most older people are in good health."

These data suggest that corporate and union officials tend to approach the collective bargaining table with very different impressions about the health status and work capabilities of older employees. Unfortunately, those charged with representing the interests of these older workers in the collective bargaining situation appear to hold the least favorable image about the physical capabilities of aging individuals. The union local presidents, for example, were far more likely than other decision-makers to suggest that poor health was the primary reason that older workers retire (see Chapter 7). The perceptions of the poor health of older persons that are entertained by such union leaders undoubtedly help to mold the unions' position in favor of early retirement packages for older workers in collective bargaining negotiations.

These union local presidents may have overestimated the degree of poor health in the older population because they were generalizing from their personal experiences with retired blue-collar workers in their own union locals. National health statistics document that blue-collar workers, retiring after 40 years of physical and sometimes arduous labor on the job, experience significantly more chronic health conditions and average many more restricted-activity and bed-disability days in a year during old age than do white-collar retirees.[16] To the extent that union leaders are aware of the unusual disabilities and disadvantages their blue-collar union members and kindred lower socioeconomic individuals endure in old age, the union management officials may occupy a useful adjunct advocate role in the policy process on behalf of these less advantaged segments of the elderly population, at least in the health care policy area. The unions have been long-time supporters of national health insurance for the aged, and their organized support was instrumental in securing passage of the medicare legislation.[17] The data to be presented later in this chapter will affirm that the unions are still strong advocates for the overhaul of the medicare insurance system in its present form in order to provide more comprehensive insurance coverage to elderly beneficiaries. Possibilities for political alliances among the unions and various aging organizations in pursuit of medicare reforms are reflected in these data, and they should be noted.

The advocates for the aged and other categoric decision-makers were substantially more likely than decision-makers who worked less closely with the elderly to acknowledge the elderly's vulnerability to chronic illness (see Table 4.3). At the same time, the advocates and the aging specialists were the least likely to presume that widespread incapacity and institutionalization in the elderly population resulted from those chronic disabilities. In other words, these decision-makers possessed the most accurate information regarding the elderly's health status. In contrast, health professionals and other service providers not only relatively more often stressed the elderly's affliction with chronic conditions but also most often overestimated the percentage of institutionalized elderly. One third of the health professionals and other service providers suggested that 30 percent or more of the elderly population was so incapacitated as to require institutionalization. These professionals appeared to be inappropriately generalizing to the entire elderly population based on their experiences with the elderly in need who have sought medical assistance or services from other government social programs in the community.

The perspectives of the legislative subsample provide the final amplification in this analysis of the decision-makers' assessments of the elderly's health status. The legislators' views on the elderly's health status could conceivably influence their priorities regarding the allocation of public health care dollars in the community. Moreover, the legislators would probably operationalize different models of community social service programs to help the elderly depending upon whether they generally perceived the elderly to be in good health or in poor health. As a group, the legislators revealed relatively inaccurate information about the health status of the older population.

The vast majority of the legislators (73 percent) did not believe that most elderly enjoy good health. The majority (54 percent), however, also did not believe that most older persons suffer from chronic illness; hence, many of the legislators must have believed that the elderly's poor health derived mainly from their increased susceptibility to acute illnesses, such as the flu. These perceptions of the elderly's health conditions probably helped to fuel legislative support for President Gerald Ford's swine flu immunization program for the elderly in 1976 despite considerable division in the medical community over the advisability of the program.

The legislators also overestimated the extent of dependency in the aged population. In fact, the legislators were the least likely of the six subsamples to estimate the percentage of elderly who were institutionalized at under 10 percent. One half of the legislators believed that one in five elderly or even more were institutionalized. These exaggerated estimates of the size of the institutionalized elderly population may help to explain why legislators devote considerable attention to the study of conditions in nursing homes and then follow up by enacting volumes of legislation designed to improve the conditions that they have uncovered in the institutions.

The decision-makers interviewed in this study emphasized the elderly's health decrements and growing dependency. They are both right and wrong when they do this. Data from all available surveys repeatedly confirm that health poses serious problems for a large minority of the elderly population--perhaps as many as 35 to 40 percent of the elderly suffer some limitations on their daily activities and/or personal mobility due to deteriorations in their health status. Decision-makers' sensitivity to the health problems faced by these older people thus cannot be misplaced. The decision-makers err, however, in believing that many elderly who have trouble managing in the community are institutionalized. For the most part, the elderly who experience significant health decrements in the later years still remain in the community, settling for getting along the best they can with the resources they have. Provision thus needs to be made for these elderly in the community, not in nursing homes.

The decision-makers in this sample seemed quite unable to accept the proposition that the majority of older Americans enjoy relatively good health. The reason may be that the decision-makers judge the health status of the elderly by the standards of health more appropriately applied to middle-aged adults. There is support for this hypothesis in the data. Less than one third (31 percent) of the decision-makers believed that it was appropriate for people to relax and take life easy in old age; on the other hand, the decision-makers virtually unanimously agreed that the key to a successful old age was to stay as active as ever (see Table 2.4).

Health status, however, should be evaluated according to the individual's stage in the life cycle. It is unreasonable to expect the body at age 70 to do what it could at age 50 or age 25. Few of the decision-makers allowed for the effects of aging in their evaluation of the elderly's health status. More commonly, the decision-makers confused the effects of aging with those of pathology and reached the misleading conclusion that the majority of old is ill, rather than the more appropriate conclusion that the majority of elderly is old but in comparatively good health. Those in the gerontological and medical professions who strive to clarify and distinguish between the effects of aging and pathology on the health status of older persons have an important target group for their educational campaign in these and other decision-makers.[18]

Others in the health professions and the field of gerontology have argued strongly in favor of using a functional index of the elderly's health status rather than a measure of the extent of pathology, that is, to evaluate the elderly's health status in terms of ability to manage independently in the community whatever the signs of pathology may be.[19] Were decision-makers to focus on the health of the elderly population in terms of functional independence rather than in inventories of pathology, they might base policy decisions on more accurate information about the health status and the health needs of elderly people. Perhaps if decision-makers were more aware of precisely how the elderly person's health status mediates his ability to function in the home, in the neighborhood, and in the larger community, these decision-makers could design community social service programs that would provide elderly residents with the kind of assistance they require in order to be able to manage better on their own in the community. It would thus seem particularly important to educate decision-makers about the functional capabilities and the program assistance needs of the elderly population, and to uneducate the decision-makers from thinking about the elderly in traditional health diagnostic inventories.

DECISION-MAKERS' PERCEPTIONS OF THE BARRIERS THE AGED CONFRONT IN OBTAINING ADEQUATE MEDICAL CARE

Following upon their observations regarding the elderly's poor health status, these decision-makers could be expected to evidence considerable concern about the elderly's access to available medical care in the community. When asked to identify the major barriers that old people confront in finding good medical care, the decision-makers expressed the most concern about the cost of medical care. More than half (57 percent) of the decision-makers cited problems related to the prohibitive costs of medical care. The physical inability of many elderly to get to medical facilities in the community because of the lack of suitable transportation concerned nearly half of the decision-maker sample (48 percent).

Much smaller segments of the decision-making community focused on a variety of other problems confronting the elderly. One quarter (23 percent) of the sample believed that many elderly simply lacked information about medical services available in their community. An identical percentage criticized the quality of care that is currently available to tend to the elderly's medical needs; they commonly observed that medical personnel and medical facilities do not exist to provide elderly patients with medical treatment tailored to their special health care needs. One in six of the decision-makers (17 percent) believed that medical personnel entertain negative attitudes toward aging and/or the aged that interfere with the quality of health care services delivered to elderly patients. One in eight decision-makers (13 percent) identified a major problem in the resistance of many elderly patients to seek out medical care when it is required either because of ignorance of their health problems or because of a fear about a bad diagnosis and the threat of possible hospitalization or institutionalization. Finally, one in ten decision-makers (11 percent) suggested that barriers to the elderly's securing adequate medical care have been created by the very medical insurance system (medicare/medicaid) that was designed to facilitate the elderly's access to medical services available in the community; these decision-makers typically observed that the bureaucracy-bound insurance program caused physicians to shy away from elderly patients rather than become entangled in the red tape of medicare/medicaid reimbursement schedules.

Before looking more closely at some of the decision-makers' perspectives on the delivery of health care services to the elderly, their perceptions are checked against the complaints of elderly persons who report having problems in obtaining adequate medical care.

Interviews with elderly residents living in the community suggest that a sizable minority of them report serious problems in obtaining good medical care. In the University of Southern California companion survey of the Los Angeles County residents aged 65 to 74, one in five claimed to experience problems in securing needed medical care, and they represent the younger and presumably healthier part of the elderly population. In the nationwide Harris survey, both the young and old elderly were interviewed, and approximately one quarter of the elderly respondents affirmed that they experience serious problems in obtaining enough medical care.[20] Moreover, it is probable that many other elderly have problems getting adequate medical care, either which they do not verbalize to interviewers or which they themselves do not fully appreciate. Thus the decision-makers' sensitivity to the problems that elderly people may have in obtaining adequate medical care responds to the expressed needs of a sizable minority of the elderly population as well as the possibly latent needs of many more elderly.

As to the problems that elderly people most commonly report, the USC community survey provides additional data. In order of frequency mentioned, the problems cited by the elderly residents included the incompetence of medical personnel and poor medical treatment (39 percent); costs of medical care, including drugs (34 percent); problems processing medical insurance claims (30 percent); problems of long waits to get appointments or at the physicians' offices (15 percent); and transportation to medical facilities (4 percent). Thus in relation to these elderly community residents, the decision-makers apparently overemphasized the elderly's transportation problems. In other respects, however, the decision-makers' collective perspective on the elderly's problems getting adequate medical care seemed to be reasonably accurate perceptions of the problems that this sample of elderly in particular reported having personally experienced. Differences among the various decision-makers in their perceptions of the problems emerge more clearly when each of the identified problems is examined more closely.

The Cost Barriers

More than half of the 316 decision-makers maintained that, despite medicare and medicaid health insurance, the high costs of medical care still represented the primary barrier facing most elderly people seeking medical assistance for their health problems (see Table 4.5). Curiously, decision-makers who perceived widespread poverty in the elderly population therefore were not more likely to cite the unaffordability of medical care for elderly patients; the high costs of medical care proved to be a more universal perception in the decision-making community. Those decision-makers who were relatively more involved with aging programs and working with the elderly stressed the cost barrier somewhat less than other decision-makers. Thus, less than one half of the advocates maintained that cost was a major barrier for many elderly people seeking medical assistance. With the exception of women, a majority of all other groups in the decision-making community cited the cost barriers.

The decision-makers' perceptions of the high costs of medical care as a major barrier to the elderly's securing needed medical assistance are related to the decision-makers' perceptions of the inadequate coverage that medicare provides for elderly beneficiaries. Less than half (44 percent) of the decision-makers who believed that medicare covered nearly all health care costs for the elderly still cited the expense of health care as a major barrier to elderly people seeking medical assistance; in contrast, nearly two thirds (64 percent) of those who believed that medicare covered significantly less than half of the elderly's health care costs maintained that costs were a major barrier to elderly people seeking medical assistance.

The introductory materials of this chapter explored the concept of medicare as a national health insurance plan for the elderly and suggested that many of the elderly's most common health care costs were not included within the scope of the plan. Medicare never covered even half of the average elderly individual's annual health care bill; maximum coverage under medicare was achieved in 1969 when medicare covered 45.5 percent of the average elderly person's health bill. By 1972, inflating medical care costs forced the elderly person to pay $42 more out-of-pocket for his medical care than he

TABLE 4.5

"What Are the Major Problems Older People Face in Getting the Medical Care They Need?" (percent citing "cost of medical care" and problem's rank based on number of mentions)

	Percent	Rank
Positional Characteristics of the Decision-Makers		
Position in the Policy Process		
Legislators (N = 71)	61	1
Agency administrators (N = 70)	59	1
Service delivery personnel (N = 70)	54	1
Corporate directors of personnel (N = 35)	63	1
Union local presidents (N = 35)	60	1
Advocates for the aged (N = 35)	46	1
Responsibility for Aging Programs		
Primary function (N = 85)	51	1
Important but not central function (N = 88)	59	1
Minor function (N = 143)	60	1
Area of Program Expertise		
Health-related professions (N = 60)	58	2
Specialists in other program areas (N = 256)	57	1
Positional Characteristics of the Decision-Makers		
Age of the Respondent		
Under 45 (N = 98)	59	1
45-54 (N = 98)	56	1
55-64 (N = 90)	58	1
65 and over (N = 30)	53	1
Sex of the Respondent		
Male (N = 230)	61	1
Female (N = 86)	48	1
Ethnicity of the Respondent		
White (N = 235)	60	1
Minority (N = 81)	51	1
Educational Level of the Respondent		
High school graduate or less (N = 42)	60	1
Some college (N = 64)	53	1
College graduate (N = 99)	60	1
Postcollege professional education (N = 111)	57	1.5
Total (N = 316)	57	1

Source: Compiled by the author.

did the year before medicare was enacted. At the time of the interviews with these decision-makers in 1974, medicare covered only 40 percent of the average elderly's annual health care expenditures; the figure has since dropped below 40 percent for the first time in medicare's history to 38 percent.[21]

The decision-makers in this study were asked to evaluate the extent of coverage they believed medicare provided for elderly beneficiaries: "Would you say that medicare covers nearly all, at least half, or significantly less than half of the average older person's health care costs?" Only one in five (19 percent) maintained that medicare covers nearly all of the elderly's health care costs. Another 7 percent of the sample felt too uninformed to even hazard a guess at the scope of medicare's coverage. But the overwhelming majority of the 316 decision-makers proved to be well aware of the fact that medicare's coverage is far from comprehensive. Three quarters (74 percent) of the sample believed that medicare covered closer to half rather than all of the elderly's expenditures for health care. It is no wonder that these decision-makers stressed the cost barriers to the elderly's securing adequate medical care despite a full decade of operation of the medicare insurance program.

Even among the three quarters of the sample with relatively more accurate impressions of the coverage that medicare provides for the elderly, however, most still tended to overestimate the scope of coverage. They were nearly twice as likely to maintain that medicare covers at least half of the elderly's health care costs as to assert that medicare covers significantly less than half of those costs (48 percent versus 26 percent). In the last analysis, then, only 26 percent of the entire sample of 316 decision-makers correctly maintained that medicare covers significantly less than half of the elderly's personal health care expenditures (see Table 4.6).

The advocates for the aged were the only decision-maker group that in the majority correctly assessed the extent of medicare coverage, although one out of every seven of the advocates still insisted that medicare was a comprehensive medical insurance plan that covered nearly all of the elderly's health care costs. As a rule, categoric decision-makers closely aligned with various aging programs were far more likely than generic decision-makers to appreciate fully the limitations of medicare coverage. Health providers and legislators, on the other hand, infrequently possessed correct information about the scope of medicare's coverage. Advocates and categoric decision-makers pressing for an overhaul of the medicare system will have to begin their campaign by educating the legislators and health providers in particular about the extent of the deficiencies in the medicare insurance system. But one labor leader (I.D. 507B) warned, "Most state legislative bodies aren't sensitive to the elderly's

TABLE 4.6

"Would You Say That Medicare Covers Nearly All, at Least Half, or Significantly Less Than Half of the Average Older Person's Health Care Costs?" (percent correctly responding "significantly less than one half")

Positional Characteristics of the Decision-Makers	
Position in the Policy Process	
Legislators (N = 71)	18
Agency administrators (N = 70)	29
Service delivery personnel (N = 70)	30
Corporate directors of personnel (N = 35)	11
Union local presidents (N = 35)	14
Advocates for the aged (N = 35)	51
Responsibility for Aging Programs	
Primary function (N = 85)	45
Important but not central function (N = 88)	18
Minor function (N = 143)	19
Area of Expertise	
Health-related professions (N = 60)	20
Specialists in other program areas (N = 256)	27
Personal Characteristics of the Decision-Makers	
Age of the Respondent	
Under 45 (N = 98)	28
45-54 (N = 98)	22
55-64 (N = 90)	23
65 and over (N = 30)	37
Sex of the Respondent	
Male (N = 230)	24
Female (N = 81)	30
Ethnicity of the Respondent	
White (N = 235)	25
Minority (N = 81)	28
Educational Level of the Respondent	
High school graduate or less (N = 42)	21
Some college (N = 64)	31
College graduate (N = 99)	32
Postcollege professional education (N = 111)	18
Total (N = 316)	26

Source: Compiled by the author.

needs and the medical profession has taken a stance of nonparticipation on their problems." Advocating change may not be easy despite the widespread acknowledgment of the inadequacies in the medical insurance system.

It is significant that corporate directors of personnel and union local presidents, both of whom are in positions to promote supplemental health insurance benefits for the elderly through company or union plans, appeared the most uninformed about the inadequacies of medicare's financial coverage. Only one in nine and one in seven of these subsamples, respectively, believed that medicare covered significantly less than half of the elderly's health expenses. Operating from such a perspective, they would probably be less likely to push for supplemental insurance benefits for their retirees than they might be if they hold a more accurate image of the adequacy of the insurance coverage that is afforded the elderly by medicare. And, indeed, data presented in Tables 2.9 and 2.10 confirm that the union and corporate management officials in this sample relatively infrequently pressed for allowing retirees to remain eligible for health insurance benefits in company- and union-sponsored plans.

Additional monies to underwrite the elderly's health care costs may not solve all the problems that elderly people face in obtaining adequate medical care, but many of these decision-makers believed it would certainly help improve the elderly's access to what health care services are available. Undeniably, there is strong appeal in the frequent urgings of these decision-makers to develop a comprehensive national health insurance system. As one among many, a union local president (I.D. 531) asserted, "Expand the health insurance system to cover everything--anything else is inadequate. Remove all costs to the patient. This country should take care of its people."

Transportation to Medical Facilities

Nearly half of the decision-makers (48 percent) were concerned that many elderly could not get to medical facilities available in the community because they lacked suitable transportation (see Table 4.7). Like perceptions of the cost barriers facing elderly patients in the health services system, perceptions of the transportation barrier were also more or less universal in the decision-making community. Thus decision-makers who maintained that the majority of elderly people typically face severe transportation problems in moving around the community were not more likely to cite the elderly's transportation problems in the specific context of obtaining medical care compared to decision-makers who believed that in

TABLE 4.7

"What Are the Major Problems Older People Face in Getting the Medical Care They Need?" (percent citing "transportation" and the problem's rank based on number of mentions)

Positional Characteristics of the Decision-Makers	Percent	Rank
Position in the Policy Process		
Legislators (N = 71)	56	2
Agency administrators (N = 70)	50	2
Service delivery personnel (N = 70)	47	2
Corporate directors of personnel (N = 35)	40	2
Union local presidents (N = 35)	40	2
Advocates for the aged (N = 35)	43	2
Responsibility for Aging Programs		
Primary function (N = 85)	45	2
Important but not central function (N = 88)	56	2
Minor function (N = 143)	45	2
Area of Program Expertise		
Health-related professions (N = 60)	60	1
Specialists in other program areas (N = 256)	45	2
Personal Characteristics of the Decision-Makers		
Age of the Respondent		
Under 45 (N = 98)	45	2
45-54 (N = 98)	49	2
55-64 (N = 90)	50	2
65 and over (N = 30)	47	2
Sex of the Respondent		
Male (N = 230)	47	2
Female (N = 86)	50	2
Ethnicity of the Respondent		
White (N = 235)	51	2
Minority (N = 81)	38	2
Educational Level of the Respondent		
High school graduate or less (N = 42)	43	2
Some college (N = 64)	39	2
College graduate (N = 99)	44	2
Postcollege professional education (N = 111)	58	1.5
Total (N = 316)	48	2

Source: Compiled by the author.

general only a minority of the elderly population experiences severe transportation problems. Similarly, the decision-maker's perceptions of significant health decrements in the elderly population were not related to his perception of personal mobility and transportation problems limiting the elderly's access to available medical facilities.

Within the decision-making community, the health services providers appeared somewhat more concerned about the elderly's possible transportation problems in the specific context of seeking medical care than did the rest of the decision-making community. Among all the problems they cited, they most often focused on the elderly's transportation problems, and they mentioned the elderly's transportation problems more frequently than any other subgroups in the decision-making community.

Concern over these transportation barriers has already prompted some communities to establish "medi-transit" programs to provide elderly and handicapped residents with direct transportation service between their homes and medical facilities in the community. The development of more of these "medi-transit" programs will probably depend on the publicized success of these prototypes and the ultimate persuasion of those legislators and health professionals not yet persuaded of the need for such programs.

Minority decision-makers proved much less likely than their white counterparts to believe that transportation was a problem for elderly people in getting to medical facilities. In light of other data in the survey, this finding was the reverse of what was anticipated. Minority decision-makers tended to stress that the elderly in their respective ethnic communities were forced to rely disproportionately on public transportation to get around because they lacked other transportation alternatives.* And the responses of the elderly interviewed in the community survey suggested that the minority decision-makers' concerns were real ones. The black and Mexican American elderly were considerably more likely to identify transportation as a serious

---

*When asked which ethnic elderly group relies most on public transportation to get around, white decision-makers cited black elderly over Mexican American elderly by a proportion of two to one; black decision-makers cited black elderly over Mexican American elderly by more than three to one; but Mexican American decision-makers picked Mexican American elderly over black elderly by a margin of more than three to one. Hence the ethnic decision-makers seemed particularly sensitive to the potential dependence of the elderly on the public transportation system within their own ethnic communities.

problem compared to the white elderly.* Hence the highlighting of the elderly's transportation problems in the medical context by white more than by minority decision-makers is an inexplicable reversal of expectations.

It is probably obvious, but it nevertheless bears repeating: "Doctors do not make house calls, and so the older person has to find a way to get to the doctor" (president of a public employees' union, I.D. 517). For the sizable number of elderly people who no longer drive, transportation may become a problem on occasion. Nationwide, approximately half of all households headed by an elderly person own no automobile;[22] these elderly must rely on friends or family to drive them to medical facilities in the community or take public transportation as a last resort. In Los Angeles County, the site of this study, public transportation means bus, and as one psychiatric nurse (I.D. 317) reminded, "It takes a lot of energy to get dressed and get on a bus to go to the doctor" (implication: many elderly do not bother to go to the doctor because it is so much trouble for them). For the 5 percent of the elderly who are in a wheelchair, the head of a homemaker services program observed, "In a city like this, how can you get in a taxi or on a bus? Most buildings aren't built for wheelchairs. We deal with many in this condition. We hear their complaints; streets are a problem--even restrooms."

It is true that few of the elderly residents in the companion community survey identified transportation as a major barrier to their obtaining adequate medical care. Perhaps it is because most of the elderly also seem to get to the doctor's office one way or another, at least when it is absolutely necessary. One local aging committee president (I.D. 619) concurred in this opinion: "The elderly need to be able to get to the doctors, but I feel they could get there if they had to or really wanted to." Many more decision-makers, however, are concerned about the elderly who do not go to the doctor

---

*Black elderly were more than twice as likely as either white or Mexican American elderly to report using public transportation regularly as a means to get around in the community. Nearly half (44 percent) of the Mexican American elderly interviewed, however, complained about living too far away from public transportation facilities. The majority of the Mexican American elderly (54 percent) relied on members of their immediate families to drive them where they needed to go. Whereas two thirds of the white elderly reported driving themselves around town, less than half (43.4 percent) of the black elderly and less than one quarter of the Mexican American elderly reported that they still drove.

this and the next day because "it's a chore to get there" (a social worker, (I.D. 316). For them, the latent demand in the elderly population for direct transportation service between home and medical office may indeed warrant the development of more "meditransit" programs in local communities across the country. A financial counselor in a retirement income program (I.D. 346) suggested, "I would add a transportation component to all health care facilities. I hear about those problems from our members from time to time." The head nurse in a convalescent facility (I.D. 341A) wondered, with transportation being "critical" to the elderly's access to medical services in the community, "if all communities have dial-a-ride programs or not?"

Alternatively, but suggested far less often by these decision-makers as a means of ensuring the elderly's access to good medical care when they experience serious transportation or mobility problems, is bringing the physician to the elderly patient. A national legislator (I.D. 164A) fantasized, "I'd like to see a system of a roving medical care where doctors visit homes when the elderly can't get out." There was a time when home visits were the primary mode of delivery of health services to the population in general, but the nascent organization and increasing institutionalization of the medical profession back in the 1920s spelled the demise of the physicians' home visit and marked the beginning of the patients' treks to the physician's office.[23] And for 90 to 95 percent of the general population, seeing patients in an office may be an efficient way to deliver medical services, but for the 5 to 10 percent of the patients who are relatively homebound (and many of them would be elderly patients), home health care with home visits by medical personnel may be a more efficient way to deliver health services. It is a proposition that deserves more attention than it has received or than it appears it will receive. If the opinions of these 316 decision-makers represent a fair sampling of the climate of decision-making, then few decision-makers are thinking seriously about home health care options for elderly patients. This point can be made again and again in these data.

The Aged's Lack of Information about Available Health Care Services

For one quarter of the decision-makers, transportation to medical facilities is almost beside the point because they believed that many elderly do not know where to go in the community to obtain medical assistance appropriate to their specific health needs (Table 4.8). That only 23 percent cited this problem is somewhat

TABLE 4.8

"What Are the Major Problems Older People Face in Getting the Medical Care They Need?" (percent citing "lack of information about health services" and problem's rank)

	Percent	Rank
Positional Characteristics of the Decision-Makers		
Position in the Policy Process		
Legislators (N = 71)	15	4
Agency administrators (N = 70)	29	4
Service delivery personnel (N = 70)	26	3
Corporate directors of personnel (N = 35)	23	3
Union local presidents (N = 35)	29	3
Advocates for the aged (N = 35)	20	4
Responsibility for Aging Programs		
Primary function (N = 85)	20	4
Important but not central function (N = 88)	28	3
Minor function (N = 143)	22	3
Area of Program Expertise		
Health-related professions (N = 60)	32	3
Specialists in other program areas (N = 256)	21	4
Personal Characteristics of the Decision-Makers		
Age of the Respondent		
Under 45 (N = 98)	22	4
45-54 (N = 98)	27	3
55-64 (N = 90)	21	4
65 and over (N = 30)	23	4
Sex of the Respondent		
Male (N = 230)	21	4
Female (N = 86)	30	3
Ethnicity of the Respondent		
White (N = 235)	21	4
Minority (N = 91)	30	3
Educational Level of the Respondent		
High school graduate or less (N = 42)	14	5
Some college (N = 64)	23	3
College graduate (N = 99)	29	3
Postcollege professional education (N = 111)	23	3
Total (N = 316)	23	3.5

Source: Compiled by the author.

surprising, because elsewhere in the interview, nearly all of the 316 decision-makers (93 percent) agreed with the proposition that it is sometimes difficult to reach the elderly with information about programs and policies that affect them. Most of these decision-makers apparently did not believe that the lack of information about community health services in particular was a serious problem for most elderly residents.

The legislators were one such group in the decision-making community who did not stress this information problem. In contrast, many of the health professionals who staff various community medical facilities did perceive the elderly's lack of information about community health services as a major barrier to the elderly's utilizing available programs and facilities. The head nurse in a community health center (I.D. 311) advocated one proposal, "Somewhere we need some type of national health system. An educational component has to be built into the system for laymen. They need to know about alternatives to solve their own health problems." These health professionals are undoubtedly closer to the problem and hence should have a more accurate reading of the magnitude of the information barrier. It would appear that they confront a task of educating the legislators about the information barriers limiting the elderly's access to available health care resources in the community.

The minority decision-makers in this sample were more concerned than the white decision-makers about possible information barriers that would restrict the elderly's use of medical facilities in the community. Most of the 316 decision-makers (78 percent) were agreed that ethnic elderly have special problems in learning about new programs and policies that could affect them. These minority decision-makers may thus be exhibiting sensitivity to a problem that may be more acute in their respective ethnic communities than in the general population. It's hardly surprising, for example, that a Mexican American employment office manager (I.D. 252) would say of the elderly's problems obtaining adequate medical care: "The main one is the language barrier with the Mexican Americans. There is a lack of knowledge of services available to them. They are uninformed in these matters." But it was the black, not the Mexican American, decision-makers who proved to be the most concerned about the information problem in the context of the elderly's securing adequate medical care.* Black decision-makers frequently cited

---

*Forty percent of the black decision-makers compared to 25 percent of the Mexican American decision-makers asserted that lack of information about health care services available in the community was a major barrier to the elderly's securing adequate medical care.

the minorities' lack of education generally as creating special problems for ethnic people in old age. The information referral problem mentioned here in the context of securing adequate medical care may be one such instance.

The Lack of Adequate Health Care Services

Less than a quarter of the sample of 316 decision-makers challenged the adequacy of medical care supplied to elderly patients in the health services delivery system, although this appeared to be a major concern of elderly residents in the community who were dissatisfied with the health care they received (Table 4.9). The list of issues related to the quality of health care actually provided to the elderly that could have but tended not to occupy the attention of these decision-makers is a long one. Only a few of the more important oversights are highlighted here.

Few talked about the priority that health care for the elderly receives in the health services delivery system. One local legislator (I.D. 123) did pointedly observe, "If they are 16 years of age, there are plenty of agencies to help them; but at 60, 70, or 80, I don't know if there are those agencies and then they may be too proud to go and ask for more help." Only a handful of the decision-makers even touched on the concept of a "continuum of care" for the elderly, let alone placed the emphasis on the concept that gerontologists do. The supervisor in a district Social Security office (I.D. 348) was one of several who did underscore the problem, "They are not sick enough to be in nursing homes but they need help. We should pay more attention to home health care instead of hospitalization." A few others cited the lack of geriatric medical programs and facilities and the absence of preventive health programs, such as community health screening clinics designed especially for the elderly population. One psychiatric nurse (I.D. 327) observed that "most doctors don't know enough about geriatrics to treat some of these people"; a corporate personnel director added, "Most doctors specialize in treating babies, but not in treating old people."

The critical point that bears repeating is that only a minority of the decision-makers in this sample actually criticized the quality of health care that the elderly receive. The decision-makers typically expressed more concern for increasing the elderly's access to available medical care than they did for restructuring the existing medical programs in order to serve better the specific health care needs of the elderly patient. The detractors of medicare appear to be right when they claim that the health insurance program has done little to modify either the mode or nature of health services delivered

TABLE 4.9

"What Are the Major Problems Older People Face in Getting the Medical Care They Need?" (percent citing "inadequate medical services" and problem's rank based on number of mentions)

	Percent	Rank
Positional Characteristics of the Decision-Makers		
Position in the Policy Process		
Legislators (N = 71)	20	3
Agency administrators (N = 70)	31	3
Service delivery personnel (N = 70)	16	6
Corporate directors of personnel (N = 35)	14	5
Union local presidents (N = 35)	20	4
Advocates for the aged (N = 35)	37	3
Responsibility for Aging Programs		
Primary function (N = 85)	34	3
Important but not central function (N = 88)	25	4
Minor function (N = 143)	15	4.5
Area of Program Expertise		
Health-related professions (N = 60)	18	5.5
Specialists in other program areas (N = 256)	24	3
Personal Characteristics of the Decision-Makers		
Age of the Respondent		
Under 45 (N = 98)	26	3
45-54 (N = 98)	16	5.5
55-64 (N = 90)	29	3
65 and over (N = 30)	30	3
Sex of the Respondent		
Male (N = 230)	24	3
Female (N = 86)	20	5.5
Ethnicity of the Respondent		
White (N = 235)	22	3
Minority (N = 91)	25	4
Educational Level of the Respondent		
High school graduate or less (N = 42)	24	3
Some college (N = 64)	20	4
College graduate (N = 99)	28	4
Postcollege professional education (N = 111)	20	4
Total (N = 316)	23	3.5

Source: Compiled by the author.

to the elderly population but in essence has changed only the way that health services to the elderly are financed.

The advocates for the aged expressed the most dissatisfaction with the quality of health care the elderly are receiving under the existing health care system, and in this regard they appropriately reflected the discontent of their elderly constituents. The mid- and top-level agency administrators were only somewhat less outspoken in their criticism of the available health care programs. As a general rule, the more closely involved the decision-maker was with aging programs of any kind, the more likely he was to criticize existing health care services for the elderly.

But those adopting the critical perspective have a monumental education and lobbying effort ahead of them if they hope to restructure the health care system so that it will deliver a more appropriate range of health services to elderly patients. The earlier experiences with medicare and national health insurance confirm the health bureaucracy's resistance to change. Furthermore, the critics of the health care system proper would seem to have few fellow supporters among the legislators or health professionals, the first groups who would have to be persuaded to favor reform.

Attitudes of Medical Personnel toward the Aged

One in six of the decision-makers alleged that the elderly do not receive good treatment from medical professionals when they do seek medical assistance and that repeated negative experiences with the medical professions could subsequently deter elderly patients from seeking medical care (Table 4.10). The criticism focused primarily on what one specialist in transportation for the handicapped (I.D. 334) called "the abuse of doctors that take care of them in mass production." As the director of an upper middle-income retirement residence (I.D. 319A) remarked, "No one likes to be treated like cattle." Others suggested that the response of the medical profession to elderly patients should be characterized more as non-treatment; a psychiatric nurse in a senior citizens health screening clinic (I.D. 310) asserted, "Doctors usually attribute aches and pains to advancing old age," and a corporate personnel director (I.D. 415) concurred, "Many times doctors think because the patient is old, they cannot do much for them."

The health professionals themselves were even more likely than most other subgroups in the decision-making community to admit that the attitudes of health service providers could be a major factor deterring the elderly from seeking needed medical care. Professional schools in the health field seem to afford the most direct

TABLE 4.10

"What Are the Major Problems Older People Face in Getting the Medical Care They Need?" (percent citing "attitudes of medical personnel" and problem's rank based on number of mentions)

	Percent	Rank
Positional Characteristics of the Decision-Makers		
Position in the Policy Process		
Legislators (N = 71)	14	5
Agency administrators (N = 70)	24	5
Service delivery personnel (N = 70)	17	5
Corporate directors of personnel (N = 35)	17	4
Union local presidents (N = 35)	14	5
Advocates for the aged (N = 35)	14	5
Responsibility for Aging Programs		
Primary function (N = 85)	19	5
Important but not central function (N = 88)	20	5
Minor function (N = 143)	15	4.5
Area of Program Expertise		
Health-related professions (N = 60)	22	4
Specialists in other program areas (N = 256)	13	5
Personal Characteristics of the Decision-Makers		
Age of the Respondent		
Under 45 (N = 98)	17	5
45-54 (N = 98)	18	4
55-64 (N = 90)	16	5
65 and over (N = 30)	20	5
Sex of the Respondent		
Male (N = 230)	17	5
Female (N = 86)	20	5.5
Ethnicity of the Respondent		
White (N = 235)	18	5
Minority (N = 91)	15	5
Educational Level of the Respondent		
High school graduate or less (N = 42)	19	4
Some college (N = 64)	14	5.5
College graduate (N = 99)	17	5
Postcollege professional education (N = 111)	19	5
Total (N = 316)	17	5

Source: Compiled by the author.

means to resocialize the attitudes of these health professionals. At present, however, school curriculums appear to do little to alter the aversion that most of their young students feel about working with elderly patients. The professional schools will need to assume a more active role in shaping their students' attitudes toward caring for elderly patients before the medical and allied health professions will be properly sensitive to the health care needs of elderly patients. Such changes in the delivery of health care services to elderly patients would be difficult, if not impossible, to mandate from outside the health care system; it more appropriately belongs to the domain of professional socialization.

While only one in six of the 316 decision-makers believed that the attitudes of medical personnel were a major barrier to the elderly's securing adequate medical care, many more of the decision-makers apparently believed that the attitudes of the medical profession toward elderly patients did constitute a problem, albeit perhaps of some lesser importance. When asked whether they believed many physicians are reluctant to treat elderly patients, a majority (60 percent) of the sample of 316 decision-makers responded affirmatively (Table 4.11). The advocates and categoric decision-makers were the most likely to believe that medical personnel simply "don't like old people" (a senior citizens affairs official, I.D. 263).

When asked why physicians were reluctant to treat the elderly (Table 4.12), nearly two thirds of the sample (64 percent) replied that it was because elderly patient care was financially unrewarding: "The doctors are profit oriented, and the elderly are less profitable to treat" (director of an employment program for the elderly, I.D. 348). One union local president (I.D. 512) charged, "The medical profession is a disgrace to the country, not only to the elderly, but to all. They can't draw as much money from the elderly as from the young, so the elderly come second rather than first." Similar indictments of the medical profession were leveled repeatedly by these 316 decision-makers, even by the health providers themselves on occasion. Significantly, however, health providers were only half as likely as the rest of the decision-makers to say that physicians don't treat old people because it is unprofitable.

Problems with reimbursement of fees under the medicare and medicaid (MediCal, the State of California medicaid program) insurance programs were deemed an integral part of the financial picture. The head of one local labor organization (I.D. 520B) answered, "The doctors are worried about getting their money and they don't want to be bothered with medicare and MediCal (medicaid) patients." The head of a manufacturing union local (I.D. 529) concurred, "Doctors are not too interested in elderly patients if they are not covered by insurance or medicare. . . . They don't even treat emergencies

TABLE 4.11

"Do You Think Many Physicians Are Reluctant to Treat Aged Patients?"
(percent responding "yes")

Positional Characteristics of the Decision-Makers	
Position in the Policy Process	
Legislators (N = 71)	52
Agency administrators (N = 70)	66
Service delivery personnel (N = 70)	63
Corporate directors of personnel (N = 35)	51
Union local presidents (N = 35)	54
Advocates for the aged (N = 35)	71
Responsibility for Aging Programs	
Primary function (N = 85)	75
Important but not central function (N = 88)	59
Minor function (N = 143)	51
Area of Expertise	
Health-related professions (N = 60)	65
Specialists in other program areas (N = 256)	59
Personal Characteristics of the Decision-Makers	
Age of the Respondent	
Under 45 (N = 98)	53
45-54 (N = 98)	65
55-64 (N = 90)	60
65 and over (N = 30)	63
Sex of the Respondent	
Male (N = 230)	57
Female (N = 86)	66
Ethnicity of the Respondent	
White (N = 235)	57
Minority (N = 81)	67
Educational Level of the Respondent	
High school graduate or less (N = 42)	57
Some college (N = 64)	67
College graduate (N = 99)	58
Postcollege education (N = 111)	57
Total (N = 316)	60

Source: Compiled by the author.

TABLE 4.12

Decision-Makers' Perceptions of the Reasons Why Physicians Are Reluctant to Treat the Aged

Decision-Makers' Positional and Personal Characteristics	Financially Unrewarding Patient Care (percent)	Time-Consuming Patient Care (percent)
Positional Characteristics		
Position in the Policy Process		
Legislators (N = 37)*	76	11
Agency administrators (N = 46)	52	30
Service delivery personnel (N = 44)	55	32
Corporate directors of personnel (N = 18)	67	17
Union local presidents (N = 19)	74	11
Advocates for the aged (N = 25)	53	20
Responsibility for Aging Programs		
Primary function (N = 64)	70	23
Important but not central function (N = 52)	63	19
Minor function part (N = 73)	59	23
Area of Program Expertise		
Health-related professions (N = 39)	36	31
Specialists in other program areas (N = 151)	71	23
Personal Characteristics		
Age of the Respondent		
Under 45 (N = 52)	58	23
45-54 (N = 64)	59	25
55-64 (N = 54)	72	15
65 and over (N = 19)	74	32
Sex of the Respondent		
Male (N = 132)	65	20
Female (N = 57)	61	28
Ethnicity of the Respondent		
White (N = 135)	64	21
Minority (N = 54)	63	26
Educational Level of the Respondent		
High school graduate or less (N = 24)	75	8
Some college (N = 43)	63	23
College graduate (N = 58)	72	29
Postcollege education (N = 68)	50	19
Total (N = 189)	64	22

*Base N for percentages = number who in previous question asserted that physicians are reluctant to treat the aged.

Why Physicians Are Reluctant to Treat the Elderly			
Reluctance to Treat Chronic Diseases (percent)	Aged Patients Irritable, Boring (percent)	Physicians' Lack of Training in Geriatrics (percent)	Miscellaneous Other Problems (percent)
16	30	5	5
35	22	11	7
25	32	14	18
22	33	11	6
26	21	0	5
16	20	4	4
23	25	11	6
25	31	8	12
25	25	7	8
33	36	13	7
22	24	7	5
40	21	2	10
25	22	14	8
15	37	11	11
5	26	0	0
29	22	8	18
14	37	11	5
29	30	7	9
13	19	13	7
12	17	0	0
19	34	5	9
24	19	9	10
31	29	13	10
24	26	8	8

Source: Compiled by the author.

unless the money is there, insurance or cash." In a position better able to observe the problem, the operations supervisor of a district Social Security office (I.D. 352) affirmed, "We get calls from many doctors wanting verification of medicare before treatment. Doctors are reluctant to treat MediCal (medicaid). The cards have stickers on them indicating what they are good for . . . after they have used them for a month, they are thrown out." The administrator of a large long-term care hospital (I.D. 206) acknowledged that he found some physicians to be reluctant to take elderly patients "if the patients are on MediCal (medicaid). They don't want to be bothered with the paperwork and small payment."

One in five decision-makers (22 percent) asserted that elderly patient care often requires more time and patience than a busy physician is willing to give to his patients. The health professionals, in particular, but also others involved with various government social service programs, be it in administrative or service delivery capacities, were the most likely to cite this factor in the physicians' reluctance to treat the elderly. Thus, one housing administrator (I.D. 229) described a physician's office, "It's like a machine, and if you're not there on time . . . ." A psychiatric social worker (I.D. 316) explained, "You have to get a lot of information about the elderly. You have to be careful administering drugs because the drugs might conflict. Most of the elderly require a lot of time, and the doctor does not have that time." A housing referral counselor (I.D. 335) noted, as did many others in the sample, "A lot of older people use a doctor's visit as a social occasion and go with the slightest ache--a lot of doctors don't have time for that." The director of a retirement residence (I.D. 319A) concurred, "Doctors don't take time to listen and help emotionally. Offices should use paramedics and nurse practitioners for the elderly."

Some focused on the psychosocial relationship between physician and patient to highlight reasons why doctors are reluctant to treat the elderly: the physician's attitude toward old people, the physician's attitude toward chronic and terminal diseases, and so forth. They spoke of the elderly patient as a "subconscious reminder of their oncoming old age" (head nurse in a senior citizens health clinic, I.D. 310). Others suggested that it was hard for "newer, younger doctors--they don't have rapport with older people" (head nurse on a hospital geriatric ward, I.D. 303). Physicians' reluctance to treat the elderly was blamed on old people being "crochety," "chronic complainers," "lonely and looking for attention"; one psychiatric social worker (I.D. 320) alleged, "Their personal hygiene is not the best, so doctors dislike to treat them." Health providers were somewhat more likely than other decision-makers to discuss the doctors' dislike of old people.

Other respondents suggested that it was not that physicians disliked old people but merely that they disliked treating the elderly's chronic and terminal diseases. A senior citizens affairs official (I.D. 263) and many others analyzed the problem this way: "It's a question of chronic versus acute cases. Acute case patients get better and that makes the doctor feel better." A union local president (I.D. 521) concurred, "There's no cure and doctors don't like a losing proposition. They can only fight for a holding pattern for old people's health." A housing administrator (I.D. 228) summed it up this way, "The elderly have too many ills and a lot of them just can't be cured--a doctor hates to see them walk through the door." A senior citizens affairs official (I.D. 265) maintained, "The elderly are old and so physicians feel that there is no hope and time is only being wasted on the elderly. Did you ever hear of a transplant on an 80-year-old?" But a social security administrator (I.D. 236) reminded, "The elderly in the twilight of their careers are concerned with their productivity as individuals. Physicians are insensitive to the needs of the aged."

As far-reaching and wholly indicting as were their criticisms of the medical profession's treatment of the elderly in general, it is surprising that only a scant one in six of the total sample believed that the attitudes of medical personnel posed a major barrier to the elderly's securing adequate medical care (Table 4.10).

The Aged Person's Reluctance to Seek Medical Treatment

Most people do not like to visit doctors, but according to one in eight of these decision-makers elderly people are particularly reticent to seek medical assistance even when it is plainly required (Table 4.13). The president of a service union local (I.D. 534) suggested it was because of the "lack of people caring, fear of hospitalization and the inability to cope without feeling manipulated or confused." A psychiatric social worker (I.D. 316) maintained that the elderly's reticence was "a fear of the unknown--they are afraid to find out what is wrong." A district health officer (I.D. 215) blamed "the elderly's lack of awareness of health needs--they don't know if they are just getting old or if there is really something wrong with them. They shrug off health problems as old age." A few noted that some elderly view any kind of help, even medical care, as charity or welfare and refuse. "The elderly are very proud--they don't want handouts" (a local legislator, I.D. 122).

The staff in sampled government agencies, both the service providers and the various agency and program administrators, were

TABLE 4.13

"What Are the Major Problems Older People Face in Getting the Medical Care They Need?" (percent citing "elderly's reluctance to seek help" and problem's rank by number of mentions)

	Percent	Rank
Positional Characteristics of the Decision-Makers		
Position in the Policy Process		
Legislators (N = 71)	10	6
Agency administrators (N = 70)	19	6
Service delivery personnel (N = 70)	21	4
Corporate directors of personnel (N = 35)	9	6
Union local presidents (N = 35)	6	6
Advocates for the aged (N = 35)	6	6
Responsibility for Aging Programs		
Primary function (N = 85)	18	6
Important but not central function (N = 88)	12	6
Minor function (N = 143)	11	6
Area of Program Expertise		
Health-related professions (N = 60)	18	5.5
Specialists in other program areas (N = 256)	12	6
Personal Characteristics of the Decision-Makers		
Age of the Respondent		
Under 45 (N = 98)	11	6
45-54 (N = 98)	16	5.5
55-64 (N = 90)	12	6
65 and over (N = 30)	13	6
Sex of the Respondent		
Male (N = 230)	10	6
Female (N = 86)	21	4
Ethnicity of the Respondent		
White (N = 230)	13	6
Minority (N = 81)	14	6
Educational Level of the Respondent		
High school graduate or less (N = 42)	10	6
Some college (N = 64)	14	5.5
College graduate (N = 99)	15	6
Postcollege professional education (N = 111)	13	6
Total (N = 316)	13	6

Source: Compiled by the author.

the most sensitive to the resistance many elderly might show to seeking needed medical care. Perhaps these agency personnel were extrapolating from some of their personal experiences with elderly recipients in their own service delivery programs. Many of the health providers did concur in those observations however. One in five of the health professionals interviewed asserted that a minority of the elderly population is very reticent to seek medical care of any kind. Moreover, if the elderly patient's initial reluctance to seek medical care is buttressed by negative experiences with medical personnel when he finally does seek medical assistance, the result may be a doubly reinforced resistance in the elderly patient to seeking any further medical care. This is obviously an outcome to be avoided.

Summary

The decision-makers in this sample more frequently identified the major barriers to the elderly's obtaining adequate health care in the subsidiary rather than in the primary operations of the health care system; that is, they focused mostly on problems that were external to the individual and the health care services he received when they discussed the obstacles most elderly people face in obtaining adequate medical care. Specifically, the decision-makers seemed more concerned with the problems of financing medical care costs and eliminating bureaucratic inefficiencies in the health insurance programs, transporting the elderly to existing health care services, and informing the elderly about available health care services than they did with any intrinsic operations of the medical care delivery system that directly involved the nature and quality of the health care services actually provided to the elderly. Many decision-makers seemed to presume that the elderly would receive top-quality care in the health care system if only the barriers external to the actual medical visit--for example, cost, information referral, and transportation problems--were solved.

Specification of ways in which the health care system itself was not adequately responsive to the particular health care needs of the elderly was noticeably lacking in the responses of these decision-makers. Among the issues one might have expected to receive more attention from these decision-makers were the lack of geriatric training of medical personnel, the frequent insensitivity of the medical personnel to the total psychosocial needs of the elderly patient, the lack of geriatric treatment facilities, the lack of outreach and home health care programs, and the lack of preventive medicine programs tailored specifically for elderly residents in the community.

Some of the decision-makers were relatively more sensitive to these inadequacies in the health care that the U.S. medical bureaucracy provides for its elderly patients. Decision-makers in the health services delivery system and decision-makers who worked closely with the elderly in other program contexts relatively were more likely to be critical of the level and kind of care that the elderly are receiving in the existing health care system. But these decision-makers comprise only a minority. The majority of all groups in the decision-making community was focused mainly or exclusively on barriers external to the medical practice situation, on the assumption that if they can guarantee the elderly person's presence in the medical facility, he will be well taken care of once there.

MODIFYING MEDICARE TO ADDRESS BETTER THE AGED'S HEALTH CARE NEEDS

It is clear from the foregoing data that this sample of decision-makers is still most concerned with the problems involved in financing affordable medical care for the elderly. Medicare covers only a portion of the elderly's health care costs and what is not covered may mount to a tidy sum. In 1973, for example, the average elderly beneficiary under medicare had to pay $311 out of his own pocket to cover his health care costs.[24] For those stricken by chronic diseases or long-term illnesses requiring extended medical care, the annual bill for health care would, of course, be much higher. The impact of medicare's limited coverage on the elderly's already shaky financial status was plain to these decision-makers, and many of them pondered the obvious question: How many of the elderly simply do not seek medical care out of fear of what it could cost them?

Aside from the direct impact of deductibles or copayments on the elderly's financial status, these decision-makers also believed that medicare mediated the response of the medical and allied health professions to elderly patients. Specifically, physicians did not want to treat the elderly because they did not like the fee rate at which their services were compensated under the program and they felt further aggravated by the volume of paperwork required to get reimbursed for services rendered to medicare's beneficiaries. The decision-makers feared that many physicians would refuse to treat elderly patients.

In the context of the decision-makers' own assessment of the central role of medicare in ensuring the elderly's access to good medical care, the decision-makers were asked to recommend changes they considered important to make in the medicare insurance program. As would be expected from their prior criticisms of the insurance program, they recommended numerous changes in order to improve the elderly's coverage under the program.

Almost one quarter of the sample urged making medicare a comprehensive national health insurance plan that would cover all of the health care costs for older Americans (see Table 4.14). But only among the union local presidents was a substantial minority (37 percent) in favor of such a sweeping proposal. Union organizations were largely responsible for the enactment of the original legislation in 1965, and once again, in the mid-1970s, they have emerged in the forefront advocating reform of the medicare system to provide better health care insurance coverage to older Americans. Advocates for the aged and categoric decision-makers involved with aging programs and health professionals also were all relatively more likely to support a radical overhaul of the medicare system, but the prospects for making a comprehensive insurance package for the elderly are dim when less than one in seven of the legislators support the proposition.

Legislators proved to be the least supportive of the comprehensive national health insurance concept in the whole decision-making community. A national legislator (I.D. 161) commented, "I wouldn't expand it, I would reduce it if I could," and a state legislator (I.D. 130A) postulated, "If it gets any more costly, the young will rise in revolt--medicare is almost double what it would cost for first-class private insurance." Similar perceptions led another (I.D. 115) to suggest that "the solution lies in working a unified program with private industry for health care, not expanding medicare further." Their perceptions were a small minority in the decision-making community, but they were clustered in the legislative subsample. At the same time, far fewer legislators than other decision-makers supported the comprehensive health insurance concept.

Among those decision-makers who do not endorse turning medicare into a comprehensive national health insurance program for the aged there is still considerable sentiment for expanding medicare to cover many of the elderly's more common health care costs that are not now covered. The most popular suggestions for expanding medicare included dental and eye care (24 percent); drug prescriptions (21 percent); convalescent and long-term care (21 percent); preventive health care, including routine diagnostic laboratory tests and annual medical examinations (24 percent); and in-home support services (10 percent).

If such a list of suggested modifications were effected in medicare coverage, the health care costs that burden many elderly would be eased significantly. Consider the elderly's out-of-pocket expenses for drugs not now covered under medicare. Among those elderly enrolled in the supplementary medical insurance program (part B

TABLE 4.14

Decision-Makers Who Maintain That Medicare Should Provide Comprehensive National Health Care to the Aged Population
(percent)

Positional Characteristics of the Decision-Makers	
Position in the Policy Process	
Legislators (N = 71)	14
Agency administrators (N = 70)	23
Service delivery personnel (N = 70)	26
Corporate directors of personnel (N = 35)	17
Union local presidents (N = 35)	37
Advocates for the aged (N = 35)	31
Responsibility for Aging Programs	
Primary function (N = 85)	28
Important but not central function (N = 88)	15
Minor function (N = 143)	26
Area of Program Expertise	
Health-related professions (N = 60)	28
Specialists in other program areas (N = 256)	22
Personal Characteristics of the Decision-Makers	
Age of the Respondent	
Under 45 (N = 98)	24
45-54 (N = 98)	23
55-64 (N = 90)	21
65 and over (N = 30)	27
Sex of the Respondent	
Male (N = 230)	23
Female (N = 86)	24
Ethnicity of the Respondent	
White (N = 235)	21
Minority (N = 81)	30
Educational Level of the Respondent	
High school graduate or less (N = 42)	26
Some college (N = 64)	23
College graduate (N = 99)	23
Postcollege professional education (N = 111)	23
Total (N = 316)	23

Source: Compiled by the author.

of medicare), 7 percent paid drug costs in excess of $180 in 1971, 18 percent in excess of $100, and 60 percent in excess of $50.[25] Coverage of dental care could be equally important to the elderly, nearly half of whom are edentulous. It comes as no surprise that the dental visits of older persons are more likely to be for expensive denture work rather than for the routine and inexpensive periodic checkups or teeth cleaning, which characterize the dental visits of younger people. That half of the older population have not seen a dentist in five years or more is undoubtedly a result of the fact that medicare does not currently cover either dental care or dentures.[26] A similar picture of need emerges with respect to eye care. Approximately 92 percent of persons 65 years of age or over wear eyeglasses or contact lenses, but currently eye care expenses are borne chiefly out-of-pocket by the elderly.[27]

Advocates for the aged most often urged the expansion of medicare coverage to include first the elderly's drug prescription costs and second their dental and eye care expenses. The legislators, however, were not particularly supportive of any of the proposed modifications in medicare, with the exception of eye and dental care coverage, which approximately one quarter (27 percent) of the legislators endorsed adding to medicare. A bare 1 out of 12 of the legislators, for example, considered it important to add the elderly's prescription drug costs to the list of reimbursable expenditures under medicare. Many of the other legislators may simply believe that such basic health care costs are already covered by medicare (the legislators, it will be recalled, were among the subsamples least likely to recognize that medicare covers significantly half of the elderly's health care costs). In any event, it appears that the advocates will have to work hard to achieve their priorities for reforms in medicare coverage.

In overview, then, the decision-makers tended to overrate the efficiency with which medicare absorbs the health care costs of the elderly population. At the same time, they seemed to recognize that medicare is far from comprehensive and that it should be expanded to cover more of the elderly's pressing health care costs. There was a small core of support for making medicare into a comprehensive health insurance plan for the aged. While the majority of the 316 decision-makers favored more limited expansions of the medicare program that would cover some of the more common of the elderly's health care costs not yet included under the program, there was no overwhelming agreement among the decision-makers regarding which expansions should have priority. Less than one quarter of the sample, for example, cited either drug costs or dental and eye care as top priority for reform. Perhaps the most important factor in medicare reform will be the lack of leadership for reform among the legislators. Nearly one third of legislators were unaware of the major deficiencies that exist in the medicare insurance program in its present form.

One final observation that deserves a passing note. Although the trend in recent Republican administrations has been to increase the elderly's deductible payments under medicare, thus forcing them to bear more of their own health costs out-of-pocket, very few of the decision-makers in this survey recommended cutting back on the coverage medicare provides to elderly beneficiaries. Rather, the decision-makers spoke almost unanimously of increasing the coverage afforded the elderly under medicare.

HEALTH CARE PLANNING FOR THE AGED: IMPLICATIONS OF THESE DATA

The decision-makers appeared to have an overly pessimistic view of the older persons' functional capabilities. They not infrequently overestimated the size of the institutionalized elderly population by as much as five or six times its actual number. Such misperceptions in the decision-making community undoubtedly contribute to the dominant focus in U.S. health care policy for the aging on institutional care rather than on in-community and in-home support programs. The decision-makers may benefit from learning to think about the elderly in functional rather than medical terms, to evaluate the elderly's health status in terms of the aged person's ability to manage independently at home and in the community rather than in terms of inventories of pathology. Perhaps if decision-makers had more accurate information regarding the functional capabilities of elderly people, they could develop a range of community-based social service programs that would better serve the needs of elderly and other community residents who are suffering from health decrements of a temporary or permanent nature. Given that most elderly in frail health try to maintain independence in their homes and their communities, these decision-makers should be more oriented to developing program supports to assist these elderly within those environs. These data do not reveal that kind of focus in the decision-makers' analysis of the health care system.

The decision-makers commonly acknowledged that many elderly experience severe transportation problems getting to medical facilities, and yet the decision-makers persisted in pondering how to get the elderly patient to the physician without giving the alternative serious consideration--bringing the physician to the elderly patient. Home health care apparently continues to be challenged as a legitimate health care expense. Many elderly who suffer from poor health fear hospitals and other institutional settings and would surely prefer treatment at home if practical. Medicare, on the other hand, forces institutional care, and relatively few elderly can afford on their own to pay for the home health care that they would prefer. Nevertheless, the data indicate that establishment of a supplemental system of home health care services for immobile elderly persons appears politically remote at the present time.

Similarly, medicare currently makes no provisions for preventive health care. Nearly one quarter of this sample of decision-makers urged converting medicare into a comprehensive national health insurance plan to cover all the elderly's health care costs. But most of the decision-makers interviewed here still conceived of the elderly's health problems more in terms of custodial care rather than preventive care. Health care services for the elderly will continue to be fragmented and relatively less effective until the decision-making community begins to think in terms of a continuum of care to protect the elderly that would supplement custodial care in institutional settings with a variety of ancillary medical services, including home health care, medical transportation, preventive health care, and so on. Based upon the climate of decision-making reflected in the responses of the 316 respondents interviewed in this study, the need for a full continuum of care is not commonly perceived or accorded priority in structuring the delivery of health care services to elderly residents in the community.

As would be expected from their views of the elderly's poor health status, the decision-makers were concerned about the elderly's access to available health care services in the community. Cost and transportation were the major barriers perceived by most decision-makers. Most decision-makers acknowledged that medicare did an inadequate job of guaranteeing the elderly access to affordable medicare. They perceived that copayments and deductibles meant that many elderly still had to pay large sums out-of-pocket to secure needed medical care. But equally of concern to these decision-makers were their perceptions of the physicians' reluctance to treat medicare patients because of limited reimbursement allowances and extraordinary amounts of paperwork involved in filing claims. These decision-makers agreed for the most part that the way to improve the elderly's access to health care services is to improve the medicare insurance program. A minority of the decision-makers was thus in favor of converting medicare into a comprehensive insurance plan that would cover all of the elderly's health care expenses; nearly all of the other decision-makers were in favor of expanding medicare coverage at least to cover some of the elderly's more common health care expenditures that were not then covered by medicare.

Empirical studies suggest, however, that physicians are reluctant to treat the elderly at least as much for personal psychological reasons as for financial ones. Physicians prefer to treat young people and acute illness as opposed to old people and chronic illness. Physicians don't like to treat the elderly because they are repeatedly reminded of their own mortality when they do. Physicians believe it is a waste of time to treat the elderly because they are going to die soon anyway; they would rather treat the young who have a long time to live. Hence it is a questionable proposition whether increasing the lucrativeness of the medicare medical insurance provisions would attract more practitioners in the health fields into specialization for work with the elderly.

The decision-makers' focus on improving the elderly's access to existing medical services by restructuring the medicare insurance program appeared to draw the decision-makers' attention away from other issues germane to the delivery of health care services to elderly patients. The quality of medical care the elderly receive is determined almost as directly by allocations of money to research to search for breakthroughs in the treatment of degenerative and chronic diseases that commonly afflict the elderly. And yet very few of these decision-makers mentioned the priority of aging-related medical research as a serious limitation on the quality of medical care now available to help elderly patients who have serious health problems. But then most (83 percent) of these 316 decision-makers are convinced that major medical breakthroughs in aging diseases will come within the next 30 years, so conceivably, these decision-makers felt that aging research is sufficiently well funded at this time.

Along with priorities for research in diseases of the aging, priorities need to be given to training practitioners in the medical and allied health professions for specialized work with elderly patients. Physicians and other health personnel need special medical training in order to give elderly patients the best medical care that science can make available. Health personnel must be capable of distinguishing between "normal" aging and decrements induced by pathological conditions. The range of "normality" is not easily established for the elderly patient, but it is certainly different in many instances from standards of "normality" established for middle-aged adults. The general physician whose practice consists mainly of middle-aged adults may thus lack the experience to make medical judgments about the health status of his aged patients. The ramifications of this problem in diagnostic and treatment situations pertaining to elderly patients are numerous.

European medicine appears significantly in advance of the U.S. medical profession in offering a geriatric specialization for health care personnel. This fact, however, should come as no surprise, since Europe pioneered as well in income-maintenance and health insurance programs for its elderly citizens well in advance of implementation of similar programs in the U.S. system. The crucial question is how long will it be before the U.S. health care system provides formal education and socialization of health personnel to the special medical needs of the elderly. Currently, the U.S. decision-making community, at least as illustrated by this sample, has inadequately assessed the real barriers to developing a corps of medical personnel to serve the elderly. The decision-makers tend to believe that making treatment of the elderly at least competitively lucrative will entice medical professionals into providing treatment to elderly patients without discrimination. But even assuming that the promise of a more lucrative medicare practice will entice more health professionals to treat the elderly, few of the decision-makers have questioned whether the professionals willing to treat the elderly would be qualified to provide "the best medical treatment available" to those patients. The decision-making community seems to be viewing only the tip of the iceberg on this health care issue.

The leadership role in planning modifications in the delivery of health services to the aged will have to come from the decision-making community in general, because the initiative for change and actual planning of change will probably come directly from only very few elderly residents. Decision-makers need to be sensitive not only to the quality of health care services that are actually received by the elderly client today but to the potential range of care that could be provided were those service delivery systems modified with the special health care needs of the elderly in mind.

In this context, then, it is disconcerting that these decision-makers were not as a whole more sensitive to some very basic issues that challenge the mode, nature, and quality of health care currently being administered to the elderly. Some sectors of the decision-making community show initiative in lobbying for such changes in health care services for the elderly. Data presented in this chapter suggest that many professionals who work closely with the elderly in the course of their jobs and many individuals from the health-related professions are dissatisfied with the current quality of health services being delivered to the elderly. Social service agency personnel, both administrators and providers, plus advocates for the elderly and health professionals, articulate proposals for change in health care services in the future. Agency personnel and health professionals, however, may be expected to advocate change that would protect their vested interests in the organization of health care services. While this may not preclude their consideration of proposals for a radical reorganization of the health care delivery system, it certainly does cloud the prospect that any such future reorganization of health services will be dictated by the health needs of the elderly. And, as will be the subject of a later chapter, the elderly and their spokesmen currently possess too little political clout to force the changes in the organization of health care services to meet on a more rational basis the health care needs of the elderly basis.

The best that can probably be hoped for, in the short run, is the expansion of medicare coverage to cover some of the more common expenses confronting the elderly--drug costs, dental and eye care, long-term and convalescent care, and so on. But, given that legislators are relatively unenthusiastic supporters of even these incremental changes in medicare, the work of the advocates winning these modifications in health care policy may be considerable.

In the long run, perhaps the issues of health care for the elderly are wrapped up in issues of national health insurance for the general public. If so, the merging of health insurance plans will probably not eliminate, but rather may very well only exacerbate, the problems of designing a health care program that will serve the special needs of the elderly. If the special health needs of the elderly receive inadequate attention under the categoric medicare program, why is there reason to believe they will receive more careful scrutiny under a generic national health insurance program?

In any event, national health insurance and/or new medicare proposals will be deliberated by the same actors that forged the first national health plan in the country, medicare, enacted in 1965. The decision-making climate does appear to be reassessing federal responsibility in guaranteeing access to adequate health care, not just for elderly but for all Americans. The actual health insurance proposals that will be hammered out in the future will surely, however, reflect the basic values and social arrangements pertinent to health in the U.S. system. Within that, however, there is considerable latitude for the operation of interest-group influence and rational needs to dictate the form of the final proposals. If the elderly and their spokesmen do not lobby for the changes they desire to see implemented in the organization of health care services, no one else will represent their interests. Without that input, there is little likelihood that U.S. health care policy in the future will any more adequately meet the needs of the elderly than it does now under the existing medicare program. And nearly unanimously, the decision-makers agreed--that is not enough.

NOTES

1. When asked to describe the worst things about being over age 65, poor health was mentioned by 61 percent of the public aged 18 to 64 and by 70 percent of those 50 years of age and older. Health was mentioned far more often than the second problem, loneliness, which was cited by 36 percent of the public aged 18 to 64 compared to only 20 percent of the older public aged 50 plus. Poverty trailed third, mentioned by 29 percent of the younger but only 17 percent of the older respondents. Louis Harris and Associates, The Myth and Reality of Aging in America (Washington, D.C.: National Council on the Aging, 1975), pp. 19-20.

2. Eighty percent of American men and 83 percent of American women aged 45 to 64 report no limitation on their activities due to chronic ailments; over age 65, only 54 percent of the men and 60 percent of the women report no limitation on their activities. Men and women aged 45 to 64 each report approximately 20 days of restricted activity and 7 to 8 days of bed disability in a year. Men over age 65, on the other hand, report an average of 32 restricted-activity days and 13 bed-disability days, while elderly women report an average of 36 restricted-activity days and 14 bed-disability days in the year. National Center for Health Statistics, Health in the Late Years of Life (Washington, D.C.: U.S. Government Printing Office, 1971), pp. 32, 36.

3. The elderly, who make up 10 percent of the population, accounted for more than 28 percent of the $80 billion spent for personal health care costs in 1972. The elderly's average annual medical bill was $1,052 compared to $384 for the population aged 19 to 64 and $167 for the under-19 age group. In keeping with aggregate figures, the elderly's hospital bills and physicians' fees averaged three times that of the younger population for the year. Ethel Shanas and George L. Maddox, "Aging, Health and the Organization of Health Resources," in Handbook of Aging and the Social Sciences, ed. Robert H. Binstock and Ethel Shanas (New York: Van Nostrand-Reinhold, 1976), p. 594.

4. Some of the fundamental political issues in the delivery of health care services for the elderly have been delineated by Carl Eisdorfer, "Issues in Health Planning for the Aged," Pt. I, Gerontologist 16, no. 1 (February 1976): 12-16; and Shanas and Maddox, "Aging, Health, and the Organization of Health Resources."

5. Theodore R. Marmor, The Politics of Medicare (Chicago: Aldine, 1973).

6. Ibid., p. 90.

7. The story of the politics of medicare makes good reading. See ibid.; and James L. Sundquist, Politics and Policies: The Eisenhower, Kennedy and Johnson Years (Washington, D.C.: Brookings Institution, 1968).

8. For a good sampling of the debated issues, skim the record of extensive legislative hearings conducted by the U.S. Senate Special Committee on Aging entitled, "Barriers to Health Care for Older Americans," Hearing before the Subcommittee on Health of the Elderly, 93d Cong., 1st and 2d Sessions (Washington, D.C.: U.S. Government Printing Office, 1973-74).

9. Ibid., Pt. I, March 1973, p. 8.

10. Frances M. Carp, "The Mobility of Retired People," in Transportation and Aging: Selected Issues, ed. Edmund J. Cantilli and June L. Schmelzer (Washington, D.C.: U.S. Government Printing Office, 1970), pp. 23-41.

11. A Duke University study found that more than 39 percent of a sample of persons 60 years of age and older who claimed to be in good health actually were found to be suffering from chronic illnesses and other pathological conditions when they were examined by physicians. Much of what elderly subjects consider normal aging, physicians consider pathology and hence amenable to treatment. George L. Maddox and Elizabeth B. Douglass, "Self-Assessment of Health," in Normal Aging, II, ed. Erdman Palmore (Durham, N.C.: Duke University Press, 1974), pp. 346-64.

12. See, for example, Rodney M. Coe, "Professional Perspectives on the Aged," Pt. I, Gerontologist 7, no. 2 (June 1967): 114-19; Donald L. Spence and Elliott M. Feigenbaum, "Medical Students' Attitudes toward the Geriatric Patient," Journal of the American Geriatric Society 16, no. 9 (September 1968): 976-83; Phyllis Mutschler, "Factors Affecting Choice of Social Work with the Aged," Pt. I, Gerontologist 11, no. 3 (Autumn 1971): 231-41; and Tom Hickey, William Rabowski, David F. Hultsch, and Betty J. Fatula, "Attitudes toward Aging as a Function of In-Service Training and Practitioner Age," Journal of Gerontology 31, no. 6 (November 1976): 681-86.

13. U.S. Department of Health, Education and Welfare, Facts About Older Americans: 1975, DHEW Publication No. OHD 75-20006, 1975.

14. Bernice L. Neugarten, "Age Groups in American Society and the Rise of the Young-Old," Annals of the American Academy of Political and Social Science 415 (September 1974): 187-98.

15. Robert C. Atchley, The Social Forces in Later Life (Belmont, Calif.: Wadsworth, 1972), pp. 123-24.

16. The number of days in a year in which at least half of the daylight hours were spent in bed or in the hospital is inversely

related to income in all age and sex groups between the ages of 25 and 74. Over age 74, the inverse relationship between disability and socioeconomic status does not hold. See Lenore A. Epstein and Janet H. Murray, The Aged Population in the U.S.: The 1963 Social Security Survey of the Aged (Washington, D.C.: U.S. Government Printing Office, 1967). A similar inverse relationship is seen between income and limitation on major physical activity of noninstitutionalized older persons due to chronic conditions. Forty-six percent of older persons with incomes of less than $3,000 experience limited mobility compared to only 30 percent of those with incomes exceeding $15,000. See Office of Management and the Budget, Executive Office of the President, Social Indicators, 1973 (Washington, D.C.: U.S. Government Printing Office, 1973).

17. Marmor, Politics of Medicare, p. 24.

18. See, for example, Ruth B. Weg, "Changing Physiology of Aging: Normal and Pathological," in Aging: Scientific Perspectives and Social Issues, ed. Diana S. Woodruff and James E. Birren (New York: D. Van Nostrand, 1975), pp. 229-56; and Herbert A. DeVries, "Physiology of Exercise and Aging," ibid., pp. 256-76.

19. Shanas and Maddox, "Aging, Health, and the Organization of Health Resources," p. 596.

20. Harris and Associates, Myth and Reality of Aging in America, p. 32.

21. U.S. Senate Special Committee on Aging, "Barriers to Health Care for Older Americans," Pt. 8, March 12, 1974, 93d Cong., 2d sess., Report No. 34-275 (Washington, D.C.: U.S. Government Printing Office, 1974), p. 678.

22. U.S. Department of Housing and Urban Development, Tomorrow's Transportation: New Systems for the Urban Future (Washington, D.C.: U.S. Government Printing Office, 1968).

23. Talcott Parsons, "Social Change and Medical Organization in the United States," Annals of the American Academy of Political and Social Science 346 (March 1963): 21-33.

24. Shanas and Maddox, "Aging, Health and the Organization of Health Resources," p. 594.

25. U.S. Senate Special Committee on Aging, "Barriers to Health Care for Older Americans."

26. U.S. Department of Health, Education and Welfare, Facts About Older Americans: 1975.

27. Ibid.

5 Housing for the Aged: Prospects for a Coherent National Policy

TWO DECADES OF HOUSING ASSISTANCE PROGRAMS TO HELP THE AGED: THE NEED FOR REDIRECTIONS IN THE FUTURE

Housing environment assumes a critical role in the lives of many elderly people. In contrast to younger generations, many elderly spend the majority of their waking hours in or around their homes.[1] It should thus come as no surprise that social science research has begun to document in rather convincing fashion the effects that the housing environment of the elderly person may have on his lifestyle, on his morale, and even on his physical well-being.[2] Similarly, the elderly are considerably more dependent than younger age groups on support services, for example, shopping, transit, and medical services, which are immediately available in the surrounding neighborhood.[3]

Residing in a good neighborhood translates into personal safety, shopping convenience, freedom of movement, engaging friendships--all providing a headstart for a generally satisfying way of life for the older person. Residing in a less desirable neighborhood can mean criminal victimization, inaccessible community resources, lack of mobility, social disengagement--the ingredients for an impacted and unsatisfying lifestyle for the older person. Delegates to the 1971 White House Conference on Aging analyzed the impact of housing environs on the quality of life enjoyed by older persons in this way: "Aside from his spouse, housing is probably the single most important element in the life of an older person."[4]

Despite the critical role of adequate housing in structuring a good quality of life in the later years, many elderly are ill-housed. The first national annual housing survey conducted in 1973 by the

U.S. Bureau of Census under contract to the U.S. Department of Housing and Urban Development (HUD) revealed that only 10 percent of the elderly households in this country live in dwellings free of structural and/or neighborhood defects.[5] At the other end of the spectrum, one in five live in substandard housing that lacks basic heating and/or plumbing facilities.[6] Many elderly are trapped in deteriorating structures in decaying inner-city neighborhoods. Many more elderly live in "service-poor" suburban neighborhoods. Still others encounter increasing difficulty in functioning independently in their homes and neighborhoods because of growing sensory and motor decrements that are the result of chronic and acute ailments in advancing old age. Most elderly people already spend a disproportionate amount of their small retirement incomes to cover expenses in their present living arrangements, and hence they can ill-afford to move in order to improve their housing situation.[7]

The need for more and better retirement housing options has grown increasingly apparent in the decades since World War II. Dramatic increases in life expectancy have meant that more Americans are surviving to and well into old age. Couples today may anticipate a decade or two together after the last child has grown to adulthood and left home, and the surviving spouse is likely to live well into his 80s and possibly his 90s.[8] Older couples and widowed or single elderly require housing that is at once moderately priced, desirably situated near community services and facilities, and designed to accommodate their changing functional capacities in late life.

The private housing industry in the United States has been very slow to develop as an integral part of the normal housing market, housing that is specifically designed to satisfy the needs of the retired and elderly population.[9] Even so, most elderly people, upwards of 90 percent, live in the ordinary housing available in the existing private housing market. How well this housing meets their particular housing needs is not well researched, but evidence is accumulating to document that the lack of viable housing alternatives in the community has forced the premature institutionalization of many elderly people who are no longer able to cope with the demands of fully independent living. Anywhere from 15 to 40 percent of the residents now located in proprietary nursing homes could continue to live more or less independently in the community with the support of well-designed structural and service environments. There are additional estimates that between 10 and 15 percent of the elderly population (approximately 3 million older people) who currently reside in their own homes in the community also require supportive housing environments in order to avoid or at least postpone institutionalization in long-term care facilities.[10]

Confronted with growing numbers of ill-housed elderly and the persistent unresponsiveness of the private housing industry to the needs of the older population, Congress was ultimately faced with the responsibility to underwrite better housing opportunities for the nation's senior citizens. But the U.S. government was late in responding to the special housing needs of its senior citizens, especially when contrasted with the development of public housing programs for the elderly in Western European countries.[11] It was not until 1956 that Congress finally initiated a special incentive program to spur home purchases by elderly Americans.[12] That legislation marked the first explicit commitment of national resources to a program designed exclusively to address the special needs found in the elderly population. By 1970, HUD administered more than 20 different programs providing some form of housing assistance to elderly persons.[13]

After two decades of concerted federal activity to procure more adequate housing opportunities for senior citizens, many policy analysts are agreed that the federal government has yet to develop a coherent national policy on housing for the aged, that is, a policy focused upon providing a number of housing options for individuals from all walks of life that will accommodate their evolving housing needs throughout the later years of life. Housing the elderly is no single undertaking. The elderly are a diverse population in terms of income resources, health status, family circumstances, and lifestyle preferences; and housing needs and preferences of the older population mirror this diversity in their personal and social circumstances. Critics allege that the existing array of federal housing programs to assist the elderly does not adequately take into account this diversity in the housing needs and preferences of the retired and elderly populations.

The dominant emphasis in federal housing programs for the elderly has centered on meeting the pressing shelter needs of low-income elderly housed in substandard dwelling units. Thus, three quarters of all new housing units designated for elderly occupancy under HUD programs throughout the 1960s were low-rent public housing units.[14] Nevertheless, only 3 percent of the elderly population had been rehoused in these new projects by the early 1970s, and estimates range up to another 4 million, or 20 percent, of the elderly population who would like to have access to such housing projects as an alternative to their present housing that is seriously deficient for their needs.[15]

The vast majority of elderly (more than 70 percent) are homeowners, however, who are not benefited by the low-rent public housing projects that have been the mainstay of federal housing assistance programs for the elderly. While increasing numbers of elderly are losing their homes because of inflated taxes and escalating home maintenance and home repair costs, only a small fraction of federal housing assistance monies has gone to help these elderly homeowners. The investment in shoring up elderly homeowners has so far been negligible in comparison to the multibillion dollar investment the government has devoted to the construction of low-rent public housing units for the elderly.[16]

Until recent years, the housing needs of the frail and ill elderly were also largely ignored by the government, even though these elderly are probably the most in need of rehousing in projects operated under various HUD programs. As a way to keep down per-unit housing costs and to encourage independent living among elderly residents, official federal housing policy throughout the 1960s formally discouraged the provision of on-site supportive services (for example, hot meals, housekeeping or medical services) in age-congregate housing projects. Frail and ill elderly thus were effectively denied occupancy in these new projects. Ironically, the healthy elderly initially recruited to occupy the housing units aged during successive years and eventually required those very same supportive services.[17]

Official housing policy inevitably reversed its position in the early 1970s. Both the Housing and Urban Development Act of 1970 and the Community Development Act of 1974 approved construction of congregate housing projects that would offer a range of supportive physical and service environments to elderly residents in frail health. But it proved a costly lesson of unenlightened federal housing policy for the aged. Retroactive design of existing dwelling units to provide barrier-free environments for elderly residents has been far more expensive than if the barrier-free features had been included in the original design and construction of the buildings.[18]

Federal housing programs for the aged have also been criticized for moving elderly people into age-segregated congregate housing environments as opposed to maintaining these elderly in their own homes within an age-integrated community setting.[19] A federal housing policy that emphasizes relocating the elderly in centralized projects contradicts the decided preference of elderly individuals to remain in their own homes in their familiar neighborhoods. For many elderly, moving means disrupting comfortable routines, losing contact with long-time friends and neighbors, feeling lost and confused by new surroundings, and so forth. The elderly typically prefer to make do in their present housing and move only as a last resort, either when they can no longer afford their housing expenses or when they can no longer continue to function independently in their homes.[20]

Nevertheless, the lion's share of federal subsidies in housing programs for the elderly still goes to housing developers to build new multiple-unit projects rather than directly to elderly individuals who might then make individual decisions about improving their housing situation involving either repairs on their present dwellings or moving to more suitable housing in the same or another area. There are many who believe that federal housing programs for the elderly would be more effective in guaranteeing the elderly access to decent housing suited to their personal needs if supplemental housing allowances were issued directly to ill-housed elderly who were then allowed to shop for better housing in an open market; others, however, fear that the housing supplements would not be spent to improve deficient housing circumstances and hence opposed the direct subsidy arrangements.

Two decades of federal experience in managing housing programs for the elderly have left federal housing officials searching for better solutions to the elderly's most pressing housing problems. In recent years, HUD has experimented with supplemental housing allowances, home repair and home maintenance programs, and other program innovations. A well-balanced program of housing assistance to the elderly will require significant expansion and institutionalization of these experimental programs to make them an integral part of a coherent national housing program for the aged.

Gerontologists underscore the need for a coherent national housing policy for the aged that more adequately addresses the diverse housing needs in the older population. They urge the development of housing subsidy programs that will maximize choice for the older individual. They advocate housing assistance programs that will enable aging individuals to remain in their own homes in familiar neighborhood surroundings. They advance the concept of a continuum of living arrangements in the community ranging from housing designed for fully independent living to fully supportive physical and service environments for the elderly in declining health. The mistakes of an uninformed housing policy for the aged, they argue, are very costly, both in terms of dollars and cents and in terms of human inconvenience. One gerontologist who is a specialist in housing for the elderly summarizes present housing policy in this way:

> On the research side there is clear documentation that housing can have decisive impact upon the life-styles and well-being of older persons; and on the policy and service side, there is a growing commitment to provide adequate housing for the elderly. With regard to coordinate efforts on the part of planners, service providers, and researchers, progress seems less clear. Moreover, despite the activity, housing remains a major problem among the old, and the best solutions remain to be specified.[21]

The data from the interviews with the 316 decision-makers surveyed in this study offer an opportunity to explore how the decision-making community in the mid-1970s proposes to assist the elderly in finding better housing in the community. The central question is whether decision-makers appear more responsive to the housing needs and preferences of the elderly population than past housing policies suggest they have been in prior decades. Are these decision-makers cognizant of diverse housing needs and preferences in the elderly population or do they persist in focusing almost exclusively on the shelter needs of the elderly poor? Do the problems of the elderly homeowners have greater visibility to decision-makers in this decade or do decision-makers still generally believe that the foundation of housing policy for the aged lies in an expanded low-rent public housing program? Do these decision-makers emphasize the role that suitable housing environments might assume in fostering independent living for frail and ill elderly in the community at large; that is, do they commonly advocate the need for more carefully designed supportive physical and service environments to house the elderly?

The decision-makers were asked to enumerate what they perceived to be the most serious problems elderly people face in finding housing adequately suited to their needs. The decision-makers were then asked about how best to improve the bad housing situation confronting these ill-housed elderly. Do the decision-makers envision assistance to these elderly that would maintain them in their present housing units or do they advocate relocating the elderly in new housing structures? How do the decision-makers evaluate the success of age-segregated living arrangements and multigeneration households? But, more important, do the decision-makers' preferences among alternative modes of housing assistance and alternative models of living arrangements for the later years match the preferences expressed by elderly residents living in the community?

Finally, as they project to the year 2000 and beyond, how do these decision-makers envision future generations of elderly will be housed? Do they believe that the majority of elderly will continue to reside independently in their own households in the community, or do they believe that alternative living arrangements will become considerably more common in the later years of life? For example, do these decision-makers predict increases or decreases in the percentage of elderly living alone or in multigeneration households, or those residing in nursing homes or in retirement communities?

Accepting that the functional life of a dwelling unit built today is on the average one-half century, it seems obvious that housing for these future generations of elderly must be planned today in light of the best knowledge available. New housing for the elderly should thus be designed on the basis of the emerging scientific information base that specifies particular characteristics of the living environment that contribute to good person-environment interaction in the later years of life. Moreover, new housing construction should logically correspond to the expressed housing needs and preferences of aging residents in the community, for they are the future residents of these new dwelling units. The data that follow here reflect on the prospects for developing a coherent national policy on housing for the aged that will ensure suitable housing alternatives for this and future generations of older Americans.

DECISION-MAKERS' ANALYSES OF THE AGED'S MOST PRESSING HOUSING PROBLEMS

When asked to identify the three greatest problems facing elderly residents of Los Angeles County, nearly one third (30 percent) of the 316 decision-makers cited the elderly's housing problems (see Table 5.1). As such, it was ranked behind the elderly's financial problems, their physical and mental health problems, and their transportation problems. After two decades of federal assistance programs to help the elderly secure better housing, a large segment of the decision-making community still defines inadequate housing as a serious problem confronting many elderly people.

Among the original six subsamples, advocates for the aged and union local presidents were considerably more likely than others to assert that housing remains a major problem for many elderly in the 1970s. As of 1970, labor unions managed 7 percent of the nonprofit housing for the elderly that had been constructed under the Section 202 construction program administered by HUD.[22] Hence, union officials generally have been aware of the elderly's housing problems for quite some time, and not a few unions have already taken some action to remedy identified housing problems in their constituent retiree population. Nevertheless, many of the union local presidents believed housing still represents a common problem among elderly residents living in the community at large.

As a general rule, only those decision-makers closely involved with aging programs frequently cited housing as a major problem for old people. Senior citizens affairs specialists inside and outside of government underscored the elderly's housing problems as did the directors of recreation programs organized for elderly participants. Finally, elderly decision-makers were also relatively more likely to believe that housing posed serious problems for many elderly people in the community.

When surveys are made of the expressed needs of older people living in the community, housing is only infrequently mentioned among

TABLE 5.1

"What Would You Say Are the Three Greatest Problems Facing People in Los Angeles Who Are Age 65 and Older?"
(percent mentioning "housing" as a problem and problem's rank based on number of mentions)

	Percent	Rank
Positional Characteristics of the Decision-Makers		
Position in the Policy Process		
Legislators (N = 71)	30	5
Agency administrators (N = 70)	29	5
Service delivery personnel (N = 70)	27	5
Corporate directors of personnel (N = 35)	14	6
Union local presidents (N = 35)	40	2.5
Advocates for the aged (N = 35)	46	4
Responsibility for Aging Programs		
Primary function (N = 85)	38	5
Important but not central function (N = 88)	25	5
Minor function (N = 143)	29	4.5
Area of Program Expertise		
Health (N = 37)	32	4
Mental health (N = 23)	17	4
Housing (N = 29)	28	4
Employment (N = 92)	26	4
Income maintenance (N = 26)	27	5
Recreation/leisure (N = 18)	44	3
Senior citizens affairs (N = 49)	43	4
Generalists (N = 42)	26	5
Personal Characteristics of the Decision-Makers		
Age of the Respondent		
Under 45 (N = 98)	22	5
45-54 (N = 98)	34	4
55-64 (N = 90)	28	5
65 and over (N = 30)	50	4
Sex of the Respondent		
Male (N = 230)	30	5
Female (N = 86)	31	5
Ethnicity of the Respondent		
White (N = 235)	29	5
Minority (N = 81)	32	5
Educational Level of the Respondent		
High school graduate or less (N = 42)	43	3
Some college (N = 64)	30	5
College graduate (N = 99)	29	5
Postcollege professional education (N = 111)	26	5
Total (N = 316)	30	5

Source: Compiled by the author.

their top-priority problems (see Table 2.6). Seldom do even 5 percent of the elderly residents volunteer housing as a major problem; even when probed more directly about their satisfaction with their existing living arrangements, only 10 to 15 percent typically indicate serious dissatisfaction.[23] One reason uncovered by empirical research for the lack of greater expressed dissatisfaction over housing arrangements in the community is that characteristics of the neighborhood (for example, friendship and neighbor relationships, availability of transportation service, access to stores and medical facilities, and personal safety factors) appear to be more decisive in determining the elderly's overall satisfaction with their present housing than simply the character of the physical dwelling unit, per se.[24] Thus many elderly lodged in obviously substandard housing that lacks basic heating and/or plumbing facilities nevertheless rate their housing as "good" or "fair."

The author of the Background and Issues housing report prepared for the 1971 White House Conference on Aging appropriately cautioned, "It would be ill-advised to accept the lack of expressed dissatisfaction with their housing as a measure of whether or not older people are well or healthfully housed."[25] Other data suggest that substantial unmet housing needs and/or latent housing dissatisfaction do exist in the elderly population. One study, for example, found that one in four older persons living in Los Angeles County was sufficiently dissatisfied with their housing to consider moving, although in the following year, only one half of these elderly were successful in finding housing better suited to their needs. The remainder continued to live in housing that failed to satisfy their personal needs.[26]

If as many as one quarter of the elderly population express discontent with their housing arrangements and if as many as one fifth of the elderly reside in substandard housing units, the decision-makers cannot be incorrect in identifying housing as a major problem for many elderly people. Such numbers alone could justify considering housing a serious problem in the elderly population. But considering the critical role that housing environment may play in structuring the quality of life enjoyed by the older person, decision-makers would seem entirely justified in devoting considerable attention to whatever housing problems they identify in the elderly population.

Moreover, because many of the ill-housed elderly are not vocal about their housing dissatisfactions and/or they are unable to change unsatisfactory living arrangements, the decision-making community would seem to bear a heavier burden for developing housing opportunities that will meet the latent housing needs of these ill-housed elderly. If the elderly themselves are unlikely to protest the need for housing better suited to the demands of living in the late years of life and if the private housing industry persists in shunning the potential market for retirement housing, opportunities for the elderly conceivably will come only from inside the decision-making community. In this context, the elite decision-makers' perspectives on the elderly's housing situation assume a dimension of added importance.

More than three quarters of the decision-makers sampled in this survey continued to focus on the excessive costs of housing as a major problem for elderly people who are typically trying to manage on small retirement incomes (see Table 5.2).* More than one in four of the decision-makers (29 percent) concentrated on the problem of skyrocketing rents. Advocates for the aged, service providers in government social agencies, and other decision-makers who reported working closely with the elderly all tended to stress the elderly's problems in the rental housing market in particular. A large percentage (34 percent) of the rest of the decision-making community, however, voiced explicit concern about the plight of the elderly homeowner, with attention being equally divided between the problems posed by high mortgage payments and upkeep costs and the problems created by rising property taxes. But the common theme expressed by all of these decision-makers was that the elderly are being priced out of the housing market on their small retirement incomes. In nearly all corners of the decision-making community, respondents were almost twice as likely to cite cost barriers to the elderly's finding suitable housing as to identify any other barrier confronting the elderly in the housing market. Such cost considerations were virtually a universal concern of the corporate directors of personnel in particular. Concern over the costs of housing obviously dominated the decision-makers' perceptions of the elderly's most pressing housing problems.

---

*Curiously, however, there was no consistent relationship between the decision-makers' perceptions of widespread poverty in the elderly population and their identification of excessive housing costs as a major barrier to the elderly securing adequate housing. The only statistical relationship that emerged in the data found that those who believed half or more of the elderly lived in dire poverty were somewhat more likely to cite high rents as a problem for the elderly than decision-makers who believed poverty was less widespread in the elderly population. The perceptions of poverty in the elderly population and the perceived problems created by excessive housing costs would thus seem to be independently rather than jointly held perceptions.

TABLE 5.2

Decision-Makers' Perceptions of the Major Housing Problems Confronting Los Angeles County Aged

Decision-Makers' Positional and Personal Characteristics	Excessive Housing Costs (percent)	High Rental Costs (percent)
Positional Characteristics		
Position in the Policy Process		
Legislators (N = 71)	77	20
Agency administrators (N = 70)	51	27
Service delivery personnel (N = 70)	41	41
Corporate directors of personnel (N = 35)	71	23
Union local presidents (N = 35)	57	29
Advocates for the aged (N = 35)	51	43
Responsibility for Aging Programs		
Primary function (N = 85)	53	41
Important but not central function (N = 88)	64	20
Minor function (N = 43)	57	29
Area of Program Expertise		
Housing planners (N = 29)	59	28
Specialists in other program areas (N = 287)	58	30
Personal Characteristics		
Age of Respondent		
Under 45 (N = 98)	63	28
45-54 (N = 98)	62	27
55-64 (N = 90)	52	32
65 and over (N = 30)	43	43
Sex of Respondent		
Male (N = 230)	64	26
Female (N = 86)	41	41
Ethnicity of Respondent		
White (N = 235)	59	29
Minority (N = 81)	54	33
Educational Level of the Respondent		
High school graduate or less (N = 42)	40	43
Some college (N = 64)	67	30
College graduate (N = 99)	59	30
Postcollege professional education (N = 111)	59	25
Total (N = 316)	58	30

Source: Compiled by the author.

The Elderly's Most Pressing Housing Problems as Cited by the Decision-Makers

Inadequate Housing Supply Generally (percent)	Insufficient Low-Cost Housing (percent)	Insufficient Housing Designed for the Elderly (percent)	Housing Located Too Far from Needed Services (percent)	Housing Located in High-Crime Areas (percent)	Lack of In-Home Support Services (percent)
48	17	10	34	8	7
43	29	24	37	17	13
50	16	23	46	16	13
29	20	9	34	20	11
34	31	6	29	29	3
54	29	6	26	20	14
45	27	18	38	9	14
52	23	15	40	15	8
39	20	13	32	22	10
41	14	28	55	3	14
45	23	14	34	18	10
43	21	16	36	17	9
45	28	15	35	13	10
43	19	14	38	19	11
50	20	10	33	20	13
42	22	11	35	17	8
50	23	26	37	17	16
39	24	13	36	18	10
59	17	21	36	14	11
43	24	2	24	26	12
41	25	6	33	19	11
47	16	16	42	11	10
44	26	23	36	17	10
44	22	15	36	17	10

Many of the decision-makers maintained that, apart from the issue of being able to afford housing on the open market, there was simply insufficient low-cost housing available in the normal housing supply.* Legislators considered the problem more in terms of a general housing shortage that affected the entire market and not just low-cost housing units. Their dominant response to solving the shortage of housing for the elderly, however was a recommendation to build more low-cost housing.

In light of the decision-makers' common perceptions regarding the elderly's poor health, it is very surprising that more decision-makers did not cite the lack of housing architecturally designed to accommodate the elderly's changing functional capacities as a major barrier to old people locating housing that would be suited to their special needs in later life.† Only one in seven of the sample of 316 decision-makers noted the lack of housing specially designed for senior citizens. Housing planners were considerably more likely than the rest of the decision-making community to affirm the elderly's need for architecturally supportive physical housing environments. Agency administrators and service delivery personnel in government social agencies were also substantially more sensitive than other decision-maker groups to the elderly's special housing needs for barrier-free living environments. In-home support services provide an alternative to physical supports in the elderly's housing environment. However, even fewer of the decision-makers registered concern about the lack of in-home support services than raised questions about the lack of architecturally designed housing environments for the elderly.‡ Decision-makers as a group paid

*Concern over the lack of low-cost housing alternatives on the housing market would seem to accord with the decision-makers' perceptions of widespread poverty in the elderly population and their concern about excessive housing costs pricing the elderly out of the housing market. However no statistical relationship emerged to suggest that these perceptions were jointly held.

†Moreover, the decision-maker's perceptions of the elderly's health status did not determine whether or not he cited the lack of supportive physical environments in housing normally available on the open market as a major barrier preventing elderly people from finding housing suited to their special needs.

‡Once again, a decision-maker's perceptions of the elderly's poor health status did not predict whether he would identify the lack of in-home support services as a major barrier to elderly people finding suitable living arrangements in their later years of life.

far less attention to the health-related housing problems of the elderly than they did to the cost factors as they assessed the major barriers that older people face in finding housing adequately suited to their specific housing needs.

A little more than one third of the decision-makers (36 percent) believed that many elderly live in service-poor neighborhoods. Of most concern was the elderly's isolation from medical facilities and shopping centers, which was cited by more than one sixth of the sample of 316 decision-makers. Housing located too far from public transportation service concerned only half as many of the decision-makers. As could be expected, service delivery personnel were the most sensitive of all the decision-maker subgroups to the elderly's isolation from important life-support and community facilities. Housing planners were also acutely aware of the problems created for many elderly residents who live in service-poor neighborhoods. Other decision-makers assessed the problems with location of the elderly's housing in terms of older people being forced to find housing in slum and high-crime neighborhoods because it is the only housing they could afford on their limited incomes. In general, however, poor location of the elderly's housing concerned these decision-makers far less than either cost or availability factors.

An overview of the decision-makers' assessments of the elderly's housing situation finds that all but one of the 316 decision-makers interviewed in this study believed that elderly people face serious problems in finding housing suited to their needs, but that less than one third of these decision-makers believed that housing thus represents one of the three most pressing problems facing elderly people in general. The majority of the decision-makers asserted that high housing costs posed serious problems for elderly homeowners and renters alike. The general housing shortage worried many of the decision-makers. The isolation of the elderly's housing in service-poor and otherwise undesirable neighborhoods concerned a minority of the decision-makers. The lack of service and/or architecturally designed supports in housing environments for the elderly concerned relatively few decision-makers, which is especially surprising considering the negative profile on the elderly's health status described by the majority of these decision-makers. The decision-makers as a group thus seem to believe that the elderly do not require special housing environments, but rather that all the elderly need is a chance to compete effectively on the open market for their housing. That is, with sufficient money to spend on housing and with good housing available on the market, most elderly should have no problems finding housing suited to their needs. The decision-makers' recommendations for improving the housing opportunities available to senior citizens are considered in the following section.

DECISION-MAKERS' RECOMMENDATIONS FOR IMPROVING THE HOUSING SITUATION OF THE AGED

Two alternative public policy strategies to improve the elderly's housing situation dominated the thinking of these 316 decision-makers: construct more housing and provide housing subsidies directly to the elderly (see Table 5.3). Looked at one way, the decision-makers were merely approaching the supply and demand problem in the housing market from opposite ends. Those urging construction of more housing could be seeking to enlarge the supply of available housing, whereas those urging housing subsidies administered directly to elderly people could be seeking to improve the elderly's purchasing power within the existing housing market.

But fundamental differences also divide the two approaches to solving the elderly's housing problems. For example, constructing new housing often entails subsidizing middleman developers and contractors in the private housing industry more than the elderly residents themselves; and too often the middleman sponsors of the housing redevelopment projects raise prices of the new housing units in order to cover construction and operating expenses, and the low- and middle-income elderly are thereby effectively priced out of the new housing. This has been the history of many housing projects for the elderly constructed with the help of government subsidies, and this experience led one state legislator (I.D. 140) to observe: "We should try to put as much emphasis on maintenance of the elderly in their homes as possible, rather than the demolition and clearing away of homes. Give the elderly incentives so they can maintain their homes, rather than tearing down the old and building anew. Often older people can't afford the new modern apartments that we put up to replace their homes." Constructing new housing also entails moving the elderly into new surroundings, often in unfamiliar neighborhoods, whereas providing subsidies directly to elderly residents gives the elderly the choice of whether to improve their present dwelling units or move into other housing. Because of these and other basic differences in the two policy approaches, many of the decision-makers clearly preferred one over another. This was especially true in the legislative subsample and only somewhat less so in the corporate subsample.

Considerable diversity of opinion is masked by the initial choice to build more housing for the elderly or conversely to provide housing subsidies to the aged. For example, those decision-makers preferring more housing construction do not agree on the kind of new housing required. Some (22 percent) believe the elderly's needs could be met by shoring up the housing market in general,

TABLE 5.3

Decision-Makers' Preferences among Alternative Strategies to Improve Housing for the Aged: Housing Construction versus Housing Subsidies

	Construct More Housing (percent)	Provide Housing Subsidies Directly to the Aged (percent)
Positional Characteristics of the Decision-Makers		
Position in the Policy Process		
Legislators (N = 70)	61	56
Agency administrators (N = 70)	80	44
Service delivery personnel (N = 70)	80	41
Corporate directors of personnel (N = 35)	66	49
Union local presidents (N = 35)	77	43
Advocates for the aged (N = 35)	77	43
Responsibility for Aging Programs		
Primary function (N = 85)	80	53
Important but not central function (N = 88)	75	44
Minor function (N = 143)	69	44
Area of Program Expertise		
Housing planners (N = 29)	79	41
Specialists in other program areas (N = 287)	73	47
Personal Characteristics of the Decision-Makers		
Age of the Respondent		
Under 45 (N = 98)	74	48
45-54 (N = 98)	74	49
55-64 (N = 90)	72	43
65 and over (N = 30)	70	43
Sex of the Respondent		
Male (N = 230)	72	50
Female (N = 86)	77	37
Ethnicity of the Respondent		
White (N = 235)	71	44
Minority (N = 81)	79	54
Educational Level of the Respondent		
High school graduate or less (N = 42)	60	45
Some college (N = 64)	73	47
College graduate (N = 99)	72	42
Postcollege professional education (N = 111)	80	50
Total (N = 316)	73	47

Source: Compiled by the author.

others (45 percent) urge that the building emphasis be placed on low-cost housing, and still others (37 percent) stress the need for more barrier-free housing (see Table 5.4). Similarly, decision-makers who prefer giving housing subsidies directly to the elderly do not agree on whether the elderly should be aided through supplemental housing allowances to renters and homeowners alike (30 percent) or whether they should be subsidized in their homes through utility rate reductions and tax exemptions (23 percent).

Decision-makers' proposals for improving the housing situation of elderly residents depended on both their position in the policy process and their personal characteristics. Union local presidents, for example, strongly favored the construction of more low-cost housing units for the elderly. This policy preference is consistent with the union leaders' common perception of widespread poverty in the elderly population (see Table 3.2). Service delivery personnel, on the other hand, were most concerned about constructing barrier-free environments for the elderly. Their policy preference for specially designed senior housing is similarly consistent with their emphasis on the poor health status of old people; the reader may recall that these service providers were the most likely of all the subsamples to overestimate the number of elderly people who are institutionalized.*

Apparently these service providers believed that if there were more supportive physical and service environments available, elderly persons in frail or declining health could maintain residence in their own homes in the community rather than move into institutional settings as they do now for the lack of such housing alternatives in their communities. Housing planners and decision-makers with college and/or professional degrees were also considerably more supportive of the idea of building more housing that was designed specifically to accommodate the elderly's changing functional capacities in late life.

In contrast to designing architectural supports in the elderly's housing environments, which had the endorsement of a sizable segment of the decision-making community, development of in-home support services to assist frail elderly with household chores of home repairs and home maintenance did not prove to be a popular idea with this sample of decision-makers. Home-based support

---

*More than one third (34 percent) of the service delivery personnel believed that one in every three of the elderly population or even more were institutionalized because they could no longer function independently in their homes or in their communities.

services, like home-based health care, still seem to be challenged as a legitimate cost.[27] At the same time, however, the cost to support the institutionalized aged population in this country is approaching $7 billion per year, with much of that cost already covered by government subsidies. Ironically, recent cost-analysis studies have begun to document that the per-patient costs of institutionalization far exceed those of home-delivered support services.[28] When the cost advantages of in-home support services are added to the social-psychological benefits that social science has confirmed accrue to the older person who is able to remain in the familiar surroundings of his home and neighborhood, it seems reasonable to conclude that support services to assist the elderly in their own homes should be expanded to become an integral part of housing programs for the elderly. But the political feasibility of a greatly enhanced program of home-delivered services to assist the elderly is not promising based on an assessment of the climate of decision-making as it is reflected in the thinking of this cross section of the decision-making community.

Legislators proved to be the only subgroup in the decision-making community that was not significantly more committed to construction of new housing than to providing housing subsidies directly to the elderly as the primary means for solving the elderly's most pressing housing problems. Legislators were the most supportive of providing housing subsidies directly to elderly people both in the form of reduced taxes and discounts on utility bills and in the form of housing allowances to supplement their small retirement incomes. Of the two alternatives, most of the decision-making community preferred straight supplemental housing allowances over miscellaneous tax exemptions and discounts. The proportion favoring the housing allowances approached or exceeded two to one among the service providers and the advocates, as well as among female and high school educated decision-makers.

To recap briefly the decision-makers' preferences among alternative public policy strategies to improve the housing situation of older people, many of the decision-makers still think primarily in terms of constructing more housing, particularly more low-cost housing to fit the elderly's limited income resources. A sizable segment of the decision-making community, however, is focused on the need to build more housing that is architecturally designed to accommodate the elderly's declining functional capacities in late life. In-home support services, which might be used to complement barrier-free living environments or to compensate for unmodified structural environments, were rarely identified by this sample of decision-makers as a feasible policy alternative in future expansion of housing programs to assist the elderly. Of greater promise in the thinking

TABLE 5.4

Decision-Makers' Recommended Solutions for the Aged's Major Housing Problems

Decision-Makers' Positional and Personal Characteristics	Construct More Housing Generally (percent)	Construct More Low-Cost Housing (percent)
Positional Characteristics of the Decision-Makers		
Position in the Policy Process		
Legislators (N = 71)	20	41
Agency administrators (N = 70)	33	49
Service delivery personnel (N = 70)	20	41
Corporate directors of personnel (N = 35)	17	34
Union local presidents (N = 35)	9	60
Advocates for the aged (N = 35)	26	51
Responsibility for Aging Programs		
Primary function (N = 85)	26	48
Important but not central function (N = 88)	24	48
Minor function (N = 143)	18	42
Area of Program Expertise		
Housing planners (N = 29)	17	45
Specialists in other program areas (N = 287)	22	45
Personal Characteristics of the Decision-Makers		
Age of Respondent		
Under 45 (N = 98)	19	38
45-54 (N = 98)	28	50
55-64 (N = 90)	16	49
65 and over (N = 30)	30	43
Sex of Respondent		
Male (N = 230)	21	47
Female (N = 86)	24	42
Ethnicity of Respondent		
White (N = 235)	23	44
Minority (N = 81)	19	48
Educational Level of Respondent		
High school graduate or less (N = 42)	12	45
Some college (N = 64)	20	47
College graduate (N = 99)	18	46
Postcollege professional education (N = 111)	30	43
Total (N = 316)	22	45

Source: Compiled by the author.

Recommended Solutions for the Elderly's Major Housing Problems					
Construct More Housing Designed for the Elderly (percent)	Repair the Elderly's Existing Housing (percent)	Reduce Tax, Utility, et cetera Rates for the Elderly (percent)	Income Supplements for the Elderly (percent)	In-Home Support Services for the Elderly (percent)	No Public Policy Solution (percent)
28	7	31	35	8	7
41	6	26	21	11	9
50	1	17	34	14	6
37	3	26	29	9	14
26	0	20	29	3	9
31	11	17	31	20	0
41	7	28	28	19	5
36	6	23	30	10	10
35	3	21	32	7	7
48	3	28	24	14	7
36	5	23	31	11	7
38	5	28	34	10	11
36	3	26	29	11	3
41	7	18	29	11	9
27	3	20	27	13	3
33	4	27	30	8	8
48	7	13	31	19	5
34	3	22	28	9	7
44	9	27	36	16	7
19	10	17	38	17	12
30	6	27	23	13	3
40	2	26	26	10	9
45	5	22	34	9	6
37	5	23	30	11	7

of these decision-makers were housing allowances to supplement the elderly's limited incomes or a package of tax exemptions and utility rate discounts to ease the toll that housing expenses take on the elderly's diminishing income resources. One advantage of these latter policy options is that they would permit the elderly to continue living in their present housing environment if that is their personal preference.

Questions should surface regarding the extent to which these decision-makers are sensitive to housing needs and preferences that the elderly themselves have expressed. Do these decision-makers articulate housing problems and propose policy solutions that accord with the verbalizations of elderly residents in the community, or do these decision-makers mandate housing programs and policies with little awareness of and/or little regard for the elderly's own preferences? Do ill-housed elderly prefer to move to new housing or stay where they are and repair their present dwellings? If the former, then the decision-makers' emphasis on building new housing for the elderly is appropriate; if the latter, then decision-makers might appropriately focus more than they have on providing housing subsidies directly to the elderly that would enable them to fix up their present homes. Questions such as these are explored in the following section, which examines the congruence of the decision-makers' perceptions regarding the elderly's housing situation with those of elderly residents living in the community.

CONGRUENCE BETWEEN THE DECISION-MAKERS' AND THE AGED'S PERCEPTIONS OF HOUSING NEEDS AND PREFERENCES IN OLD AGE

The Expressed Housing Needs and Problems of the Aged

The basis for an informed and potentially effective housing policy for older Americans would be a relatively accurate understanding on the part of decision-makers of both the elderly's housing needs or problems and their apparent preferences among various forms of housing assistance that might be offered to them. Data from both the USC companion survey of Los Angeles County elderly residents aged 65 to 74 and the nationwide survey conducted for the National Council on the Aging by Louis Harris and Associates provide an opportunity to compare the decision-makers' observations on the elderly's housing situation with those expressed by the elderly themselves.

Data from both surveys confirm the findings of other studies that were noted earlier in this chapter: that relatively few elderly volunteer housing as one of their most pressing problems. In the nationwide Harris survey, approximately one third of the elderly (34 percent) believed that housing posed a "very serious" problem for "most" people aged 65 and older. This figure roughly corresponds to the three out of ten decision-makers in this study who identified housing as one of the three most serious problems commonly confronting people in old age. However, only 4 percent of the elderly interviewed in the Harris survey asserted that housing was personally "a very serious problem" and only another 7 percent labeled housing as "a somewhat serious problem."[29] In the Los Angeles County survey, even fewer of the elderly residents cited housing as a major problem. Only 11 percent believed that housing posed a major problem for most older people, and only 7 percent volunteered housing as one of their own worst problems.

Nevertheless, on more detailed examination of the housing situation of these very same Los Angeles County residents, serious problems do emerge. More than one in eight of these elderly (13 percent) felt burdened by the excessive costs of housing (rent or mortgage payments and property taxes). One in five (19 percent) acknowledged that their homes were in poor condition and in need of substantial repairs. Other elderly residents acknowledged that the location of their present housing posed various problems. One in nine (11 percent) complained that their homes were too far away from stores; nearly one in five (18 percent) asserted that their homes were too far from public transportation service; nearly one in four (23 percent) complained about residing in high-crime areas; and nearly one in eight (12 percent) complained about living too far away from family and friends. In all, 58 percent of the sample of elderly interviewed in the USC study cited one or more of these problems with their current living arrangement.

Other data gathered in these interviews confirmed that declining health also poses a problem for many of these elderly in their homes and the surrounding neighborhood. One in five acknowledged that their health created problems for their moving around in the community or neighborhood outside their homes; nearly one in four (23 percent) reported problems climbing stairs, which could be a problem in anything but ground-floor living quarters; and nearly one in five (19 percent) complained that their health interfered with their performing basic household chores. All of these are problems that would certainly be more common and more serious among the elderly who are in advanced old age (aged 75 and older) who were not interviewed in this USC study.

In comparison with the elderly's self-assessed housing problems, the decision-makers appeared to far overestimate the problems of excessive costs. At the same time, they substantially underestimated problems associated with physical aspects of the elderly's housing environment, including, specifically, access to community facilities and services from the elderly's residence, location of the elderly's home in a high-crime area, and the ability of the elderly person to do basic household chores and home maintenance to keep his housing in good condition. In other words, the decision-makers apparently have not yet developed a full appreciation of the complex interrelationship between the neighborhood and the physical dwelling unit, on the one hand, and the maintenance of an independent lifestyle for the elderly individual, on the other.

These data further confirm the need for supportive physical and service housing environments that are designed to accommodate the elderly's changing functional capabilities in advancing old age. Although many decision-makers appeared sensitive to the need for new housing environments that are barrier free for the elderly, relatively few decision-makers accepted the need for in-home support services to assist the elderly in maintaining their residence within the community. The data from the USC survey suggest that such in-home support services may, in fact, be one of the most valuable and most desired forms of housing assistance that could be provided to elderly people trying to maintain their own homes in the community at large. Gerontologists, advocates for the aged, and housing specialists will need to launch an extensive promotional campaign to influence others in the decision-making community to think more favorably about home-delivered support services for the elderly, because at the present time, the political prospects for significantly expanding in-home support programs are very dim.

The Desire to Move versus the Desire to Stay

For those elderly who are ill-housed, the question becomes whether to repair their present homes or to move into new housing. The elderly residents of Los Angeles County interviewed in the USC study were asked, "If government funds were available, and needed by you for housing, would you prefer to have these funds used to repair your present residence or to help you get other housing?" Nearly one third (32 percent) of the elderly residents insisted that they had no need of such government housing assistance money. Two thirds of the remainder of the sample (66 percent) preferred monetary assistance to help repair their present dwellings, whereas the remaining one third (one fifth of the total sample) preferred government assistance to help them find new housing.

The decision-makers in this study were also asked directly, "Given the choice and need, do you think elderly people would prefer that the government provide funds to repair present housing or to make other housing available?" In response to this question, the majority of the sample of 316 decision-makers (58 percent) acknowledged that most elderly would prefer to use the government money to repair their present housing rather than to relocate in other housing (see Table 5.5). Less than one in four of the decision-makers (23 percent) responded that the elderly would want the money used to make other housing available. Service delivery personnel and women decision-makers were the most sensitive to the elderly's desire to remain in their present housing. Union local presidents, on the other hand, were the most likely to say that the elderly would like to find new housing; earlier in the interview the union leaders had similarly urged construction of more low-cost housing projects to accommodate the needs of ill-housed elderly people in the community.

For many decision-makers, their response to this question was to the effect that they believed elderly people would prefer to repair their present housing rather than move to new housing and thus represented a reversal of their earlier position when they focused on more housing construction as the best way to solve the elderly's most pressing housing problems (see Table 5.3). Some of the decision-makers acknowledged this tension in their contrasting responses, noting that although the elderly's preference would probably be to repair their old housing, in their professional opinion it was still better to rehouse the elderly in new or at least more adequate structures.

A few of their comments are illustrative of the themes in their responses. A state legislator (I.D. 150A) observed, "I would rather see new housing as a first choice, but I suppose that the person who owns his own home would like to repair it." A local legislator (I.D. 107) noted, "Repair would be less expensive but I think senior homes are good. Seniors need to be watched and protected; they shouldn't be left alone. Many times they hurt themselves and need somebody to keep an eye on them." Another state legislator (I.D. 133) worried about the costs to repair the elderly's present housing. "The large percentage of the people would like money to repair their present housing, but we have no idea of the costs involved." Some city councilmen suggested that repairing structures was out of the question in the decaying inner-city areas: "In older parts of the city, repairing never works. Public housing is needed there" (I.D. 111A). "Repairing is simply inadequate; it is a stopgap measure only" (I.D. 113A).

TABLE 5.5

"Given the Choice and Need, Do You Think Elderly People Would Prefer the Government Provide Funds to Repair Housing or to Make Other Housing Available?"
(percent responding "to repair present housing")

Positional Characteristics of the Decision-Makers	
Position in the Policy Process	
Legislators (N = 71)	51
Agency administrators (N = 70)	53
Service delivery personnel (N = 70)	74
Corporate directors of personnel (N = 35)	57
Union local presidents (N = 35)	51
Advocates for the aged (N = 35)	60
Responsibility for Aging Programs	
Primary function (N = 85)	65
Important but not central function (N = 88)	55
Minor function (N = 143)	57
Area of Program Expertise	
Housing planners (N = 29)	55
Specialists in other program areas (N = 287)	59
Personal Characteristics of the Decision-Makers	
Age of the Respondent	
Under 45 (N = 98)	64
45-54 (N = 98)	50
55-64 (N = 90)	60
65 and over (N = 30)	60
Sex of the Respondent	
Male (N = 230)	53
Female (N = 86)	72
Ethnicity of the Respondent	
White (N = 235)	59
Minority (N = 81)	57
Educational Level of the Respondent	
High school graduate or less (N = 42)	55
Some college (N = 64)	59
College graduate (N = 99)	63
Postcollege professional education (N = 111)	54
Total (N = 316)	58

Source: Compiled by the author.

Age-Segregated versus Age-Integrated Housing Communities

For those elderly who choose to relocate or who are forced by circumstances to relocate in new housing, is their dominant preference to live in age-integrated communities or in age-graded communities comprised solely of late middle-aged and older adults? As noted earlier, nearly all new housing construction for the elderly subsidized by public monies has provided only age-graded housing environments for the elderly, leaving those who prefer age-integrated surroundings to find housing adequately suited to their needs in the normal supply of housing available in their community. When asked whether they would prefer to live near people their own age or people of all ages, the overwhelming majority (82 percent) of the elderly interviewed in Los Angeles County preferred age-integrated neighborhoods. Only one in ten opted for age-segregated housing; an additional 8 percent asserted that they had no preference in the matter. Similarly, when asked whether it would be better for most older people to live in residential units with other people their own age, more than three quarters (77 percent) of these elderly respondents disagreed, while less than one in seven concurred.

The majority of decision-makers (57 percent) interviewed here acknowledged that most older people would prefer to live in age-integrated neighborhoods (see Table 5.6). Once again, service delivery personnel and female decision-makers were the most cognizant of the elderly's expressed housing preferences. In contrast, among the corporate directors of personnel and the union local presidents in the private sector, the respondents were almost evenly split in their perceptions of the elderly's preferences for age-integrated versus age-segregated living environments. Thus, nearly half of these two subsamples believed that most elderly would prefer to live in age-segregated housing complexes. Of greater significance to the future of public housing programs for the elderly, however, is the identical perception held by many of the housing planners located in various government housing agencies. Nearly four out of ten (39 percent) of the housing planners interviewed in this sample of decision-makers maintained that the elderly would prefer to live in age-graded housing environments; only a slightly larger percentage of the housing planners (45 percent) correctly interpreted the elderly's preference to live in age-integrated neighborhoods.

The majority of the decision-makers in this cross section of the decision-making community correctly acknowledged that most elderly residents prefer to live in age-integrated housing environments. The major thrust in current public housing programs to

TABLE 5.6

"Do You Think Most Older People Would Prefer to Live Near People Their Own Age or among People of All Ages?" (percent responding "among people of all ages")

Positional Characteristics of the Decision-Makers	
Position in the Policy Process	
Legislators (N = 71)	50
Agency administrators (N = 70)	57
Service delivery personnel (N = 70)	73
Corporate directors of personnel (N = 35)	46
Union local presidents (N = 35)	51
Advocates for the aged (N = 35)	57
Responsibility for Aging Programs	
Primary function (N = 85)	62
Important but not central function (N = 88)	57
Minor function (N = 143)	55
Area of Program Expertise	
Housing planners (N = 29)	45
Specialists in other program areas (N = 287)	59
Personal Characteristics of the Decision-Makers	
Age of the Respondent	
Under 45 (N = 98)	62
45-54 (N = 98)	59
55-64 (N = 90)	53
65 and over (N = 30)	46
Sex of the Respondent	
Male (N = 230)	52
Female (N = 86)	71
Ethnicity of the Respondent	
White (N = 235)	56
Minority (N = 81)	62
Educational Level of the Respondent	
High school graduate or less (N = 42)	50
Some college (N = 64)	59
College graduate (N = 99)	59
Postcollege professional education (N = 111)	57
Total (N = 316)	57

Source: Compiled by the author.

construct age-segregated congregate housing arrangements for the elderly runs counter to the expressed housing preferences of the vast majority of elderly residents living in the community. But in light of the persistent belief of many housing planners in government housing agencies who assert that most elderly would prefer to live in age-segregated housing, the emphasis on age-graded living environments is likely to persist in public housing programs for the elderly.

Racially Integrated versus Racially Segregated Neighborhoods

The racial and socioeconomic composition of neighborhoods has long been a public policy concern. In new public housing projects, the opportunity--indeed, the responsibility--exists to achieve socially integrated housing environments. Achieving social integration, however, has generally been viewed as an unpopular public policy goal.[30] Because much of the new housing constructed for the elderly is multiple-unit or congregate-type housing projects, the social and racial mixes of the new projects are relevant policy questions.

When asked if they would prefer to live near people of similar or different social and racial backgrounds, nearly half (48 percent) of the Los Angeles County elderly residents interviewed in the USC study elected to live among neighbors of similar background. More than one third (36 percent) of the elderly respondents, however, asserted that they would prefer to live among neighbors of mixed social and ethnic backgrounds, and another one in six (16 percent) replied that they had no preference. The majority of the elderly residents thus expressed no preference for segregated living arrangements.

But the vast majority of decision-makers (82 percent) believed that the elderly typically prefer to live among those having similar social backgrounds. Only one in eight of the decision-makers suggested that most elderly would choose to live in socially integrated neighborhoods (see Table 5.7).

Most housing for the elderly constructed to date under Section 231, 202, and 236 programs has tended to segregate residents according to income and race. For example, only 3 percent of 202 housing tenants are black, and the majority of these black tenants live in 202 projects sponsored by black organizations. Moreover, the 202 projects housed lower-middle-income elderly almost exclusively until the rent supplement program provided access for some welfare tenants into these projects. Administrators of the 202 housing projects differed in their evaluation of the desirability of this

TABLE 5.7

"Do You Think Most Older People Would Prefer to Live Near People Who Are Similar to Them in Social and Racial Background or Near People from Various Social and Racial Backgrounds?"
(percent responding "near people from various social and racial backgrounds")

Positional Characteristics of the Decision-Makers	
Position in the Policy Process	
Legislators (N = 71)	10
Agency administrators (N = 70)	17
Service delivery personnel (N = 70)	14
Corporate directors of personnel (N = 35)	9
Union local presidents (N = 35)	14
Advocates for the aged (N = 35)	14
Responsibility for Aging Programs	
Primary function (N = 85)	18
Important but not central function (N = 88)	14
Minor function (N = 143)	10
Area of Program Expertise	
Housing planners (N = 29)	0
Specialists in other program areas (N = 287)	15
Personal Characteristics of the Decision-Makers	
Age of the Respondent	
Under 45 (N = 98)	7
45-54 (N = 98)	17
55-64 (N = 90)	14
65 and over (N = 30)	17
Sex of the Respondent	
Male (N = 230)	13
Female (N = 86)	14
Ethnicity of the Respondent	
White (N = 235)	13
Minority (N = 81)	14
Educational Level of the Respondent	
High school graduate or less (N = 42)	26
Some college (N = 64)	14
College graduate (N = 99)	12
Postcollege professional education (N = 111)	9
Total (N = 316)	13

Source: Compiled by the author.

income mix between welfare-poor and stable income elderly in planned housing environments. While the majority approved of the resulting income mix, a substantial minority did not, observing that tenants do not look favorably on living with people "who have not put money away for the future."[31]

Planned housing for the elderly has not and probably will not conduct large-scale experiments in social integration. But then public housing policy has generally proved to be an unsuccessful vehicle for structuring more integrated social environments in communities across the country.[32] Because many of the housing officials interviewed in this study believe that most elderly prefer age-segregated and socially homogeneous housing environments, there is little reason to expect housing policy will produce anything else. The future of housing policy, at least in this regard, appears mirrored in the past.

Living with Adult Children in a Multigeneration Household

There are many who maintain that the changes in family structure are responsible for many of the problems that old people face today. They point to some mythical time in the past when the elderly were safely ensconced in multigeneration households, cared for and protected by younger family members. Historical analyses, however, document that multigeneration households, though somewhat less common today than at the turn of the century, have always been an atypical housing arrangement in the United States. Until 1950, approximately 16 percent of the elderly lived with an adult child; today, only 9 percent do.[33] The majority of elderly today as in the past live with their spouse in independent households in the community.

The elderly residents interviewed in the USC study overwhelmingly rejected the multigeneration household as a desirable living arrangement. Nearly seven out of eight (86 percent) of the elderly respondents agreed that "It usually does not work out too well for older people to live with their children and grandchildren." Only 6 percent believed that multigeneration households provided suitable living arrangements for all members of the family. There was one notable exception, however, to the general agreement about the undesirability of multigeneration living. More than half (51 percent) of the Mexican American elderly believed that multigeneration households were completely satisfactory living arrangements. In contrast, three quarters of the black elderly and nine in ten of the white elderly opposed the idea of multigeneration living.

Because of their feelings about the negative effect of multigeneration living on family relationships, the vast majority of the elderly interviewed in the USC study did not foresee the prospect of moving into their children's households even if the time came when they could no longer live alone. Seven percent of the elderly respondents already lived with one of their adult children. Another one in seven believed that they probably would move in with one of their children if the time ever arrived when they could no longer manage independently on their own. But the overwhelming majority (78 percent) did not foresee moving into their children's household under any circumstances. Consistent with their endorsement of multigeneration living arrangements, Mexican American elderly were more likely than either black or white elderly to be living with one of their adult children already or to predict moving in with one of their adult children at some future time.*

The decision-makers interviewed in this study by and large agreed with the semtiments expressed by the elderly residents in the community. More than seven out of ten of these decision-makers agreed that "It usually doesn't work out too well for older people to live with their children and grandchildren" (see Table 5.8). But more than one in four of the 316 decision-makers (28 percent) believed that multigeneration living arrangements were frequently successful.

Legislators were the most likely to endorse multigeneration living arrangements. Four out of ten believed that multigeneration households offered good housing arrangements for the elderly, and

---

*Among the Mexican American elderly, nearly one in three (32 percent) reported that they expect to live with one of their children if the time ever comes when they can no longer live alone; another one in four of the Mexican American elderly (24 percent), however, were already living with one of their children at the time of the interview. Among the black elderly interviewed, 39 percent said that they expected to live with one of their children if the time ever came when they could not manage on their own; in contrast to the Mexican American elderly, only 6 percent of the black elderly were already living with one of their children at the time of the interview. Among the white elderly interviewed, only 12 percent anticipated living with one of their children if they could not manage on their own sometime in the future, and only 5 percent were living with one of their children at the time of the interview. Thus, multigeneration living arrangements were most common for the Mexican American elderly and least common for the white elderly.

TABLE 5.8

"It Usually Doesn't Work Out Too Well for Older People to Live with Their Children and Grandchildren" (percent responding in agreement)

Positional Characteristics of the Decision-Makers	
Position in the Policy Process	
Legislators (N = 71)	56
Agency administrators (N = 70)	70
Service delivery personnel (N = 70)	74
Corporate directors of personnel (N = 35)	77
Union local presidents (N = 35)	77
Advocates for the aged (N = 35)	80
Responsibility for Aging Programs	
Primary function (N = 85)	72
Important but not central function (N = 88)	66
Minor function (N = 143)	73
Area of Program Expertise	
Housing planners (N = 29)	76
Specialists in other program areas (N = 287)	70
Personal Characteristics of the Decision-Makers	
Age of the Respondent	
Under 45 (N = 98)	61
45-54 (N = 98)	69
55-64 (N = 90)	77
65 and over (N = 30)	87
Sex of the Respondent	
Male (N = 230)	71
Female (N = 86)	70
Ethnicity of the Respondent	
White (N = 235)	74
Minority (N = 81)	59
Educational Level of the Respondent	
High school graduate or less (N = 42)	86
Some college (N = 64)	66
College graduate (N = 99)	74
Postcollege professional education (N = 111)	65
Total (N = 316)	71

Source: Compiled by the author.

they rejected the idea that including a grandparent in the household impacted negatively on other family members. One way to encourage multigeneration living would be to offer attractive tax exemptions for adult children who provide live-in housing arrangements and attendant care for their elderly parents. The substantial legislative sentiment in favor of multigeneration living arrangements should translate into considerable legislative support for such tax proposals. Prospects for the tax-exemption dim, however, when it becomes apparent that advocates for the aged, reflecting the sentiment of their elderly constituency, are among those in the decision-making community who are the most opposed to the concept of multigeneration living arrangements. Four out of five of the advocates interviewed in this study agreed that "It usually doesn't work out too well for older people to live with their children and grandchildren," and nearly half of these advocates strongly affirmed their beliefs on this matter. They are unlikely to push tax exemptions for multigeneration households to the top of their list of legislative priorities.

Among the community residents aged 45 to 74 who were interviewed in the USC companion study, all age groups were similarly agreed on the desirability of living close to but apart from their adult children after retirement.* In the decision-making community, however, middle-aged decision-makers were considerably less opposed to multigeneration living arrangements than were older decision-makers. Unlike differences manifest along the age dimension, however, comparison between the decision-makers and the elderly residents in the community along ethnic lines revealed a more congruent attitude structure. Minority decision-makers, like minority residents in the community, were considerably less likely than their white counterparts to condemn multigeneration living arrangements as unsatisfactory.†

---

*Ninety-four percent of the 65- to 74-year-olds, 97 percent of the 55- to 64-year-olds, and 98 percent of the 45- to 54-year olds said that they would prefer to live apart from their children after retirement. At the same time, 63 percent of the 65- to 74-year-olds, 55 percent of those 55 to 64, and 57 percent of those 45 to 54 would prefer to live in the same general neighborhood as at least one of their children after retirement. Thus, living close to but separate from adult children is the preference of all adults, not just the elderly.

†Only 23 percent of the white decision-makers believed that multigeneration living arrangements typically worked out satisfactorily as compared to 36 percent of the Mexican American and 40 percent of the black decision-makers.

For the most part, however, sentiment in both the general public and the decision-making community ran counter to the concept of multigeneration living arrangements. The question then arises of how to care for frail elderly when they are no longer able to manage independently in their own homes in the community. If these frail elderly are not going to be housed and cared for in the households of their adult children, where will they be housed and cared for?

The Alternative of Living in a Nursing Home

Living in a nursing home is typically viewed as the housing alternative of last resort. One reason for this prevailing attitude toward nursing homes can undoubtedly be traced to the adverse publicity that nursing homes often receive in the media when attention is being drawn to the poor care patients receive in some of the homes. Nursing home scandals have surfaced in the news regularly over the years, and the public has developed an image of life in the nursing home that is none too pleasant to contemplate.

More than half of the 45- to 54- and the 55- to 64-year olds living in Los Angeles County who were interviewed in the companion USC survey asserted that it was somewhat or very likely that they would someday live in a nursing home. Less than one third of the elderly residents, however, speculated that they might live in a nursing home at some future time; more than two thirds of the elderly respondents (68 percent) insisted that it was not at all likely that they would ever live in a nursing home.

The horns of the dilemma emerge clearly. If the elderly do not want to live with their adult children, if the elderly furthermore do not expect ever to live with their adult children, even if they arrive at the point of being unable to care for themselves, and if, at the same time, the elderly do not accept the idea of going to a nursing home, then where are the elderly going to live if and when their health begins to fail them in advanced old age? The majority of elderly is hopeful of being able to live out their lives in the comfort of their own homes.

The need to develop a comprehensive housing-services continuum as an integral part of a national policy on housing for the aged thus emerges once again as crucial for ensuring a good quality of life for the elderly during the last years of their lives. Given a choice, most elderly would choose to remain in their own homes, but as their health fails, they can maintain themselves in their own homes only with the assistance of multiple social service supports. Unless public housing policies for the aged seek to develop and underwrite a comprehensive continuum of social service support programs to assist the elderly in their homes, the frail and ill elderly will continue to face involuntary eviction from their homes and their communities. The social and psychological trauma commonly experienced by these elderly in relocating to a nursing home or other institutional setting is well documented in the gerontological literature.[34]

The decision-makers in this study did not seem unaware of the problems associated with living in a nursing home. As much as they were agreed that it usually does not work out too well when older people live with their children and grandchildren, these 316 decision-makers concurred by a margin of more than two to one that it is better for the aged person to live with his family than to live in a home for the aged (see Table 5.9). Among the original six subsamples, only the union local presidents were split more or less evenly in their preference for multigeneration living versus life in a home for the aged, when independent living proved to be no longer possible for the older person (46 percent opted for living in a nursing home compared to 51 percent who chose living with adult children).

The more closely involved the decision-maker was with aging programs of various kinds, the more likely he was to favor the frail and ill elderly taking up residence with an adult child as opposed to moving into a nursing home. Housing planners in government agencies were less committed to the proposition that it is always better for the elderly person to live with his family than in a home for the aged; in fact, more than two in five of the housing planners disagreed with that observation.

With strong sentiment in both the general public and the decision-making community against placing the elderly in nursing homes and against the elderly moving into the households of adult children, it is surprising that public housing assistance programs have not developed a major component of home-delivered support services to help maintain frail and ill elderly in their own homes in the community. But, as these data have shown, few decision-makers, even today, think seriously about the need to expand social services to the elderly in their homes. Home-delivered services continue to be challenged as a legitimate health care and/or housing cost.[35]

DECISION-MAKERS' PROJECTIONS ON HOUSING FOR THE AGED IN THE YEAR 2000

Planning for the housing needs of future generations of elderly must be undertaken today, because dwellings built to house the elderly today will last well into the next century. A corollary proposition is that mistakes made today in planning housing for the future generations of elderly will have impact on cohorts for the next half-century.

TABLE 5.9

"It Is Better for an Older Person to Live with His Family Than in a Home for the Aged"
(percent responding in agreement)

Positional Characteristics of the Decision-Makers	
Position in the Policy Process	
Legislators (N = 71)	72
Agency administrators (N = 70)	71
Service delivery personnel (N = 70)	69
Corporate directors of personnel (N = 35)	69
Union local presidents (N = 35)	51
Advocates for the aged (N = 35)	71
Responsibility for Aging Programs	
Primary function (N = 85)	73
Important but not central function (N = 88)	69
Minor function (N = 143)	65
Area of Program Expertise	
Housing planners (N = 29)	55
Specialists in other program areas (N = 287)	70
Personal Characteristics of the Decision-Makers	
Age of the Respondent	
Under 45 (N = 98)	71
45-54 (N = 98)	67
55-64 (N = 90)	63
65 and over (N = 30)	76
Sex of the Respondent	
Male (N = 230)	67
Female (N = 86)	72
Ethnicity of the Respondent	
White (N = 235)	66
Minority (N = 81)	74
Educational Level of the Respondent	
High school graduate or less (N = 42)	67
Some college (N = 64)	66
College graduate (N = 99)	66
Postcollege professional education (N = 111)	73
Total (N = 316)	68

Source: Compiled by the author.

Social science research has shown not only that housing arrangements are crucial to the maintenance of an independent lifestyle and a sense of well-being for the older person but that housing and neighborhoods can even be planned so as to stimulate good person-environment interaction. The scientific base is thus emerging upon which to develop an informed national policy on housing that can provide not only for this but for future generations of the elderly as well.

A good start in planning for the housing of future generations of elderly requires accurate predictions about the likely housing needs and preferences of these groups as they move into old age. To know where and in what kinds of dwellings these future aged will prefer to reside is a step in the direction of allocating resources to meet the anticipated needs. Such was the observation made recently by one researcher at a symposium organized to consider the needs of the elderly population in the year 2000: "A failure to consider how the residential distribution of the elderly will change in the future may result in a less efficient allocation of available resources to this group. The success of any program will depend largely on whether it is correctly designed for the elderly consumer group it is intended to serve."[36]

Some of the decision-makers interviewed in this study foresaw serious housing problems in several decades if medical breakthroughs succeeded in significantly extending life expectancy (see Table 2.12). The majority of the decision-making community, however, while still anticipating a greatly enlarged elderly population in future decades, did not consider large-scale housing crises a likely problem. Planning housing for future generations of elderly thus may not have the proper attention of decision-makers at the present time. Unfortunately, the political character of the democratic decision-making processes in this country mitigates against planning for long-term needs even when those long-term needs have been properly identified.[37] This fact of political life may be operating here.

The 316 decision-makers interviewed in this study were asked to speculate about future trends in housing for the elderly. The decision-makers largely concurred that the percentage of elderly living in nursing homes and in retirement communities would increase by the year 2000 (see Table 5.10). But, even with dramatic increases in the number of elderly residing in these age-graded environments, only a small minority of the total elderly population would be lodged in these congregate settings two to three decades hence. Decision-makers displayed considerably less agreement about housing trends in the living arrangements of the vast majority of elderly who live in age-integrated community settings, that is, who live independently in their own households with their spouse (currently 56 percent), who live alone or with nonrelatives (currently 29 percent), or who live with relatives (currently 11 percent). A majority of the decision-makers (60 percent) did agree, however, that the small percentage of elderly individuals now living with other family members (usually adult children or siblings) would decrease in future decades, and a near majority (46 percent) maintained that the proportion of elderly living with spouse in independent households in the community would similarly decrease.

For the most part, there was relatively little variation in the pattern of predictions offered by various subgroups in the decision-making community; but among the differences that did emerge, some are worth noting more closely.

Projections of substantial increases in the institutionalized elderly population were generally related to perceptions that a large institutionalized elderly population already existed. Those who believed 25 percent or more of the elderly population were institutionalized in the mid-1970s were nearly half again as likely to project future increases in this institutionalized elderly population as decision-makers who presently estimated the institutionalized elderly population at under 10 percent (77 versus 56 percent). In other words, most of those decision-makers who visualized old age in terms of decrement and functional dependency believed that medical breakthroughs would, in the last analysis, succeed only in extending the years lived in decrepit old age. Such underlying perceptions may help to explain why categoric decision-makers, those closely involved with programs for the elderly, were less likely to project an increase in the nursing home population in future decades, while at the same time, housing planners in government agencies were relatively more likely to predict increases in the institutionalized elderly population. (The reader should recall data presented earlier in this chapter that highlight the relatively accurate impressions about the size of the institutionalized elderly population held by the categoric decision-makers and the starkly inaccurate impressions entertained by the housing planners.)

As could well be expected, predictions regarding the proportion of elderly who would be living in their own independent households by the year 2000 were also correlated with perceptions of dependency in the present elderly population. Decision-makers who estimated the present institutionalized elderly population at under 10 percent of the total age group were nearly twice as likely as decision-makers estimating the institutionalized elderly at 25 percent or more to project an increase in the proportion of independent elderly households in the community and only half as likely to project a decrease in such independent living arrangements.* Probably for this reason, advocates

---

*Among those who estimated that under 10 percent of the elderly were presently institutionalized, 46 percent predicted an increase

TABLE 5.10

Decision-Makers' Perceptions of the Trends in Housing for the Aged: Projections to the Year 2000

Decision-Makers' Positional and Personal Characteristics	Nursing Homes (currently 4 percent)			Retirement Communities (currently 1 percent)		
	Increase	Remain the Same	Decrease	Increase	Remain the Same	Decrease
Positional Characteristics of the Decision-Makers						
Position in the Policy Process						
Legislators (N = 71)	74	20	6	77	21	0
Agency administrators (N = 70)	73	20	9	85	13	0
Service delivery personnel (N = 70)	73	14	13	83	13	4
Corporate directors of personnel (N = 35)	83	11	6	94	0	5
Union local presidents (N = 35)	82	11	6	89	6	6
Advocates for the aged (N = 35)	66	17	14	89	6	2
Responsibility for Aging Programs						
Primary function (N = 85)	64	16	19	84	12	4
Important but not central function (N = 88)	81	14	6	84	12	2
Minor function (N = 143)	77	17	5	86	11	2
Area of Program Expertise						
Housing planners (N = 29)	79	21	0	86	14	0
Specialists in other program areas (N = 287)	74	16	10	85	12	3
Personal Characteristics of the Decision-Makers						
Age of the Respondent						
Under 45 (N = 98)	69	19	11	88	8	4
45-54 (N = 98)	77	18	4	85	13	0
55-64 (N = 90)	79	12	7	86	11	3
65 and over (N = 30)	70	7	23	73	20	3
Sex of the Respondent						
Male (N = 230)	78	14	7	85	12	2
Female (N = 86)	65	21	13	84	12	3
Ethnicity of the Respondent						
White (N = 235)	76	17	6	86	11	2
Minority (N = 81)	69	15	16	83	14	4
Educational Level of the Respondent						
High school graduate or less (N = 42)	79	10	12	86	12	2
Some college (N = 64)	72	19	9	83	12	5
College graduate (N = 99)	77	10	12	86	10	2
Postcollege professional education (N = 111)	73	23	5	90	12	2
Total (N = 316)	75	16	9	85	12	3

Source: Compiled by the author.

Percentage of Elderly in Each Type of Housing Arrangement in the Year 2000 Relative to 1970								
Alone or with Nonrelatives (currently 29 percent)			With Relatives (currently 11 percent)			Independently in Own Households (currently 56 percent)		
Increase	Remain the Same	Decrease	Increase	Remain the Same	Decrease	Increase	Remain the Same	Decrease
37	28	34	15	31	52	28	15	55
41	29	29	13	20	67	33	23	44
43	26	31	11	27	61	33	29	38
40	17	43	17	23	60	23	23	54
9	43	46	17	29	51	20	20	59
40	23	37	14	14	69	43	29	29
41	24	34	14	18	68	33	33	33
40	24	35	16	19	65	26	19	54
32	32	35	13	32	52	31	19	49
41	28	31	14	17	69	17	34	48
36	28	35	14	25	59	31	21	45
37	22	40	18	28	54	35	16	49
37	29	34	13	26	59	27	19	53
37	33	29	12	21	67	27	30	42
36	23	40	10	23	63	37	33	30
35	26	38	16	26	57	27	21	51
42	31	26	9	21	69	39	28	32
35	30	34	19	21	60	26	24	49
42	20	38	12	26	60	42	20	38
21	40	36	19	26	50	30	29	38
34	23	42	16	27	58	25	22	52
34	23	37	16	23	60	32	19	48
41	28	27	10	24	65	31	25	44
37	28	35	14	25	60	30	23	46

for the aged were the most likely to predict an increase in independent living arrangements for the elderly by the turn of the century, while housing planners were the most likely to predict a decrease in the number of elderly households in the community.

Advocates for the aged were among those in the decision-making community who most strongly opposed multigeneration living arrangements for the elderly. They were also the most likely to predict a decrease in the proportion of elderly who would be living with their adult children or other family members in future decades. As a general rule, the more closely a decision-maker worked with aging problems and elderly people, the more likely he was to believe that multigeneration living would continue to decrease over future decades. Similarly, the more education the decision-maker had, the more likely he was to predict a continued decrease in merged family households.

Predictions that the percentage of elderly living alone or with unrelated roommates would increase by the turn of the century were correlated with the perception that most elderly people retain good health in the later years coupled with the belief that neither nursing homes nor multigeneration living provide adequate housing arrangements for the elderly. In the entire decision-making community, only the corporate directors of personnel did not believe the proportion of elderly living alone or with nonrelated roommates would increase by the turn of the century.

An overview of the decision-makers' projections on housing for the elderly in the year 2000 suggests that they anticipate a decreasing proportion of elderly households living in the general community matched by an increase in age-segregated and age-congregate living arrangements. To this extent, the decision-makers' projections on the future counter the expressed housing preferences of elderly and pre-retired residents living in the community.

---

and 28 percent predicted a decrease in the proportion of elderly people who would be living in independent households in the year 2000. But among those who estimated that 25 percent of the elderly or more were presently institutionalized, only 29 percent predicted an increase in the proportion of elderly who would be maintaining independent households in the year 2000, while nearly half (49 percent) predicted a decrease in such independent living arrangements by the turn of the century.

THE FUTURE: PROSPECTS FOR A COHERENT NATIONAL POLICY ON HOUSING THE AGED

Housing the elderly is no single undertaking; the elderly's housing needs and preferences are as diverse as their personal and social circumstances. Moreover, the elderly's housing needs typically change as they move into advanced old age. The recent growth in both the newly retired population and the very old population suggests the need to develop more diverse housing options for the older population. Both the private housing industry and public housing programs, however, have been slow to respond to the need for more retirement housing.

Rational planning for the elderly's housing needs in the immediate and future decades suggests the need to develop a continuum of housing-services options, from which the elderly can choose according to their own needs and preferences. The decision-makers in this study, however, persist in thinking about rehousing the elderly in age-segregated and age-congregated housing environments; that is, they continue to think first and foremost about solving the elderly's housing problems by constructing more subsidized housing, particularly low-cost congregate housing projects designated strictly for elderly occupancy. A minority of the decision-makers stressed the need to design new housing for the elderly that would be barrier free to accommodate changes in the elderly's health status without jeopardizing their opportunities for independent living. But the decision-makers stopped far short of endorsing the idea of a housing-services continuum; only a small minority pressed for an expansion of home-support services to assist the frail and ill elderly to maintain in their homes. As a group, the decision-makers were preoccupied with the excessive costs of housing and problems related thereto, relegating to secondary consideration the housing problems caused by changes in the elderly's health status that frequently accompany advancing old age.

Although the decision-makers acknowledge that nursing homes and multigeneration living do not offer satisfactory housing arrangements for older persons who are in frail health, the decision-makers are not yet seriously committed to finding ways to maintain these elderly in their homes in the community. Although the decision-makers acknowledge the desire of elderly people to continue residing in their own homes in the community, they often challenge the expense that would be entailed to underwrite the extensive home repair and home maintenance programs that would be required. Decision-makers still seem to prefer the administrative ease and ostensibly cost-efficient manner of meeting the elderly's needs for special support services in congregate housing environments, and hence public housing programs continue to subsidize the construction of new housing projects in contrast to helping the elderly stay in their present housing when that is the elderly's preference.

Housing construction is big business and its output visible for all to see. The elected officials like to see housing built, because they can point to the new elderly-designated units in the projects and gain votes among their elderly constituencies. The housing agencies, local, state, and federal, like housing construction programs because they have the opportunity to manage more monies and staff within the government maze. The builders and sponsors and unions like housing construction programs because it means money and jobs. Consequently, the initial response to identified needs of ill-housed elderly is to build more low-cost housing. It surely is not the only answer. It may not even be the right answer. But it is the program response that the decision-making community is structured to give.

Responses of the elderly themselves do not, however, support this narrow statement of desirable housing policy. They voice preferences for alternate programs. To gain due consideration for other housing program initiatives in the prevailing climate of decision-making will take persuasive lobbying on the part of aging professionals and articulate advocates on the elderly's behalf. Home health services, home repair and home maintenance services, door-to-door community transportation services, and the like will never be institutionalized and operative on a large scale until they can be proven feasible, cost-effective, administratively efficient, and socially desirable. The task of advocates is to demonstrate the foregoing conclusively. Only in this way can the prevailing climate of decision-making concerning housing for the elderly be changed.

NOTES

1. Empirical studies show that elderly people typically become more home oriented in their daily activity routines beginning in their late 60s or early 70s. For a review of the literature, consult Matilda White Riley and Anne B. Foner, eds., Aging and Society, Vol. I, An Inventory of Research Findings (New York: Russell Sage Foundation, 1968). For a more recent confirmation of these findings, see Chad Gordon and Charles M. Gaitz, "Leisure and Lives: Personal Expressivity across the Life Span," in Handbook of Aging and the Social Sciences, ed. Robert H. Binstock and Ethel Shanas (New York: Van Nostrand-Reinhold, 1976), pp. 310-41.

2. A cursory but representative survey of the social science literature can be found in Frances M. Carp, "Housing and Living

Environments of Older People," in Handbook of Aging and the Social Sciences, ed. Robert H. Binstock and Ethel Shanas (New York: Van Nostrand-Reinhold, 1976), pp. 244-71. For readers interested in pursuing the subject in more depth, a selected sampling of the literature is noted here: Wilma T. Donahue, ed., Proceedings of the International Symposium for Housing and Environmental Design for Older Adults (Washington, D.C.: International Center for Social Gerontology, in press); Isaac Green et al., Housing for the Elderly: The Development and Design Process (New York: Van Nostrand-Reinhold, 1975); M. Powell Lawton, Planning and Managing Housing for the Elderly (New York: Wiley, 1975); Louis E. Gelwicks and Robert J. Newcomer, Planning Housing Environments for the Elderly (Washington, D.C.: National Council on the Aging, 1974); Ira S. Robbins, Housing the Elderly: Background and Issues, 1971 White House Conference on Aging (Washington, D.C.: U.S. Government Printing Office, 1971); Frances M. Carp, ed., Patterns of Living and Housing of Middle Aged and Older Adults (Washington, D.C.: U.S. Government Printing Office, 1966).

3. Most elderly, for example, rarely shop outside a six-block radius from their homes. M. Powell Lawton and Thomas O. Byerts, eds., Community Planning for the Elderly (Washington, D.C.: U.S. Department of Housing and Urban Development, 1973). See also Victor Regnier, "Neighborhood Planning for the Urban Elderly," in Aging: Scientific Perspectives and Social Issues, ed. Diana S. Woodruff and James E. Birren (New York: Van Nostrand, 1975).

4. Proceedings of the 1971 White House Conference on Aging: Toward a National Policy on Aging, Vol. II, November 28-December 2, 1971 (Washington, D.C.: U.S. Government Printing Office, 1973), p. 30.

5. Raymond J. Struyk, "The Housing Situation of Elderly Americans," Gerontologist 17, no. 2 (April 1977): 130-39.

6. Carp, "Housing and Living Environment of Older People," p. 249.

7. More than one third (34 percent) of the average retired couple's budget is spent on housing. The Federal Housing Administration recommends that housing expenditures should be no more than 25 percent of the family's monthly income to remain a comfortably affordable expense. Robbins, Housing the Elderly, pp. 15-22.

8. Herman B. Brotman, "Life Expectancy: Comparison of National Levels in 1900 and 1974 and Variations in State Levels, 1969-1971," Gerontologist 17, no. 1 (February 1977): 12-22.

9. C. Everett Ashley III and M. Carter McFarland, "The Need for Research toward Meeting the Housing Needs of the Elderly," in Social and Psychological Aspects of Aging, ed. Clark Tibbitts and

Wilma Donahue (New York: Columbia University Press, 1962), pp. 303-26.

10. Robert Morris, "The Development of Parallel Services for the Elderly and Disabled," Gerontologist 14, no. 1 (February 1974): 15-19; Donahue, Proceedings of the International Symposium.

11. Carp, "Housing and Living Environments of Older People."

12. The 1956 amendments to the National Housing Act liberalized the provisions of the long-established FHA mortgage insurance program (Section 203) so that persons 62 years or older could borrow money for the down payment and closing costs from an FHA-approved source as long as the elderly could meet the monthly mortgage payments and maintain their property. Robbins, Housing the Elderly, p. 44.

13. For an overview of these housing programs, see ibid.

14. Ibid.; Lawton, Planning and Managing Housing for the Elderly.

15. Lawton, Planning and Managing Housing for the Elderly.

16. Ibid.

17. Donahue, Proceedings of the International Symposium; M. Powell Lawton, "Supportive Services in the Context of Housing Environment," Gerontologist 9, no. 1 (February 1969): 15-19.

18. Green et al., Housing for the Elderly.

19. Lawton, Planning and Managing Housing for the Elderly; Irving Rosow, "Retirement Housing and Social Integration," in Social and Psychological Aspects of Aging, ed. Clark Tibbitts and Wilma Donahue (New York: Columbia University Press, 1962), pp. 327-39.

20. Robbins, Housing the Elderly, p. 40.

21. Carp, "Housing and Living Environments of Older People," p. 244.

22. Robbins, Housing the Elderly, p. 48.

23. These percentages have shown considerable stability over several decades. Compare the data reported in Rosow, "Retirement Housing and Social Integration," with that reported in a recent nationwide survey conducted by Louis Harris and Associates, The Myth and Reality of Aging in America (Washington, D.C.: National Council on the Aging, 1975), pp. 31-32.

24. Carp, "Housing and Living Environments of Older People"; Robert J. Havighurst, "Research and Development Goals in Social Gerontology. A Report of a Special Committee of the Gerontological Society," Pt. II, Gerontologist 9, no. 4 (Winter 1969): 1-90; Frances M. Carp, A Future for the Aged (Austin: University of Texas Press, 1966).

25. Robbins, Housing the Elderly, p. 13.

26. Calvin Goldscheider, "Differential Residential Mobility of the Older Population," Journal of Gerontology 21, no. 1 (January 1966): 103-08.

27. Carl Eisdorfer, "Issues in Health Planning for the Aged," Pt. I, Gerontologist 16, no. 1 (February 1976): 13.

28. Morris, "The Development of Parallel Services."

29. Harris and Associates, The Myth and Reality of Aging in America, pp. 31-32, 36.

30. The best documented case study of public housing programs from conceptualization to ground-breaking ceremonies is still Martin Meyerson and Edward C. Banfield, Politics, Planning, and the Public Interest (New York: Free Press, 1955).

31. Lawton, Planning and Managing Housing for the Elderly, p. 36.

32. Meyerson and Banfield, Politics, Planning, and the Public Interest.

33. Stephen M. Golant, "Residential Concentrations of the Future Elderly," Pt. II, Gerontologist 15, no. 1 (February 1975): 16-23.

34. Although only 4 percent of the elderly population are resident in nursing homes and other institutional facilities at any one point in time, one study suggests that a much larger proportion of old people (close to one in four) will spend at least some time in the last year of their lives in a nursing home, and that 23 percent rather than 4 percent of the deaths of elderly people occur in these nursing home and extended care settings. Robert Kastenbaum and Sandra E. Candy, "The Four Percent Fallacy: A Methodological and Empirical Critique of Extended Care Facility Population Statistics," Aging and Human Development 4, no. 1 (1973): 15-21. Another study, however, confirms that nearly half of these nursing home deaths occur in the first month after admission to the home. Harold J. Wershow, "The Four Percent Fallacy: Some Further Evidence and Policy Implications," Pt. I, Gerontologist 16, no. 1 (February 1976): 52-55.

35. Ironically, in-home support services fall in the political no-man's land between the central functions of the health and housing agencies in government. In times of budget cutbacks, the agency administrators frequently try to stretch their budget dollar by eliminating the "frills" in their program. For the health agency director, this means eliminating home-care programs that he can easily redefine as a housing department responsibility. But in the housing department, the agency directors are making the identical decision--to eliminate the home-support services as more properly belonging to the domain of the health and welfare agencies. The result is the demise of one home-support program after another, to the detriment of the frail and ill elderly who require such supports to maintain themselves in their homes. Eisdorfer, "Issues in Health Planning for the Aged," p. 14.

36. Golant, "Residential Concentrations of the Future Elderly," p. 16.

37. It is always hard to justify planning for long-term needs in the population when immediate needs are pressing to be satisfied. It is difficult, for example, for a congressman to sell his constituency on his dedication to planning housing for the year 1990 when 20 percent or more of his constituency presently live in substandard housing. Some of the political dilemmas created by trying to engage in long-term planning are nicely spelled out in Robert H. Binstock and Martin A. Levin, "Political Dilemmas of Intervention Policies," in Handbook of Aging and the Social Sciences, ed. Robert H. Binstock and Ethel Shanas (New York: Van Nostrand-Reinhold, 1976), pp. 511-35.

6 Transportation Services for the Aged: Special Transportation Problems . . . Special Transportation Programs?

Transportation is an important mediator between the elderly person and his environment. Continued participation in community affairs and social activities depends on his having suitable transportation to community facilities and to the homes of friends and relatives. Continued independent living throughout the years of advancing old age depends on his being able to reach food, medical, and miscellaneous shopping facilities in neighborhoods close to his home. Emphasizing the need for good transportation services to underwrite the opportunities that all Americans should enjoy for social involvement, freedom of choice, and utmost independence in old age, the delegates to the 1971 White House Conference on Aging concluded, "To the extent the aged are denied transportation services, they are denied full participation in meaningful community life."[1]

The U.S. Senate Special Committee on Aging was similarly developing an awareness of how critical the elderly's transportation problems were. In congressional hearings held throughout the 1960s to monitor the progress of various public policies and social programs in redressing the elderly's most pressing problems and unmet needs, the legislators heard over and over again about the elderly's transportation problems in getting to services and facilities that were already available to them in the community: "It mattered little what the subject of the hearing was: transportation inadequacy was mentioned again and again as a complicating factor in other problems affecting the elderly."[2] In 1970, the U.S. Senate Special Committee on Aging declared that a "crisis in mobility" confronted many elderly Americans.[3]

Transportation problems plague elderly people living in diverse economic and social circumstances. For the elderly who are fortunate enough to own and operate a car, insurance and other maintenance costs for the vehicle consume an excessive share of their small retirement incomes. Moreover, self-imposed limitations on their driving behavior are common. As much as possible, they avoid driving at night or on freeways or downtown. But as many as half or more of the elderly do not drive a car regularly. According to the 1970 U.S. Census, nearly half (45 percent) of the elderly households in the country own no car and less than half (47 percent) of the elderly are licensed to drive. Without a car, these elderly necessarily must rely on other means of transportation--relatives or friends to drive them, walking, taxis, or public transportation.[4] But the desire to remain totally independent or to avoid becoming a burden on someone else inevitably leads many nondriving elderly to stay at home rather than ask a friend or relative to drive them.

At the same time, the very factors that forced the elderly to relinquish use of his automobile--typically, cost- and/or health-related reasons--similarly interfere with his ability to rely on walking or public transportation to satisfy his ordinary transit requirements. Elderly people rarely express satisfaction with walking or public transportation as a primary means of getting around in the community; most miss the comfort and convenience of door-to-door service that their automobiles once provided them.[5] It is not surprising, then, that empirical studies confirm that elderly people often forego trips in the community beoause of inadequate transportation.[6] The "crisis in mobility" identified by the U.S. Senate Special Committee on Aging is thus a widespread and multifaceted problem that impacts directly on the disparate lives of many millions of older people.

Congressional response to the perceived crisis in mobility was immediate. In 1970, Congress issued the following policy statement (Section 1612) as an amendment to the 1964 Urban Mass Transportation Assistance (UMTA) Act:

> It is hereby declared to be the national policy that elderly and handicapped persons have the same right as other persons to utilize mass transportation facilities and services; that special efforts shall be made in the planning and design of mass transportation facilities and services so that the availability to elderly and handicapped persons of mass transportation which they can effectively utilize will be assured; and that all Federal programs offering assistance in the field of mass transportation (including the programs under this act) should contain provisions implementing this policy.[7]

The amendment authorized $46.5 million to begin the task of modifying existing transit systems to take into account the special needs of the elderly and handicapped.[8]

Congress enacted several other major pieces of legislation in the early 1970s that were intended to make equal access to public transportation a growing reality for the country's aged, infirmed, and handicapped citizens. The Older Americans Comprehensive Services Amendments of 1973, Title IV, Part 3, Section 412, authorized experimentation with new methods of providing transportation to these transit-dependent groups, including use of demand-actuated services or direct payments to individuals to enable them to buy the transportation services they need.[9] Title III of the Federal-Aid Highways Act Amendments of 1973 (Public Law 93-87) required buses and other transit vehicles operating with any federal financial assistance to be designed for easy utilization by the elderly and handicapped. This act further authorized federal grants and loans to private, nonprofit organizations engaged in developing transportation subsystems specifically designed to serve the handicapped and the isolated elderly. Finally, the 1975 amendments of Title III in the Older Americans Act of 1965 specified transportation services as one of four priority areas for the Area Agencies on Aging, which are charged with the responsibility of overseeing the delivery of coordinated social services to elderly residents in their service area.

Although the congressional mandate for action to improve transportation services for the elderly has been indisputably clear and persistent, there has been widespread disillusionment over what has been accomplished in reality. About the time of the present study, the U.S. Senate Special Committee on Aging launched a program of extensive hearings on the subject of "Transportation and the Elderly: Problems and Progress" in order to assess problems in the implementation of their mandates. Many criticized Congress for financing mandated programs for the elderly with discretionary monies, the expenditures of which are subject to the approval of the head official of the Department of Transportation (DOT) or the Administration on Aging (AOA). The critics suggested that failure to implement the programs mandated by Congress should be traced to the low priority given program development in these areas by DOT and AOA at the federal level rather than to the priorities accorded these programs by local agencies. Others complained that the patchwork of research and demonstration projects sponsored by AOA and DOT is simply too fragmented to supply adequate transportation services tailored to the needs of the elderly and handicapped populations in the country.

Public policy directives and program development in response to the transportation problems identified in the elderly and handicapped populations have come largely from the federal government. But, while legislation and regulations may be written mostly in Washington, implementation is accomplished largely at the local level. Turning attention to Los Angeles County, the site of this study, is thus instructive. This study coincided in time with fervent political activity to muster public support in the county for the construction of a rapid mass transit system to serve the county residents. In the course of this research, three different referendums to finance construction of three different concepts of a countywide mass transit system were successively defeated by the voters. County officials today remain under considerable pressure to develop a rapid mass transit system that will efficiently serve the residents of Los Angeles County. It is therefore more than an academic question to ask how decision-makers in the county define the transportation needs of the elderly and how those needs can be met by a mass transit system if and when it is implemented.

Los Angeles County has a reputation for being very much an automobile-oriented society. The residents of Los Angeles are wedded to their automobiles because of the great distances they typically must cover (the Los Angeles Standard Metropolitan Statistical Area covers 4,069 square miles) and because public transportation is usually inadequate to their transit needs. (Bus service is currently the only mode of public transportation service, and it takes several hours and many bus transfers to cross town.) Despite its reputation nationwide, the Los Angeles transit experience is not unique. A pair of transportation analysts recently observed about Los Angeles together with other urban areas that

> The United States' major metropolitan areas, and even many of its minor ones, are in a state of crisis. While the extent of the problem may differ, the basic symptoms are the same everywhere. . . . It is our contention that the urban crises which manifest themselves in so many different ways have at least one common root. This is the increasing reliance on the automobile. In every urban area the automobile has become the only means of transportation by which every part of the region can be reached. In addition, metropolitan activity and land-use patterns have become so dispersed that neither the automobile nor any public transit system can furnish the mobility required by every individual to function with reasonable ease in the activities their respective social, economic and physical well-being demands.[10]

Thus Los Angeles County suffers the problems of developing an efficient mass transit system to serve the needs of its residents in more exaggerated dimensions, but its problems are shared with most or all U.S. urban communities, large or small, which must serve a diverse locale and population through a single large transit network. At the very least, all of these metropolitan areas must develop their mass transit systems under the same set of federal guidelines and regulations. Hence, to be able to study Los Angeles County decision-makers' attitudes and perceptions of the transportation problems of the county's elderly at the very time that they are actively engaged in long-range transportation planning for the county as a whole is a unique research opportunity.

Planning for the transportation of the elderly is already under way in the county. The Federal-Aid Highway Act of 1962 requires all areas with a population over 50,000 to have a regional transportation plan in order to qualify for federal transportation assistance; that plan is to be comprehensive (covering all modes of transportation), continuing (with a continuously updated data base against which the regional transportation plan can be periodically reevaluated), and cooperative (involving both state and local officials). In order to comply with federal Urban Mass Transportation Assistance (UMTA) Act amendments that require all public transportation operators using federal subsidies to modify their systems to accommodate elderly and handicapped passengers, the Southern California Rapid Transit District and Southern California Association of Governments are in the process of updating Los Angeles County's regional transportation plan to be specifically cognizant of the needs of elderly and handicapped citizens in the ongoing long- and short-range planning of transportation service for county residents. This is the context in which the responses of the decision-makers sampled in this study are examined as they discuss the transportation problems and prospects for Los Angeles County's elderly population.

The 316 respondents representing a broad cross section of the decision-making community were asked to assess the extent of transit dependence in the elderly population as well as to estimate the size of the elderly group who regularly experience severe transportation problems getting to places they want to go. The decision-makers were also asked to specify what they believed to be the major obstacles preventing older people from getting around as they might like to. Developing transit programs tailored to the particular needs of this age group in response to federal mandates ideally should begin with an accurate understanding of the nature and magnitude of the transportation problems afflicting this age group. The accuracy of the decision-makers' analyses of the problems will be checked against information obtained in interviews with elderly community residents in a companion survey.

The decision-makers were encouraged to recommend timely and practical solutions to the transportation problems that they had identified. The decision-makers' perspectives on serving the elderly's transit needs effectively and efficiently through a central mass transit system versus supplemental door-to-door services are closely examined. Similarly, the decision-makers' support for subsidizing the providers as opposed to subsidizing the elderly riders directly are considered. In conclusion, the interdependence of the decision-makers' perceptions of the problems and their policy preferences is discussed from the standpoint of developing transit programs that will effectively and efficiently serve the elderly population in the community.

DECISION-MAKERS' PERCEPTIONS OF THE PREVALENCE OF TRANSPORTATION PROBLEMS AMONG THE AGED

The elderly's transportation problems had considerably visibility to the decision-makers interviewed in this study. In the leadoff question of the interview, when the decision-makers were asked to identify what they consider to be the three greatest problems facing people 65 years of age or older residing in Los Angeles County, nearly one third of the decision-makers (32 percent) identified transportation as a major problem for the elderly residents (see Table 6.1). As such, it was the fourth most frequently cited problem of older people, ranking behind the problems of income, health, and psychosocial adjustment to aging. The percentage of decision-makers identifying transportation as a problem for the elderly in this study is probably much higher than it would have been in similar interview circumstances five or ten years earlier; the same probably could not be said for the identification of income, health, housing, or psychosocial adjustment problems, which probably would have been cited more or less as frequently 5, 10, or 20 years ago as they are today. But in the mid-1970s, the transportation problems of the elderly appear to have a fair amount of visibility to those in the decision-making community.

Within the decision-making community, some were more sensitized to the elderly's transportation problems than others. Most closely attuned to the elderly's mobility problems were the advocates for the aged and the recreation center directors; more than two out of three of these decision-makers mentioned transportation among the elderly's three major problems. Senior citizens affairs

TABLE 6.1

"What Would You Say Are the Three Major Problems Facing People Living in Los Angeles County Who Are 65 Years of Age or Older?" (percent mentioning "transportation" and problem's rank based on number of mentions)

	Percent	Rank
Positional Characteristics of the Decision-Makers		
Position in the Policy Process		
Legislators (N = 71)	38	3
Agency administrators (N = 70)	34	4
Service delivery personnel (N = 70)	30	4
Corporate directors of personnel (N = 35)	26	3
Union local presidents (N = 35)	31	4.5
Advocates for the aged (N = 35)	69	2
Responsibility for Aging Programs		
Primary function (N = 85)	49	3
Important but not central function (N = 88)	38	4
Minor function (N = 143)	29	4.5
Area of Program Expertise		
Health (N = 37)	24	5
Mental health (N = 23)	13	5
Housing (N = 29)	21	5
Employment (N = 92)	28	4
Income maintenance (N = 26)	38	4
Recreation/leisure (N = 18)	67	2
Senior citizens affairs (N = 49)	61	3
Generalists (N = 42)	48	3
Personal Characteristics of the Decision-Makers		
Age of the Respondent		
Under 45 (N = 98)	42	3
45-54 (N = 98)	32	5
55-64 (N = 90)	29	4
65 and over (N = 30)	60	2
Sex of the Respondent		
Male (N = 230)	35	4
Female (N = 86)	41	4
Ethnicity of the Respondent		
White (N = 235)	36	4
Minority (N = 81)	40	3
Educational Level of the Respondent		
High school graduate or less (N = 42)	40	4
Some college (N = 64)	34	4
College graduate (N = 99)	35	4
Postcollege professional education (N = 111)	38	4
Total (N = 316)	37	4

Source: Compiled by the author.

specialists and decision-makers who themselves were elderly were also more than twice as likely as most other subgroups in the decision-making community to focus on transportation as one of the elderly's most serious problems. Most of these decision-maker groups ranked the elderly's transportation problems second only to their financial problems. The rest of the decision-making community accorded the elderly's transportation problems considerably lower priority. This does not mean that they believed the elderly had few transportation problems, for as the following paragraphs confirm, these decision-makers typically believed that many elderly people experience serious transportation problems getting around in the community. Hence, the elderly's transportation problems had less visibility to some decision-makers, only because income or health or housing problems had greater visibility; many decision-makers were nevertheless still aware of the elderly's transportation problems.

When the decision-makers were asked to estimate the percentage of Los Angeles County elderly residents who "have severe transportation problems getting to places they want to go," the mean response from this sample of 316 decision-makers was 49 percent; in other words, the collective perception of this cross section of the decision-making community was that nearly half of the elderly population experienced severe transportation problems. One third of the decision-makers (34 percent) maintained that 60 percent of the elderly or more had serious mobility problems and one quarter of the sample (24 percent) said 70 percent or more of the elderly had such problems.

The union local presidents and the advocates for the aged were the most likely of the original six subsamples to suggest that the majority of elderly people experienced serious transportation problems (see Table 6.2). The corporate directors of personnel, in comparison, deemphasized the prevalence of transit problems in the elderly population. They collectively estimated that only one third of the elderly population experienced serious mobility problems in getting to places where they wanted to go, and only two suggested a figure as high as 60 percent of the elderly.

Minority decision-makers were much more likely than white decision-makers to allege widespread transportation problems in the elderly population. Whereas less than half of the white decision-makers maintained that the majority of old people experienced serious mobility problems, nearly two thirds of the minority decision-makers believed transit problems affected the majority of the aged. Perhaps the minority decision-makers were reflecting on the transportation situation of the elderly in their respective minority communities. Data from interviews with elderly residents in the county revealed

TABLE 6.2

"Roughly What Percentage of Older People Would You Say Have Severe Transportation Problems Getting to Places That They Want to Go?"
(percent estimating 50 percent of the elderly or more)

Positional Characteristics of the Decision-Makers	
Position in the Policy Process	
Legislators (N = 71)	48
Agency administrators (N = 70)	57
Service delivery personnel (N = 70)	53
Corporate directors of personnel (N = 35)	46
Union local presidents (N = 35)	69
Advocates for the aged (N = 35)	69
Responsibility for Aging Programs	
Primary function (N = 85)	59
Important but not central function (N = 88)	53
Minor function (N = 143)	47
Area of Program Expertise	
Health (N = 37)	51
Mental health (N = 23)	61
Housing (N = 29)	49
Employment (N = 92)	46
Income maintenance (N =,26)	38
Recreation/leisure (N = 18)	79
Senior citizens affairs (N = 49)	65
Generalists (N = 42)	48
Personal Characteristics of the Decision-Makers	
Age of the Respondent	
Under 45 (N = 98)	51
45-54 (N = 98)	53
55-64 (N = 90)	49
65 and over (N = 30)	60
Sex of the Respondent	
Male (N = 230)	50
Female (N = 86)	56
Ethnicity of the Respondent	
White (N = 235)	48
Minority (N = 81)	64
Educational Level of the Respondent	
High school graduate or less (N = 42)	50
Some college (N = 64)	47
College graduate (N = 99)	47
Postcollege professional education (N = 111)	59
Total (N = 316)	52

Source: Compiled by the author.

that black and Mexican American elderly reported many more transportation problems than did their white age peers. When asked about the problems they experienced in getting around in the community, the majority of white elderly respondents reported having no problems. In contrast, less than one third of the black elderly (31 percent) and less than one quarter of the Mexican American elderly maintained that they experienced no problems getting around in the community. To the extent that minority and white decision-makers represent different constituencies in the elderly population, their mismatched perceptions of the elderly's transportation problems may nevertheless be accurate.

One reason, and probably an important reason, why many decision-makers alleged widespread transit problems in the elderly population is their perception of the elderly's dominant reliance on public transportation as a means to get around in the community. The mean estimate of the sample of 316 decision-makers was that 62 percent of the elderly rely primarily on public transportation to get around in Los Angeles. Nearly three quarters (73 percent) of the 316 decision-makers believed that a majority of the elderly (50 percent or more) rely mainly on public transportation, and more than a third (35 percent) of the decision-makers believed 70 percent or more of the elderly relied on the public transportation system. The decision-makers collectively pictured the elderly population as heavily dependent on public as opposed to private means of transportation.

Legislators were the least likely to find a majority of the elderly relying on the public transportation system for most of their transportation needs (see Table 6.3). The corporate directors of personnel, the health professionals, and the income-maintenance specialists were the only other decision-maker subgroups in which a majority estimated that only a minority of the elderly relied heavily on the public transportation system to satisfy their ordinary transit needs. In contrast, recreation center and senior citizens club directors were the most likely by far to stress the elderly's heavy dependence on public transportation to get around. They were half again as likely as any other subgroup in the decision-making community to believe that the clear majority of the elderly (60 percent or more) rely first and foremost on public transportation to get around in the community.

Minority decision-makers also stressed the elderly's dependence on public transportation modes. Nearly two thirds of the minority decision-makers, compared to only half of the whites, maintained that 60 percent of the elderly or more relied primarily on public transportation to get around in the community. Data from the community survey again confirm that minority elderly rely more

TABLE 6.3

"What Percentage of People over 65 Would You Estimate Rely Primarily on Public Transportation to Get Around in Los Angeles?" (percent estimating 60 percent or more of the elderly)

Positional Characteristics of the Decision-Makers	
Position in the Policy Process	
Legislators (N = 71)	41
Agency administrators (N = 70)	63
Service delivery personnel (N = 70)	60
Corporate directors of personnel (N = 35)	49
Union local presidents (N = 35)	60
Advocates for the aged (N = 35)	60
Responsibility for Aging Programs	
Primary function (N = 85)	61
Important but not central function (N = 88)	50
Minor function (N = 143)	55
Area of Program Expertise	
Health (N = 37)	41
Mental health (N = 23)	52
Housing (N = 29)	62
Employment (N = 92)	59
Income maintenance (N = 26)	46
Recreation/leisure (N = 18)	89
Senior citizens affairs (N = 49)	59
Generalists (N = 42)	43
Personal Characteristics of the Decision-Makers	
Age of the Respondent	
Under 45 (N = 98)	53
45-54 (N = 98)	53
55-64 (N = 90)	57
65 and over (N = 30)	63
Sex of the Respondent	
Male (N = 230)	52
Female (N = 86)	64
Ethnicity of the Respondent	
White (N = 235)	51
Minority (N = 81)	65
Educational Level of the Respondent	
High school graduate or less (N = 42)	64
Some college (N = 64)	61
College graduate (N = 99)	51
Postcollege professional education (N = 111)	52
Total (N = 316)	55

Source: Compiled by the author.

on public transportation than white elderly do, but not to the extent envisioned by either the minority or the white decision-makers. Approximately one in five of both the black and Mexican American elderly were mostly dependent on the bus for transportation compared to only 8 percent of the white elderly.

The decision-makers' overview of the prevalence of transportation problems in the elderly population is partly accurate and partly inaccurate. The decision-makers seemed correctly sensitive to the fact that a sizable minority of the elderly population (perhaps as high as 45 percent or even higher) experiences significant transportation barriers in getting to places they want to go in the community. Despite the decision-makers' proper identification of serious transportation problems afflicting many of the elderly residents in the county, the decision-makers for the most part defined the elderly's transportation problems as less pressing than the elderly's income and physical or mental health problems. But, in this regard, the decision-makers reflected the priorities that elderly residents themselves assign to these problems (see Table 2.6). Hence the decision-makers' overview of the elderly's transportation problems is to this point congruent with the problems volunteered by elderly residents living in the community.

Where the decision-makers seriously err in their overview of the elderly's transportation problems is in assuming that the majority of the elderly relies on public transportation to get around in the city and in subsequently concluding that the primary reason elderly people experience serious transportation problems is because they rely on a public transportation system that does not accommodate their special transit needs. In the companion survey of elderly residents, less than one in seven reported riding the bus as often as once a week; in contrast, more than five out of six maintained that they hardly ever or never used the bus for transportation. Rather than bus, these elderly relied on the automobile as their primary means of transportation. Most of the elderly (64 percent) still drove themselves, but if they could not, then their spouses or other family members would generally drive them to their destination. This inaccurate bias in the decision-makers' perceptions conceivably could have a detrimental impact on planning transit programs tailored to the elderly's special transportation needs. To the extent that these decision-makers focus primarily on improving public transportation service, they may help only a small minority of the elderly population who currently experience transportation problems rather than the vast majority of the elderly who many of these decision-makers might believe they were helping. This proposition receives closer scrutiny throughout the rest of the chapter.

DECISION-MAKERS' PERCEPTIONS OF THE BARRIERS TO TRANSPORTATION EXPERIENCED BY THE AGED

The Problem of Inadequate Public Transportation

What specific obstacles do these decision-makers identify as "preventing older people from getting around Los Angeles as they might like to"? As could be predicted from the decision-makers' definition of the elderly as a transit-dependent population, nearly three quarters of the sample of 316 decision-makers (71 percent) identified deficiencies in the public transportation system as a primary contributor to the elderly's loss of mobility in the later years (see Table 6.4). A state legislator (I.D. 140) cited the availability of public transportation close to the elderly's home, "Older people can't walk great distances to get to it." But that's only half the problem; a corporate personnel officer (I.D. 423) observed, "Often the buses don't go where the elderly want to go." The head of a local committee on aging (I.D. 619) complained additionally that "public transportation is bad on weekends." A local legislator (I.D. 121) blamed the elderly's transportation problems on "the lack of a comprehensive rapid transit system" in the county, noting that it was "too lengthy a trip across town" for most elderly people to make on their own. A counselor who helped to place nursing home patients (I.D. 345) concurred, "It's a complicated bus system--sometimes the elderly have to transfer three times" in a single trip.

From his own experience a recreation center director (I.D. 369) affirmed the elderly "cannot cope with transfers" on the buses. Still others mentioned problems created for elderly passengers by the structural design of the buses: "The elderly don't have mobility within the aisles" (a local legislator, I.D. 123), and "the elderly can't get up the tall steps of the bus" (a psychiatric social worker, I.D. 318). Whatever the precise nature of their complaints with the Los Angeles bus system, all of these decision-makers could agree with a federal legislator (I.D. 169) who summarily observed that "public transportation is not geared to the elderly."

The advocates for the aged, followed by the legislators, were the most critical of the way in which the existing public transportation system served the elderly's transportation needs. In general, those decision-makers whose jobs brought them into frequent contact with elderly people were more likely to criticize the existing public transportation as a major obstacle to the continued mobility of elderly people in their later years. Thus, the senior citizens affairs officials and the senior citizens club directors were also relatively more critical of public transportation than the rest of the decision-making community.

TABLE 6.4

Decision-Makers' Perceptions of the Obstacles Aged People Face in Getting around Los Angeles County

Decision-Makers' Positional and Personal Characteristics	Inadequate Public Transportation System (percent)	Excessive Transportation Costs (percent)
Positional Characteristics of the Decision-Makers		
Position in the Policy Process		
Legislators (N = 71)	79	54
Agency administrators (N = 70)	61	51
Service delivery personnel (N = 70)	67	64
Corporate directors of personnel (N = 35)	69	51
Union local presidents (N = 35)	69	54
Advocates for the aged (N = 35)	86	37
Responsibility for Aging Programs		
Primary function (N = 85)	79	41
Important but not central function (N = 88)	78	57
Minor function (N = 143)	62	59
Area of Program Expertise		
Health (N = 37)	65	57
Mental health (N = 23)	61	65
Housing (N = 29)	69	52
Employment (N = 92)	64	57
Income maintenance (N = 26)	77	54
Recreation/leisure (N = 18)	89	67
Senior citizens affairs (N = 49)	86	33
Generalists (N = 42)	69	57
Personal Characteristics of the Decision-Makers		
Age of the Respondent		
Under 45 (N = 98)	76	60
45-54 (N = 98)	72	57
55-64 (N = 90)	63	50
65 and over (N = 30)	73	30
Sex of the Respondent		
Male (N = 230)	73	54
Female (N = 86)	65	51
Ethnicity of the Respondent		
White (N = 235)	73	50
Minority (N = 81)	65	63
Educational Level of the Respondent		
High school graduate or less (N = 42)	67	50
Some college (N = 64)	66	48
College graduate (N = 99)	75	52
Postcollege professional education (N = 111)	72	59
Total (N = 316)	71	53

Source: Compiled by the author.

Obstacles to the Elderly's Getting around as Perceived by Decision-Makers			
Health-Related Mobility and Transportation Problems (percent)	Various Environmental Obstacles to Mobility, Travel (percent)	Fear of Crime and Other Fears for Personal Safety (percent)	Lack of Private Means of Transportation (percent)
38	23	11	17
44	21	20	37
59	11	19	37
40	23	3	31
40	23	6	29
43	11	26	17
49	14	24	29
38	23	14	23
47	19	10	32
46	14	16	32
57	13	13	39
55	21	21	41
43	21	9	30
46	27	19	27
28	22	11	22
41	12	22	18
45	21	14	24
40	22	18	35
43	16	15	26
49	17	11	27
57	20	13	27
43	21	12	28
51	13	22	30
45	19	12	24
46	17	22	42
55	14	10	29
47	16	14	27
36	21	19	33
48	20	14	26
45	19	15	29

The Problem of High Transportation Costs

The high cost of transportation was the only other major obstacle to the elderly's getting around in the community that was cited by a majority of the decision-makers (53 percent). Most of the decision-makers spoke generally about the high cost of transportation or the inability of the elderly to afford the cost of transportation on their small retirement incomes. Less than one in five of the decision-makers specified whether they were thinking primarily about "the cost of maintaining a private vehicle" (a city councilman, I.D. 118A) or the fact that the elderly "can't afford the bus or taxi" (administrator of a long-term care hospital, I.D. 206). In all, less than 5 percent of the total sample expressed specific concern about the rising costs of owning and operating a car on small retirement incomes. This seems to be a serious oversight in the decision-makers' perceptions of the elderly's transportation problems, for five out of six of the elderly residents interviewed in the USC companion survey reported having a car in their household, which means having to contend with the rising costs of owning and operating that car within their limited household budgets.

In general, the more closely involved a decision-maker was with aging programs and elderly constituents, the less likely he was to cite the cost barriers among the elderly's transportation problems. Advocates for the aged and senior citizens affairs officials were by far the least likely in the decision-making community to highlight the cost problems. Decision-makers who belonged to the elderly age group also deemphasized the cost barriers as a serious obstacle in preventing elderly people from getting around as they might like to.

In contrast, respondents who had to wait for the elderly to come to see them in their own office or facility on a walk-in basis--the service providers in general, but the mental health counselors and the recreation center and senior citizens club directors in particular--were the most likely in the decision-making community to believe that transportation costs do seriously inhibit elderly people making unnecessary trips in the community. Their contrary perceptions of the barriers on travel imposed by high costs are probably justified within the limited context of their service delivery environment. The elderly clientele who walk into public health and/or social service agencies for assistance tend to be from low- to moderate-income backgrounds because of the income-based eligibility requirements of these service programs, and for the elderly, costs may indeed be a deterrent to travel in the community. Similarly, the participants at the recreation centers and senior citizens clubs sponsored by the city and county tend to be from low- to moderate-income backgrounds, and these elderly would probably be likely to forego trips to the recreation center whenever their limited budget became stretched.[11]

For many such elderly living on modest monthly incomes, the rising costs of public and private transportation could impose a serious barrier to their making trips in the community. In 1970, more than one dime in every dollar of the average retired couple's budget went to transportation; only food and housing regularly accounted for larger outlays from the elderly's pocket.[12]

The Problems Created by Poor Health

Cited by nearly half (45 percent) of the 316 decision-makers were the obstacles to mobility created by the elderly's "own state of health" (an employment program administrator, I.D. 245). A senior citizens club director (I.D. 365) commented, "A lot of the seniors are handicapped. They need help getting to a bus or wherever they are going." A housing program administrator (I.D. 227) agreed, "Partially blind, physically unable, many elderly are handicapped and need special assistance." A senior citizens affairs official (I.D. 269) remarked about the "lack of escort services for those elderly who require special services to get around." But a nursing home administrator (I.D. 231) doubted the physical ability of at least some elderly individuals "to get around with or without the aid of others."

Service providers among the original six subsamples were the most concerned about the health impediments to the elderly's continued mobility in the later years of life. In particular, mental health counselors and housing planners worried about the mobility implications of the elderly's poor health. Decision-makers who themselves belonged to the elderly age group also stressed the barriers to mobility created by the health decrements that often accompany old age. For this subgroup alone in the entire decision-making community were the health barriers to the elderly's continued mobility in their own neighborhood and beyond generally considered more serious than the limitations imposed on travel by the high cost of transportation.

In contrast, the recreation specialists, who had disproportionately criticized the inadequacy of public transportation and the barriers created by high costs, only infrequently cited the problems that declining health status posed for continued mobility in the later years. Conceivably, the elderly who regularly attend activities scheduled at these recreation centers enjoy reasonably good health, and the problems they have in coming to the center are mainly with the bus system and the cost of transportation, of which the recreation center directors were well aware; but perhaps the recreation center directors were not fully attuned to the many other elderly who might attend those programs but for physical infirmities and difficulties of getting to such recreational centers in the community. A majority or near majority of most subgroups in the decision-making community, however, was acutely aware of the health-related problems that limit the elderly's mobility in the community.

The Problems Created by Environmental Obstacles

A minority of the decision-makers referred to environmental obstacles that posed major barriers to the elderly's mobility in the community. The majority of these decision-makers focused on the sprawl of the Los Angeles metropolitan area. A federal legislator (I.D. 168) summarized the feelings of others, "Los Angeles is very spread out. Places are too far away. Living areas, for example, are too far from shopping areas, and the elderly are afraid to drive on busy, fast highways or freeways to get there. The traffic scares them." A Social Security office manager (I.D. 241) observed that "Not all the elderly can live near a plaza."

A senior citizens affairs official blamed at least part of the elderly's transportation problems on poor community planning and "the lack of centralized facilities and activities." Some of the other decision-makers focused on physical obstructions in the neighborhood intervening between the elderly person in his home and his desired destination, as opposed to the obstacle of distance, per se. The chief administrator of a long-term care hospital (I.D. 206), for example, pointed to "curbs and steps which impair movement of wheelchairs," and a social worker (I.D. 312) underscored the "lack of special facilities for the elderly, such as ramps for the handicapped."

Fear for Personal Safety as an Inhibitor of the Aged's Mobility

An even smaller percentage of the decision-makers (only one in seven) acknowledged the role that fear for personal safety may play in keeping the elderly at home. Some believed it was the fear of "exposure to criminal acts of violence" (a hospital administrator, I.D. 209). A state legislator (I.D. 136), for instance, noted that because of their physical handicaps elderly women were "virtually defenseless against purse snatching." Others suggested that the elderly don't go out often because they fear getting into uncomfortable or unfamiliar situations. A Social Security office supervisor (I.D. 348) commented that from his experience with the elderly, "They don't like to go out because they fear masses of people." The administrator of a long-term care hospital (I.D. 205) elaborated on the elderly's problems moving around in the neighborhood with "crowding and pushing because of the lack of youngsters' respect." An insurance company executive (I.D. 409) noted the problem of "overcrowded buses and rude bus drivers." The observations of these decision-makers may help to respond to the challenge issued by a district health officer (I.D. 215) who complained that the elderly "lack initiative--they don't try to find ways of getting to places." More than motivation problem, it may be a problem of fear for personal safety.

The decision-making community was selectively sensitive to the elderly's perspective on travel as one characterized by fear and anxiety. Advocates for the aged and social agency personnel were relatively more aware of the elderly's fears of traveling in the community. In general, the more closely involved in working with the elderly that a decision-maker was, the more likely he was to be aware of the elderly's perspective on the hazards of traveling outside the immediate neighborhood. Corporate personnel directors and union local presidents, on the other hand, rarely interpreted fear of crime or fear of the unknown as a major barrier to the elderly's moving around freely in the community.

The Lack of Private Means of Transportation

Nearly one third of the decision-makers summarily traced the elderly's transportation problems to their "not having their own means of transportation like cars" (director of personnel in an insurance corporation, I.D. 409); to having "no one they can depend on for transportation" (a psychiatric nurse, I.D. 323) after "they have to give up their licenses" (head of a local committee on aging, I.D. 614).

Searching for alternative modes of community-based, door-to-door transportation service that could substitute for the convenience of private methods of transportation, the decision-makers were disappointed. A local legislator (I.D. 104) criticized the "lack of feeder systems" to link local neighborhoods and communities with the central public transportation. Others commented on the sparsity of "dial-a-ride," "mini-bus," and jitney services in local areas. While the flexibility of taxi service was perceived to suit the elderly's needs for door-to-door service, a number of decision-makers dismissed taxi service as too expensive for the elderly to afford, and a state legislator (I.D. 151) implied that social agencies were derelict in having "no taxi service through agencies to adequately serve the elderly population."

The feeling of these decision-makers seemed to run throughout the responses of many more in the sample. Because of health problems that often make walking, standing, and waiting difficult and that also make the elderly especially vulnerable to juvenile assaults or injury in crowded situations, the elderly need door-to-door transportation service in order to remain active in the community and independent in their home. Without good transportation, the elderly will tend to sit home more and more in the later years, going out for a trip in the community only when driven to it by necessity.

DECISION-MAKERS' RECOMMENDATIONS FOR IMPROVING TRANSPORTATION SERVICE TO AGED RESIDENTS IN THE COMMUNITY

The decision-makers were asked to recommend ways to ease the elderly's transportation problems. Their responses are summarized in Table 6.5. A quick glance at the table confirms that these decision-makers were far more concerned about the needs of transit-dependent elderly residents in the community than they were about the problems of the elderly car owner or the elderly driver. The decision-makers commonly focused on ways to improve the public transportation and often volunteered suggestions for the development of supplemental community-based transportation services. In contrast they rarely proposed to underwrite some of the costs of insurance, gasoline, or vehicle repairs for the elderly car owner, or alternatively, to supplement the elderly's income to help cover the rising costs of private transportation that are consuming a disproportionate share of their retirement incomes. The decision-makers' emphasis on public transportation solutions to the elderly's transportation problems is completely consistent with their commonly held beliefs that the overwhelming majority of the elderly relies primarily on public transportation to get around in the community. That their perceptions do not completely accord with reality is a policy consideration that is temporarily set aside until after a more thorough analysis of the decision-makers' perspectives on solving the elderly's transportation problems.

Improving the Public Transportation System

Nearly half of the 316 decision-makers (47 percent) recommended solving the elderly's transportation problems by improving the central public transportation system in the county: "I think the area has to develop a better transportation system--rapid transit, subway, monorail or what-have-you. It's totally inadequate now," observed the personnel director in a medical organization (I.D. 423). But rapid mass transit is not a panacea for the elderly's transportation problems. First there are questions about what kind of public transportation system. Then there are questions about whether a public transportation system could adequately serve the elderly population. Would the system go where the elderly want to go? Would the system have to be specially designed to accommodate the needs of frail elderly passengers? In the last analysis, is barrier-free mass transit a cost-efficient way to solve the elderly's transportation problems?

Although a near majority of the decision-makers in this sample agreed that one solution to the elderly's transportation problems lay in designing a better mass transit system to serve all areas of the county, they were far from agreement on what kind of mass transit system Los Angeles County should have. A housing planner (I.D. 230) maintained, "A fixed rail public transportation system is still needed." A district health officer (I.D. 214) remarked, "You see the need of a modern mass transit system. Whether it be monorail or subway, it should be easy to get to." But the head of a professional association (I.D. 516) protested, "There has to be an expansion of the bus transportation system. We don't have the population density to support a subway system." A housing counselor who worked extensively with elderly clients (I.D. 335) concurred and added, "extend and expand the bus service. Maybe more mini-buses should be used." A local legislator (I.D. 125) suggested a compromise, "an improved combination of rail and bus." Another city councilman (I.D. 124) urged the county to "try new modes of transportation." A state legislator (I.D. 127) agreed with him, "Increase the types of transportation. Evaluate bringing in street cars or monorail. The county doesn't have to be locked into the bus, but if we are, then increase service and the number of buses."

This diversity of opinion in the decision-making community only reflects the diversity of opinion in the population. During the course of this research from initial funding to final writing, the county voters defeated three different ballot propositions that would have financed three different models of mass transit; one offered an enlarged bus system, another a fixed rail system. All were soundly defeated by the voters.

It is important not to lose sight of one critical element of the decision-making climate in which mass transportation systems are planned and implemented. Mass transit systems are usually designed to serve first and foremost the needs of the business community, most specifically, by facilitating commuting trips for suburbanites

TABLE 6.5

Decision-Makers' Recommendations for Improving the Aged's Mobility in the Community

Decision-Makers' Positional and Personal Characteristics	Improved Public Transportation Systems (percent)	Development of Demand-Response Transportation Services (percent)
Positional Characteristics of the Decision-Makers		
Position in the Policy Process		
Legislators (N = 71)	55	21
Agency administrators (N = 70)	46	34
Service delivery personnel (N = 70)	40	53
Corporate directors of personnel (N = 35)	40	14
Union local presidents (N = 35)	54	11
Advocates for the aged (N = 35)	46	46
Responsibility for Aging Programs		
Primary function (N = 85)	41	51
Important but not central function (N = 88)	55	24
Minor function (N = 143)	45	26
Area of Program Expertise		
Health (N = 37)	49	35
Mental health (N = 23)	26	49
Housing (N = 29)	66	28
Employment (N = 92)	47	23
Income maintenance (N = 26)	38	23
Recreation/leisure (N = 18)	61	56
Senior citizens affairs (N = 49)	41	45
Generalists (N = 42)	50	24
Personal Characteristics of the Decision-Makers		
Age of the Respondent		
Under 45 (N = 98)	51	33
45-54 (N = 98)	46	31
55-64 (N = 90)	43	28
65 and over (N = 30)	47	47
Sex of the Respondent		
Male (N = 230)	50	24
Female (N = 86)	38	52
Ethnicity of the Respondent		
White (N = 235)	51	29
Minority (N = 81)	35	41
Educational Level of the Respondent		
High school graduate or less (N = 42)	55	29
Some college (N = 64)	34	41
College graduate (N = 99)	53	26
Postcollege professional education (N = 111)	46	33
Total (N = 316)	47	32

Source: Compiled by the author.

Development of Other Supplemental Transportation Programs (percent)	Development of Senior Citizen Neighborhoods with All Services (percent)	Reduced Fares for Elderly Passengers (percent)	Income Supplements for the Elderly (percent)	No Solution (percent)
10	20	30	13	7
17	29	31	21	10
21	27	37	13	6
23	20	23	11	26
11	20	23	23	9
20	26	23	9	6
18	32	25	14	6
14	22	39	11	7
18	21	27	18	13
8	24	30	11	8
13	22	30	13	4
28	21	34	17	14
20	21	23	21	13
31	35	42	7	4
6	33	44	22	6
14	31	20	10	4
12	17	36	14	14
14	30	29	17	12
16	22	32	21	8
17	22	31	11	8
27	17	20	0	10
15	23	29	17	10
22	27	30	10	7
16	19	29	12	11
19	38	32	23	6
14	14	17	21	2
17	27	33	9	6
19	24	35	9	13
15	26	27	22	11
17	24	29	15	9

Solutions to the Elderly's Transportation Problems Volunteered by the Decision-Makers who work in the downtown area; the needs of all other user groups are clearly a secondary consideration in planning the systems.[13] The elderly are one of the secondary user groups who are typically left to adapt to using public transportation facilities on a "take it or leave it" basis in the nonpeak hours. Most of the elderly's trips are limited to short distances, most often within single or adjacent neighborhoods.[14]

None of the mass transit systems proposed for Los Angeles County in the past decade would have improved intraneighborhood transportation services; the emphasis in each proposal was, predictably, on rapid conveyance from suburb to hub. Hence, it is a questionable assumption that a central public transportation system in the county could satisfy the elderly's ordinary transit needs. The personnel manager in a utility company (I.D. 404) minimized the problems facing elderly passengers who have to rely on the public transportation system to get around in the community, "The elderly have lots of time. Where you have a spread-out community, you can't have direct routes everywhere."

There is no doubt that a public transportation system relying on buses is more flexible and hence more adaptable to changing population needs than is one designed around a fixed rail system. Buses are far more easily rerouted than are rail lines. An expanded bus system would offer considerably greater flexibility for serving the needs of the elderly population in particular than would any fixed rail system. An advocate for the elderly (I.D. 602) urged, for example, "There should be more bus routes where a high density of senior citizens live," and a federal legislator (I.D. 169) suggested that "between nine o'clock and four o'clock, buses ought to be rerouted to take the elderly to recreation centers in the community."

Of those decision-makers urging improvement of the existing public transportation system as a means of improving transportation services in the community for the elderly residents, more than one in five (22 percent) maintained that the public transportation system would have to be designed barrier free to accommodate handicapped passengers. A senior citizens affairs official (I.D. 263) affirmed, "We need redesigned buses. We have some--the city has six of them--but we need hundreds of them. All of the buses should be available to seniors and the handicapped." A district health officer (I.D. 214) looking forward to a new public transportation system in the county in the not too distant future warned, "I think in any new system, you should be able to get right into them--no stairs. There should be some kind of hydraulic lift or escalator so that the older person could get right in. You'd think some of our engineering geniuses would come up with something."

Barrier-free mass transit has been mandated by federal and state legislation in California, and the specifications for barrier free facilities and vehicles have been outlined along with deadlines for their implementation. The Southern California Rapid Transit District has been studying the cost and feasibility of retrofitting its existing fleet of more than 2,000 buses to meet the new specifications for door and aisle widths and seat spacing. Estimates for the complete retrofitting job range between $11 and $41 million. This is an expensive bill when it is not clear how many passengers the redesign will actually benefit. The data presented in this chapter confirm that the overwhelming majority of elderly in Los Angeles County does not now regularly use the bus system to get around town; rather they rely on the private automobile, either driving themselves or being driven by spouse, other family members, or friends. Would these elderly residents use public transportation more often if the system were modified to be barrier-free? It is an unanswered question. Transportation planners admit that "the extent to which the characteristics of existing transportation systems constrain the mobility of the elderly is largely unknown."[15] At the same time, transportation analysts remain confident: "Chances that improvements in public transit facilities and services would bring about higher rates of utilization seem good."[16]

Beyond cost considerations in retrofitting old systems or designing new systems to be barrier free, coupled with the uncertain return on that investment in terms of increased utilization of the barrier-free system by frail, infirmed, or handicapped passengers, the ultimate question remains whether it is economically efficient to intend for a single transit system to serve everyone in the community. The results of one recent study are eye-opening. To provide comprehensive service to all passengers, including those in wheelchairs, would require stretching the average time per stop from 10 to 15 seconds for nonhandicapped passengers to 4 to 6 minutes for wheelchair passengers. The inescapable conclusion of the study was that "In busy systems where 10 to 15 minute headways are used [headway is the time between buses], this would disrupt the entire system making it untenable for public service."[17]

This is not to say that barrier-free mass transit is not the answer to the elderly's transportation problems, but rather than barrier-free mass transit may be only part of the answer. It is likely, for example, that the vast majority of the elderly and handicapped populations (more than 90 or 95 percent) could adequately be served by a barrier-free public transit system, while the remaining 5 percent, who make up the most frail and handicapped passengers, would be served more appropriately by the implementation of a supplementary transportation program providing door-to-door transportation services.[18]

Demand-Response and Other Programs to Provide Community-Based Transportation

Concerned that mass transit will never adequately serve the needs of many transit-dependent elderly, either because reasonably direct service is not available to destinations where the elderly want to go and/or because the system is not adequately redesigned to accommodate the health decrements that often come in old age, another near majority of the decision-makers urged the development of community-based transportation systems to provide neighborhood transportation service for the elderly (see Table 6.5). The head of a local committee on aging (I.D. 629B) maintained, "More personal attention has to be paid to the elderly's needs such as the development of dial-a-ride type programs to meet the needs of disabled elderly." The head nurse in a retirement home (I.D. 341A) observed, "I think the dial-a-ride would be the best solution for those who can ambulate even a little."

Service providers and advocates for the aged particularly favored the development of dial-a-ride transportation programs to serve the elderly's ordinary transit needs. Decision-makers who reported working primarily in connection with various aging programs were twice as likely as decision-makers who worked less closely with the elderly age group to favor the development of dial-a-ride programs as one part, if not the central part, of a transportation system to serve the elderly's particular transit needs. Decision-makers who themselves were elderly also lobbied more often for the implementation of dial-a-ride programs than did younger decision-makers, who focused more often instead on meeting the elderly's transit needs through the development of a rapid mass transit system that would service the entire population in the metropolitan region. Women and minority decision-makers were similarly much more likely to favor dial-a-ride programs over mass transit solutions for the elderly's special transit needs, while men and white decision-makers, in contrast, more often favored barrier-free mass transit solutions for the elderly's transit needs.

Women and ethnic elderly, however, have special problems in relying on public transportation to get around in the community. As the head of a local committee on aging (I.D. 614) explained, "Not all women our age drive cars, and they have lost their husbands." Many of the elderly women in this situation are reluctant to ride buses around town for fear of "getting hit over the head or having their purse snatched," said the head of another local aging committee (I.D. 619). Dial-a-ride would ensure safe transit to elderly women. Minority elderly are also disadvantaged in relying on public transportation to get around in their communities, because bus service is generally considered to be less adequate in the Mexican American and/or black areas than in other parts of the county. "Blacks and Mexican Americans lack auto transportation by private cars. They rely more on public transportation than the whites. They need more bus service in those areas" (a senior citizens affairs official, I.D. 266). Dial-a-ride would offer these minority elderly convenient neighborhood transportation. Women and minority decision-makers seemed to be sensitive to the special transit needs or problems of these subgroups in the elderly population.

Dial-a-ride was the most commonly suggested alternative transportation program, but certainly not the only one. A state legislator (I.D. 151) suggested intracommunity transit systems using "neighborhood buses underwritten by government or private agencies." A seasoned advocate for the elderly (I.D. 601) urged creation of an "escort system manned by volunteer groups to take the elderly out." The personnel director in a public service corporation (I.D. 404) concurred in finding that the solution was in "People helping people. Government can't do it all. Families need to help their own older members especially." A health services administrator (I.D. 203) favored "taxicab services or taxicab-like services," with emphasis on the desirable flexibility of door-to-door transportation service for the elderly. A senior citizens affairs official (I.D. 260) believed the elderly's neighborhood transit needs would be very well satisfied by a "good mini-bus system." The director of a long-term care hospital (I.D. 205) believed that "more shuttle-type transportation in shopping areas within communities" was particularly important. A mental health counselor (I.D. 323) asserted that "public agencies should provide transportation for the elderly," and a senior citizens director (I.D. 365) agreed, emphasizing that "every hospital should have vans and buses to bring senior citizens to the health program. It should be available 24 hours a day so that they can call on it when they need it."

Although the responses were varied as to the mode of transportation service, all of these decision-makers were agreed about the need to improve intracommunity (as opposed to cross-town) transportation service for elderly residents; of particular concern to these decision-makers was improving the elderly's access to shopping and/or medical facilities in nearby locations.

The idea of demand-response and other special neighborhood-based transportation programs is not new. At the time of this study, more than 1,000 such demand-response systems across the nation were operating or in the planning stage.[19] Moreover, in recent years, the development of door-to-door transit programs has been given top priority by the area agencies on aging in response to the congressional mandate issuing from the 1975 Older Americans Comprehensive Services amendments.

In order to assess the receptivity of this cross section of the decision-making community to the concept of demand-response transportation service, the interviewer inquired of the respondents, "Do you think some kind of door-to-door system of transportation such as dial-a-ride is a feasible solution to transportation problems older people face?" Nearly three out of four (74 percent) of the 316 decision-makers responded affirmatively (see Table 6.6). As to be expected on the basis of earlier responses, service delivery personnel and advocates for the aged were the most supportive of the dial-a-ride concept. Women and minority decision-makers similarly remained more in favor of demand-response transportation services than did their male or white counterparts.

But many decision-makers who endorsed the concept challenged its feasibility. Thus, a city councilman (I.D. 125) noted "Yes, it's feasible, but not for taxpayers. Studies in this area indicate it would need a significant subsidy." Another city councilman (I.D. 102B) concurred based on his own experience in another city, "I favor it. However, the cost is almost prohibitive. We took a look at it in this city. But at the same time, I have reservations about rapid transit as the total solution." Because of these cost considerations, some favored the development of demand-response transportation programs "only as a secondary thing. The development of a rapid transit system is first and foremost" (head of a craft union local, I.D. 535). A city councilman (I.D. 107) similarly believed that demand-response service would be "some solution, but for many seniors, it's expensive and I don't know if they can afford it. I would rather see the seniors get more buses in the area. When you get door-to-door service, you can pay as high as $18. They would rather save the money and go a cheaper way."

Others concluded conversely: "Dial-a-ride is not feasible financially--too costly" (an employment counselor, I.D. 357). Alternatively, a recreation center director (I.D. 369) concluded, "There are too many older people; dial-a-ride would not be feasible." And finally, "Dial-a-ride will not work in such a large area like Los Angeles" (a local legislator, I.D. 101). A retirement income counselor (I.D. 346) asserted simply, "The idea seems totally impractical to me. I would prefer to see a much more extensive bus system." A recreation center director (I.D. 364) spoke from practical experience in condemning the dial-a-ride programs as unfeasible, "It isn't working at all in our community."

But these views were clearly in the minority in the decision-making community. More commonly the decision-makers felt not only that demand-response transportation was a desirable solution to some of the elderly's transportation problems but that it was also a feasible idea: "It's one of the options that must be considered" (a

TABLE 6.6

"Do You Think Some Kind of Door-to-Door System of Transportation Such as Dial-a-Ride Is a Feasible Solution to Transportation Problems Older People Face?"
(percent responding "yes")

Positional Characteristics of the Decision-Makers	
Position in the Policy Process	
Legislators (N = 71)	72
Agency administrators (N = 70)	76
Service delivery personnel (N = 70)	84
Corporate directors of personnel (N = 35)	57
Union local presidents (N = 35)	66
Advocates for the aged (N = 35)	80
Responsibility for Aging Programs	
Primary function (N = 85)	80
Important but not central function (N = 88)	77
Minor function (N = 143)	69
Area of Program Expertise	
Health (N = 37)	76
Mental health (N = 23)	87
Housing (N = 29)	76
Employment (N = 92)	67
Income maintenance (N = 26)	65
Recreation/leisure (N = 18)	83
Senior citizens affairs (N = 49)	76
Generalists (N = 42)	79
Personal Characteristics of the Decision-Makers	
Age of the Respondent	
Under 45 (N = 98)	77
45-54 (N = 98)	76
55-64 (N = 90)	70
65 and over (N = 30)	73
Sex of the Respondent	
Male (N = 230)	69
Female (N = 86)	87
Ethnicity of the Respondent	
White (N = 235)	71
Minority (N = 81)	84
Educational Level of the Respondent	
High school graduate or less (N = 42)	74
Some college (N = 64)	72
College graduate (N = 99)	68
Postcollege professional education (N = 111)	81
Total (N = 316)	74

Source: Compiled by the author.

city councilman (I.D. 109). One of his colleagues (I.D. 111A) approved the idea of demand-response transportation services in the community, but added, "they are too costly to run on a city-wide basis. If federally subsidized okay, but not just city-sponsored."

The problems of establishing demand-response transportation service in Los Angeles County are admittedly multiplied by the urban area sprawl. In theory and in practice, demand-response systems are most likely to succeed in areas with population densities of 2,000 to 4,000 persons per square mile and where demand density ranges from 20 to 100 demands per square mile per hour.[20] In Los Angeles County, three demand-response programs have been in operation for several years. Although the service demands per 1,000 population and the passengers per vehicle per hour are low relative to programs in other parts of the country, the cost factors are not too much higher in comparison. One report thus concludes that the existing demand-response transportation programs in Los Angeles County are reasonably successful.[21] The report does caution, however, that some areas in the county could better support such specialized transit programs than others, and careful planning is therefore required in developing demand-response transportation services to ensure their successful operation.

If cost-benefit studies suggest such demand-response programs are economically feasible, and if the decision-making community is generally supportive of the concept of dial-a-ride programs, as these data suggest, perhaps the time is not far off when neighborhood transportation systems will be an integral part of the county's overall transportation plan rather than constituting the transportation system of last resort.

Community Reorganization to Locate Services Near the Aged

One in four of the decision-makers (24 percent) thought about minimizing the elderly's need to travel by reorganizing communities to bring services closer to elderly residents living in the community (Table 6.5). For some decision-makers, community reorganization meant infusing new services and facilities into residential areas with a high concentration of elderly residents. A city councilman (I.D. 107), for instance, lobbied for "more regional mini-hospitals and clinics in more areas with especially high concentrations of elderly." A suburban city councilman (I.D. 121) saw the problem differently; he complained that the problem was to "get people to stay within their own communities. The older person doesn't need to go to a doctor in L.A."

Other decision-makers felt that it would be best to rehouse the ill and frail elderly in "more centralized communities for the elderly" (a Social Security program administrator, I.D. 237). A lower echelon operations supervisor in a branch Social Security office (I.D. 348) agreed, "We need communities for elderly people where they don't have to go far. Older people in England are really not lonely. They congregate together in neighborhood pubs--there is something for them to do." A housing program administrator (I.D. 227) justified rehousing the frail elderly in congregate living arrangements: "Concentrate the handicapped in locations so that special bus service can be provided. Assign an attendant to assist these elderly. Use a mutual aid system whereby nonhandicapped elderly can be assigned to help the handicapped."

In the entire decision-making community, minority officials were the most likely to recommend large-scale community reorganization in order to minimize the elderly's need to travel great distances to secure those goods and services necessary for life support. Perhaps their experience with urban renewal projects in the central downtown areas (where, by the way, many elderly live) has given these minority decision-makers hope that old communities may be redesigned or new communities built with the living requirements of resident populations in mind. Large-scale community reorganization is the most ambitious and long-term proposal that was offered for altering the elderly's transit-disadvantaged status. Certainly the more carefully housing environments are planned, the more transportation problems can be minimized. But planned communities will rarely eliminate the need to travel completely, and when the need to travel arises, the question remains of how to ensure the elderly's access to suitable transportation service.

Breaking the Cost Barriers Limiting the Aged's Access to Transportation Services

A little more than one half (53 percent) of the sample believed the high cost of transportation limited the elderly's mobility in the local community and beyond (see Table 6.4). In response to this problem, nearly half of the decision-making community (44 percent) recommended either reduced fares for elderly passengers using various modes of transportation and/or supplements in the elderly's income to cover the rising costs of transportation (see Table 6.5). By a ratio of two to one, the decision-makers thought in terms of reduced fares on public transportation systems as opposed to income supplements that the elderly might spend on private travel means.

Looked at one way, it could be said that the decision-makers think more often in terms of subsidizing the public transit providers in a middleman role than directly subsidizing the elderly passenger. One result is that the elderly person who is struggling to continue operating his private automobile in the face of mounting costs for insurance, gasoline, and repairs is given little support in his endeavors to remain transportation independent; without income or indirect subsidies, the elderly car owner could be forced to give up his private means of transportation prematurely, only to become one of the transit-dependent population whom decision-makers seem more willing to subsidize. Among the minority who advocated income supplements be given directly to transit-deprived elderly residents, an employment program administrator (I.D. 245) suggested, "The best way would be to give them a sufficient transportation allowance right in their social security benefits. In this way, you give them dignity." Cash supplements also give the elderly person the freedom to choose whatever transportation is best suited to his own needs and capacities.

To test the limits of the decision-makers' support for reduced fares for the elderly, the sample was asked if they favored free transit for the elderly. Two out of three of the decision-makers not only supported reduced fares for elderly passengers on all public transportation systems but actually favored elimination of all fares for elderly passengers (see Table 6.7). A national legislator (I.D. 165) professed, "I would saturate the streets and freeways with no-fare buses. We should operate a simple system paid by taxes like other services." Support for the no-fare proposal was relatively evenly distributed throughout the decision-making community; but it still might be noted that legislators were among those segments of the decision-making community least in favor of the plan.

Many of the decision-makers who were not in favor of the complete elimination of fares for elderly passengers still believed that the elderly should travel for reduced fares. The operations supervisor of a branch Social Security office (I.D. 348) suggested that the elderly be allowed to travel for 10 cents as a token fare. A local legislator (I.D. 104) explained his rationale for the same position. "There should be a minimum 10-cent fare. In that way, there will be some awareness as well as some participation and that will make the elderly feel more comfortable." A city councilman (I.D. 112A) concurred, "I really don't think older people want everything free." As with dial-a-ride, some decision-makers, particularly the local legislators, worried about "where is the money going to come from?" (a city councilman, I.D. 102B). Some said that they favored the idea of free transit for the elderly, but to actually get such a program in operation would "depend on the costs" (a city councilman, I.D. 112A).

TABLE 6.7

"Would You Favor Free Transit for the Elderly?"
(percent responding "yes")

Positional Characteristics of the Decision-Makers	
Position in the Policy Process	
Legislators (N = 71)	59
Agency administrators (N = 70)	74
Service delivery personnel (N = 70)	66
Corporate directors of personnel (N = 35)	60
Union local presidents (N = 35)	71
Advocates for the aged (N = 35)	71
Responsibility for Aging Programs	
Primary function (N = 85)	71
Important but not central function (N = 88)	67
Minor function (N = 143)	64
Area of Program Expertise	
Health (N = 37)	57
Mental health (N = 23)	83
Housing (N = 29)	66
Employment (N = 92)	66
Income maintenance (N = 26)	62
Recreation/leisure (N = 18)	89
Senior citizens affairs (N = 49)	71
Generalists (N = 42)	57
Personal Characteristics of the Decision-Makers	
Age of the Respondent	
Under 45 (N = 98)	73
45-54 (N = 98)	68
55-64 (N = 90)	60
65 and over (N = 30)	60
Sex of the Respondent	
Male (N = 230)	67
Female (N = 86)	65
Ethnicity of the Respondent	
White (N = 235)	61
Minority (N = 81)	83
Educational Level of the Respondent	
High school graduate or less (N = 42)	62
Some college (N = 64)	67
College graduate (N = 99)	67
Postcollege professional education (N = 111)	68
Total (N = 316)	67

Source: Compiled by the author.

Each of the decision-makers was also asked, "Would you favor subsidization of neighborhood transportation systems, such as jitneys or taxi services, if they were to provide reduced fares for the elderly?" More than five out of six of the decision-makers (84 percent) responded affirmatively (see Table 6.8). These transportation programs would provide the elderly with good service in their immediate neighborhoods at a price they could afford to pay for transportation. Such service could undoubtedly serve the large majority of transit-dependent elderly quite effectively, but it is unlikely that taxis or jitneys would be able to serve the handicapped elderly population adequately. This thinking may have led one local legislator (I.D. 126), among others, to conclude, "This plan is a modification of dial-a-ride, and I prefer dial-a-ride." As with the no-fare proposal, this subsidy plan had less support among the legislators than in any other subgroup in the decision-making community save the corporate directors of personnel. Presumably the dissenting legislators are most concerned about what kind of financial arrangements are going to be made to underwrite the subsidies to the taxicab and jitney companies that are going to offer the reduced fares to elderly passengers; they probably realized that the bill is going to stop for payment at their office.

TRANSPORTATION SERVICES FOR THE AGED: SOCIAL PRIORITIES AND POLITICAL COMMITMENT

Over and over again, the decision-makers interviewed in this study expressed support for proposals to provide special transportation services to elderly residents in the community contingent on what the programs would cost. Transportation officials ponder the costs of retrofitting an existing bus fleet of more than 2,000 vehicles in order to make the vehicles relatively barrier free for elderly and handicapped passengers using the system. Legislators worry about the size of the subsidies required to offer elderly passengers reduced fares on buses or neighborhood transportation systems, including taxis or jitneys. Decision-makers support the concept of dial-a-ride programs but worry that the per-passenger costs may be prohibitive.

Ironically, communities across the country already subsidize transportation service for the overwhelming majority of the citizenry. The decision-making community easily accepts the idea of large subsidies to the private automobile user (for example, trust funds for highway construction, oil depletion allowances and gasoline tax write-offs, selective automobile insurance rates for certain classifications of drivers),[22] and the decision-making community has readily accepted the responsibility to underwrite the costs of public transportation

TABLE 6.8

"Would You Favor Subsidization of Neighborhood Transportation Systems, Such as Jitneys or Taxi Services, if They Were to Provide Reduced Fares for the Elderly?"
(percent responding "yes")

Positional Characteristics of the Decision-Makers	
Position in the Policy Process	
Legislators (N = 71)	72
Agency administrators (N = 70)	89
Service delivery personnel (N = 70)	100
Corporate directors of personnel (N = 35)	69
Union local presidents (N = 35)	86
Advocates for the aged (N = 35)	83
Responsibility for Aging Programs	
Primary function (N = 85)	91
Important but not central function (N = 88)	82
Minor function (N = 143)	81
Area of Program Expertise	
Health (N = 37)	92
Mental health (N = 23)	91
Housing (N = 29)	90
Employment (N = 92)	78
Income maintenance (N = 26)	81
Recreation/leisure (N = 18)	100
Senior citizens affairs (N = 49)	86
Generalists (N = 42)	74
Personal Characteristics of the Decision-Makers	
Age of the Respondent	
Under 45 (N = 98)	86
45-54 (N = 98)	83
55-64 (N = 90)	86
65 and over (N = 30)	77
Sex of the Respondent	
Male (N = 230)	80
Female (N = 86)	93
Ethnicity of the Respondent	
White (N = 235)	81
Minority (N = 81)	93
Educational Level of the Respondent	
High school graduate or less (N = 42)	86
Some college (N = 64)	81
College graduate (N = 99)	86
Postcollege professional education (N = 111)	83
Total (N = 316)	84

Source: Compiled by the author.

systems. Yet the decision-makers balk at the prospect of underwriting transportation programs to serve the most frail and handicapped members of the population with the door-to-door service that is required to satisfy their special transit needs. Transportation is a social commodity; it is the "bloodline" of society. For that reason, private as well as public transportation has been heavily subsidized in this country.

Until the policy statement issued by Congress in the 1970 amendments to the Urban Mass Transit Assistance Act, which read, "It is hereby declared to be the national policy that elderly and handicapped persons have the same right as other persons to utilize mass transportation facilities and services," the implicit transportation policy of the country was to subsidize only that 90 to 95 percent of the citizenry who could operate a car or ride public transit. For the 5 to 10 percent of the population too incapacitated to drive a car or use public transit, neither the government nor the community was under a legal or seemingly even a moral obligation to provide transportation services suited to their special needs. The policy statement issued in the 1970 amendments thus constituted a major step forward in the conceptualization of the rights of elderly and handicapped citizens to public transportation in this country. The commitment of dollars to support the requisite door-to-door services as an adjunct to the primary public transportation system in communities across the country has been slow to follow, however. Door-to-door transportation service for the handicapped population, like home health care programs and in-home support services, is still challenged as a legitimate expense in the public sector.

Although demand-response transportation programs are clearly a valuable community service, they have yet to amass the institutional support at the community level that is necessary to guarantee the programs' survival more than a few years. Public officials overwhelmingly approve of the idea for such programs, but demand-response transportation programs tend to be very costly to operate, and they almost always fade into oblivion when federal subsidies dry up. The federal government provides two to three years of initial funding for these transportation projects in order to get them started, with the expectation that the local communities will continue to finance the new demand-response programs after they have become fully established. But local communities are consistently unwilling or unable to finance the programs in the absence of these sizable federal subsidies, and hence the programs lapse at the end of the research and demonstration project phase. Most demand-response transportation programs simply never achieve the requisite stage of institutionalization where they could legitimately be defined as demand-response transportation service systems serving an adjunct role to the central public transportation system in the community.

What remains now is to develop the commitment to finance neighborhood demand-response transportation service as an institutionalized system that is as permanent in structure and operation as the central public and mass transit systems that have operated in U.S. cities for a century or more. When financial commitment follows upon the growing public moral support for providing public transportation to all citizens, then and only then will the transportation needs of the frail and handicapped elderly be adequately served by community transportation systems. It is not a matter of technology; it is a matter of social priorities and economic commitments. It is a political decision to be made at the federal, state, and local levels of government, and it is a decision that can be influenced by persuasive lobbying both by and on behalf of the elderly.

Decision-makers are aware of the elderly's transportation problems and perceive the need for demand-response transportation service to serve regularly the special transit needs of certain elderly and handicapped citizens in the community. But persuasive lobbying is required to convince the legislators and public agency personnel that the rights of these citizens to public transportation service are no less than those of any other citizen in the community who is already heavily subsidized as a car owner or a transit rider. The moral argument must be made strong enough to overcome the economic concerns of the decision-makers. As the sentiment in the decision-making community runs strongly in favor of developing special transit programs for elderly residents, the elderly and their advocates begin their promotional campaign with good advantage. But the task of persuasion remains theirs. Institutionalized demand-response programs will appear in their communities only at the stubborn insistence of their rights to adequate (or if not adequate, at least parity) transportation service.

The decision-makers in this sample think of the elderly almost exclusively in transit-dependent terms. They appear little aware of the special problems confronting the elderly driver, and they seem even less concerned about providing assistance to the elderly car owner that would enable him to keep the transportation-independent status he enjoys so long as he is able to continue operating his car. By not providing income supplements to low- and moderate-income elderly who find the expense of maintaining a private vehicle too prohibitive, the decision-makers seem to be implicitly fostering premature transit dependence in the elderly population.

Conceivably, decision-makers would like to lure the elderly out of their cars and attract them to public transportation instead; and conceivably, they rationally propose to accomplish this transition by making public transportation convenient and easy to use. Or, alternatively, the decision-makers' emphasis on public transportation solutions to the elderly's transportation problems may be attributed to their misperception of the current measure of transit dependence in the elderly population and their consequent belief that by improving public transportation service to the transit-dependent elderly they are in effect improving the transportation situation of the vast majority rather than a small minority of the elderly. In the latter policy-making context, existing transportation policy would inadvertently rather than rationally foster transit dependence in the elderly population, and the subsequent growth of transit dependence in the aged population could be an undesirable spin-off of existing policies rather than a consciously sought outcome of rationally designed programs.

The alternative interpretations of the decision-making context have considerable implications for advocacy on behalf of future program outcomes. If decision-makers are not deliberately trying to foster transit dependence in the elderly population, then advocates may be able to muster support in the decision-making community for additional subsidies to low- and moderate-income elderly households in the interest of underwriting sustained transit independence in the elderly age group. The advocates' first task would be to reeducate key decision-makers about the relative size of the elderly population who continue to operate their own cars and to underscore for the decision-makers the implicit drive of existing policies to foster premature transit dependence in the elderly population.

If, on the other hand, decision-makers are consciously seeking to entice the elderly out of their cars into the public transportation system, then advocates may better devote their efforts to spurring decision-makers to consider barrier-free mass transit and supplemental demand-response neighborhood transportation systems that can adequately serve the transit needs of all elderly in the community. The advocates' task would become one of reminding the decision-makers of their public responsibility to provide adequate public transportation to elderly residents in the community who have been pressured into giving up their private transportation means.

Only one in four of these decision-makers (26 percent) believed that transportation would become a rallying issue that would spur the elderly on to greater political activism on behalf of their own interests (see Table 9.4). But, without an active lobbying effort by the elderly and their advocates, it is unlikely that transportation programs better suited to their special transportation needs will soon emerge. The elderly and their advocates have the task of persuading community decision-makers that elderly residents, even the most infirmed or handicapped, have a moral, and increasingly a legal, right to parity private as well as public transportation service in their community. The development of an integrated package of transportation programs and policies that will ensure all elderly residents adequate transportation at least to destination in the surrounding community will come only at the insistence of the elderly and their advocates.

NOTES

1. *Toward a National Policy on Aging: Proceedings of the 1971 White House Conference on Aging*, November 28-December 2, 1971 (Washington, D.C.: U.S. Government Printing Office, 1973), p. 65.

2. U.S. Congress, Senate, *Developments in Aging, 1969*, Report of the U.S. Senate Special Committee on Aging, 91st Cong., 2d sess. (Washington, D.C.: U.S. Government Printing Office, 1970).

3. U.S. Congress, Senate, *Older Americans and Transportation: A Crisis in Mobility*, Hearings before the Special Committee on Aging, 91st Cong., 2d sess. (Washington, D.C.: U.S. Government Printing Office, 1970).

4. K. H. Schaeffer and Elliot Sclar, *Access for All: Transportation and Urban Growth* (Baltimore: Penguin Books, 1975); John C. Falcocchio and Edmund J. Cantilli, *Transportation and the Disadvantaged* (Lexington, Mass.: Heath, 1974); William G. Bell and William T. Olsen, "An Overview of Public Transportation and the Elderly: New Directions for Social Policy," *Gerontologist* 14, no. 4 (August 1974): 324-30; Edmund J. Cantilli and June L. Shmelzer, eds., *Transportation and Aging: Selected Issues* (Washington, D.C.: U.S. Government Printing Office, 1970).

5. Frances M. Carp, "On Becoming an Ex-Driver: Prospect and Retrospect," Pt. I, *Gerontologist* 11, no. 2 (Summer 1971): 101-03; Frances M. Carp, "Walking as a Means of Transportation for Retired People," Pt. I, *Gerontologist* 11, no. 2 (Summer 1971): 104-11; Frances M. Carp, "Public Transit and Retired People," in Cantilli and Shmelzer, *Transportation and Aging*, pp. 82-92.

6. Bell and Olsen, "An Overview of Public Transportation and the Elderly," p. 325; Frances M. Carp, "The Mobility of Retired People," in Cantilli and Shmelzer, *Transportation and Aging*, pp. 23-41.

7. U.S. Congress, Senate, *Transportation and the Elderly: Problems and Progress*, Pt. 1, Hearings before the Special Committee on Aging on February 25, 1974, 93d Cong., 2d sess. (Washington, D.C.: U.S. Government Printing Office, 1974), p. 4.

8. Ibid., p. 29.

9. Ibid., p. 163.

10. Schaeffer and Sclar, *Access for All: Transportation and Urban Growth*, p. 103.

11. Thomas Tissue, *Social Class and the Senior Citizen Center* (Washington, D.C.: Administration on Aging, Department of Health, Education and Welfare, 1969).

12. Joseph S. Revis, *Transportation: Background and Issues*, 1971 White House Conference on Aging (Washington, D.C.: U.S. Government Printing Office, 1971), pp. 1-2.

13. J. Allen Whitt, "Means of Movement: Some Political Aspects of Modern Transportation Systems" (Paper presented at the 69th Annual Meeting of the American Sociological Association, Montreal, August 29, 1974).

14. Martin Wachs, ed., *Transportation Patterns and Needs of the Elderly Population in Los Angeles* (Los Angeles: University of California at Los Angeles, School of Architecture and Urban Planning, 1974).

15. W. L. Garrison, "Limitations and Constraints of Existing Transportation Systems as Applied to the Elderly," in Cantilli and Shmelzer, *Transportation and Aging*, p. 100.

16. Carp, "Public Transit and Retired People," p. 91.

17. J. J. Jontig, ed., *Transportation for the Elderly and Handicapped*, Transit Advisory Committee Report (Los Angeles: Southern California Association of Governments, November 20, 1974), p. 16.

18. This is the conclusion reached by the Southern California Association of Governments in its cost-benefit analyses. It concluded that the vast majority of the elderly and handicapped population (more than 95 percent) could be adequately served by the implementation of a barrier-free public transit system, while the remaining 5 percent, representing the most frail and handicapped passengers, would best be served by the implementation of a supplementary demand-response system. Ibid.

19. U.S. Congress, Senate, *Transportation and the Elderly: Problems and Prospects*, Pt. 5, Hearings before the Special Committee on Aging, 94th Cong., 1st sess. (Washington, D.C.: U.S. Government Printing Office, July 29, 1975), p. 376.

20. Wachs, *Transportation Patterns and Needs*.

21. Ibid.

22. Schaeffer and Sclar, *Access for All*, pp. 134-44.

7 Employment and Retirement in the Later Years: The Aged's Opportunities for Continued Involvement

Retirement is essentially a twentieth-century innovation of industrial societies. It was not until well into the 1900s that the cumulative impact of various forces set in motion by the industrial revolution between 1750 and 1850 created the social and economic conditions in the modernizing countries that were essential to supporting a nonworking aged population.[1] Medical breakthroughs in these technologically advanced countries meant that increasing numbers in their populations survived well into old age. The numbers who were simply too old or incapacitated to continue working productively in the labor force increased substantially, and governments were increasingly pressed to find some way to support them outside the labor force. At the same time, technological advances (for example, automation) in the economic sectors of these societies fostered rapid economic growth and provided the necessary economic surplus in the social system to support through various income transfer programs older and disabled workers who were unable to continue earning their own livelihood.

The Social Security Act of 1935 represented the first attempt to institutionalize retirement or withdrawal from the labor force for aging workers in U.S. society. As twentieth-century technology streamlined the means of economic production and machines replaced men in jobs, the competition for jobs grew keener. Employers sought younger workers, who they assumed were better trained and healthier and hence more productive than older workers. Assured that older workers would be eligible for retirement benefits under social security, business and industrial organizations increasingly applied mandatory retirement policies to ensure a turnover of jobs from older to younger workers. Discouraged that many older workers were still reluctant to relinquish their jobs even when eligible for social security benefits, many employers and unions developed private pension plans to raise the prospective retirement incomes of their older employees to levels where the workers would finally be enticed to retire in their early 60s or even earlier.

The combined efforts of government, unions, and business management have quite successfully fashioned retirement into a normal and anticipated stage of the life cycle. The percentage of men continuing in active employment beyond age 65 has dropped from 67 percent in 1900 to 20 percent in 1974.[2] Moreover, as of 1970, more than half (53 percent) of the new social security beneficiaries were retiring before age 65.[3] The emergence of the institution of retirement implying a prolonged postemployment stage of life as a normal and expected part of the human life cycle thus is quite literally a social invention of only the last 100 years of human history.[4]

Although the social institution of retirement is relatively new and hence still evolving, it has become a permanent part of the fabric of U.S. society, and as such, it must be seriously examined in the projection of social and economic growth moving into the twenty-first century. It is thus important to understand how decision-makers responsible for formulating and implementing social policy for the aging segments of the population conceptualize retirement in U.S. society. How do they evaluate the increasing institutionalization of the retirement process? For example, do they perceive the transition from working to retired status as a relatively smooth or severely traumatic one for most workers? What do they think about the increasing application of mandatory retirement age policies in the economic sector? How do they assess the macro- and microsocial implications of the apparently increasing trend toward early retirement in this country? These are important policy questions that will be receiving increasing attention in the last quarter of this century in preparation for the year 2010, when the first of the postwar "baby boom" cohort reaches age 65 and swells the ranks of retirees to numbers heretofore unimagined.

The decision-makers sampled here are among those who will be debating these issues in future years and formulating new policies that will impact on the future institutionalization of the retirement process in U.S. society. Their perspectives on the problems of retirement in this country will thus constitute an important backdrop against which various specific policy issues and proposals will be debated. This chapter examines how these decision-makers perceived the problems attendant to the retirement transition. How much freedom of choice is involved in the older worker's decision to retire? What opportunities exist for continued employment past age 65? What other options besides employment exist to give older people an active and continuing role in community life after retirement?

Specific policy issues that will receive attention in this chapter include the desirability of mandatory retirement practices, the feasibility of older worker retraining programs, the implications of early retirement policies for individuals and the society, and the need for pre-retirement preparation programs. As a prelude to the discussion of those issues, however, it is important to understand decision-makers' perceptions of the nature of the retirement event in the lives of older workers, because their perception of the problem can be expected to influence their policy stance.

DECISION-MAKERS' PERCEPTIONS OF THE RETIREMENT EVENT

Retirement is frequently characterized as a time for social and personal reorganization for the individual who must reshape his life without work as the fulcrum of his daily activities. Posited on assumptions about the centrality of the work role in shaping an individual's self-concept and social identity, in structuring his lifestyle, and in integrating him into the social fabric of the society, the model hypothesizes that the individual who relinquishes this central work role necessarily suffers social and personal disorganization. Cut off from the economic, social, and psychological benefits that derive from having a stable work role in society, the retiree is presumed to face substantial loss of opportunities for social participation with a commensurate loss in social identity, as well as to suffer considerable personal trauma or psychosocial disorientation over this inability to continue his involvement in the socially productive endeavors that earlier gave his life meaning and value.[5]

Any large-scale reorganization of life is to be considered potentially traumatic for the individual. The crisis implications of the retirement transition are heightened, however, by what many gerontologists have referred to as the essential "rolelessness" or "normlessness" of old age.[6] At the very time when the individual is called upon by his retirement to forge substantial changes in his lifestyle, experts point out that he is given few viable models or guidelines for what he should accomplish with the change to retired status or how to accomplish the necessary changes. The individual thus arrives at retirement with little preparation for the changes he must make, thereby aggravating the potential crisis inherent in the outwardly simple act of his terminating employment. Many have suggested the need for greater "socialization to old age" in order to facilitate transition from working to retired status.

Given the emphasis in U.S. culture on the value of work and meaningful social engagement, there is considerable intuitive appeal for this crisis model of the retirement transition in U.S. society.

Indeed, for many years, gerontological research seemed to confirm substantial problems for many U.S. workers in adjusting to retired status. The first studies on retirement relied on cross-sectional data that compared retirees and still-employed workers at the same point in time on a number of health, activity, and morale measures. The results quite consistently revealed that retirees on the average had poorer health, lower morale, and so forth than did workers of the same age who were still employed. The conclusion of these studies was that the act of retirement itself was a direct contributor to the consistently disadvantaged status of the retirees vis-a-vis the employed.

Beginning in the 1960s, however, research findings from longitudinal research designs that followed a single panel of employees through the last few years of working life into the first few years of retirement began to negate the impression that retirement constitutes a crisis event in the lives of most workers. After a six-year study that monitored the adjustment to retirement made by more than 2,800 older workers (aged 63 to 65 at first interview) who were employed in diverse occupations, the senior researchers concluded:

> Retirement does not have the broad negative consequences for the older person that we had expected. The cessation of the work role results in a sharp reduction in income, but there is no significant increase in "worry" about money in the impact year of retirement. There is no sharp decline in health, feelings of usefulness, or satisfaction in life after retirement. Neither do respondents suddenly think of themselves as "old" when they stop working.[7]

They challenged the notion that retirement precipitates a crisis for retiring individuals because of the sudden disruption of adult role set configurations. They concluded that the typical adult role set contains many statuses or positions, the work role being only one among the many, and that, in fact, most older people handle role realignment upon cessation of working quite adequately (at least insofar as physical and mental health indicators confirm). The researchers also challenged the notion of retirement and old age as a roleless stage of life, stressing that continuity rather than discontinuity and crisis characterize the retirement transition for the majority of the working population.

Despite mounting scientific evidence to the contrary, the decision-makers in this sample still believed that retirement poses a crisis for many, if not most of the older workers in the U.S. labor force. The 316 respondents were asked to speculate about the potential crisis that might be created for some individuals on the occasion of their retirement from the labor force: "Retirement is usually associated with many changes in a working person's lifestyle. Do you think that retirement precipitates a crisis in the lives of most, many, some or few workers?" Nearly one half of the sample of decision-makers (45 percent) believed that retirement occasioned a crisis for most workers leaving the labor force, and more than three quarters (76 percent) believed that at least many workers would confront a serious personal crisis upon their retirement (see Table 7.1).

Advocates for the aged were the most likely of the original six subsamples to believe that retirement poses a crisis for most, or at least many, retiring workers. Union local presidents and corporate directors of personnel, on the other hand, were the least likely to define retirement crises as that widespread among older workers in the labor force. Fully 40 percent of the union local presidents and 30 percent of the corporate personnel directors insisted that only a rather small minority of the retiring workers actually confronts personal crises because of the retirement transition. It is worth noting that the business and labor officials have their closest professional contact with older persons who are still actively employed and hence merely looking ahead to retirement, whereas the advocates for the aged have their closest professional contact with older persons who are already retired and currently confronting the realities of retirement living.

It was true in all sectors of the decision-making community that the more closely involved with aging programs a decision-maker was, the more likely he was to believe that retirement crises were widespread in the older population. Mental health counselors, senior citizens affairs officials, and senior citizen club directors were particularly concerned about the prevalence of retirement adjustment problems. In contrast, decision-makers most closely involved with establishing employment and retirement policies--retirement income program administrators, employment counselors, personnel managers, union officials, and legislators staffing employment/retirement policy committees in local, state, and national legislatures--tended to deemphasize the incidence of retirement crises among older workers.

Social science has rather consistently documented that individuals who retire voluntarily from the labor force show higher morale and life satisfaction in retirement than do those who have been retired involuntarily from the labor force.[8] Perhaps the decision-makers' perceptions that retirement poses a crisis for many or most workers is linked to their perception that retirement is typically an involuntary decision for these individuals and therefore

TABLE 7.1

"Retirement Causes a Crisis in the Lives of Many Workers"
(percent responding in agreement)

Positional Characteristics of the Decision-Makers	
Position in the Policy Process	
Legislators (N = 71)	76
Agency administrators (N = 70)	80
Service delivery personnel (N = 70)	79
Corporate directors of personnel (N = 35)	69
Union local presidents (N = 35)	60
Advocates for the aged (N = 35)	86
Responsibility for Aging Programs	
Primary function (N = 85)	84
Important but not central function (N = 88)	80
Minor function (N = 143)	69
Area of Program Expertise	
Health (N = 37)	73
Mental Health (N = 23)	83
Housing (N = 29)	72
Employment (N = 92)	66
Income maintenance (N = 26)	73
Recreation/leisure (N = 18)	89
Senior citizens affairs (N = 49)	88
Generalists (N = 42)	81
Personal Characteristics of the Decision-Makers	
Age of the Respondent	
Under 45 (N = 98)	81
45-54 (N = 98)	75
55-64 (N = 90)	70
65 and over (N = 30)	83
Sex of the Respondent	
Male (N = 230)	74
Female (N = 86)	80
Ethnicity of the Respondent	
White (N = 235)	76
Minority (N = 81)	77
Educational Level of the Respondent	
High school graduate or less (N = 42)	64
Some college (N = 64)	72
College graduate (N = 99)	77
Postcollege professional education (N = 111)	82
Total (N = 316)	76

Source: Compiled by the author.

a situation the older employees would tend to dislike and resist. The overwhelming majority of the sample of decision-makers (71 percent) said that most workers retire "because they are required to by company policy," in contrast to a mere 17 percent who maintained that most workers retired "because they want to." A very small minority (4 percent) identified poor health as the main reason for workers' retirement and an additional 7 percent cited some combination of the aforementioned reasons (see Table 7.2).

As suggested, decision-makers who perceived retirement as a crisis for many or most workers were significantly more likely to identify forced retirement by company policy as the primary reason most workers retire than were decision-makers who believed retirement poses a crisis for only a small minority of workers in the labor force. At the same time, decision-makers who deemphasized the incidence of retirement crises were almost twice as likely as the decision-makers who believed the retirement crisis to be more widespread to say that the decision to retire most often occurred as the individual's own option.*

In this context, it becomes more apparent why the union local presidents were the least likely of all the decision-maker subsamples to consider retirement crises widespread. They were the most likely to perceive the retirement decision as voluntary. Whereas approximately three quarters of all the other subsamples reported that mandatory retirement policies were the most common reason for retirement, less than one third of the union officials (31 percent) maintained that company policies promoted involuntary retirements. In contrast, nearly one half of the union leaders (43 percent) identified the retirement decision as purely elective on the individual's part; less than 20 percent of all other subsamples believed this desirable situation prevailed. In other segments of the decision-making community, too, perceptions of the voluntary versus involuntary nature of the retirement decision paralleled decision-makers' perceptions

---

*Among those who believed that retirement crises were widespread in the older worker population, 14 percent said older workers retire because they want to, 5 percent said they retire for reasons of poor health, and 76 percent said they retire because they are required to retire by company policy. By contrast, among those decision-makers who believed that retirement crises affected only a minority of retiring workers, 27 percent said that older workers retire because they want to, 4 percent said they retire because of failing health, and 58 percent said they retire only because they are forced to retire by company policy.

TABLE 7.2

Decision-Makers' Perceptions of the Primary Motivation in the Retirement Decisions of Older Workers

Decision-Makers' Positional and Personal Characteristics	They Want to (percent)
Positional Characteristics of the Decision-Makers	
Position in the Policy Process	
Legislators (N = 71)	20
Agency administrators (N = 70)	4
Service delivery personnel (N = 70)	10
Corporate directors of personnel (N = 35)	17
Union local presidents (N = 35)	43
Advocates for the aged (N = 35)	14
Responsibility for Aging Programs	
Primary function (N = 85)	12
Important but not central function (N = 88)	18
Minor function (N = 143)	19
Area of Program Expertise	
Health (N = 37)	8
Mental health (N = 23)	4
Housing (N = 29)	3
Employment (N = 92)	29
Income maintenance (N = 26)	27
Recreation/leisure (N = 18)	6
Senior citizens affairs (N = 49)	14
Generalists (N = 42)	12
Personal Characteristics of the Decision-Makers	
Age of the Respondent	
Under 45 (N = 98)	14
45-54 (N = 98)	13
55-64 (N = 90)	22
65 and over (N = 30)	20
Sex of the Respondent	
Male (N = 230)	22
Female (N = 86)	4
Ethnicity of the Respondent	
White (N = 235)	19
Minority (N = 81)	10
Educational Level of the Respondent	
High school graduate or less (N = 42)	26
Some college (N = 64)	19
College graduate (N = 99)	16
Postcollege professional education (N = 111)	12
Total (N = 316)	17

Source: Compiled by the author.

What Is the Primary Reason Older Workers Retire?		
Forced to by Poor Health (percent)	Forced to by Company Policy (percent)	Combinations of These Reasons (percent)
3	70	6
4	76	10
6	80	4
0	74	9
9	31	17
6	80	0
6	79	4
6	68	7
3	68	10
14	81	3
9	78	9
3	86	7
3	55	12
4	54	15
6	89	0
6	80	0
5	77	5
4	74	7
5	71	10
4	64	8
3	77	0
1	65	9
6	86	3
4	69	7
6	77	7
7	57	10
6	64	11
4	74	5
3	78	6
4	71	7

regarding how widespread retirement crises were. Thus, categoric decision-makers, consistent with their concern for the far-reaching proportions of the retirement crisis, were more likely than generic decision-makers to emphasize mandatory retirement policies and less likely to emphasize free choice in the retirement decision. Similarly, administrators of employment retirement policies and programs, who were more likely to minimize the retirement crisis, were nearly three times more likely than other decision-maker groups to suggest that individuals generally retire by choice.

Given the dual perceptions held by the majority of these decision-makers, first, that most workers are forced to retire by their employers' mandatory retirement policies, and second, that most workers face a crisis in their personal lives when they cease working, it is not surprising to learn that the decision-makers believed that the overwhelming majority of older persons would prefer to continue working at least part time rather than retire from the labor force. One half of all the decision-makers (50 percent) estimated that three out of four or even more of the older population would prefer to continue working at least part time (see Table 7.3). As predicted, decision-makers who identified an element of compulsion in the individual's decision to retire, be it due to poor health or mandatory retirement policies, generally maintained that the overwhelming majority of the elderly retired population (three quarters or more) would prefer to keep working, whereas decision-makers who perceived the retirement decision as strictly voluntary for most workers believed that only a small minority of the retired population (one quarter or less) would prefer to keep working.* Similarly, decision-maker groups who had minimized the prevalence of a transition crisis for retirees also significantly minimized estimates of the proportion of elderly who would prefer to keep working.

Thus, union local presidents estimated the proportion of elderly who would like to continue working to be considerably lower than did their colleagues in the decision-making community. Union local presidents were twice as likely as the rest of the decision-making community to aver that only one quarter of the elderly or less would desire to keep working at least part time. Their picture of the

---

*The majority (51 percent) of those who believed that most older workers retire because they want to retire maintained that one quarter or less of the retirees would prefer to keep working. The majority of those who believed that older workers retire involuntarily because of poor health or company policy conversely maintained that three out of four or more of the retirees would prefer to keep working.

TABLE 7.3

"What Proportion of Older People Would You Estimate Would Prefer to Keep Working, at Least Part Time, after Retirement?"
(percent estimating three quarters of the aged or more)

Positional Characteristics of the Decision-Makers	
Position in the Policy Process	
Legislators (N = 71)	55
Agency administrators (N = 70)	46
Service delivery personnel (N = 70)	59
Corporate directors of personnel (N = 35)	46
Union local presidents (N = 35)	40
Advocates for the aged (N = 35)	49
Responsibility for Aging Programs	
Primary function (N = 85)	44
Important but not central function (N = 88)	51
Minor function (N = 143)	54
Area of Program Expertise	
Health (N = 37)	51
Mental health (N = 23)	65
Housing (N = 29)	55
Employment (N = 92)	47
Income maintenance (N = 26)	50
Recreation/leisure (N = 18)	56
Senior citizens affairs (N = 49)	49
Generalists (N = 42)	57
Personal Characteristics of the Decision-Makers	
Age of the Respondent	
Under 45 (N = 98)	57
45-54 (N = 98)	55
55-64 (N = 90)	39
65 and over (N = 30)	47
Sex of the Respondent	
Male (N = 230)	50
Female (N = 86)	51
Ethnicity of the Respondent	
White (N = 235)	47
Minority (N = 81)	59
Educational Level of the Respondent	
High school graduate or less (N = 42)	43
Some college (N = 64)	44
College graduate (N = 99)	55
Postcollege professional education (N = 111)	53
Total (N = 316)	50

Source: Compiled by the author.

retirement transition as founded in the workers' own voluntary decision and hence relatively problem free may accord well with the experience of their own union members, who, after 40-odd years of hard manual labor, may indeed be looking forward to a life of relaxation and leisure in retirement and who may have little or no desire to continue working even on a part-time basis.

When asked why older people would prefer to keep working, the majority of decision-makers (51 percent) replied that the employment was primarily for the purpose of remaining active; only 19 percent contended the primary purpose was to earn extra money to supplement deficient retirement incomes (see Table 7.4). An additional 29 percent asserted that both factors were important motivations in the elderly's seeking a continued role in the labor force. Nearly twice as many of the decision-makers thus averred that staying active was an important reason for the elderly remaining in the labor force as asserted earning extra income was a primary motivation.

Advocates for the aged were the least likely of the subsamples to emphasize the activity element in the elderly's persistence in the employment role. Rather, these advocates (who more than all the other subsamples stressed retirement as a widespread crisis precipitated by the mandatory retirement practices of the employers) were considerably more likely to believe that the elderly desire to remain in the labor force primarily because they need to supplement their income. In fact, the advocates for the aged were the only subsample to emphasize financial motivations more than activity incentives.

The corporate directors of personnel and union local presidents continued to exhibit differences in their perceptions of the retirement transition that are interesting to explore. The union local presidents, the only subsample that had emphasized the limited incidence of crisis at the retirement transition and in the plurality cited the individual's option in the retirement decision, were significantly more likely than all the other subsamples with the exception of the advocates for the aged to believe that the need for extra income was a significant factor motivating elderly persons to stay in the labor force. In contrast, the corporate directors of personnel, who had underscored retirement as a crisis because it was most often a decision forced on the individual by his employer, were the most likely of the subsamples to believe the elderly person will seek to remain employed at least part time because he wants to stay active, not because he needs extra income. Thus, the union local presidents perceived a limited incidence of crises in the retirement transition and characterized the existing crises, at least in an important part, financial in nature; in contrast, the corporate directors of personnel perceived more widespread crises occasioned by retirement that they characterized

TABLE 7.4

Decision-Makers' Perceptions of the Reasons Why the Aged Would Prefer to Continue Working

Decision-Makers' Positional and Personal Characteristics	Why Would the Elderly Prefer to Keep Working? They Need the Money (percent)	They Prefer to Remain Active (percent)	Both Reasons Are Important (percent)
Positional Characteristics of the Decision-Makers			
Position in the Policy Process			
Legislators (N = 71)	20	48	30
Agency administrators (N = 70)	14	51	34
Service delivery personnel (N = 70)	16	60	24
Corporate directors of personnel (N = 35)	6	60	34
Union local presidents (N = 35)	31	51	17
Advocates for the aged (N = 35)	37	31	31
Responsibility for Aging Programs			
Primary function (N = 85)	25	41	34
Important but not central function (N = 88)	16	59	24
Minor function (N = 143)	18	52	29
Area of Program Expertise			
Health (N = 37)	8	70	22
Mental health (N = 23)	13	61	26
Housing (N = 29)	7	52	41
Employment (N = 92)	20	54	26
Income maintenance (N = 26)	27	58	12
Recreation/leisure (N = 18)	28	44	28
Senior citizens affairs (N = 49)	35	29	37
Generalists (N = 42)	14	48	36
Personal Characteristics of the Decision-Makers			
Age of the Respondent			
Under 45 (N = 98)	16	51	33
45-54 (N = 98)	23	53	21
55-64 (N = 90)	18	54	28
65 and over (N = 30)	20	37	43
Sex of the Respondent			
Male (N = 230)	20	56	29
Female (N = 86)	16	50	28
Ethnicity of the Respondent			
White (N = 235)	18	49	31
Minority (N = 81)	22	57	21
Educational Level of the Respondent			
High school graduate or less (N = 42)	21	45	33
Some college (N = 64)	20	55	23
College graduate (N = 99)	23	51	26
Postcollege professional education (N=111)	14	51	33
Total (N = 316)	19	51	29

Source: Compiled by the author.

almost exclusively as a problem of social-psychological adjustment in retired status.

Categoric decision-makers who dealt almost exclusively with elderly persons in their jobs were more likely than decision-makers who worked less closely with the elderly to cite the importance of financial needs in the elderly's quest for employment. Hence, senior citizens affairs officials and senior citizens club directors underscored the financial motives more than other decision-makers did.

DECISION-MAKERS' PERCEPTIONS OF THE RETIREMENT TRANSITION COMPARED TO THE AGED'S OWN DESCRIPTIONS

To what extent are the decision-makers' majority perceptions of the retirement transition accurate reflections of the experiences that the elderly themselves report? To begin with, the decision-makers seem to vastly overestimate the proportion of involuntary retirements. Nearly three quarters of the 316 decision-makers presumed that most older workers retire because they are required to by company policy. In the companion USC survey of elderly residents in Los Angeles County, 42 percent of the 312 who reported themselves as retired said that they had retired because they wanted to retire. Nearly one third of the elderly respondents (31 percent) identified poor health as the primary reason for their retirement, but only one in nine (11 percent) suggested that the mandatory retirement policy of their employer had been the primary reason. Data from the nationwide Harris poll confirm these findings. They reported that 61 percent of those over age 65 who were retired indicated that they had retired by choice, whereas 37 percent of the retirees maintained that they had been forced to retire (exact reason not specified).[9] Hence, the decision-makers collectively appeared to far underestimate the prevalence of voluntary retirements among older workers. Nevertheless the decision-makers were quite properly sensitive to the fact that many workers do not retire for strictly voluntary reasons, although the decision-makers generally incorrectly ascribed the element of compulsion to mandatory retirement policies, whereas older workers attributed their involuntary retirement to failing health.

Recognizing that the decision-makers generally failed to appreciate the proportion of voluntary retirements among older workers, it is not surprising to learn that these decision-makers also far overestimated the proportion of retirees who would prefer to continue working at least part time. The Harris poll was conducted in mid-1974 at the height of the recession. They found 12 percent of the elderly population employed at least part time, 6 percent unemployed, and 63 percent retired (an additional 17 percent were housewives). Of the 69 percent who were retired or unemployed, 65 percent asserted that they would not like to return to work; in contrast, nearly one third (31 percent) reported that they would like to return to work and another 4 percent said they might consider returning to work under selected circumstances.[10] Data from the USC survey of Los Angeles elderly residents, which was conducted at approximately the same time, confirm the Harris poll results.

At the time of the interviews, nearly one quarter (23 percent) of the elderly respondents were already working at least part time. Among those elderly not working, more than one third (35 percent) said they would prefer to be working; of that group, nearly one quarter (23 percent) affirmed that they would like to find full-time employment. One quarter of the elderly who expressed a desire to return to work cited the need for extra income as the primary motivation. A considerably larger percentage (39 percent) maintained that they sought employment primarily for the reason of staying active. An additional 36 percent identified both reasons as important motivations. In all, three quarters of the elderly who seek employment do so at least in part in order to stay active, whereas a little less than two thirds (61 percent) suggested that financial considerations were important.

Because the decision-makers as a group overestimated the prevalence of retirement crises and did not correctly understand the factors typically precipitating the workers' retirement decision, the decision-makers typically overestimated the elderly's desires to continue working and misjudged the elderly's motivations in seeking a continued employment role. The implications of the decision-makers' misperceptions on retirement policies and program planning are the subject of the remainder of this chapter.

DECISION-MAKERS' FEELINGS ABOUT MANDATORY RETIREMENT PRACTICES

Given that most of the decision-makers in the sample believed that retirement is forced on older workers by the employer's mandatory retirement policy and that the transition from working to retired status is traumatic for at least many workers, it is not surprising that these decision-makers overwhelmingly agreed, "There should be no required retirement age; older people should be allowed to work as long as they want to and are able to." Nearly three quarters (74 percent) of the decision-makers expressed agreement with that statement; more than half (51 percent) even expressed strong agreement with it (see Table 7.5). One in twelve of the decision-makers strongly disagreed and one in six mildly disagreed with the statement, implying thereby at least some endorsement of employers' mandatory retirement practices. As anticipated, those who emphasized the prevalence of retirement crises also showed greater support for the abolition of mandatory retirement policies.*

Opposition to mandatory retirement practices was stronger in some segments of the decision-making community than others. For example, corporate directors of personnel, who are responsible for the execution of their companies' mandatory retirement provisions, were the most in favor of retaining those employment practices. Similarly, employment counselors and retirement income specialists were relatively more supportive of employers' mandatory retirement practices. In contrast, advocates for the aged, who purport to represent the elderly's point of view, were particularly strongly opposed to those employment policies. Decision-makers who themselves were elderly were the most strongly opposed to mandatory retirement among all the decision-makers interviewed in this study.

On the issue of abolishing mandatory retirement, these decision-makers and the community residents seemed to agree on the whole. In response to the identical statement--"There should be no required retirement age; older people should be allowed to work as long as they want to and are able to"--Los Angeles County residents aged 45 to 74 registered levels of support for the elimination of such practices, similar to their decision-makers. More than eight out of ten (81 percent) of these community residents agreed that mandatory retirement practices should be eliminated. Only 11 percent voiced disagreement with the statement, thereby implying support for mandatory retirement policies; and an additional 8 percent of the sample guarded their response with "depends." Middle-aged (45 to 54 years of age), pre-retirement (55 to 64), and elderly (65 and over) respondents expressed virtually identical levels of support for the abolition of mandatory retirement. In a similar question included in the recent nationwide Harris poll, 86 percent of the general public 18 years of age or older agreed that "Nobody should be forced to retire because of age, if he wants to continue working and is still able to do a good job." Even the 18 percent of their sample who reported having some

---

*More than three quarters (78 percent) of the decision-makers who perceived widespread retirement crises agreed that there should be no mandatory retirement age, whereas only two thirds (67 percent) of the decision-makers who perceived a more limited incidence of retirement crises favored abolition of mandatory retirement practices.

TABLE 7.5

"There Should Be No Required Retirement Age; Older People Should Be Allowed to Work as Long as They Want to and Are Able to" (percent responding in agreement)

Positional Characteristics of the Decision-Makers	
Position in the Policy Process	
Legislators (N = 71)	69
Agency administrators (N = 70)	76
Service delivery personnel (N = 70)	81
Corporate directors of personnel (N = 35)	54
Union local presidents (N = 35)	74
Advocates for the aged (N = 35)	83
Responsibility for Aging Programs	
Primary function (N = 85)	85
Important but not central function (N = 88)	74
Minor function (N = 143)	67
Area of Program Expertise	
Health (N = 37)	86
Mental health (N = 23)	91
Housing (N = 29)	93
Employment (N = 92)	64
Income maintenance (N = 26)	46
Recreation/leisure (N = 18)	83
Senior citizens affairs (N = 49)	84
Generalists (N = 42)	62
Personal Characteristics of the Decision-Makers	
Age of the Respondent	
Under 45 (N = 98)	73
45-54 (N = 98)	68
55-64 (N = 90)	74
65 and over (N = 30)	90
Sex of the Respondent	
Male (N = 230)	70
Female (N = 86)	84
Ethnicity of the Respondent	
White (N = 235)	71
Minority (N = 81)	80
Educational Level of the Respondent	
High school graduate or less (N = 42)	71
Some college (N = 64)	72
College graduate (N = 99)	76
Postcollege professional education (N = 111)	74
Total (N = 316)	74

Source: Compiled by the author.

responsibility in their position for hiring and firing other employees overwhelmingly agreed (79 percent) in favor of abolishing mandatory retirement policies.[11]

The strong consensus of both public and decision-makers' opinions in opposition to existing mandatory retirement practices helps to explain the growing trend toward abolishing these employment practices. Since the completion of this study, California has adopted a new law prohibiting employers from forcing their employees to retire at age 65 unless the employer can demonstrate that the employee is no longer capable of doing his job.

Nor is California the only state to have adopted a law prohibiting compulsory retirement; 13 other states also have some kind of ban on forced retirement. Additionally, the prospects are good that a new federal law will be enacted in 1978, which, while not eliminating mandatory retirement practices altogether, will place restrictions on the way employers use such policies to force employees to retire. For example, it appears that the federal legislation is going to ban mandatory retirement policies in the private sector if they require the worker to retire before age 70. Although employers may be expected to oppose these legislative developments, the rest of the decision-making community and the general public appear to stand solidly behind these reforms in employers' retirement practices.

DECISION-MAKERS' PERSPECTIVES ON EARLY RETIREMENT PRACTICES

The 316 decision-makers interviewed in this study evidently considered the prospects remote for the relaxation or elimination of mandatory retirement policies and the consequent extension of the elderly's employment careers because they overwhelmingly forecast the continuation of the recent trend toward early retirement for at least the foreseeable future. More than five out of six (84 percent) of the decision-makers believed that the recent trend toward early retirement is going to continue unabated in future decades (see Table 7.6).

The decision-makers who did predict a continuation of the early retirement trend were asked to discuss the implications of early retirement that they perceived for the retiring individual, on the one hand, and the economic and social system, on the other. The decision-makers' responses suggested that they expected more problems than benefits from the early retirement practice, both for the retiring individual and for society supporting the enlarged retired population.

TABLE 7.6

"Do You Think the Trend toward Early Retirement Is Likely to Continue?"
(percent responding "yes")

Positional Characteristics of the Decision-Makers	
Position in the Policy Process	
Legislators (N = 71)	80
Agency administrators (N = 70)	87
Service delivery personnel (N = 70)	86
Corporate directors of personnel (N = 35)	77
Union local presidents (N = 35)	91
Advocates for the aged (N = 35)	74
Responsibility for Aging Programs	
Primary function (N = 85)	80
Important but not central function (N = 88)	85
Minor function (N = 143)	84
Area of Program Expertise	
Health (N = 37)	81
Mental health (N = 23)	83
Housing (N = 29)	76
Employment (N = 92)	87
Income maintenance (N = 26)	88
Recreation/leisure (N = 18)	89
Senior citizens affairs (N = 49)	78
Generalists (N = 42)	83
Personal Characteristics of the Decision-Makers	
Age of the Respondent	
Under 45 (N = 98)	85
45-54 (N = 98)	82
55-64 (N = 90)	88
65 and over (N = 30)	70
Sex of the Respondent	
Male (N = 230)	84
Female (N = 86)	81
Ethnicity of the Respondent	
White (N = 235)	82
Minority (N = 81)	88
Educational Level of the Respondent	
High school graduate or less (N = 42)	79
Some college (N = 64)	78
College graduate (N = 99)	83
Postcollege professional education (N = 111)	88
Total (N = 316)	83

Source: Compiled by the author.

For the retiring individual, the decision-makers first and foremost predicted an increase in leisure time. Considering the decision-makers' dominant impressions of the retirement transition as one characterized by crises and trauma, it is not surprising to learn that more than two out of three of the 147 decision-makers citing increased leisure time resulting from early retirement believed that the increased leisure time would be a problem for the individual. Responses in the same vein as this one offered by a local legislator (I.D. 107) were frequently volunteered, "Boredom. When you are retired, you have nothing to do. That's when you have problems." Only a small minority of the decision-makers perceived the increased leisure time in positive terms for the individual. A union local president (I.D. 506) was one of a few who suggested that "the individual is free to pursue other avenues that are fulfilling." An advocate for the aged (I.D. 621) averred that early retirement is "a second honeymoon for older ones--they can travel and see a different view on life when they are not pinched for time and money." Most, however, believed that the increased leisure time caused by early retirement constituted a problem with which the individual must somehow cope.

Not surprisingly, a large percentage of the decision-makers (nearly one third) believed that early retirees would have problems adjusting to retirement living. The decision-makers perceived these emotional adjustment problems ranging from low morale ("a lot of unhappy people," according to a nursing supervisor in a large hospital, I.D. 304) to more severe mental crises among the retirees (a psychiatric social worker, I.D. 316, predicted "more mental illness because they are not active. The suicide rate will rise"). Agency personnel, both agency and program administrators and service providers, were particularly likely to emphasize such emotional adjustment problems in the early retiree population. In contrast, a mere 2 percent of the decision-maker sample predicted that mental health advantages accrue to early retirees.

In reduced dimensions the same picture emerges in the decision-makers' impressions about the physical health aspects of early retirement. The decision-makers were five times as likely to cite negative as positive outcomes of early retirement on the retiree's physical health status. A hospital director (I.D. 221) noted, for example, "Early retirement puts a burden on health services because the retirees have more time to think about their health and this magnifies their aches and pains." Along with real or imaginary health problems, higher death rates among early retirees was considered a problem. A geriatric nurse (I.D. 302) observed that early retirement means "an earlier death rate due to retirement." Many decision-makers were agreed that early retirement means too much time on the retirees' hands and that "inactivity leads to emotional and physical problems" (director of a special services program, I.D. 234).

One in four of the decision-makers (28 percent) believed that early retirees would face serious income problems trying to live on a relatively fixed income in an inflating economy. Despite their concerns over inflation in the economy, the legislators were only half as likely as any of the other five subsamples to suggest that the erosion of early retirement pensions by inflation could prove to be a very serious problem for early retirees who failed to take proper account of inflation effects in their retirement budget planning. One in seven of the decision-makers thus believed that retirement planning was even more important for the individual considering early retirement.

Finally, more than one in five decision-makers (22 percent) believed that early retirees would in increasing numbers seek additional employment opportunities, ranging from second and third careers through consultant or advisory roles to minimal part-time engagement in employment. Corporate directors of personnel were most likely to predict early retirees returning to the labor force in some capacity. Almost one third of the personnel directors compared to less than one quarter of all the other decision-maker subsamples predicted this continued employment role. This is important, because corporate directors of personnel are in the single most advantageous position to support the efforts of early retirees to reengage in the labor force by hiring such older workers in their own companies. The personnel director in a large manufacturing and distribution company (I.D. 431) proposed, "I would like to hire people 65 and over because they are usually good workers. There is a need to form a retirement work force and catalog the retirees' capabilities. Private industry has not provided for this to date. It is the job of private industry, not the government's job."

Thus, as expected from their predominant impression of the retirement transition as fraught with crises and trauma for many older workers, these decision-makers also characterized the early retirees' lives as fraught with problems rather than filled with pleasures. If these decision-makers are correct in their perceptions, then it is ironic that most people retire early because they want to pursue other interests while they are in sufficiently good health and financial position to enjoy them.[12] There are insufficient data available on the early retirement experiences of older Americans to say whether the workers' positive or the decision-makers' negative expectations are borne out in the realities of early retirement, but it is an empirical question well worth investigating if the trend toward early retirement is going to continue.

In contrast to the implications of the elderly retirement trend for retiring individuals, which the decision-makers viewed largely in negative terms, they viewed the implications of early retirement for the economic and social system in more mixed terms. They thought mainly in terms of the impact on the labor market and on the income maintenance system. Nearly half of the sample (41 percent) mentioned each of these impacts on the social system. Many cited the effect that early retirements would have on the turnover of jobs between old and young workers, but they disagreed about whether this turnover was good or bad for the economy. One in five believed the turnover was good for the economy because it offered mobility opportunities to the young and infused new thinking and innovation into the established ways of doing business. One in five, however, believed this accelerated turnover of jobs between young and old was bad for the economy: "There would be a lack of brain-power and know-how. Turning the economy over to 25- to 50-year-olds to run is not a good idea" (according to an operations supervisor in a branch Social Security office, I.D. 348). These decision-makers typically focused on the loss of the older workers' skills in the economy occasioned by the workers' premature retirement. Some (8 percent) wondered if the labor market would make adequate provision for second career and part-time employment options for early retirees who wanted to come back into the labor force.

Alternatively, the decision-makers focused on the strain that massive early retirements would place on the income maintenance system. In particular they feared depletion of the retirement plans' financial resources or growing tax burdens on the younger working population. The manager of a Social Security district office (I.D. 243) maintained, "There are going to be fewer and fewer basic producers and many who are supported as nonproducers. Younger people will have the burden of carrying these nonproducers." Corporate personnel directors and government agency personnel were significantly more concerned about these issues than were union local presidents, legislators, or advocates for the aged. It is a little puzzling that the legislators were not more sensitive to these issues; not only are they the architects of U.S. tax policies but they are also the most likely to feel directly (that is, by not getting reelected) any backlash of workers when they grow displeased over the tax burden being placed upon them.

The only other impact of mass early retirements on the social system perceived by these decision-makers concerned the elderly's role as consumers in the society. For the most part, these decision-makers believed the impact would be negative on the theory that because the elderly would have less money, they would be able to spend less. According to a social worker (I.D. 325), "There will be less buying because of fixed incomes; necessities will become luxuries." A few saw bright spots however, and the observation of one advocate for the aged (I.D. 609) was typical of their responses, "It will mean a booming business for companies in recreation." But only one in ten of the decision-makers predicted the emergence and growth of a new leisure ethic in U.S. society spurred by the trend in early retirements. More commonly the decision-makers imagined early retirees living a spartan existence in an effort to make ends meet on a skimpy monthly retirement income.

As negatively as the majority of these decision-makers perceived the impact of early retirement on both the individual and the social system, it is not surprising to learn that many of them opposed the widespread practice of early retirement implemented by businesses and unions to solve the problem of skills obsolescence in older workers. The decision-makers were presented with the following dilemma: "From the standpoint of the national economy, if a change of jobs becomes necessary for a worker in his 50s, do you think it would be more feasible to update his skills for a second career or to retire him with an adequate income?" Overwhelmingly, this cross section of the decision-making community opted for retraining the older worker rather than retiring him. Seventy-six percent favored retraining, whereas a mere 13 percent preferred retirement (see Table 7.7). The decision-makers' preference for retraining rather than retiring older workers is completely consistent with their emphasis on the elderly person's desire to keep working.

There were, however, some important dissenters from this perspective. The union local presidents opted in large numbers for retiring the older worker with an adequate income rather than retooling him for a second career. Comments such as those offered by the head of a public employees union official (I.D. 503A) were quite common in the union subsample: "Older people have slipped mentally and physically; they are not able to take the pressure. They just can't do the job as well. We have to let young people into the labor force." It is this kind of thinking that undoubtedly has spearheaded the unions' drive for early retirement provisions for older workers in collective bargaining pacts.[13]

Generally speaking, employment counselors, labor and industry officials, and retirement income program administrators in the decision-making community were far less likely than decision-makers with other areas of expertise to promote the need to retrain older workers who are faced with the loss of their job. These decision-makers were typically more willing to consider the idea of retiring the displaced older worker on an adequate income even though the worker might only be in his 50s. Nevertheless, even the majority of these employment/retirement specialists still maintained that it would be more desirable from an economic and/or humanistic perspective to prepare the older worker for a second career rather than to retire him at that age.

TABLE 7.7

Decision-Makers' Preferences for Early Retirement versus Retraining for Older Workers

Decision-Makers' Positional and Personal Characteristics	From the Standpoint of the Economy, If a Change of Jobs Becomes Necessary for a Worker in His 50s, Do You Think It Would Be More Feasible . . .		
	To Update His Skills for a Second Career (percent)	To Retire Him with an Adequate Income (percent)	It Would Depend on the Particular Situation (percent)
Positional Characteristics of the Decision-Makers			
Position in the Policy Process			
Legislators (N = 71)	70	14	15
Agency administrators (N = 70)	76	10	14
Service delivery personnel (N = 70)	93	7	0
Corporate directors of personnel (N = 35)	71	6	23
Union local presidents (N = 35)	57	37	6
Advocates for the aged (N = 35)	80	14	6
Responsibility for Aging Programs			
Primary function (N = 85)	80	12	8
Important but not central function (N = 88)	74	15	11
Minor function (N = 143)	76	13	12
Area of Program Expertise			
Health (N = 37)	86	11	3
Mental health (N = 23)	96	4	0
Housing (N = 29)	86	10	3
Employment (N = 92)	68	18	13
Income maintenance (N = 26)	57	12	31
Recreation/leisure (N = 18)	94	6	0
Senior citizens affairs (N = 49)	73	14	12
Generalists (N = 42)	74	14	14
Personal Characteristics of the Decision-Makers			
Age of the Respondent			
Under 45 (N = 98)	77	11	12
45-54 (N = 98)	74	15	10
55-64 (N = 90)	77	14	9
65 and over (N = 30)	80	10	10
Sex of the Respondent			
Male (N = 230)	72	15	13
Female (N = 86)	88	8	4
Ethnicity of the Respondent			
White (N = 235)	74	13	12
Minority (N = 81)	81	14	5
Educational Level of the Respondent			
High school graduate or less (N = 42)	76	21	2
Some college (N = 64)	75	14	11
College graduate (N = 99)	80	8	12
Postcollege professional education (N = 111)	74	14	12
Total (N = 316)	76	13	10

Source: Compiled by the author.

Here, again, existing employment practices run counter to the prevailing opinion of the decision-making community. The reason is to be found in economic factors external to the specific policy issue under consideration in another illustration of the discussion of the first chapter pertaining to external social, economic, and political constraints on policy enactment. Employers seek to maintain the manpower resources of their organization in ways that are maximally cost-efficient to that firm. To the extent that it is more costly to the employer to retrain an older worker than it is to retire him on a small monthly pension and hire a younger worker to replace him, the practice of early retirement of older workers will continue in accord with the principle of economic efficiency.

Currently it is the broader social system, not individual employers or unions, that must assume the primary economic costs incurred by the practice of large-scale early retirement of older workers. To begin with, the cost of supporting early retirees falls mainly to public income maintenance systems, not to corporate or union pension plans. (More than one half of all social security beneficiaries in 1970 were drawing their retirement benefits before age 65.[14]) Moreover, it has not been an uncommon practice for employers to retire or terminate older workers before the employees have acquired vested interests in the company or union pension plan; in that way, the companies frequently escape any pension obligations to the terminated older worker.[15] Finally, society subsidizes education and training of young workers just entering the labor force but not workers already well advanced in their work life. Thus, when corporations and/or unions retire an older worker and hire a young entry into the labor force, they obtain the training of the young worker at little cost to the organization in contrast to having to pay for retraining the older worker; moreover, the organization can look forward to drawing on the young worker's education for many years without facing the costs of replenishing it by retraining.

Until such time as employers and unions are required to assume a greater proportion of the costs created by the practice of forced early retirements of obsolete older workers, there will be no incentive for employers or unions to change their procedures. The recently enacted pension reform legislation (the Employees' Retirement Income Security Act, enacted in 1974) represents one effort of the federal government to ensure that employers and unions in the private sector assume a greater share of the pension costs for supporting retired workers. It is still too soon to know, however, whether one effect of the legislation will be to slow the pace of forced early retirement of older workers witnessed in recent decades.

Nevertheless, the retraining versus early retirement issue is probably best tackled from the other direction, that is, developing, and more importantly, institutionalizing, retraining and/or continuing education programs for older workers in the labor force. Half of the labor force is currently over the age of 45; the economy cannot afford to discard them or relegate them en masse to less technological positions in business and industry. It is clear, however, that until business, unions, and government are equal partners in revitalizing older workers' resources through the joint funding of various retraining and continuing education programs, the society's manpower resources will continue to be seriously mismanaged, at a cost more to the broader society than the private sector organizations who are primarily responsible for creating the problem of misused manpower resources.

The repeated congressional defeats of several versions of the Mid-Career Development Program legislation in the early to mid-1970s suggest that policy action is not soon forthcoming on this issue. The federal government itself emerges reluctant to commit the necessary fiscal resources to support an extensive career development program for middle-aged and older workers in the economy. Policy action once again lags far behind opinion formation in the decision-making community; midcareer training programs remain bogged in the politics of legislative infeasibility.

DECISION-MAKERS' PERCEPTIONS OF THE OPPORTUNITIES FOR CONTINUED EMPLOYMENT PAST AGE 65

The decision-makers concluded in the majority that many elderly would prefer to keep working rather than retire to a life of leisure. But how did the decision-makers assess the elderly's opportunities for finding suitable employment?

The decision-makers largely concurred that "in most jobs, older people can perform as well as younger people." Nearly two out of three (65 percent) of the decision-makers evaluated the elderly worker's job performance on a par with that of younger workers (see Table 7.8, part A). The legislators were most likely to disagree with the assertion that elderly people usually perform a job as well as younger ones. Nearly four out of ten of the legislators felt that the elderly's on-the-job performance was less satisfactory if compared to that of a younger worker. Service delivery personnel were also somewhat more likely to discount the older worker's job performance. In contrast, categoric decision-makers were considerably more likely to strongly agree that older people generally performed on a par with younger people than were decision-makers who had professional responsibilities extending beyond just the elderly.

TABLE 7.8

Decision-Makers' Assessments of Older Workers' Capabilities and Opportunities to Perform in the Employment Role Past Age 65

Decision-Makers' Positional and Personal Characteristics	Percent Agreeing with Each of the Following Statements		
	A. "In Most Jobs, Older People Can Perform as Well as Younger People"	B. "Most Older People Cannot Find a Job Even Though They Are Able and Willing to Work"	C. "Most Older People Can Do a Job as Well as Younger Persons, But Are Not Given an Opportunity to Show What They Can Do"
Positional Characteristics of the Decision-Makers			
Position in the Policy Process			
Legislators (N = 71)	62	92	82
Agency administrators (N = 70)	70	97	81
Service delivery personnel (N = 70)	64	99	83
Corporate directors of personnel (N = 35)	74	100	80
Union local presidents (N = 35)	11	97	77
Advocates for the aged (N = 35)	74	97	80
Responsibility for Aging Programs			
Primary function (N = 85)	74	94	80
Important but not central function (N = 88)	64	93	84
Minor function (N = 143)	60	96	74
Area of Program Expertise			
Health (N = 37)	65	100	84
Mental health (N = 23)	65	91	83
Housing (N = 29)	59	93	83
Employment (N = 92)	70	96	78
Income maintenance (N = 26)	46	92	58
Recreation/leisure (N = 18)	72	100	94
Senior citizens affairs (N = 49)	71	91	82
Generalists (N = 42)	60	93	71
Personal Characteristics of the Decision-Makers			
Age of the Respondent			
Under 45 (N = 98)	74	95	84
45-54 (N = 98)	58	97	76
55-64 (N = 90)	68	97	82
65 and over (N = 30)	80	93	83
Sex of the Respondent			
Male (N = 230)	67	95	79
Female (N = 86)	71	99	86
Ethnicity of the Respondent			
White (N = 235)	68	96	81
Minority (N = 81)	68	95	81
Educational Level of the Respondent			
High school graduate or less (N = 42)	64	98	79
Some college (N = 64)	66	94	78
College graduate (N = 99)	70	97	85
Postcollege professional education (N = 111)	69	95	80
Total (N = 316)	65	95	78

Source: Compiled by the author.

As might be expected, those decision-makers who were themselves elderly were by a significant margin the strongest proponents of the elderly's capacity to perform equally in most jobs.

It is particularly interesting that employment counselors and union and corporate management officials showed considerable agreement regarding the capacity of the elderly to perform on a par with younger persons in most jobs, because these are decision-makers who would be instrumental in hiring elderly persons for available employment opportunities. The head of a craft union local (I.D. 518A) described his experience with older workers, "We have a person 78 in our place, and he is the best worker around here. I wish we had more like him." The income maintenance program administrators were the only subgroup in the entire decision-making community in which a majority maintained that the elderly's job performance was generally inferior to that of a younger worker. This attitude is undoubtedly part of the reason why income maintenance specialists were by far the least likely in the whole decision-making community to endorse elimination of the mandatory retirement practices in order to allow older workers to continue working as long as they would like (see Table 7.5).

In spite of the fact that they generally believed that the elderly had the capability to perform adequately on the job, the decision-makers nearly unanimously (95 percent) agreed that "most older people cannot find a job even though they are able and willing to work" (see Table 7.8, part B). The reason that older people typically cannot find jobs is that they are not given an opportunity to work and show what they can do; the elderly simply are not hired for the available jobs, according to the predominant opinion of these decision-makers (see Table 7.8, part C). Nearly four out of five (78 percent) of the 316 decision-makers agreed that "Most older people can do a job as well as younger persons, but they are not given an opportunity to show what they can do."

If older people are equally qualified for jobs as younger persons but the older person is not hired because of his advanced age, the employer is guilty of practicing age discrimination, which is now against the law. The federal law, the Age Discrimination in Employment Act (ADEA), and most state laws, however, define discrimination as illegal only when it operates to the detriment of workers between 40 and 65 years of age. Workers over age 65 are not protected by the act. Hence if an employer refuses to hire an elderly person because of the applicant's advanced age, he is within the law in doing so, and the elderly job applicant has no legal recourse. Several bills have been introduced in Congress and various state legislatures to eliminate the upper age limit on their age discrimination laws and consequently to make those laws apply equally to all those past the age of 40, including those that society labels elderly after age 65. Until such time as the laws are changed, however, age discrimination in employment against elderly workers will probably continue unchecked. Even if the laws are changed to afford the elderly greater protection, it is doubtful that the age discrimination practices of employers against the elderly workers will ever be successfully curbed or eliminated.[16]

The decision-makers were asked to analyze the obstacles they foresaw to hiring more elderly persons in the labor force (see Table 7.9). The most common responses included the workers' poor health and consequent absenteeism on the job (cited by 34 percent of the sample); the older workers' skills obsolescence as well as their tendency to cling to old ways of doing a task rather than experimenting to find new and better ways to do the job (cited by 27 percent of the sample); the employers' higher contributions to insurance, workmen's compensation, and retirement pension plans for older as opposed to younger workers (cited by 29 percent of the sample); the companies' mandatory retirement policies prohibiting employment of most or all persons past a certain age (cited by 22 percent of the sample); and the employers' preference for hiring younger as opposed to older workers whenever a choice exists (cited by 29 percent of the sample).

The health professionals were the only subgroup in the decision-making community who in the majority cited the elderly's own health status as the major barrier to continuation in the employment role past age 65. The health providers were nearly twice as likely to focus on the health barriers as to mention any other obstacle to hiring older workers. Advocates for the elderly also stressed that potential health problems would make elderly applicants less desirable to hiring officials. Union and corporate management officials, however, tended to minimize these problems more than nearly any other segment of the decision-making community. The head of a retail store chain (I.D. 407B) offered this perspective on hiring older workers: "We have changed our retirement plan. Employees may now request to keep working. If their general health is good, we retire them and hire them back part time."

Union local presidents were also the least concerned about the problem of skills obsolescence in older workers; less than one in seven of the union local presidents focused on the skills obsolescence problem in hiring older workers. The head of a public employees' union (I.D. 504) observed that rather than there being problems in hiring older workers, there were "many advantages--older workers have something to offer." The personnel director in a large merchandising corporation (I.D. 411A) concurred, "Providing they are in good health and have the skills, there are no obstacles in hiring

TABLE 7.9

Decision-Makers' Perceptions of the Potential Obstacles to Employing More Older Workers Past Age 65

Decision-Makers' Positional and Personal Characteristics	Older Workers' Poor Health (percent)	Older Workers' Skills Obsolescence (percent)
Positional Characteristics of the Decision-Makers		
Position in the Policy Process		
Legislators (N = 71)	30	25
Agency administrators (N = 70)	31	26
Service delivery personnel (N = 70)	43	33
Corporate directors of personnel (N = 35)	26	31
Union local presidents (N = 35)	26	14
Advocates for the aged (N = 35)	46	31
Responsibility for Aging Programs		
Primary function (N = 85)	38	25
Important but not central function (N = 88)	33	31
Minor function (N = 143)	32	27
Area of Program Expertise		
Health (N = 37)	54	27
Mental health (N = 23)	30	17
Housing (N = 29)	31	31
Employment (N = 92)	24	27
Income maintenance (N = 26)	38	27
Recreation/leisure (N = 18)	39	44
Senior citizens affairs (N = 49)	37	27
Generalists (N = 42)	33	24
Personal Characteristics of the Decision-Makers		
Age of the Respondent		
Under 45 (N = 98)	33	33
45-54 (N = 98)	39	28
55-64 (N = 90)	29	23
65 and over (N = 30)	37	20
Sex of the Respondent		
Male (N = 230)	31	25
Female (N = 86)	40	33
Ethnicity of the Respondent		
White (N = 235)	33	27
Minority (N = 81)	37	27
Educational Level of the Respondent		
High school graduate or less (N = 42)	24	21
Some college (N = 64)	42	22
College graduate (N = 99)	28	33
Postcollege professional education (N = 111)	38	27
Total (N = 316)	34	27

Perceived Obstacles to Employers' Hiring More Older Workers		
Employers' Cost for Insurance, Pensions, et cetera (percent)	Company and Union Mandatory Retirement Policies (percent)	Employers' Preference to Hire Younger over Older Workers (percent)
34	20	31
23	31	31
24	29	26
26	14	26
34	6	34
37	23	23
25	29	25
26	20	26
33	20	33
30	24	24
26	52	35
24	14	24
29	14	32
38	27	35
22	17	22
33	33	24
24	17	31
21	24	32
34	27	29
29	17	28
33	20	23
31	20	29
23	30	28
30	22	29
26	23	27
33	12	21
30	17	20
29	22	30
26	30	35
29	22	29

Source: Compiled by the author.

workers past the age of 65." The head of a local committee on aging (I.D. 617) similarly noted, "The people they retire today are more adequate and more experienced, but still they retire them at age 65."

The senior citizens club and recreation center directors were the only subgroup in the decision-making community in which a near majority (44 percent) cited skills obsolescence as a major barrier to the hiring of more older workers. These recreation specialists were one of only a few subgroups in the decision-making community who were nearly unanimous about the need to update the skills of older workers by retraining programs. They showed less support than any other group in the decision-making community for retiring older workers because of possible skills obsolescence (see Table 7.7).

Legislators, union officials, and advocates for the aged were all more likely than the corporate personnel directors to cite the employers' added expenses in retirement plan contributions and insurance premiums as a result of hiring older as opposed to younger workers. The head of a craft union local (I.D. 530A) commented, for example, "There's a prejudice on the part of employers against employing older people because of workmen's compensation and health plan insurance. You can hardly beat that one. I don't really see any other obstacle." The head of an insurance corporation (I.D. 409) replied, however, "I can see no obstacle to hiring more older workers." Pension program administrators were the most likely in all of the decision-making community to focus on the employers' added financial burdens in hiring older as opposed to younger workers. Pensions would be one of those extra costs assumed by the employer; hence, it was natural for the retirement income specialists to be particularly sensitive to the possible barriers these added pension and insurance plan costs might raise to employers' hiring more older workers.

Mental health professionals were the most likely to blame the existing mandatory retirement policies of employers and labor unions for creating serious barriers for older workers who wish to remain or reenter in the labor force after age 65. Mental health professionals were, at the same time, the most likely group in the decision-making community to insist that older people retire because they are forced to by company policies, not because they do so by choice (see Table 7.2). These mental health counselors were also the most likely of the decision-maker subgroups to believe that the overwhelming majority of the older workers (three quarters or more) would prefer to continue working at least part time rather than retiring completely from the labor force (see Table 7.3). The mental health counselors' dominant concern for the barriers that existing mandatory retirement policies pose to elderly job applicants is thus totally consistent with their impressions about the nature of the retirement transition as it is experienced by the retiring worker.

Between one fifth and one third of all of the decision-maker subgroups cited the employers' illicit preference for hiring younger as opposed to older workers as a serious barrier to the elderly's continued employment past age 65. The head of personnel for a service organization (I.D. 402A) observed that many employers feel "that older people are not harmonious with the other employees. Younger people plain dislike older people." The head of a public employees' union (I.D. 505) suggested that employers prefer young workers "because employers have long-term interest in new employees." An advocate for the elderly (I.D. 604) explained the problem this way, "You have youth culture image in our society today, so companies need to have young people in management positions." Another advocate (I.D. 610) added other information to the composite picture, "The attitude of young personnel in the company who might resent the old fogies is a problem." A local legislator (I.D. 119) observed, "Another possible obstacle is that there are only so many jobs available and you have to keep people employed who have family obligations."

Whatever the precise reason for the employers' bias, these decision-makers could at least agree that employers prefer to hire younger over older workers, which places each elderly job applicant in a disadvantaged position. The vast majority of the decision-makers was aware of the problems that elderly job applicants confront in finding jobs, that there are many elderly who would like to work but are unable to find employment because they are never hired and given the opportunity to show what they can do (see Table 7.8); but only a minority of these decision-makers evidently believed that the employers' preferences for hiring younger workers constituted a major problem preventing more employment of elderly workers.

A minority of the decision-maker sample cited some additional barriers to hiring more elderly employees (not reported in Table 7.8). One in nine mentioned the lack of jobs specifically designed to fit the changing capabilities of the older worker. A state legislator (I.D. 127) noted, for instance, "Older people have accidents on the job. A good personnel manager would be able to fit the person to the job and not let this happen." Another common criticism was "the inability of our present manufacturing and production systems to break down jobs to part time for older persons" (offered by a housing program administrator, I.D. 230). An additional one in nine of the sample of 316 decision-makers spoke about the lack of enough jobs generally and the high unemployment rate throughout the 1970s. The observation of a city councilman (I.D. 117) was typical of their comments, "With the high unemployment you can't bring in the young and keep the old." A mere 4 percent of the sample suggested that the retirement means test under the social security system inhibited employment past age 65 because it limited what the older person could earn before his social security benefits were reduced. Problems created by the retirement means test did not have significant visibility to the decision-makers in this sample, despite the repeated efforts of gerontologists and advocates for the elderly to make the earnings limitation an important policy issue. Finally, 7 percent of the decision-makers perceived no problems whatsoever in hiring more older workers. More commonly, however, the decision-makers cited multiple obstacles to the older workers' continued employment past age 65.

The decision-makers perceiving obstacles to the elderly's continuing in the employment role past age 65 were asked to suggest ways to remove these obstacles and improve the elderly's access to available job opportunities. The most frequent recommendation, offered by one in three of the decision-makers, involved relocating older workers in new jobs better suited to their slowing work pace and generally declining health status. One common suggestion was "to implement programs of part-time jobs for seniors" (a senior citizens affairs official, I.D. 269). A housing program administrator (I.D. 230) observed, "I think a lot of governmental jobs can be broken down to create part-time employment. Also they could provide more jobs like crossing guards. I think most government offices could provide such jobs." The personnel director of a computer firm (I.D. 419) suggested that "Companies can identify certain positions in the firm that would afford opportunities for the elderly."

An employment counselor specializing in older workers (I.D. 357) reminded, "An older person is capable of holding down a job like a younger man. An older person can do many jobs well. Some can't do physical work, but then they can do many things better than young people because they have had more experience." Of the 30 percent of the sample who urged relocating elderly workers in jobs better suited to their capabilities, many believed that the government would have to serve as the employer of last resort for the elderly. The observation of a health clinic nurse (I.D. 313) was implicit in the comments of others, "I think maybe the government is going to have to step in and make jobs available--on the basis of a community project."

In contrast to the large number recommending transfer of the elderly to new jobs as declining capabilities require, very few of the decision-makers (only 7 percent) suggested redesigning the elderly's existing job to fit his present capabilities. The idea of retiring the elderly and rehiring them in new jobs was far more ingrained in the decision-makers' thinking than was the concept of job redesign. Job redesign has the advantage of keeping the older worker in a job setting with which he is familiar, and also saving him from the agony of a potentially long search for a new job elsewhere. The idea of job redesign is practiced much more extensively in Europe, but the idea still has not gained much popularity in the United States.

One in seven of the decision-makers believed that a massive media-based educational campaign about the value of older workers ought to be directed toward employers of all kinds in the business world. A city councilman (I.D. 119) affirmed "that it's a matter of information dissemination to publicize the fact that there's still a lot of zip in old bodies yet. I suppose there are a lot of agencies or service organizations that could publicize the idea through the media." A continuing education program administrator (I.D. 261) concurred, "We need to educate businesses and industries to the fact that older people are good and safe workers." But a small minority of the decision-makers (6 percent) believed that the educational campaign ought to be directed toward the elderly themselves rather than the employers. Illustrative of their point of view was the recommendation of the president of a manufacturing union local (I.D. 508), "Do a P.R. job on the elderly: show them alternatives to full-time employment such as areas of hobby development or social direction."

Another one in seven of the decision-makers urged stricter enforcement of existing age discrimination laws together with implementation of new laws that would improve the economic feasibility of hiring older workers. Several union local presidents began from a position of "enforcement of the present laws that forbid discrimination because of age" (head of a public employees' union, I.D. 502). A state legislator (I.D. 157) recommended modification of existing age discrimination laws to remove the upper age limit on the protection afforded older workers: "Make it illegal to reject or refuse employment to anyone past retirement age based solely on age. And the employee should be able to appeal." A senior citizens affairs official (I.D. 264), like many others, suggested "declaring mandatory retirement illegal by legislation and allowing our older citizens the right of choice." The corporate personnel officer in a financial organization went so far as to lobby for "an affirmative action program like for minorities and women which would require corporations to hire a certain number of seniors." A number of decision-makers also believed that the added costs confronting the employer who hires older as opposed to younger workers could be similarly corrected by legislation. The personnel manager for a large retail store chain (I.D. 408) suggested, for example, "The government could pick up the costs of workmens compensation at, say, age 62." The head of a craft union local (I.D. 530A) suggested that by subsidization, "the employer who's willing to hire, say, 50 percent or more older people would get a different consideration on claims and rates."

To summarize the decision-makers' perspectives on continued employment for the elderly, the decision-makers expressed much concern that in spite of the trend toward early retirement, many elderly do not care to retire, but that after age 65 these elderly face tremendous barriers to continuing in the retirement role. On the one hand, the decision-makers identified age discriminatory attitudes and behavior on the part of employers. For this, they urge adoption and enforcement of more stringent laws prohibiting age discrimination, as well as more positive educational measures taken to persuade employers of the positive attributes of older workers. On the other hand, the decision-makers cited physical decline and skills obsolescence and other characteristics of the older worker that make him apparently a less desirable employee than one who is younger and likely to be better trained and in better health. To minimize these problems, the decision-makers recommended the creation of more varied employment options, including part-time opportunities and jobs designed or redesigned to take into account the older persons' changing capabilities.

For the most part, however, the decision-makers perceived that the elderly person who wishes to persist in the employment role will encounter considerable, if not finally insurmountable, obstacles to finding employment suited to his needs and desires at least for some time to come. While the decision-makers are confident that persistence on the part of the elderly and their advocates could eventually improve the employment opportunities for elderly people, the decision-makers evidently believe the changes will be a long time in coming, because the overwhelming majority of these decision-makers asserted that the recent trend toward early retirement is likely to continue unabated at least in the foreseeable future. The next section probes potential retirement roles for the elderly who wish to remain active in community affairs but either cannot or do not wish to find paid employment positions.

DECISION-MAKERS' SUGGESTIONS FOR ALTERNATIVE RETIREMENT ROLES

The decision-makers were asked to speculate about alternative uses the elderly could make of their free time in their retirement years. "After retirement some people experience difficulty in finding meaningful ways to use their time. Do you have any suggestions regarding programs or organized community activities that would address this problem?" (see Table 7.10).

By far and away the most popular response offered by the decision-makers (40 percent) concerned the engagement of retirees

TABLE 7.10

Decision-Makers' Recommendations for Providing Meaningful Retirement Roles for the Aged

Suggestions for Programs or Organized Community Activities That Could Help Older People Find Meaningful Ways to Spend Their Time	Decision-Makers' Position in the Policy Process: Legislators (N = 71) (percent)	Agency Administrators (N = 70) (percent)	Service Delivery Personnel (N = 70) (percent)	Corporate Directors of Personnel (N = 35) (percent)	Union Local Presidents (N = 35) (percent)	Advocates for the Aged (N = 35) (percent)	Total Per-cent	Total No.
Volunteer projects	39	47	43	23	29	51	40	127
Organized recreation programs	35	31	23	20	23	37	29	91
Senior citizens clubs and centers	32	15	30	11	20	49	26	83
Adult or continuing education	14	24	23	6	11	31	19	60
Getting involved in programs to help the young	20	14	21	0	11	9	15	46
Church activities for seniors	9	9	20	3	14	43	13	40
More employment program options for seniors	3	13	7	9	6	9	11	34
More political organizations among the elderly	13	10	4	0	14	23	10	32
Better dissemination about organized activities that already exist for the elderly	10	17	11	14	9	11	10	31
Individual has to find meaningful retirement roles for himself	11	10	11	14	9	0	13	42
Already plenty of activities providing meaningful involvement available in the community	23	15	15	9	4	9	15	47

Source: Compiled by the author.

in volunteer and community service projects. Many gerontologists have also suggested that the elderly adopt a civic commitment in lieu of the role of worker when they are retired, and devote themselves to political and social activities on behalf of the broader social community.[17] One in seven of the decision-makers thought that the elderly would be particularly useful in working with very young children and adolescent youth, either in schools as teachers' aides or in day-care centers as babysitters and companions. Many of the decision-makers cited the foster grandparent program as a good example of how to use the elderly's skills and resources in a manner productive for the society and rewarding for the individual as well. Slightly more than one quarter of the sample (29 percent) believed organized recreational activities could lend meaning to the elderly's lives in retirement.

In a similar vein, slightly more than one quarter (26 percent) of the sample mentioned that the elderly should join senior citizens clubs and organizations where, among their age mates, they would find meaningful involvement in a range of activities. One in five (19 percent) of the decision-makers insisted that older people should take advantage of their free time and return to the classroom to further their intellectual development and/or to learn new hobbies and avocational skills. One in eight believed that the church should play a prominent role in organizing activities and orchestrating meaningful involvement for the elderly within the church purview. Finally, one in ten (10 percent) were optimistic that new politically oriented organizations based on age-group interests would develop and engage the elderly themselves in working actively on behalf of others in their age group. Some of the decision-makers' recommendations are examined more closely in light of data from empirical studies that suggest how feasible their recommendations may be.

The Aged's Engagement in Volunteer Work

The decision-makers felt strongly that the elderly with their large bloc of free time would be an extremely useful asset to society if they would apply themselves to volunteer work or in some other community service capacity. A recent national survey confirmed that apart from any work they are paid for, more than one in five of the elderly (22 percent) report they are engaged in some kind of volunteer work, and among the young-old (65 to 69 years of age), 28 percent currently do volunteer work. Thus, in real numbers, the current volunteer force among the elderly is 4.5 million strong. Moreover, another 10 percent of the 65 and over population is interested in doing volunteer work, bring the total volunteer force in the elderly population to 6.6 million people.[18]

Among the elderly, first preference for volunteer service included health and mental health work (working in hospitals and clinics) and providing transportation to the aged and handicapped or others in need. Following in popularity were engagement in civic affairs activities (voter registration and lobbying and advocacy by issues), participation in social support services (making visits to the homebound, staffing outreach programs, running telephone referral and counseling services, and so on), and working in charity and give-away programs, such as thrift shops and emergency food programs. The decision-makers' image of the elderly volunteer force meshed well with the realities as they were reported by the elderly themselves.

The advocates for the aged in the majority (51 percent) and the administrative agency and program heads in a near majority (47 percent) asserted that the elderly should explore opportunities to volunteer their time and energy for community service needs. The corporate directors of personnel and the union local presidents from the private sector were the only subsamples not strongly oriented toward encouraging the elderly to assume an active volunteer role. Legislators and service providers were most likely to assert that the natural affinity between young and old might be developed by having the elderly volunteer to assist in working with children in specific social settings such as schools or child-care centers. Surprisingly, a mere 2 percent of the decision-makers suggested that elderly volunteers should work to help other elderly people in need; the decision-makers far more often thought of the old helping the young than of the old helping the old.

Traditionally, volunteer work has been considered work that an individual devotes to a cause without pay reimbursement for the services rendered. Precisely because many of the elderly are so poor and unable to find jobs even though willing to work, the federal government has sought to subsidize the elderly with small monetary payments for the time and energy that they contribute in community service activities. When asked, "If an older person works in a community service type program, do you think he should be paid for it?", more than three out of four (76 percent) of the 316 decision-makers asserted that the elderly should be paid (see Table 7.11). The personnel in the government social agencies, administrators and service providers alike, were most likely to endorse paying the older person for his community service work; the legislators and advocates for the aged were least in favor of the practice, although even two out of three of these subsamples favored paying the elderly volunteers for their work.

The decision-makers were asked to specify the level of payment they would support for reimbursing the elderly person who

TABLE 7.11

"If an Older Person Works in a Community Service Type Program, Do You Think He Should Be Paid for It?" (percent responding "yes")

Positional Characteristics of the Decision-Makers	
Position in the Policy Process	
Legislators (N = 71)	65
Agency administrators (N = 70)	86
Service delivery personnel (N = 70)	81
Corporate directors of personnel (N = 35)	74
Union local presidents (N = 35)	77
Advocates for the aged (N = 35)	69
Responsibility for Aging Programs	
Primary function (N = 85)	82
Important but not central function (N = 88)	70
Minor function (N = 143)	76
Area of Program Expertise	
Health (N = 37)	76
Mental health (N = 23)	87
Housing (N = 29)	66
Employment (N = 92)	77
Income maintenance (N = 26)	77
Recreation/leisure (N = 18)	78
Senior citizens affairs (N = 49)	76
Generalists (N = 42)	74
Personal Characteristics of the Decision-Makers	
Age of the Respondent	
Under 45 (N = 98)	82
45-54 (N = 98)	67
55-64 (N = 90)	78
65 and over (N = 30)	83
Sex of the Respondent	
Male (N = 230)	75
Female (N = 86)	79
Ethnicity of the Respondent	
White (N = 235)	73
Minority (N = 81)	86
Educational Level of the Respondent	
High school graduate or less (N = 42)	81
Some college (N = 64)	70
College graduate (N = 99)	79
Postcollege professional education (N = 111)	75
Total (N = 316)	76

Source: Compiled by the author.

contributed his time and energy in community service activities (see Table 7.12). Nearly half of the sample (47 percent) agreed that the elderly ought to have a wage calculated at the prevailing rate for similar services in the community. This would in effect make the government the "employer of last resort" for the elderly. This decision on the part of the sample reflects their conviction that elderly people do want to work and remain contributing and productive members within society, but they simply are denied, for all practical purposes, any real opportunity to hold regular, full-time, salaried jobs in business and industry because of the age discriminatory attitudes and practices of the employers, the lack of part-time job opportunities, and the like.

Service providers were the most likely to express the prevailing wage rate in the private sector as the appropriate mode of payment for the elderly volunteer. Conceivably, many of the elderly volunteers might be doing work nearly comparable to that of the counselors and staff members in this subsample, and they simply felt that elderly volunteers should be paid accordingly for performing genuinely valuable work functions. Somewhat surprising is that decision-makers with generic responsibilities were significantly more likely than those with categoric responsibilities to believe the elderly should be paid according to the prevailing rate for comparable work in the community. Similarly, younger decision-makers were considerably more in favor of this mode of payment than were the older decision-makers. College-educated decision-makers far more than those with only a high school education believed the elderly's work deserved payment comparable to the prevailing rate for similar work in the community, the sort of objective measure of work's worth that one might expect a professional would assign. Women and minorities far more than men and whites were also in favor of paying the elderly volunteers at the prevailing rate.

Roughly one in seven of the decision-makers supported each of a number of alternative modes of payment to the elderly for their volunteered services: 14 percent favored repayment only of the elderly's out-of-pocket expenses, 15 percent favored a payment equal to the amount allowed under the social security retirement means test, and 14 percent favored payment of the elderly according to the minimum wage rate. But no segment of the decision-making community collectively endorsed any one of these payment methods even half as often as they insisted on payment of the elderly at the prevailing wage rate for comparable work in the broader community.

For all intensive purposes, then, these decision-makers translated volunteer work for the elderly into the sort of part-time work opportunity that the elderly would like to find in the private sector but seem unable to secure. In this sense, the government would become the employer of last resort for the elderly.

TABLE 7.12

Decision-Makers' Recommendations for Paying Older People Who Are Involved in Community Service Work

Decision-Makers' Positional and Personal Characteristics	Out-of-Pocket Expenses Only (percent)
Positional Characteristics of the Decision-Makers	
Position in the Policy Process	
Legislators (N = 46)*	11
Agency administrators (N = 60)	15
Service delivery personnel (N = 57)	14
Corporate directors of personnel (N = 26)	8
Union local president (N = 27)	22
Advocates for the aged (N = 24)	13
Responsibility for Aging Programs	
Primary function (N = 74)	16
Important but not central function (N = 19)	11
Minor function (N = 115)	14
Area of Program Expertise	
Health (N = 28)	14
Mental health (N = 20)	5
Housing (N = 19)	26
Employment (N = 71)	13
Income maintenance (N = 20)	15
Recreation/leisure (N = 14)	29
Senior citizens affairs (N = 37)	11
Generalists (N = 31)	10
Personal Characteristics of the Decision-Makers	
Age of the Respondent	
Under 45 (N = 85)	9
45-54 (N = 76)	14
55-64 (N = 72)	19
65 and over (N = 25)	16
Sex of the Respondent	
Male (N = 186)	14
Female (N = 72)	13
Ethnicity of the Respondent	
White (N = 185)	15
Minority (N = 73)	10
Educational Level of the Respondent	
High school graduate or less (N = 35)	21
Some college (N = 52)	16
College graduate (N = 82)	15
Postcollege professional education (N = 89)	8
Total (N = 240)	14

*Base N for percentage = Number who believed that the aged should be paid for their community service work.

Source: Compiled by the author.

How Much Should the Elderly Be Paid for Their Community Service Work?			
Amount Equal to Social Security Income Exemption (percent)	Amount Calculated on Minimum Wage Rate (percent)	Amount Calculated on Prevailing Wage Rate (percent)	Miscellaneous Payment Suggestions (percent)
13	15	37	24
12	20	45	8
14	9	61	2
19	0	50	23
19	19	41	0
21	21	38	8
17	17	43	7
15	13	42	19
14	13	52	7
18	14	46	7
5	20	70	0
0	5	58	11
18	13	47	8
20	20	35	10
14	7	50	0
19	16	46	8
13	16	32	29
12	3	65	11
9	21	44	11
20	17	36	7
24	24	24	12
15	17	41	13
15	7	60	4
14	15	43	13
19	11	56	4
21	29	26	3
16	18	44	7
15	9	47	13
12	11	55	13
15	14	47	10

Involvement in Senior Citizens Clubs and Organizations

The decision-makers agreed in substantial numbers that the elderly should find many opportunities for meaningful involvement by joining a senior citizens club or organization (see Table 7.10). Nearly half of the advocates for the aged (49 percent) endorsed greater involvement of the aged in these valuable senior clubs and organizations. To quote the head of one local senior citizens organization (I.D. 603), "Get into a senior citizen organization and they won't need anything else. We keep them so busy, they won't have time for anything else." On the other hand, a California state legislator observed, "I think most people in this country are rather individualistic and therefore plans after retirement are sort of vague and it's pretty hard to get them involved in group action."

It is estimated that 50 percent of the public 55 years of age and over have a senior citizens club or center located conveniently near them. In the nationwide Harris poll, 18 percent of the public 65 years of age and older (approximately 3.7 million people) and another 8 percent of those 55 to 64 (an additional 1.4 million people) reported that they had attended a senior citizens center within the past year.[19] The percentage of older people who attend such group meetings regularly or somewhat regularly is probably considerably smaller. Estimates have been made of 5 to 10 percent of the elderly population in reasonably regular attendance at such organizations.

The decision-makers for the most part held reasonably accurate estimates of the elderly's level of involvement in various senior citizens organizations (see Table 7.13). Nearly half of the decision-makers (45 percent) estimated that less than 20 percent of the elderly belonged to any senior citizens organization, and only one third of the sample estimated the figure as high as 30 percent of the elderly. Service delivery personnel, along with the advocates for the aged, both tended to overestimate the percentage of elderly belonging to various elderly organizations far beyond what available data would suggest. For example, nearly half (44 percent) of the advocates thought at least half of the elderly belonged to such age-graded organizations and nearly one in five (19 percent) of these advocates believed 70 percent or more of the elderly belonged to such groups. This is clearly an inaccurate estimate. Recreation and leisure specialists also overestimated the percentage of the elderly population who are involved in their senior clubs and activities. Nearly half (43 percent) of the recreation center directors believed that one half or more of the elderly population attended meetings and activities organized for seniors. Older decision-makers tended, relative to younger ones, to overestimate the level of involvement of senior

TABLE 7.13

"What Percentage of Older Persons Living in Los Angeles Would You Estimate Are Involved in Any Senior Citizens Organizations?" (percent estimating 20 percent or under)

Positional Characteristics of the Decision-Makers	
Position in the Policy Process	
Legislators (N = 71)	48
Agency administrators (N = 70)	56
Service delivery personnel (N = 70)	30
Corporate directors of personnel (N = 35)	57
Union local presidents (N = 35)	51
Advocates for the aged (N = 35)	31
Responsibility for Aging Programs	
Primary function (N = 85)	38
Important but not central function (N = 88)	49
Minor function (N = 143)	49
Area of Program Expertise	
Health (N = 37)	43
Mental health (N = 23)	52
Housing (N = 29)	45
Employment (N = 92)	49
Income maintenance (N = 26)	54
Recreation/leisure (N = 18)	17
Senior citizens affairs (N = 49)	39
Generalists (N = 42)	50
Personal Characteristics of the Decision-Makers	
Age of the Respondent	
Under 45 (N = 98)	48
45-54 (N = 98)	44
55-64 (N = 90)	47
65 and over (N = 30)	37
Sex of the Respondent	
Male (N = 230)	53
Female (N = 86)	26
Ethnicity of the Respondent	
White (N = 235)	48
Minority (N = 81)	38
Educational Level of the Respondent	
High school graduate or less (N = 42)	26
Some college (N = 64)	48
College graduate (N = 99)	43
Postcollege professional education (N = 111)	52
Total (N = 316)	45

Source: Compiled by the author.

citizens in these age-graded organizations, as did women compared to men, minorities as opposed to whites, and college-educated relative to high school educated decision-makers.

The decision-makers are appropriately concerned about increasing the elderly's participation in these age-graded organizations. In the Harris poll, 19 percent, or one in five, of the public 55 years of age and over said that they would like to attend such a senior citizens center, but often asserted either that they did not know about any such center near their home (29 percent), they had no transportation to the nearest center (20 percent), or their poor health and limited mobility prevented them from getting to the center (16 percent).[20] The majority of those interviewed (57 percent), however, said they had no interest in attending such a senior club or center. Advocates for the aged and the recreation centers directors should be the most concerned about increasing the elderly population's participation in these age-graded groups and organizations. Unfortunately, however, these are the very decision-makers who are very likely to believe that the majority of the elderly population already does belong to these organizations, and this perception undoubtedly weakens their drive to interest the remaining nonjoiners in becoming involved in the activities of these senior groups.

The Aged's Involvement in Political Activism on Behalf of Their Age Group

A minority of the decision-making community (one in ten) believed strongly that the elderly should get involved in politically motivated groups and agitate for change in the community. As one senior citizens affairs official (I.D. 270) commented, "Get the elderly involved with tasks in communities--giving input into what happens. Enhance their role in organized ways, such as the Gray Panthers. The name turns people off, but the idea is great." A veteran of advocacy and negotiation, one union local president (I.D. 535) remarked on the natural link between senior citizens clubs and organizations and grass-roots political action by the elderly on behalf of the elderly: "Senior citizens are great and they should get involved with local park and recreation departments. They should get more involved and they can get together to form political groups."

The advocates for the aged, however, were considerably more likely than the rest of the decision-making community to urge senior citizens to develop a political self-consciousness. The head of one local committee on aging (I.D. 635) exclaimed, "The elderly should become active in some kind of community program before retirement. They should take more interest in their community and get to know the state, county, and city structure--just get involved!"

Chapter 9 of this volume is devoted to a more thorough analysis of the decision-makers' perspectives on the emerging political consciousness among the aged and their assessments of the impact that the activist elderly could have on the outcome of the politics of distribution in the U.S. policy process.

The Aged's Enrollment in Continuing or Adult Education

Some of the decision-makers (one in five) believed that the elderly's free time during the retirement years might be well spent in returning to school and taking classes to enrich the mind, to learn new crafts or avocations, to learn about aging, or whatever depending on the individual's preferences. Once again, advocates for the aged were considerably more likely than all the other decision-maker groups to recommend continuing education as a useful and meaningful way for the elderly person to structure his free time in the retirement years. The corporate directors of personnel, followed by the union local presidents and the legislators, were relatively less likely to see continuing education as a viable retirement activity for senior citizens in general.

Indeed, available statistics suggest that few, probably less than 400,000 older people, are currently enrolled in courses at educational institutions. In the Harris poll, less than 5 percent of those 55 to 64 years of age and a mere 2 percent of those 65 or older were enrolled in school or taking courses. Among the 65 and over group, 7 percent of those with a college degree had returned to school, whereas only 1 percent of those with less than a high school diploma had renewed contact with the classroom; and 63 percent of those 65 years and over never graduated from high school.[21] It thus seems unrealistic to think that these elderly will return to the classroom to pursue educational pursuits of any sort. It is conceivable, however, that future generations of retirees, who will be better educated than the present cohorts, will view continuing education as a desirable and worthwhile retirement activity.

Summary of the Decision-Makers' Views on the Aged's Continued Social Participation

The decision-makers typically believed that retirement poses a crisis for many older persons because they are psychologically unprepared to substitute the work role with other activities that can equally provide meaning, value, and structure to the individual's retirement. The decision-makers tended to look at the retirement years not in terms of the "harvest years" when the elderly would reap the gains of a lifetime of hard work in delightful consummation of the pleasant experiences that life can offer, but rather the decision-makers pictured a crisis related to whiling away the hours and the days until death by keeping busy and/or amused.

The decision-makers saw little future for the elderly persisting in the employment role past age 65 unless the world of business and industry was radically altered. Out of a fear that the elderly terminated from their major role in society (that is, work) would continue to withdraw more and more from other forms of social participation and gradually dismiss all the major bases of social integration to the broader society, the decision-makers advocated reemploying the elderly in community service work, paid for by the government at the prevailing wage rate for similar work performed in the community by private or public organizations. The decision-makers thus saw the government as the employer of last resort on the elderly's behalf.

From one perspective, it could be argued that the decision-makers have thus subverted the leisure ethic into the instrumental prescriptions of the work ethic. The elderly must stay involved in meaningful, socially constructive political and social activities in their retirement years. To relax and take life easy in old age, fishing, reading, golfing, and so forth, and engaging in purely self-indulgent activities for entertainment is somehow a less viable role for the elderly in the minds of many, if not most of these decision-makers. Activity and engagement are prescribed for the elderly's lifestyle in retirement; retirement and withdrawal, even in old age, are deemed antisocial and hence rejected as socially unacceptable.

DECISION-MAKERS' PERCEPTIONS OF THE NEED FOR PRE-RETIREMENT PREPARATION PROGRAMS

The decision-makers' image of retirement living was not infrequently negative. The actual decision to retire was thought to be made more by corporate and union caveat rather than personal choice. Many retirees were perceived to be relegated to living on inadequate retirement incomes and unable to find even part-time jobs to supplement their poverty or near poverty-level incomes. Shut out of the labor market and not motivated to join community organizations or social groups, the elderly were frequently imagined to be bored, lonely, isolated, and generally unhappy with their lot. With this picture of life in retirement, it is no wonder that the decision-makers believed that it was very important to make as much preparation for the retirement years as possible. Many expressed confidence that with adequate planning beforehand, many employees would make a good transition to retirement living. The overwhelming majority of all the decision-maker subgroups believed that retirement preparation programs are needed to help people plan for retirement (see Table 7.14).

When queried about why more companies do not offer comprehensive formal retirement preparation programs for their older employees, the decision-makers most frequently cited the costs of developing such programs or the employers' attitudes (either unawareness or indifference) regarding the need for such programs. Almost three quarters of the decision-makers (74 percent) mentioned the former consideration and more than half (56 percent) cited the latter. Among those who mentioned the employer's outlook as a barrier to the development of retirement preparation programs, most cited the employers' indifference to or refusal to respond to employees' expressed desires for such programs; fewer believed that the employers were simply unaware of employees' demands or desires for retirement programs.

A considerably smaller percentage of the decision-makers (only one in five) blamed the lack of retirement programs on the lack of concerted demand for such programs by the employees themselves or the organizations (union, advocate) that represent them. A small minority of the decision-makers (9 percent) cited logistical problems for employers in putting on retirement programs, namely, too few older workers to make a formal program feasible, too high an employee turnover to assume responsibility for preparing people for retirement, too expensive for small companies to establish a formal program, and so forth. A very small group of decision-makers (6 percent) suggested that employers desired to set up pre-retirement programs, but simply lacked the knowledge or expertise to accomplish it. Finally, a sizable number suggested that employers may genuinely feel the responsibility to establish such programs lies elsewhere--with unions, with schools, with government, or even with the individual himself.

Among the 21 decision-makers who did not believe in the need for pre-retirement programs, the vast majority said that planning for retirement was the individual's own responsibility: "People who are intelligent enough to vote can plan for themselves" (a local legislator, I.D. 127). Several others believed the responsibility for presenting these programs lay elsewhere, with schools, with the media, or with government. One state legislator (I.D. 159) suggested, however, that the whole concept of retirement planning is questionable: "I don't think the general public would accept them. It seems too far ahead to the average person. The concept of saving for a rainy day--the average person doesn't accept this too readily."

TABLE 7.14

"Do You Think Retirement Preparation Programs Are Needed to Help People Plan for Retirement?" (percent responding "yes")

Positional Characteristics of the Decision-Makers	
Position in the Policy Process	
Legislators (N = 71)	90
Agency administrators (N = 70)	99
Service delivery personnel (N = 70)	96
Corporate directors of personnel (N = 35)	89
Union local presidents (N = 35)	86
Advocates for the aged (N = 35)	100
Responsibility for Aging Programs	
Primary function (N = 85)	98
Important but not central function (N = 88)	97
Minor function (N = 143)	90
Area of Program Expertise	
Health (N = 37)	95
Mental health (N = 23)	100
Housing (N = 29)	93
Employment (N = 92)	90
Income maintenance (N = 26)	85
Recreation/leisure (N = 18)	100
Senior citizens affairs (N = 49)	100
Generalists (N = 42)	93
Personal Characteristics of the Decision-Makers	
Age of the Respondent	
Under 45 (N = 98)	96
45-54 (N = 98)	94
55-64 (N = 90)	91
65 and over (N = 30)	93
Sex of the Respondent	
Male (N = 230)	94
Female (N = 86)	94
Ethnicity of the Respondent	
White (N = 235)	92
Minority (N = 81)	98
Educational Level of the Respondent	
High school graduate or less (N = 42)	88
Some college (N = 64)	92
College graduate (N = 99)	93
Postcollege professional education (N = 111)	97
Total (N = 316)	94

Source: Compiled by the author.

The crucial question for the future development of formal, company-sponsored pre-retirement programs is whether most workers would attend pre-retirement programs if made available to them. Nearly three quarters of the sample of decision-makers (72 percent) believed that older workers would attend them (see Table 7.15). Union local presidents were the least confident of that prediction; only a little more than half of them (57 percent) asserted most workers would attend pre-retirement programs if they were available. Their perceptions of the situation, which deviated significantly from the other subsamples, cannot be taken lightly, because these union officials are in close and constant contact with older workers in the unions and thus may be registering more accurately the workers' predispositions to attend such programs. Moreover, the union officials would be in the most advantageous position to push for the establishment of such programs through collective bargaining procedures if they perceived older workers wanted and needed them. Curiously, but also well worth noting, the decision-makers who themselves were in the pre-retirement age groups (aged 55 to 64) and who themselves might be appropriate candidates for a pre-retirement program, were significantly less confident than older or younger decision-makers that other pre-retirees would attend formal pre-retirement programs if available. The overwhelming majority of all groups of decision-makers, however, believed that older workers would attend pre-retirement programs.

Would older workers attend pre-retirement programs if available to them? Data from the nationwide Harris poll suggest that both the young and middle-aged public (aged 18 to 64) and the elderly (aged 65 plus) place enrollment in retirement counseling or retirement preparation programs far down their respective list of "very important steps in preparing for the later years." Whereas 80 percent or more of both groups mentioned checking into medical and financial resources for the later years and half to three quarters of both groups mentioned giving consideration to housing and leisure-time activities, less than one quarter of the public aged 18 to 64 (23 percent) and less than one fifth of the elderly public (19 percent) mentioned enrolling in formal retirement planning programs. Moreover, only 8 percent of the public 65 years or older had actually participated in such a program.[22]

Data from the survey of Los Angeles County residents aged 45 to 74 suggest a similar pattern of engagement in pre-retirement planning courses. Of those aged 45 to 64 who are still employed, almost half (45 percent) were aware of some pre-retirement course they could attend; one third of those aged 45 to 54 and two thirds of those aged 55 to 64 said that they do plan to attend those courses. Of those who did not know of any formal pre-retirement program

+

TABLE 7.15

"If Made Available to Them, Do You Think Most Workers Would Attend Pre-Retirement Courses?"
(percent responding "yes")

Positional Characteristics of the Decision-Makers	
Position in the Policy Process	
Legislators (N = 71)	68
Agency administrators (N = 70)	80
Service delivery personnel (N = 70)	69
Corporate directors of personnel (N = 35)	80
Union local presidents (N = 35)	57
Advocates for the aged (N = 35)	77
Responsibility for Aging Programs	
Primary function (N = 85)	72
Important but not central function (N = 88)	74
Minor function (N = 143)	71
Area of Program Expertise	
Health (N = 37)	73
Mental health (N = 23)	65
Housing (N = 29)	66
Employment (N = 92)	68
Income maintenance (N = 26)	81
Recreation/leisure (N = 18)	72
Senior citizens affairs (N = 49)	78
Generalists (N = 42)	74
Personal Characteristics of the Decision-Makers	
Age of the Respondent	
Under 45 (N = 98)	78
45-54 (N = 98)	73
55-64 (N = 90)	63
65 and over (N = 30)	73
Sex of the Respondent	
Male (N = 230)	71
Female (N = 86)	73
Ethnicity of the Respondent	
White (N = 235)	70
Minority (N = 81)	77
Educational Level of the Respondent	
High school graduate or less (N = 42)	76
Some college (N = 64)	77
College graduate (N = 99)	63
Postcollege professional education (N = 111)	70
Total (N = 316)	72

Source: Compiled by the author.

they could attend, more than half of those aged 45 to 54 (58 percent) said they would like to attend such a course, whereas only slightly more than one third of those aged 55 to 64 (34 percent) asserted they would like to attend such a course if made available to them.

In sum, it is difficult to ascertain whether or not decision-makers overemphasized the need for formal pre-retirement preparation programs to help workers plan for their later years, but they do appear to overemphasize considerably the workers' intentions or predispositions to attend such programs at the present time. Empirical studies confirm considerable reluctance on the part of employees to engage in formal retirement planning. Thus it is likely that retirement preparation programs will have to be institutionalized in the personnel practices of employers and unions if they are to have the desired effect in improving older workers' preparation for and subsequent adjustment to retirement living.

In the mid-1970s, a growing number of large corporations identified pre-retirement programs as a legitimate and necessary corporate function.[23] In smaller firms, however, pre-retirement programs may continue to be challenged as a legitimate expense. Retirement preparation programs sponsored by union organizations, as well as university and adult education organizations, conceivably could serve employees in these firms. To the extent that mandatory retirement policies push older workers out of the labor force against their will and oftentimes many years ahead of the usual retirement age of 65, the employees should at least have the advantage of being able to participate in company-sponsored or company-affiliated retirement preparation programs. Empirical studies confirm that this is increasingly the attitude of large corporations that are initiating programs for their employees.[24]

RETIREMENT POLICIES: IMPLICATIONS FOR FUTURE DECADES

The institution of retirement is new and still evolving in the U.S. context. The data presented in this chapter suggest that many sectors of the decision-making community do not endorse some of the retirement policies and practices that have evolved and become commonplace in the past several decades. The cross section of the decision-making community interviewed in this study registered strong opposition to the trend toward early retirement, to involuntary retirement, and to mandatory retirement on the basis of chronological age.

These decision-makers typically believed that many, maybe even most, older workers are forced out of their jobs and eventually the labor force by the decisions of their employers and/or their union organizations and that few workers actually choose to retire in order to enjoy a life of leisure. The decision-makers generally insisted that the vast majority of elderly people would prefer to continue working at least part time. For some elderly, said these decision-makers, it is a matter of needing the extra money to make ends meet on their small monthly retirement incomes; but for many more elderly, they underscored, continued employment is desired in order to remain active and involved in community affairs. Retirement is thus perceived by many of these decision-makers to lead to enforced idleness, which is not good for the individual's physical or mental well-being.

Nor were mass retirements seen as altogether beneficial for the social system that must support the enlarging retired population. Many of the decision-makers questioned the desirability of turning the management of the economy and other sectors of the society over to 25- to 50-year-olds. Retirement of older workers means an unestimated loss of valuable skills and experience from the labor force. Additionally, these decision-makers worried about the capability of existing income-maintenance systems to support a swelling retired population. Some feared a backlash from the younger working population who might suddenly resist the ever-growing tax burdens required to support the retirement system.

On the positive side, however, some of the decision-makers maintained that retirement policies institutionalized a turnover of jobs from older to younger workers. Retirement of older workers thus ensures needed upward mobility incentives for younger workers; at the same time, the problem of skills obsolescence is eliminated when older workers are retired and replaced by younger, better trained employees. Moreover, these decision-makers observed, many workers do choose to retire if they are assured of having a retirement income that appears adequate for their needs projected through the remainder of their lives. Such perceptions have apparently fueled the unions' drive to negotiate early retirement provisions in their collective bargaining contracts with various employers, and kindred perceptions have spurred many employers to support the early retirement trend. Retirement practices and policies of the 1950s and 1960s were forged in this climate of decision-making. Mandatory retirement policies became commonplace and early retirement practices were institutionalized.

Early retirement, however, turned out not to be the workers' choice. There has been no mass exodus from the labor force under new labor contracts containing early retirement provisions, at least no mass voluntary retirements.[25] Data on the early retirements taken under relatively new social security provisions that allow retirees to begin collecting reduced retirement benefits at age 62 reveal that early retirees have had considerably more spells of long unemployment and consistently lower wages than those who retire with full benefits at 65.[26] In other words, these early retirees appeared to be forced out of the labor market into retirement only because they are unable to find new jobs after a long search. One economist observed, "The early retirees hardly conform to the picture of persons with higher income taking the opportunity to indulge in the leisure of early retirement." Early retirement policies seemed to accommodate the employers' and unions' needs more than the older workers'.

In the mid-1970s, the decision-making community appeared to be reexamining many retirement policies and practices. The decision-makers in this sample acknowledged widespread age discrimination in the labor market that has made it difficult for older workers to find jobs. The decision-makers overwhelmingly supported abolition of mandatory retirement policies and urged employers and unions to allow older employees to continue working as long as they want to or as long as they are able to work productively. The decision-makers further advocated retraining as a better way than early retirement to deal with the problem of skills obsolescence in older workers, better not only for the individual worker but for the broader society as well. The overriding concern of the decision-makers interviewed in this study appeared to be finding ways to keep the elderly employed or otherwise actively involved in community affairs.

Recent legislative developments suggest that the climate of decision-making is sufficiently altered from that of the 1950s and 1960s to produce real changes in retirement policies. A number of state legislatures (for example, New York) have successfully eliminated the upper age limit on their age discrimination laws so that an employer's refusal to hire a worker beyond age 65 solely for reasons of his advanced age constitutes age discrimination of the kind prohibited by the law. A number of bills introduced in Congress in recent years seek to accomplish the same reform with the federal ADEA (Anti-Discrimination in Employment Act) law. Judging from public opinion generally and the attitudes of many in the decision-making community in particular, the ADEA law is likely to be amended soon to provide the same coverage to workers beyond the normal retirement age as is now given to workers between the ages of 40 and 65.

At the same time, mandatory retirement policies are confronting a legislative challenge. More than one quarter of the states already have some kind of ban on compulsory retirement policies, and it appears certain that in 1978 there will be a new federal law prohibiting the application of mandatory retirement policies to workers under age 70. The climate of decision-making suggests that it is only a matter of time before the normal mandatory age will be age 70 rather than age 65. As the personnel director in a media corporation (I.D. 425) observed, "There is nothing magic about age 65. It is an individual problem." Age 65 was popularized as the normal retirement age because of a political decision made in 1935 to initiate social security retirement benefits to individuals who retired at that age. The age was not selected on the basis of scientific data that profiled declines in the worker's job performance beyond age 65. Better health care in the early and middle years of life means that many workers enjoy good health in their 60s and can continue to work at their jobs for many more years if that is their choice and employment policies permit it. Raising the mandatory retirement age to 70 or doing away with it altogether may leave the decision of whether to retire or continue to work more to the individual, who many feel should have the option to choose.

It is possible, of course, that employers will circumvent the limitations on mandatory retirement policies under a program of large-scale early retirements. The decision-makers in this sample acknowledged considerable age bias on the part of employers for younger, better trained workers. Skills obsolescence and declining health are perceived by employers and others in the decision-making community to be the major detriments of employing older workers. many of the 316 decision-makers suggested these purported obstacles to using older workers are only myths. They maintained older workers show no more absenteeism than younger workers, and possibly even less absenteeism. Others insisted that older workers can perform most jobs as well as younger workers by compensating for speed decrements with experience on the job. These decision-makers believed that the barriers to hiring older workers would be eliminated by educating employers and unions about the skills and capabilities of older workers.

Others in the decision-making community believed the obstacles to hiring older workers could be more substantial, namely, that many, maybe even most older workers do, in fact, suffer from declining health status and skills obsolescence that would affect their job performance negatively. They believed it was important to consider retraining programs to update the skills of older workers. Alternatively, they lobbied for relocating the elderly in new jobs better suited to their limited capabilities or redesigning the elderly worker's own job to accommodate his changing capabilities.

Midcareer retraining has not been extensively practiced or institutionalized in either the private or public sector. The lion's share of training monies goes to assist the young in preparing for new job assignments, with very little money being spent to train workers over the age of 45, let alone over the age of 65. Several efforts in recent years to enact a Mid-Career Development Program under the Older Americans Act have not been successful, and the prospects for establishment of a program on the scale required to deal with the problem of skills obsolescence in later life appear very remote at the present time. The problem has not been adequately defined or responsibility for its solution properly assigned. Many believe retraining of older workers to be an employer or union responsibility. As yet, however, employers and unions have not institutionalized the means to retrain their older workers. As a group, they seem to find it economically more feasible to retire the older worker and hire a young recruit directly out of the educational system than to retrain the older worker at their own expense.

Apart from the feeling that "the ability of older people to learn is diminished from that of the college grad" (a local legislator, I.D. 120), there is also a widespread sentiment that it is a waste of time and money to retrain an older person when the money could be spent to train a young person with an added work life expectancy of 20 or 30 years. Unless the federal government acts to make it more financially feasible for employers to retrain their older workers on a continuing basis, the employers' practice of large-scale early retirements is likely to continue with little abatement, despite changes worked in the employers' mandatory retirement policies by federal laws. Mandatory retirement policies will exist on paper and early retirement policies will continue in practice.

Job redesign as a way to keep older workers employed when their health begins to fail and their work performance declines has not gained much popularity in the United States. Depending upon the success European companies have with the concept, perhaps job design will be tried. Short of redesigning the content of jobs, much might still be done to make existing jobs more compatible with the changing capabilities of older workers. For example, many workers in their later years might prefer to work part time rather than full time. At present, however, the economic sector offers relatively few part-time opportunities. Even fewer workers are able to cut down to part time in their present jobs; usually, the elderly have to quit their full-time job and look for a new part-time job. Many elderly who desire to remain employed, although only on a part-time basis, want to remain employed part time in their present job, not as a school crossing guard or night watchman. Their wish is rarely fulfilled.

One decision-maker suggested that it was the "inability of our present manufacturing and production systems to break down jobs to part time for older persons" (a housing program administrator,

I.D. 230). But is it the inability of the system to develop part-time jobs or the inertia of the system? Some, at least, believe the latter and therefore believe that the employment system can be modified. On the theory that the federal government is the model employer and that private sector business and union organizations will adopt an employment policy implemented successfully in the federal government, a few bills have been introduced in Congress in past years that would mandate a percentage of all federal government positions be made part time. Although none of these bills has been successfully enacted to date, they indicate the serious consideration being given to the problem of the lack of part-time jobs in U.S. industry. If the federal government is successful in encouraging and/or mandating private industry to develop more part-time job opportunities, elderly workers will certainly be among the beneficiaries.

Many of the decision-makers seemed to question whether persistence in the employment role past age 65 would be an option open to many elderly people who would like to keep working either because they need the money or they would like to remain active. Because of the bias of private industry against older workers and because of the inflexibility of job arrangements in private industry, many of the decision-makers did not believe elderly workers would find suitable employment in the private sector. These decision-makers urged the government to act as the employer of last resort by establishing community service projects to engage elderly workers on a paid basis. They believed that it is important not to let the elderly's skills go to waste but to keep them working on community problems; at the same time, they noted, elderly who are poor can earn additional income, while elderly who want to remain active can feel they are still making a valuable contribution to the community or the larger society. Few of the decision-makers in this survey directly opposed the idea of using paid elderly volunteers in community service programs, and the trend in aging programs is to offer more such opportunities for the elderly's continued community involvement.

But one major unresolved question is how to inform retiring workers about the opportunities that exist for continued involvement in community activities. Many of the decision-makers suggested that employers as part of their pre-retirement preparation programs should inform their retiring employees about community service opportunities and encourage them to pursue such work substitutes after retirement. Decision-makers were strongly agreed about the need for pre-retirement programs to help older workers make a satisfactory adjustment to retirement, and steering retirees into community service roles was perceived to be one important function that these retirement preparation programs might serve.

The decision-making community has begun to define a new employer responsibility vis-a-vis older employees in the sponsorship of pre-retirement programs to aid the older worker in making the transition from working to retired status. The decision-makers interviewed in this study perceived widespread retirement crises among the retiring workers, and they nearly unanimously agreed that retirement preparation programs will aid workers in making the retirement transition successfully. In light of the attitudes expressed by this sample of decision-makers, it is not surprising that the California state government is beginning to consider the feasibility of requiring state agencies and departments to sponsor retirement preparation programs for their retiring employees. In the 1976 term, a bill was introduced in the state legislature requesting a comprehensive survey of the retirement counseling needs of the state employees nearing retirement. Within the state, state government operates in the role of model employer. If the state government does implement retirement preparation programs for its employees, it may spur the development of such programs in the private sector, where many employers presently have a "wait and see if they work" attitude about establishing retirement preparation programs for their own employees.

The foregoing paragraphs suggest public policy actions likely to come in the next decade as federal and state governments assume an increasing role in shaping the further institutionalization of the retirement process in U.S. society. A major longitudinal study of the retirement process conducted in the 1960s concluded: "The general economic, social and psychological situation that retirees face today is similar to that of a decade ago, particularly from the standpoint of social psychology--that is, the adaptations that must be made in coping with the cessation of employment, the decline in health, and the reduction of income have not altered greatly in the course of ten years."[27] Decision-makers apparently seek to avoid a similar indictment of the retirement transition workers must make in 1990.

NOTES

1. Fred Cottrell, "The Technological and Societal Bases of Aging," in Handbook of Social Gerontology, ed. Clark Tibbitts (Chicago: University of Chicago Press, 1960), pp. 92-119; Wilma Donahue, Harold L. Orbach, and Otto Pollack, "Retirement: The Emerging Social Pattern," in Handbook of Social Gerontology, ed. Clark Tibbitts (Chicago: University of Chicago Press, 1960), pp. 330-406; Donald O. Cowgill and Lowell D. Holmes, eds., Aging and Modernization (New York: Appleton-Century-Crofts, 1972).

2. U.S. Department of Health, Education and Welfare, Facts About Older Americans, 1975, DHEW Publication No. OHD 75-20006, 1975.

3. Julian Abbott, "Covered Employment and the Age Men Claim Retirement Benefits," Social Security Bulletin 37, no. 4 (April 1974): 3-16.

4. Frances M. Carp, ed., Retirement (New York: Behavioral Publications, 1972).

5. Ida H. Simpson and John C. McKinney, eds., Social Aspects in Aging (Durham, N.C.: Duke University, 1966); Carp, Retirement.

6. Irving Rosow, Socialization to Old Age (Berkeley: University of California Press, 1974).

7. Gordon F. Streib and Clement J. Schneider, Jr., Retirement in American Society (Ithaca, N.Y.: Cornell University Press, 1971), p. 163.

8. A. William Pollman, "Early Retirement: Relationship to Variation in Life Satisfaction," Pt. I, Gerontologist 11, no. 1 (Spring 1971): 43-47; Streib and Schneider, Retirement in American Society; H. Charles Pyron and U. Vincent Manion, "The Company, the Individual and the Decision to Retire," Industrial Gerontology 4 (Winter 1970): 1-11; Richard Barfield and James Morgan, Early Retirement: The Decision and the Experience (Ann Arbor: University of Michigan, Institute for Social Research, 1969).

9. Louis Harris and Associates, The Myth and the Reality of Aging in America (Washington, D.C.: National Council on the Aging, 1975), p. 87.

10. Ibid., p. 89.

11. Ibid., p. 213.

12. A. William Pollman, "Early Retirement: A Comparison of Poor Health to Other Retirement Factors," Journal of Gerontology 26, no. 1 (January 1971): 41-45.

13. Barfield and Morgan, Early Retirement; Wayne R. Davidson, "Some Observations about Early Retirement in Industry," Industrial Gerontology 1, no. 1 (February 1969): 26-30.

14. Abbott, "Covered Employment and the Age Men Claim Retirement Benefits."

15. U.S. Congress, Senate, Private Welfare and Pension Plan Study, Pt. I, Hearings before the Subcommittee on Labor and Public Welfare, 92d Cong., 1st sess. (Washington, D.C.: U.S. Government Printing Office, 1971).

16. Patricia L. Kasschau, "Perceived Age-Discrimination in a Sample of Aerospace Employees," Gerontologist 16, no. 2 (April 1976): 166-73.

17. Robert J. Havighurst, "The Social Competence of Middle Age," Genetic Psychology Monographs 56 (1957): 297-375; Arnold M. Rose and Warren A. Peterson, Older People and Their Social World (Philadelphia: Davis, 1965).

18. Harris and Associates, The Myth and the Reality of Aging in America, pp. 95-105.

19. Ibid., pp. 182-91.

20. Ibid., p. 188.

21. Ibid., pp. 106-10.

22. Ibid., p. 118.

23. Richard S. Prentis, National Survey of Fortune's "500" Pre-Retirement Plans and Policies (Ann Arbor: University of Michigan-Wayne State University, Institute of Labor and Industrial Relations, July 1975). The major findings of the report are summarized in a book review to be found in Industrial Gerontology 4, no. 2 (Spring 1977): 140-43.

24. Ibid.

25. Davidson, "Some Observations about Early Retirement in Industry."

26. Robinson Hollister, "Social Mythology and Reform: Income Maintenance for the Aged," Annals of the American Academy of Political and Social Science 415 (September 1974): 26.

27. Streib and Schneider, Retirement in American Society, p. vii.

8 Patterns of Informaion Seeking in the Decision-Making Community: Access to Influence the Climate of Decision-Making in the Field of Aging

DECISION-MAKING ON THE BASIS OF AVAILABLE INFORMATION: A SUBJECT IN NEED OF RESEARCH

The rational decision-making model of policy formulation--that is, planning and programming based on factual information about the problems and needs of selected target groups in the general population--has been much maligned in the social science literature. In lieu of rational planning, political and social analysts propose that political bargaining and organizational interests reign supreme in the formulation of public policy.[1] Although rational planning or decision-making may not characterize the social policy process in practice, it nevertheless appears to persist as the ideal model for policy development. Most policy analysts would still probably agree with Thomas Dye's concession to the rational decision-making model: "Social scientists simply do not know enough about individual and group behavior to be able to give reliable advice to policy-makers. . . . Although some scholars argue that no advice is better than contradictory or inaccurate advice, policymakers must still make decisions, and it is probably better that they act in light of whatever little knowledge social science can provide than that they act in the absence of knowledge at all."[2]

Recent efforts have been made to enhance rational or systematic decision-making in the public arena. The PPBS (Planning, Programming, and Budgeting System) instituted in the federal social agencies during the 1960s was one attempt to develop a sound information base about social problems and policy responses that decision-makers could then use to make decisions about programs goals and implementation. Political observers differ markedly in their evaluation of the success of PPBS and other attempts to institutionalize rational policy analysis in the mainline channels of policy formulation and implementation.[3] Still the hope persists that when scientific fact finding is injected into the political climate of decision-making, which is dominated by interest-group competition and organizational imperatives, the policy outcome will optimize improvements in the general well-being of the people living in the United States. The prevailing consensus remains that serious efforts must be made to get more and better information into the decision-making process in the hope that such information will lead to more systematic development of policy solutions to identified social needs.

Despite the growing attention to the role that factual information should assume in the development of social policies, surprisingly little empirical investigation has been made of the decision-makers' utilization of various sources of information that provide the backdrop for their social policy decisions. A significant exception is to be found in a recent study completed by the University of Michigan's Institute for Social Research.[4] Based on open-ended interviews with 200 top-level federal agency and cabinet officials, the research report reached the conclusion that "only rarely is policy formulation determined by a concrete, point-by-point reliance on empirically grounded data. Although the impact of 'soft' information (i.e., 'nonempirical') on government functioning is extremely difficult to assess, our data suggest that there is widespread use of soft information and that its impact on policy, although often indirect, may be great or even greater than the impact of hard information."[5] Because of the paucity of data from similar studies, the report cautioned that it was difficult to conclude whether the federal decision-makers made substantial or little use of the empirical knowledge base available, but the researchers did feel confident in concluding that "knowledge is used at top levels of government decision-making and probably to a greater degree than most experts in the area of utilization would expect."[6]

This chapter contributes much-needed empirical data pertaining to the sources of information that the 316 decision-makers in this study reported consulting for information about the problems and needs of the elderly. For readers perusing earlier chapters of this volume who have grown progressively anxious over how to reach key decision-makers with information about the elderly's needs that could influence the decisions those gatekeepers will make, this chapter provides some information about potential channels of access to various decision-makers. Judging from the decision-makers' expressed dissatisfaction with their available information base in the field of aging and their reported receptivity to more and better information concerning the needs and problems of the elderly, there appear to be valuable opportunities to provide key decision-makers with more and better information about aging that could be instrumental in developing a more enlightened climate of decision-making in the field of aging.

The chapter begins with the decision-makers' evaluations of the available information base in the field of aging along with their recommendations for improving that information base. The second section analyzes the sources of information these decision-makers reported consulting on a regular basis, and considers whether those who rely upon specific information sources either have more accurate information about the needs of the aged or express greater satisfaction with their current information base for the purpose of designing social intervention strategies to assist the elderly. The decision-makers' evaluation of the White House Conference on Aging as an effective planning tool in the policy process will be discussed as well as their assessment of the role that social science research can have in enlightening the climate of decision-making in the field of aging.

Finally, for those who on occasion feel personally frustrated at being unable to influence the climate of decision-making, this chapter probes the kindred feelings of these 316 decision-makers located in diverse positions within the policy process. To what extent do these decision-makers feel that they themselves have sufficient opportunity to influence policy and program outcomes, and how would they suggest ensuring greater input in policy decisions from others like themselves? Strategies for advocacy on behalf of the aged are also discussed in light of the data presented in this chapter.

THE DECISION-MAKERS' EVALUATION OF THE ADEQUACY OF THE EXISTING INFORMATION BASE IN THE FIELD OF AGING

Only one third of the 316 decision-makers interviewed in this study affirmed that they had sufficient information about the problems of the elderly to make informed decisions about programs and policies affecting that segment of the population. The remainder defined their existing information base as seriously deficient for their policy-making needs (Table 8.1). Only one subgroup in the entire decision-making community responded in the majority that their information was adequately tailored to their decision-making responsibilities vis-a-vis the aged, namely, the decision-makers who were themselves 65 years of age and older. A decision-maker's personal experience with growing old conceivably would inform him about or make him more sensitive to the problems other people face when

TABLE 8.1

"In Your Position, Do You Feel You Have All the Information You Need to Work Effectively with the Problems of Middle-Aged and Older People?"
(percent responding "yes")

Positional Characteristics of the Decision-Makers	
Position in the Policy Process	
Legislators (N = 71)	42
Agency administrators (N = 70)	39
Service delivery personnel (N = 70)	33
Corporate directors of personnel (N = 35)	29
Union local presidents (N = 35)	20
Advocates for the aged (N = 35)	34
Responsibility for Aging Programs	
Primary function (N = 85)	41
Important but not central function (N = 88)	28
Minor function (N = 143)	34
Area of Program Expertise	
Health (N = 37)	46
Mental health (N = 23)	17
Housing (N = 29)	21
Employment (N = 92)	27
Income maintenance (N = 26)	50
Recreation/leisure (N = 18)	56
Senior citizens affairs (N = 49)	39
Generalists (N = 42)	36
Personal Characteristics of the Decision-Makers	
Age of the Respondent	
Under 45 (N = 98)	22
45-54 (N = 98)	34
55-64 (N = 90)	40
65 and over (N = 30)	60
Sex of the Respondent	
Male (N = 230)	35
Female (N = 86)	33
Ethnicity of the Respondent	
White (N = 235)	38
Minority (N = 81)	25
Educational Level of the Respondent	
High school graduate or less (N = 42)	33
Some college (N = 64)	31
College graduate (N = 99)	35
Postcollege professional education (N = 111)	36
Total (N = 316)	34

Source: Compiled by the author.

they grow old. A local legislator (I.D. 112) confessed: "Maybe the biggest problem is that no one knows about the blight until we are there ourselves. . . . I am only becoming aware of some of the problems of older people now." He was 58 years old.

Among the original six subsamples, the legislators were the most likely to express satisfaction with their information base for their own policy-making needs. They also have the advantage of legislative hearings and legislative research staff to gather information on the problems confronting their aging constituency. Union local presidents were least often content with their access to information about the elderly; only one in five defined their information base as adequate for their leadership role in the union structure. Of some surprise was that two out of three advocates for the aged maintained that they did not have adequate information on which to plan effective strategies for program intervention to assist their elderly constituency.

Recommendations for improving the existing information base were sought from those 202 decision-makers who indicated that their information about the needs of the elderly was less than satisfactory for their policy-making needs. Most often the decision-makers urged the development of a comprehensive director of programs and services that are available to assist elderly residents living in the community. Many of these decision-makers thought programs might be available to help elderly persons in need with whom they came in contact in the course of performing their jobs, but they simply did not presently know where to refer these elderly for assistance. Nearly half of the service provider group and nearly four in ten of the agency administrators and advocates for the aged insisted that the lack of referral information posed a serious barrier to their providing adequate assistance to elderly people in need.

More than one quarter of the decision-makers cited the need for more and better information about the problems and needs of elderly residents living in their communities. This was of particular concern to the legislators. One in five of these legislators felt that they could gain a better understanding of the elderly's problems if they could somehow structure more direct contact with elderly residents in their jurisdiction. Legislators were also more likely than other decision-makers to ask for the results of needs assessment surveys conducted locally in order to learn more about the specific problems confronting elderly residents in their community. More commonly, however, the decision-makers looked to census data and other national statistical reports to provide them with useful information regarding the elderly's life circumstances and unmet needs. While these decision-makers liked the reliability of the national-level data, they complained that it was difficult to get regional breakdowns in the data that could provide them with accurate and detailed information about conditions in their own communities.

Policy analysts, reflecting on what they would consider to be the information needs of decision-makers engaged in developing effective program intervention strategies, usually suggest the need for well-designed evaluation research to monitor policy and program outcomes and also the need for improved channels of communication for information exchange between agencies and departments that are providing similar or related services to the same target group in the population. But these information needs were infrequently mentioned by this sample of decision-makers. Also seldom mentioned by these decision-makers was the need for any formal education in gerontology to learn what is known about aging and the aged. Despite a growing number of gerontology training programs sponsoring one-day, one-weekend, and one-week institutes on aging for professionals whose jobs bring them into contact with the elderly, most of these decision-makers were not interested in or did not think in terms of enrolling in any formal seminars or workshops on aging. The exceptions were the service providers and the advocates for the aged. One in six of each of these groups expressed an interest in attending seminars on aging to gain access to whatever information is currently available in the field of gerontology.

SOURCES OF INFORMATION ABOUT AGING THAT DECISION-MAKERS REPORTED USING OFTEN

If decision-makers are so unhappy with their present body of information about the needs of the elderly population, it bears examining where they get what information they do have. It probably will not be possible to change decision-makers' information-seeking habits. But providing data on the decision-makers' patterns of information seeking may inform advocates for the aged and others wishing to inject more information about the needs of the elderly constituency into the decision-making processes that fashion aging programs as to where they will have the greatest access to which kinds of decision-makers.

A list of eight commonly identified sources of information in the decision-making community emerged from more than 100 pretest interviews: mass media, professionals and experts in the field of aging, organizations representing the elderly, government documents and reports, legislative hearings, direct contact with older persons deriving from on-the-job experiences, and personal experiences with aging or vicarious experiences deriving from observing aging in relatives and friends. Patterns of utilization of these information sources by the 316 decision-makers in this study proved to be extremely diverse.

The overwhelming majority (71 percent) of the sample relied upon their experiences with the elderly people whom they met during the routine performance of their jobs to educate themselves about the needs and problems of elderly people so that in the future they could address the needs of elderly clients more effectively (Table 8.2). In addition, nearly six out of ten decision-makers in this sample generalized from their personal or vicarious experiences with aging in an effort to understand the special problems elderly people have so that they could take various age-related problems into account when they designed programs or delivered services. Contact with aging individuals either in the structured professional relationship or in the more informal context of family and friends thus supplied the primary body of information on the problems of growing old to most of these decision-makers who have instrumental roles in shaping policies and programs to help the elderly.

Half of the decision-makers reported learning a lot about aging from the mass media; nearly as many reported that they relied on receiving pertinent data from a variety of aging organizations. Somewhat smaller percentages reported relying on government documents and reports (40 percent), professionals and experts in the field of aging (36 percent), and legislative hearings (33 percent). Only one in five reported regularly using the findings from scientific research on aging.

These data suggest that a pattern of relatively passive information seeking tends to dominate throughout much of the decision-making community. The decision-makers in this study reported learning much of what they know about aging and the elderly from nothing more than the routine of their daily lives. This would include what they learn about aging from reading newspapers and watching television, what they learn about aging from dealing with elderly people in the performance of their jobs, and what they learn about aging as they themselves age and they watch their family and friends around them age. In contrast, many fewer decision-makers actively sought out information on aging from additional sources. Thus, if it required writing for government reports or the record of legislative hearings, contacting aging organizations, calling on professionals and experts in the field of aging, or culling out relevant findings from available scientific surveys, far fewer decision-makers were willing to make the effort. The onus of outreach thus falls to researchers and advocates if they desire to inject more and better information into the decision-making in the policy process. Moreover, it appears that outside of direct outreach to decision-makers on the job, the only way to reach the sizable number in the decision-making community who have passive information-seeking habits will be through mass media presentations in prime space or prime time ("not at 2:00 a.m.-4:00 a.m. when they are asleep" contested the president of one union local, I.D. 515).

Decision-makers' patterns of information utilization depended upon who they were and where they were positioned in the policy process. The nature of the audience relying on each of these information sources is thus examined more closely. The observation might be made at the outset that the advocates for the aged and other categoric decision-makers made relatively frequent use of nearly all of the information sources listed here, with the exception of scientific research, which was underutilized by all segments of the decision-making community. The more closely involved a decision-maker was with aging programs, the more likely he was to draw upon each of these sources of information in his professional capacity. Others in the decision-making community showed more varied information-seeking behavior, and because advocates on behalf of the elderly are often keenly interested in reaching generic decision-makers with information about the needs and problems of the elderly age group, it is appropriate to consider which decision-makers may more commonly be reached through what sources of information.

The Mass Media

The media touch on the subject of aging in diverse contexts: in the news, in science reports, in human interest stories, in entertainment shows, and in sociological or anthropological documentaries. Of the original six subsamples, only the union local presidents relatively infrequently relied on mass media reports as a primary source of information about the life circumstances of elderly people. In contrast, the corporate directors of personnel relied more often on mass media as a source of information, including experiences in their personal lives and encounters with older people in their positions as heads of the personnel departments in their companies. Agency administrators also tended to rely more heavily on the mass media presentations than did other segments of the decision-making community. Recreation program directors were more likely than specialists in other program areas to report relying on mass media portrayals of the problems of the aging.* In contrast to many

*Caution should be exercised in interpreting percentages based on small N. The data are presented to indicate possible trends in this segment of the decision-making community.

TABLE 8.2

Sources of Information Decision-Makers Reported Using "Often" to Learn about the Problems Confronting the Aged

Decision-Makers' Positional and Personal Characteristics	Mass Media (percent)	Professionals and Experts (percent)
Positional Characteristics of the Decision-Makers		
Position in the Policy Process		
Legislators (N = 71)	45	34
Administrative agency heads (N = 70)	60	34
Service delivery personnel (N = 70)	50	48
Corporate directors of personnel (N = 35)	51	11
Union local presidents (N = 35)	31	17
Advocates for the aged (N = 35)	57	63
Responsibility for Aging Programs		
Primary function (N = 85)	54	55
Important but not central function (N = 88)	51	38
Minor function (N = 143)	47	24
Area of Program Expertise*		
Health (N = 37)	54	43
Mental health (N = 23)	48	35
Housing (N = 29)	55	52
Employment (N = 92)	42	20
Income and taxation (N = 26)	50	19
Recreation/leisure (N = 18)	67	44
Senior citizens affairs (N = 49)	47	63
Generalists (N = 42)	48	29
Personal Characteristics of the Decision-Makers		
Age of the Respondent		
Under 45 (N = 98)	53	36
45-54 (N = 98)	49	31
55-64 (N = 90)	49	34
65 and over (N = 30)	47	60
Sex of the Respondent		
Male (N = 230)	52	34
Female (N = 86)	45	41
Ethnicity of the Respondent		
White (N = 235)	50	37
Minority (N = 81)	49	35
Educational Level of the Respondent		
High school graduate or less (N = 42)	48	31
Some college (N = 64)	41	39
College graduate (N = 99)	49	34
Postcollege professional education (N = 111)	58	38
Total (N = 316)	50	36

*Small base N for percentages--interpret these percentages only as a possible trend in the data.

"Often" Used Sources of Information					
Government Reports (percent)	Scientific Research (percent)	Legislative Hearings (percent)	Contact with the Elderly (percent)	Personal Experiences (percent)	Aging Organizations (percent)
37	20	51	70	58	49
63	26	37	66	57	46
31	23	21	83	64	44
26	6	9	46	49	6
26	14	26	57	49	29
46	26	43	97	63	94
57	26	46	94	67	80
41	19	38	75	65	48
29	18	22	54	48	23
41	30	19	70	70	30
29	22	17	65	61	30
55	28	31	79	52	48
33	12	26	54	49	23
46	4	46	77	73	50
33	11	33	89	61	78
51	27	47	92	59	92
31	21	45	62	55	40
31	16	31	65	51	38
34	18	31	66	61	46
53	26	30	72	56	41
50	23	57	97	73	80
41	18	37	68	56	46
35	26	23	78	63	44
42	22	32	69	58	42
35	16	36	75	56	56
41	14	36	69	57	48
44	23	28	81	61	56
36	20	31	71	51	46
41	21	36	65	62	38
40	20	33	71	58	45

Source: Compiled by the author.

other sources of information, the mass media reached large numbers in almost every segment of the decision-making community.

Professionals and Experts in the Field of Aging

Professionals and experts in the field of aging should be uniquely qualified to understand the special problems of the elderly, but outside of the advocates for the aged, only the service delivery personnel frequently reported relying on professionals and experts in gerontology for information about the elderly's needs that would permit them to do a better job in providing services to their elderly clients. The corporate directors of personnel and union local presidents, on the other hand, rarely sought out these professionals for information and consultation on matters pertaining to older workers. Housing planners, health officials, and recreation directors all displayed relatively good access to gerontology experts, whereas employment and income-maintenance specialists only infrequently consulted with gerontologists to obtain information about the elderly's special problems and needs.

Government Documents and Reports

Government reports typically offer highly detailed and statistically accurate data on the elderly's needs based on national surveys of monumental scope that no local agency could hope to duplicate even on a smaller scale within their own jurisdiction. Agency administrators understandably relied heavily on government reports; the service delivery personnel in those same government agencies made considerably less use of those government documents. Service providers were most likely to turn to gerontologists for information than to the government reports. The reason is not difficult to hypothesize. Gerontologists probably give service providers more relevant information of the sort that would facilitate the delivery of services in the interpersonal setting between service provider and aged client; the numbers and statistics on the problems of the aged that would be found in the government reports would be of more remote utility in such a face-to-face context.

The legislators also did not pay much attention to government reports. The legislators tended to be most interested in obtaining data on the specific needs of the aged constituency in their own jurisdiction as well as desiring data on the extent to which existing community programs were satisfactorily addressing those needs. Their expressed requests for such information suggest that they might not find national statistics particularly useful.

Scientific Research

Ideally, scientific research offers objective, empirical information on the problems of the elderly--at least so say these decision-makers, as will be documented later in this chapter. Regular use of scientific research findings, however, was infrequent in all segments of the decision-making community sampled in this study, but it was particularly ignored by the corporate directors of personnel, the income-maintenance specialists, and the leisure/recreation planners. In contrast, a sizable minority of the health professionals and the housing officials did frequently consult the research findings in their field. Health and housing are among the most researched of the elderly's problems. Perhaps this means that when social science can accumulate a body of specific policy-relevant data, decision-makers will consult the available scientific literature in the course of performing their jobs.

Legislative Hearings and Testimony

Published records of hearings held by legislative committees in the process of considering legislation to create or modify or terminate programs are available at little or no cost to interested professionals and they are relatively easy to obtain. For this reason they seem to have become an increasingly popular information source over the past decade as professionals have learned about their availability. The hearings provide information and data on the problems of the elderly and the effectiveness of social programs in dealing with those problems. The hearings also evaluate program innovations and discuss program oversights or dysfunctions. Additionally, demographic and statistical information on the elderly tabulated by government agencies are frequently included in the hearing record.

It could hardly be surprising that the legislative subsample was the most likely to report frequent use of this particular information source to obtain data on the needs and problems of the elderly. But the legislators proved to be the only subsample in which the majority frequently relied on hearings testimony. Outside of the advocates, only the agency administrators also took advantage of the availability of the record from these hearings in any significant number. Those agency and program heads who do regularly subscribe to these legislative hearings should find them rich in suggestions for improving programs and services to the elderly in their own departments, as the purpose of these hearings generally is to hear from program administrators about what works and what does not work in delivering services to the elderly.

Direct Personal Contact with the Aged

Direct personal contact with elderly people in the performance of professional duties provided a primary source of information about the elderly's problems for the overwhelming majority of the decision-making community. The obvious question is the extent to which the information about the elderly's problems gleaned from contacts with such a sample of older persons is accurate or representative of the range of problems extant among the elderly population with which these decision-makers may sometime have to contend. On the surface, at least, it appears not an altogether reliable source for gaining accurate information about the needs and problems that do in fact exist in the elderly population.

Advocates for the aged, of course, reported virtually unanimously that direct contact with elderly people was a primary source of information for them concerning the needs and problems of this subpopulation; in their role as advocates for this aged constituency, it is not only a totally appropriate but a prerequisite information source. Five out of six in the subsample of service delivery personnel also claimed that direct contact with elderly people was an important source of information about the elderly's needs and problems; their skill in administering to the needs of elderly clients undoubtedly comes in large part from the experience they gain from many such contacts with elderly persons in the service delivery context. Corporate directors of personnel were the only subsample in which a majority did not cite direct personal contact with elderly persons as a primary information source. Union local presidents were also considerably less likely than the other subsamples of decision-makers to identify personal contact with elderly people as an important information source in the performance of their professional duties and obligations toward older persons.

Personal Experiences with Aging and Vicarious Experiences of Family and Friends

One would expect that everyone would have at least some opportunity for fairly close observation of the aging process in those around him--family, friends, colleagues--if not in himself. Only somewhat more than half of the sample of decision-makers (58 percent), however, considered these personal observations to constitute an important source of information for them about the problems of aging and the special needs of the aged in the general population. One must ask to what extent do these decision-makers, mostly from upper-middle-class backgrounds, gain an accurate image of the range and extent of problems and needs in the general aging population, especially the disadvantaged segments of that population, from observing the experiences of their family and friends?

Reliance on personal experiences as a source of information about the problems confronting most elderly people was more or less uniformly common throughout the decision-making community. Quite understandably, the eldest decision-makers, those who themselves had passed the social marker of age 65 for old age, were far more likely than the decision-makers in early, middle, and late middle age to draw upon personal experiences for information about the problems of growing old.

Organizations of the Aged

A number of formal organizations exist to advocate and promote better programs for the elderly. They exist at the national, state, and local levels and are visible to different audiences in the decision-making community accordingly.[7] Aside from the advocates, however, no other subsample contained a majority who reported using the aging organizations as a primary information source on the needs and problems of the older population. Less than half of the legislators and agency personnel positioned at all levels in the government social agencies reported frequently using reference materials from the formal aging organizations. Only three out of ten (29 percent) of the union local presidents sought out the information provided by these aging groups, and a mere one in eighteen (6 percent) of the corporate directors of personnel found the aging organizations a good source of information on the needs of the elderly. Housing planners, income program administrators, and recreational program directors relied fairly extensively on the information supplied by various aging organizations. In contrast, health and employment specialists made relatively less use of this source of information.

Sources of Information Decision-Makers Report Never Using

For those interested in knowing how to reach decision-makers with policy-relevant information, it is equally important to know the sources of information that these decision-makers reportedly "never" use along with those they report using "often" (see Table 8.3). A few merit comment. Approximately half of the corporate directors of personnel and the union local presidents never consult various aging organizations, professionals and experts in the field of aging, or scientific research in order to learn more about the problems and the capabilities of older workers on the job. Decision-makers who have never attended college were far more likely never to use scientific research findings to learn about the elderly, and they were also more likely never to consult professionals and experts in the field or contact various aging organizations for information. For the most part, each of the information sources was used at least from time to time by most of the decision-making community. The single exception is the empirical body of information generated by scientific research, which does not appear to reach a sizable part of the decision-making community.

An Overview of Decision-Makers' Sources of Information

A decision-maker's preferred information sources depends on who he is and where he is located in the policy process. To reach decision-makers with information about the aged germane to their policy decisions, the information should be disseminated through those channels that the decision-makers consult to obtain such information. If a substantial number of decision-makers in any one segment of the decision-making community does not consult a particular information source, obviously, it is an inefficient use of time and money to seek to influence their opinions by disseminating information through that channel. Influencing the climate of decision-making depends on putting policy-relevant information into the policy deliberation process through those channels decision-makers reportedly use often. The channels of information dissemination and advocacy selected by those seeking to influence the climate of decision-making on aging policy issues will thus depend on the particular segment(s) of the decision-making community that the advocate wishes to influence, because, as the data in this chapter have shown, the modes of most convenient and efficient access vary among the various segments of the decision-making community. Professional and lay advocates should be sensitive to the information-seeking behavior of decision-makers as they seek to influence the climate of decision-making on aging issues in the policy process.

As a group, the decision-makers relied most heavily on what the Michigan researchers referred to as "soft" (nonempirical) information about the needs of the elderly--most particularly personal contact with older people in their personal and professional lives.[8] Reliance on sources of information providing "hard" (empirical) information about the needs of the elderly--government reports and scientific research findings--was relatively uncommon in this sample of decision-makers. It is interesting to speculate whether decision-makers who relied more on information sources based on scientific empiricism were more likely to hold accurate perceptions of the nature and magnitude of certain problems commonly afflicting the elderly population than were decision-makers who rely heavily on soft (nonempirical and/or lay) information sources.

Two factor scales, one for hard and one for soft information sources, were constructed.* The accuracy of the decision-maker's

---

*The eight information sources were factor analyzed. The factor analysis revealed two unrelated types of information sources utilized by the decision-makers that accorded with the prior identification of hard and soft information sources. The first factor, which was labeled hard information sources, loaded as follows: use of consultants and professionals (.64), use of government reports (.55), use of scientific research findings (.56), use of legislative hearings (.55), and use of organizations of the elderly (.43). The second factor, which was identified in contrast as soft information sources, loaded as follows: contact with older persons themselves (.61), personal experiences with family and friends (.59), and mass media (.32).

One can have some confidence in the existence of two different and unrelated modes of information seeking because each item loaded high on one factor and very low on the other. Further, looking at the distribution of items between the two factors, information sources loading high on factor one appear to represent more institutionalized channels for the collection and dissemination of information on the elderly than do those loading on factor two. It is likely that the data base collected and disseminated through these institutionalized channels is likely to provide more objective information about the needs of the elderly and hence to be more representative of the total elderly population. The decision-makers' raw scores on each of the items loading on a single factor were transformed into standard scores, weighted by their corresponding factor coefficient, and then summed. The two-scale score totals were subsequently trichotomized to reflect high, medium, or low utilization of the respective hard and soft information sources.

TABLE 8.3

Sources of Information Decision-Makers Report "Never" Using to Learn about the Problems Confronting the Aged

Decision-Makers' Positional and Personal Characteristics	Mass Media (percent)	Professionals and Experts (percent)
Positional Characteristics of the Decision-Makers		
Position in the Policy Process		
Legislators (N = 71)	7	13
Agency administrators (N = 70)	4	11
Service delivery personnel (N = 70)	9	13
Corporate directors of personnel (N = 35)	17	49
Union local presidents (N = 35)	20	49
Advocates for the aged (N = 35)	0	0
Responsibility for Aging Programs		
Primary focus (N = 85)	1	8
Important but not central function (N = 88)	5	10
Minor function (N = 143)	15	31
Area of Program Expertise		
Health (N = 37)	7	5
Mental health (N = 23)	13	9
Housing (N = 29)	7	7
Employment (N = 92)	14	42
Income maintenance (N = 26)	11	27
Recreation/leisure (N = 18)	6	6
Senior citizens affairs (N = 49)	0	0
Generalists (N = 42)	10	17
Personal Characteristics of the Decision-Makers		
Age of the Respondent		
Under 45 (N = 98)	6	24
45-54 (N = 98)	10	14
55-64 (N = 90)	11	22
65 and over (N = 30)	3	10
Sex of the Respondent		
Male (N = 230)	8	21
Female (N = 86)	9	13
Ethnicity of the Respondent		
White (N = 235)	9	21
Minority (N = 81)	9	12
Educational Level of the Respondent		
High school graduate or less (N = 42)	17	36
Some college (N = 64)	16	25
College graduate (N = 99)	4	19
Postcollege professional education (N = 111)	5	9
Total (N = 316)	9	19

Source: Compiled by the author.

"Never" Used Sources of Information					
Government Reports (percent)	Scientific Research (percent)	Legislative Hearings (percent)	Contact with the Elderly (percent)	Personal Experiences (percent)	Aging Organizations (percent)
6	30	9	0	3	3
3	17	14	0	1	9
19	31	20	3	6	13
17	51	43	11	9	54
26	67	26	14	14	40
6	14	0	3	0	0
5	21	4	0	2	2
11	32	13	1	2	9
15	39	28	8	8	28
5	19	19	0	0	5
13	17	35	4	4	22
14	24	14	0	0	7
20	52	28	10	11	39
4	35	12	4	8	4
11	44	6	0	6	0
4	12	0	2	0	0
10	33	12	0	2	10
12	38	20	4	3	15
10	33	17	3	5	13
12	30	18	6	7	23
10	20	3	0	3	3
9	34	17	4	5	16
19	27	16	4	5	16
12	34	18	4	6	19
10	27	15	4	3	6
24	52	26	12	10	31
11	33	14	2	3	17
9	32	12	4	5	17
9	24	20	2	4	9
11	32	17	4	5	16

information about basic demographic characteristics in the elderly population was then tested against the nature of his information sources. The basic demographic descriptions of the elderly population examined in this analysis included, among others, the percentage of elderly living in poverty, the percentage of elderly living in institutions, the extent of chronic illness in the elderly population, and the percentage of elderly relying on public transportation to get around in the city.

While the data are not tabulated here, reliance on hard as opposed to soft information sources did not result in a decision-maker having more accurate information about the income and health status of the elderly. Rather, those relying on hard versus soft information sources reflected equally inaccurate impressions of the problems facing the elderly population, almost always in the direction of overstating the problems. Without judging the adequacy of current public policy initiatives for redressing existing problems confronting the elderly, it is clear from these data that rational planning--developing remedial social programs on the basis of accurate information about needs and problems in the population--is not the overriding force in policy development.

If decision-makers did not necessarily possess more accurate information about the problems of the elderly when they relied more on hard, or empirical, information sources than on soft, or nonempirical, sources, perhaps the decision-makers who relied on hard data nevertheless believed their information base to be more adequate to their decision-making requirements than did the decision-makers who relied primarily on soft data resources. In item analysis, those relying heavily on scientific research findings or government reports for their information about the aging proved no more satisfied with the level of their information in their policy decision-making roles than were those who relied heavily on contact with older people and personal experiences with aging in their private lives. Use of factor analytic procedures failed as well to isolate any differences in the decision-makers' satisfaction with their information base according to their reliance on hard as opposed to soft sources of information about the elderly's problems and needs. Thus those decision-makers who rely more on soft data sources to obtain information about aging and the aged do not feel nor do they appear in fact to be unduly disadvantaged in their decision-making role by having a nonempirical information base compared to those who obtain their information more directly from empirical data sources. This must be a contradictory and disconcerting finding to proponents of the rational decision-making model.

Finally, it is surprising that the majority in the decision-making community does not count the information disseminated by aging organizations among their primary sources of information about the aging. Decision-makers in the corporate and union leadership roles in particular make infrequent use of the information aging organizations could make available to them. This suggests that aging organizations might profitably launch a campaign of dissemination to reach these decision-makers in the private sector with the relevant information on aging and the aged that they have to provide them. A similar promotional campaign might be directed toward the legislative and administrative agency arenas of decision-making as well to encourage their greater use of available information.

DECISION-MAKERS ASSESS MASS MEDIA'S TREATMENT OF THE SUBJECT OF AGING

Because half of the decision-making community has reported that they frequently rely on the mass media to obtain information about the problems of aging, a closer examination is merited of the way in which these decision-makers evaluate the effectiveness of mass media in presenting information on the subject of aging to its varied audience. Nine out of ten decision-makers in this study gleaned information on problems of the aging from mass media presentations, but less than one in four believed that the media treat the subject of aging realistically (see Table 8.4). Curiously, union local presidents, the least likely to rely heavily on the media for information about the elderly, were most likely to believe that mass media dealt reasonably realistically with the subject of aging.

Having demonstrated that the reliability of the decision-maker's information source--in this case, the mass media--correlated neither with the accuracy of his knowledge on aging matters nor with his own perceptions of the adequacy of his information, it should not be quite so discomforting to learn that many decision-makers rely on the mass media for information about the elderly when at the same time they believe that the mass media tend to treat the subject of aging stereotypically rather than realistically. Decision-makers rarely, if ever, rely solely on the mass media for information about the aging; they typically seek information from other sources as well. Hence, their aggregate data on the needs and problems of the elderly tend to be no more and no less accurate than those of decision-makers who rely less on the mass media and more on other sources to obtain information about the elderly.

Nevertheless, given that most decision-makers rely on the mass media to learn something about aging and the aged, it is not surprising that the decision-makers offered many ideas for ways in which the mass media could improve their approach to the subject of

TABLE 8.4

"On the Whole, Do You Think That the Mass Media Have Dealt with the Subject of Aging Realistically or Stereotypically?"
(percent responding realistically)

Positional Characteristics of the Decision-Makers	
Position in the Policy Process	
Legislators (N = 71)	15
Agency administrators (N = 70)	20
Service delivery personnel (N = 70)	29
Corporate directors of personnel (N = 35)	17
Union local presidents (N = 35)	34
Advocates for the aged (N = 35)	29
Responsibility for Aging Programs	
Primary function (N = 85)	24
Important but not central function (N = 88)	18
Minor function (N = 143)	26
Area of Program Expertise	
Health (N = 37)	11
Mental health (N = 23)	52
Housing (N = 29)	21
Employment (N = 92)	24
Income maintenance (N = 26)	31
Recreation/leisure (N = 18)	28
Senior citizens affairs (N = 49)	22
Generalists (N = 42)	12
Personal Characteristics of the Decision-Makers	
Age of the Respondent	
Under 45 (N = 98)	18
45-54 (N = 98)	23
55-64 (N = 90)	26
65 and over (N = 30)	30
Sex of the Respondent	
Male (N = 230)	23
Female (N = 86)	22
Ethnicity of the Respondent	
White (N = 235)	20
Minority (N = 81)	31
Educational Level of the Respondent	
High school graduate or less (N = 42)	36
Some college (N = 64)	25
College graduate (N = 99)	16
Postcollege professional education (N = 111)	23
Total (N = 316)	23

Source: Compiled by the author.

aging. When queried, "How would you suggest the mass media change their approach to the subject of aging?" one in six recommended programs about aging should be more realistic. An advocate for the aged (I.D. 609) observed, "Don't just play up the sensational aspects. After all, middle-income elderly don't scrounge in garbage cans." More than one in four of the corporate personnel directors and the advocates focused on improving the realism in the mass media's treatment of the subject of aging.

One in seven emphasized that mass media should play a more constructive role in fashioning a better image for the aging in U.S. society by focusing on the positive and constructive things that elderly people do in their daily lives. For example, a local legislator (I.D. 103) commented that mass media should "begin to publicize the usefulness that retired persons have and how useful they can be by reason of their experience and training." Corporate personnel directors were most in favor of the mass media assuming this approach to the subject of aging, which is somewhat ironic, as the corporate directors of personnel were at the same time more supportive than other segments of the decision-making community of the idea of mandatory retirement, which separates a man from his job strictly on the basis of the attainment of a specific chronological age and not on the basis of an inadequate or subpar performance of his duties and responsibilities in the job.

One in six decision-makers felt that the mass media should assume the role of educating the public about the problems of the elderly. Some believed this function could be accomplished either by continuing coverage of aging-related events in the usual news programs or through specials and documentaries. The manager of housing residences for senior citizens (I.D. 336) observed, "Sketches are not realistic. Need more programs, well-researched--social reports on aging like _60 Minutes_." Others, however, suggested that such educational efforts should be limited to noncommercial or public television programming, which is essentially educational in format.

The educational function of the mass media should not be underestimated. For most Americans it is their sole educational stimuli after completing formal schooling. If any significant reeducation of attitudes toward aging and the aged is going to occur in the adult population, it will take place primarily as a result of information disseminated through the mass media. It is thus surprising that advocates for the aged have not applied more pressure to the varied mass media to alter their format with respect to the treatment of aging.

Corporate personnel directors are appreciative of the value of advertising products and hence it is not surprising that they believed the way to improve media's treatment of aging was to portray elderly people as characters in the regular commercials as well as in various series shown during normal viewing hours of airtime on the networks. To quote the director of personnel in a chemicals manufacturing firm (I.D. 414), "There should be programs devoted to situations facing the elderly--for example, All in the Family. The theme should be how to live as an elderly person. Show the problems and solutions. Entertaining, yet teaching." A hospital administrator (I.D. 208) concurred, "They have to do it through normal programming. They just don't depict old age as it really is. You can't do that through documentaries." A local housing official (I.D. 226) observed, "There are a couple of good movies, such as Harry and Tonto. It's not something that can be put out in 5 minutes. It takes time. It would have to allow an hour to 90 minutes."

One in ten believed the mass media should assume an information referral function for the elderly residents in the community. A local legislator (I.D. 123) responded, "They should have programs for the elderly telling where facilities are, having elderly people discuss problems and how to solve them." A hospital director (I.D. 221) suggested that the mass media had a responsibility to "communicate all information to seniors as to their rights and benefits." Agency personnel and advocates for the aged in particular identified this as an appropriate role for the mass media to assume in order to serve their elderly audience more adequately.

A similar percentage believed that the mass media should hire elderly persons to plan, produce, and participate in a wide range of programming addressed to the senior citizen audience. Most felt it was very important to enlist the input of seniors in programming, ranging from the news to serials and specials. Only administrative agency heads and corporate personnel directors rarely mentioned this possible role of involvement for the elderly in the mass media.

Many decision-makers could offer no way to change the mass media, and a few felt that very little could be done to induce the mass media to change their programming so as to provide better treatment of the subject of aging. They argued the media were youth oriented because the youth, not the aged, have money to buy both the tickets of admission and the products that are advertised. No one wants to learn about aging or be confronted with aging on the screen, and the elderly cannot support programming through sponsors of age-related products. In view of the profit motive of the mass media, one in twenty decision-makers saw little hope of mass media adopting a more positive approach to the subject of aging, except possibly under influence of the elderly as a pressure group or through inducement by the government.

DECISION-MAKERS' EVALUATION OF THE ROLE OF SOCIAL SCIENCE RESEARCH IN DECISION-MAKING

The decision-makers thought quite positively about the role of social science in decision-making. When asked, "Do you think social science research can inform and be used in decision-making and program planning for older people?" nine out of ten decision-makers from all segments of the decision-making community responded affirmatively. Nearly four out of ten of the decision-makers suggested that social science research provides objective data on which to design sensible programs for the elderly. For example, the director of personnel in a large private hospital (I.D. 423) observed, "It's a scientific, objective way of getting information on which to act." A manager of housing projects for retired persons (I.D. 336) noted, "In planning and theorizing, policy-makers can only turn to professional and universities."

More than one in six of the decision-makers maintained that the primary role of social science research in the policy process is to publicize the problems of the elderly and draw public attention to their needs. Nearly one out of five of the decision-makers felt that the advantage social science research offered in the planning process was the ability to sample diverse perspectives on problems and solutions that existed in the population, and one in ten even held out the hope or expectation that somehow social science research might therein be able to locate the appropriate policy solutions to the elderly's problems.

A note of concern expressed by many of the decision-makers, however, was that social science research is useful only to the extent that the findings get disseminated to those in positions to affect policy and program outcomes. An administrator in the Labor Department (I.D. 257A) complained, "It doesn't do any good to do research and stack it up someplace." A psychiatric nurse in a community mental health center (I.D. 319) cautioned that social science research can be an effective tool in the policy process "if it is listened to. But bureaucrats are afraid to listen." And an advocate (I.D. 608) lamented, "It it's used. I'm wondering how much it is used. It's filed and forgotten too often."

The opportunities as well as the challenges would thus appear well laid out by these data for gerontologists who seek access to decision-makers to advocate the findings of their research that are relevant for program development in the field of aging. The decision-makers, as a whole, are receptive to information from social science research findings, and this is most important. Nearly all of the respondents in this study requested a copy of the findings of this research and expressed interest in attending a seminar at the university to discuss the findings of the research. At the same time, however, nearly one third of the decision-making community interviewed here paid absolutely no attention to scientific research findings, and only one in five sought frequent reference to research findings for information about the elderly's problems.

Thus a problem of dissemination of findings addresses the researcher who desires to influence the climate of decision-making in the field of aging based on the findings of his own research. Data presented here suggest that agency officials at both the administrative and service provider levels may be more receptive to working directly with social science researchers than the legislators. Legislators nevertheless may be reached perhaps more indirectly through presentations in the mass media, via testimony at legislative hearings, or through the formal dissemination efforts undertaken by aging organizations that already have channels of routine contact with legislators at various levels in government. The gerontologist should evaluate his efforts to introduce the findings of his own research into the policy process in terms of what kinds of information he wants to disseminate, to whom, and through what channels. Dissemination should be planned with the care of the original research if it is to be effective.

DECISION-MAKERS' EVALUATIONS OF THE WHITE HOUSE CONFERENCES ON AGING AS AN EFFECTIVE PLANNING TOOL IN THE POLICY PROCESS

More than half of the 316 decision-makers reported that they had on occasion referred to reports from the 1971 White House Conference on Aging. Some segments of the decision-making community were considerably more likely to use these reports for reference purposes than were others (Table 8.5). For example, nearly all the advocates for the aged had made use of these reports, whereas less than one quarter of the corporate directors of personnel had referred to the conference proceedings. More than three out of four administrative agency heads had used the reports as had half of the legislators and service delivery personnel.

The more central work with the aged was in the decision-maker's professional responsibilities, the more likely he was to use the White House Conference reports as a source of information about the aging's needs and problems. Seven out of eight of the categoric decision-makers used the reports compared to only three out of eight

TABLE 8.5

"Have You Ever Referred to Reports from the 1971 White House Conference on Aging?" (percent responding "yes")

Positional Characteristics of the Decision-Makers	
Position in the Policy Process	
Legislators (N = 71)	49
Agency administrators (N = 70)	76
Service delivery personnel (N = 70)	50
Corporate directors of personnel (N = 35)	23
Union local presidents (N = 35)	37
Advocates for the aged (N = 35)	91
Responsibility for Aging Programs	
Primary function (N = 85)	87
Important but not central function (N = 88)	53
Minor function (N = 143)	38
Area of Program Expertise	
Health (N = 37)	59
Mental health (N = 23)	43
Housing (N = 29)	69
Employment (N = 92)	40
Income maintenance (N = 26)	46
Recreation/leisure (N = 18)	67
Senior citizens affairs (N = 49)	94
Generalists (N = 42)	40
Personal Characteristics of the Decision-Makers	
Age of the Respondent	
Under 45 (N = 98)	46
45-54 (N = 98)	55
55-64 (N = 90)	57
65 and over (N = 30)	87
Sex of the Respondent	
Male (N = 230)	57
Female (N = 86)	51
Ethnicity of the Respondent	
White (N = 235)	55
Minority (N = 81)	57
Educational Level of the Respondent	
High school graduate or less (N = 42)	48
Some college (N = 64)	55
College graduate (N = 99)	51
Postcollege professional education (N = 111)	64
Total (N = 316)	56

Source: Compiled by the author.

of the generic decision-makers who work with the elderly only on infrequent occasions. Accordingly, senior citizens affairs officials almost without exception referred to these reports as did two out of three of the recreation and leisure specialists. A similar percentage of housing officials and more than half of the health professionals also reported using them. Relatively less common use was reported among all other groups of decision-makers.

These data indicate that perhaps greater efforts should be undertaken to publicize the reports to those segments of the decision-making community who currently make little use of them. For those who work only sporadically with the elderly, the White House reports would provide a distilled and relatively lucid description of the elderly's problems together with policy recommendations to address the problems. Moreover, the proceedings are organized into separate analytic reports for different substantive policy problem areas, facilitating access to materials for even those most inexperienced in dealing with the elderly's problems. The White House Conference reports thus should be publicized to local union leaders and corporate personnel officers, two groups in the decision-making community who rarely use them at the present time. Additionally, income-maintenance system personnel, employment counselors, and mental health personnel might be encouraged to refer more often to these White House materials. Although the White House Conference proceedings already have considerable visibility in most segments of the decision-making community that make decisions that directly affect the well-being of elderly persons, the reports could conceivably have application in other segments of the decision-making community if an extensive educational campaign concerning the contents and functions of these reports were directed toward those decision-makers not now using the reports.

Nearly two thirds of the decision-makers interviewed here believed that the White House Conferences on Aging do result in better programs for older people (see Table 8.6). The advocates for the aged, of course, asserted this belief most often. Only the corporate directors of personnel failed to concur in the majority opinion of the other decision-maker subsamples. Most of the corporate personnel directors did not believe the conferences influenced program outcomes in favor of the elderly. Those very groups of decision-makers who were least likely to report using the White House Conference reports were also least likely to believe that the White House Conferences accomplish any positive influence on policies and programs for the aged in the real world. Thus, income-maintenance specialists, employment counselors, and mental health professionals were least likely to use the reports and least likely to believe the proceedings of the conferences influenced policy outcomes. Among

TABLE 8.6

"Do You Feel That White House Conferences on Aging Result in Better Programs for Older People?" (percent responding "yes")

Positional Characteristics of the Decision-Makers	
Position in the Policy Process	
Legislators (N = 71)	61
Agency administrators (N = 70)	67
Service delivery personnel (N = 70)	63
Corporate directors of personnel (N = 35)	34
Union local presidents (N = 35)	60
Advocates for the aged (N = 35)	86
Responsibility for Aging Programs	
Primary function (N = 85)	81
Important but not central function (N = 88)	57
Minor function (N = 143)	55
Area of Program Expertise	
Health (N = 37)	59
Mental health (N = 23)	52
Housing (N = 29)	76
Employment (N = 92)	52
Income maintenance (N = 26)	65
Recreation/leisure (N = 18)	89
Senior citizens affairs (N = 49)	88
Generalists (N = 42)	43
Personal Characteristics of the Decision-Makers	
Age of the Respondent	
Under 45 (N = 98)	68
45-54 (N = 98)	65
55-64 (N = 90)	60
65 and over (N = 30)	77
Sex of the Respondent	
Male (N = 230)	61
Female (N = 86)	67
Ethnicity of the Respondent	
White (N = 235)	60
Minority (N = 81)	69
Educational Level of the Respondent	
High school graduate or less (N = 42)	69
Some college (N = 64)	67
College graduate (N = 99)	56
Postcollege professional education (N = 111)	64
Total (N = 316)	63

Source: Compiled by the author.

the personal characteristics of the decision-makers, only age was an unimportant differentiator of belief in the utility of the White House Conferences in the policy planning process. Women more than men, minority more than white, and high school educated more than college-educated decision-makers believed in the usefulness of White House Conferences on Aging.

The decision-makers were asked to specify why they believed these White House Conferences on Aging do or do not have an influence on policy and program outcomes favorable to the elderly population. More than half (55 percent) of those who felt favorably about the outcomes of the White House Conferences believed they served a useful function in heightening visibility of the elderly's problems to the general public, to the mass media, and to elected officials, as well as to other decision-makers in the policy process. A somewhat smaller percentage of the decision-maker sample (38 percent) suggested that the White House Conferences gather data to document the problems that face older people, and that the data can then be used as the basis for long-range coordinated planning of program intervention strategies.

A smaller percentage of the sample (21 percent) believed that the White House Conferences on Aging provided good advocacy on behalf of the elderly within the policy process. For example, some decision-makers pointed out that a White House Conference developed the ranks of leadership within the elderly constituency and led to collective, coordinated efforts by elderly people and their advocates to influence policy outcomes in the elderly's favor. Finally, a still smaller percentage (12 percent) of the decision-makers believed that the proceedings of the White House Conferences on Aging do in fact shape social policy outcomes in specific ways that are of more or less direct benefit to the elderly population. For the most part, however, the decision-makers assessed the beneficial aspects of these conferences more in terms of the publicizing and information-gathering functions than in terms of any actual role for advocating the elderly's needs within the policy process and thus, perhaps, effecting specific policy outcomes that would have favor for the elderly population directly.

Approximately one in five of the decision-makers believed that the White House Conferences on Aging did not result in better programs for the elderly. Most blamed the ineffectiveness of the conferences on the inability of participants to produce empirical data to document the urgency of needs and problems confronting elderly people. One decision-maker (I.D. 237) called these conferences nothing more than an "exchange of ignorances." Others complained of the lack of fresh and innovative approaches to analyzing and remedying the problems--"nothing new ever comes of it" (I.D.128).

Others maintained that the conferences failed to represent adequately the diversity of needs and problems evident in the elderly population. Some felt, for example, that the conferences should be conducted on the local level, not in the national arena, or at least on the local level in addition to the national arena. Others complained that the delegates to the national White House Conferences on Aging were not representative of the elderly population in general; hence they felt that the White House Conferences on Aging were fabricated events that did not grow out of and represent the elderly population in fact. Finally, a few decision-makers were concerned that inadequate dissemination of the conference proceedings prohibited the conference findings from being used appropriately in the policy planning process.

In general, however, the decision-makers endorse the White House Conferences on Aging as an effective planning tool in the policy process. The conferences provide a public forum for the discussion of the elderly's problems, they organize leadership roles and channel advocacy efforts on behalf of the elderly in the policy process, and even on occasion promote specific program outcomes favorable to the elderly. With such visibility and positive support for the White House Conferences from the decision-making community, more are likely to be sponsored in future decades. Such conferences should afford more opportunities for advocates and the elderly to influence the climate of decision-making and possibly program outcomes in directions favorable to the aged.

DECISION-MAKERS' ASSESSMENT OF THEIR OWN OPPORTUNITIES TO INFLUENCE OUTCOMES OF THE POLICY PROCESS

Frustration over the inability to influence policy outcomes is usually ascribed to lay advocates who periodically seek to influence the climate of decision-making by lobbying on behalf of a specific cause that has fired their enthusiasm. It is something of a turnabout, then, to ask these decision-makers, who are located in various positions within the policy process, to evaluate their own opportunities to affect program outcomes. Each decision-maker was asked about the following: "In your position, you have undoubtedly acquired some valuable experience in the area of social planning for middle-aged or older persons. Do you feel that you have ample opportunity to feed information about this experience to persons who design or implement policies that affect these people?" Only a slim majority of the decision-makers interviewed here responded affirmatively (see Table 8.7).

TABLE 8.7

"Do You Feel That You Have Ample Opportunity to Feed Information about Your Experiences in Social Planning for Middle-Aged or Older Persons to Persons Who Design or Implement Policies That Affect These People?"
(percent responding "yes")

Positional Characteristics of the Decision-Makers	
Position in the Policy Process	
Legislators (N = 71)	65
Agency administrators (N = 70)	59
Service delivery personnel (N = 70)	40
Corporate directors of personnel (N = 35)	37
Union local presidents (N = 35)	49
Advocates for the aged (N = 35)	69
Responsibility for Aging Programs	
Primary function (N = 85)	69
Important but not central function (N = 88)	48
Minor function (N = 143)	48
Area of Program Expertise	
Health (N = 37)	44
Mental health (N = 23)	59
Housing (N = 29)	54
Employment (N = 92)	48
Income maintenance (N = 26)	45
Recreation/leisure (N = 18)	38
Senior citizens affairs (N = 49)	67
Generalists (N = 42)	58
Personal Characteristics of the Decision-Makers	
Age of the Respondent	
Under 45 (N = 98)	40
45-54 (N = 98)	51
55-64 (N = 90)	61
65 and over (N = 30)	83
Sex of the Respondent	
Male (N = 230)	59
Female (N = 86)	40
Ethnicity of the Respondent	
White (N = 235)	54
Minority (N = 81)	52
Educational Level of the Respondent	
High school graduate or less (N = 42)	64
Some college (N = 64)	55
College graduate (N = 99)	43
Postcollege professional education (N = 111)	58
Total (N = 316)	53

Source: Compiled by the author.

Some segments of the decision-making community, of course, felt better able to influence policy and program outcomes than did others. Legislators, agency administrators, and advocates, for example, were all likely to feel positive about their ability to influence outcomes in the policy process--roughly two thirds of these subsamples felt satisfied with their ability to influence policy outcomes. Not atypical was the response of one state legislator (I.D. 143B), "I am in a position to do something. I just need to know exactly what is available and what the needs are, then I can do something. You have to be kidding, you are asking a legislator!" In contrast, less than half of the union local presidents, service delivery personnel, and corporate directors of personnel were similarly satisfied with their opportunities for feedback in the policy process.

The decision-makers were then asked, "What might be done to enhance the input of persons like yourself to the whole policy process?" One theme of responses identified the need for better communication among disparate segments of the decision-making community; one in five spoke specifically of needing to develop better lines of communication to legislators in local, state, and/or national government. More than one in eight suggested better inter- or intraagency communications were required in order to improve their opportunities to make inputs into the policy process. A number focused on the creation of a department of aging at the state level that could coordinate multiple and diverse inputs into comprehensive planning and programming for the elderly. This was the central concern of the agency administrators. Finally, still others spoke in terms of the need to open channels of communication to senior citizens, their advocate organizations, and/or professionals and experts in the field of aging.

The implicit assumption in each of these recommendations is that with increased opportunities to exchange information, these decision-makers would find the opportunity to make greater inputs into the policy planning process. Thus, the president of a manufacturing union (I.D. 531) observed, "I have never been asked by those in policy-making positions for anything. I don't know that my input is that valuable. If senior citizen groups would ask me how to go about getting something done, I could help them."

Nearly one in seven of the decision-makers believed that they would have greater input into the policy process personally if they were invited to attend and participate in conferences, seminars, and workshops on aging. Service delivery personnel, union local presidents, and advocates for the aged were the most likely to desire to participate in such conferences, hoping for an opportunity to present their views and thus influence the climate of decision-making. As a supervisor in a retirement system (I.D. 243) explained, "to participate in workshops and seminars. . . . If I have ideas, I have to go through channels with them--I cannot bring them to the attention of other people outside the county. In private industry, maybe; but in government, you can't go outside. I have to let supervisors do the job; I inform supervisors and let them go from there." Participation in community workshops provides a valuable vehicle whereby government officials can participate in informal spheres of influence and have input into the policy process beyond that formally structured in their jobs. A number of others did talk of the enhanced role they could play in the policy process by becoming involved in advisory panels and planning boards or commissions in the community. Many cited a lack of time for not having done so in the past.

The advocates for the aged were the only ones who sought access to media coverage for their efforts on behalf of the elderly. Thus one advocate (I.D. 608) related this incident: "We should be referred to more often for information and advice on the problems of the elderly. An opportunity for our representatives to reach out to the public at large through the media came a few weeks ago--this was the subject on Meet the Press. Senator Long, Wilbur Mills, Wilbur Cohen, Mrs. Griffith, and a representative from the American Medical Association were on. Actually the only proponent of proper medical care was Wilbur Cohen. When we asked them to include a senior citizen leader, they said, 'Sorry--no room on the panel.'" Advocates foresaw considerably better opportunities for advocacy if the mass media would properly publicize their efforts on behalf of the elderly.

Curiously, one in five decision-makers felt totally unable to recommend how to improve their own input into the policy process. Many of these responded that they had never thought about it and were unsure about what to suggest without giving the question considerable thought. Corporate directors of personnel were particularly inclined to offer this response.

For the most part, however, the decision-makers desired to see the policy process become a more rational decision-making process, which would cull diverse perspectives and produce a reasoned programmatic solution based on the evaluation of diverse inputs. They typically desired to have greater input in the decision-making processes and implied that programs would be better designed and more effective if the policy planning process was structured to incorporate their views as well as those of others like them.

INFORMATION DISSEMINATION TO DECISION-MAKERS: IMPLICATIONS OF THESE DATA

The data presented in this chapter challenge the premises of a rational planning model of the policy process. To be sure, most if not all of the decision-makers subscribe publicly to the desirability of rational planning to provide for the elderly's unmet needs. Many verbalize that "you have to have information before you can make decisions" (a Social Security district office supervisor, I.D. 350). Most of the decision-makers in this study, however, admitted that they must make policy decisions based on inadequate information about the needs and problems of the elderly.

What information these decision-makers do have about aging, they tend to acquire from nonempirical sources of information: the mass media, contact with elderly persons in the routine performance of their jobs, and personal experiences with aging and/or vicarious experiences in observing friends and family around them age. In the case of mass media in particular, more than nine out of ten decision-makers acquired information about aging from various mass media presentations that they in turn used in making decisions about programs and policies that directly affect the lives of older people. But less than one in four of the decision-makers believed that the mass media deal with the subject of aging realistically. The predictable result is that many decision-makers possess inaccurate information about even the most basic demographic characteristics of the elderly population, information that would be essential for developing rational program intervention strategies to assist the elderly.

Nevertheless the decision-makers seem to remain confident that decision-making in the policy process could be more rational than it is if more and better information were available that described the actual needs confronting older people. They pointed to the White House Conferences on Aging as an example. Two out of three of the decision-makers maintained that such conferences resulted directly in better programs for the elderly, and more than half of these 316 decision-makers confirmed that they themselves had used the conference reports to obtain information about the aging that they then applied in the performance of their jobs.

Similarly, the decision-makers maintained that social science research could play a useful role in designing social programs to assist the elderly. Only one in five, however, actually used scientific findings regularly as a source of information, and slightly more than one third of the sample of 316 relied extensively on statistical reports published by the government. The far lower rate of utilization of hard as opposed to soft information sources would probably surprise few, but what might have surprised many is that decision-makers who relied relatively more heavily on hard data sources were not more likely to have accurate information about the elderly's needs and problems than were decision-makers who relied primarily on soft information sources.

That finding strikes at the core assumptions of any rational planning model of the policy process. If rational programs--rational in the sense that program outcomes diminish or eliminate identified unmet needs in the target population--are the outcome of policy deliberations, they must be achieved by other than systematic decision-making that identifies the problem, studies alternative program intervention strategies, and then selects that program strategy most likely to grant the greatest relief to the most people at the least cost.

An alternative, perhaps more fruitful way to view decision-making in the field of aging is through the lens of the interest-group model of the policy process. Because all problems in the society cannot rationally be solved at the same time, the prerequisite question above all others is which problems will occupy the attention of the decision-makers this term? Defining unmet needs in a subgroup of the population, such as in the case of the elderly, is an ongoing process of claims-making--claims for the attention of decision-makers, claims for scarce dollars, and so on. The decision-makers are more passive in this perspective on the policy process. Rather than seeking out the necessary information on which to base sound decisions, decision-makers prefer to wait and let the problems come to them, let those affected by problems come forward and make their case for relief.

There is much in the data from the interviews with these 316 decision-makers to suggest that many of them do take that stance. Many of the decision-makers exhibited passive information-seeking habits, preferring to rely on whatever they learned about aging and the aged from those around them instead of seeking out documented facts from empirical sources. Thus, the decision-makers urged people to come to them with their problems. A senior citizens affairs specialist (I.D. 263) pleaded, "I need information from seniors themselves about individual or group issues." A state legislator (I.D. 140) reminded that the system works because of "the input of the people--middle aged or elderly citizens letting legislators know their concerns." One of the legislator's colleagues (I.D. 132) added, "Some of the responsibility is on myself to make myself available to them personally in order that I can best serve them. Availability is the name of the game." Another legislator (I.D. 135) asked for "more input from senior citizens organizations"; and a city councilman (I.D. 123) admonished that "government agencies like the County Department of Social Services who counsel people on welfare and have direct contact with the problems of these people should relate more to the city government." For these decision-makers, the real value of the White House Conferences on Aging and scientific research was defined not so much in terms of empirically documenting the problems confronting the elderly but more in terms of publicizing the problems and drawing the attention of decision-makers to them.

The decision-makers tend to believe that it is someone else's responsibility to bring the problems forward, document the need, and justify the expenditure of public funds to solve the problem. That someone is variously the elderly themselves, the aging organizations representing the elderly's interests, the social agencies already delivering other services to the elderly, gerontologists--anyone, in fact, who will speak on behalf of the elderly. The outreach must come from them, because it will not come spontaneously from the decision-makers who control the economic and political resources to implement social programs and policies designed to alleviate the identified social ill(s). Information will still reach the decision-makers, not as it would in the rational planning context, but by way of advocacy from different interest groups competing for scarce budget allocations. Available empirical information will be shaped to fit the advocates' appeals. It will take on color and dimension, it will no longer be neutral, "objective" data. Information dissemination is thus still as important in the advocacy context as it would be in the rational planning context. The channels of dissemination are different and the way the information is used may be different, but information is at least a part of the decision-making process.

Any significantly enhanced utilization of available information about aging in the climate of decision-making that fashions aging programs will probably come through the efforts of lay and professional advocates working on behalf of the elderly. Academic gerontologists have information-dissemination roles in teaching and research. Research does not contribute to the decision-making process so long as it is "filed and forgotten, as it most often is" (I.D. 608). Unfortunately many researchers are too busy with new research ideas to take interest in disseminating the old. The solution is to channel the research findings to others who would use and disseminate them widely--aging organizations, advocates for the elderly, and gerontology instructors. Decision-makers interviewed in this study often suggested "getting on a mailing list for research projects" (I.D. 516). A state legislator (I.D. 157) hoped that there would be "regular newsletters from research groups which would deal with practical everyday problems of senior citizens and act as an advocacy agent." If researchers do not care to develop such information-dissemination techniques themselves, then they at least owe it to their funding agencies and the potential beneficiaries of their research findings to disseminate them to advocate groups who will use and disseminate the findings more broadly.

Few decision-makers currently seem motivated to seek formal exposure to more information on aging and the aged in workshops and seminars on aging. Unless these can be institutionalized in the format of on-the-job training, relatively few in the decision-making community will enjoy an informed overview of the problems of growing old in U.S. society. The only alternative is to reach these decision-makers through informative presentations on the subject of aging in the mass media. In light of the nearly unanimous audience that the mass media holds in the decision-making community, efforts should be directed toward making the mass media responsive to the needs of educating the decision-making community and the population at large about the problems of aging. The data gathered in this study do not find the advocates for the aged fully attuned to the central role that the mass media may need to play in educating the decision-making elite in this country. Moreover, it seems clear that the mass media will not change their approach to the subject of aging until pressed to do so, in much the same way as vocal ethnic and sex minority groups succeeded in winning prime time serious discussions of their problems. The advocates for the aged exhibited no inclination to force a showdown at the present time with the mass media over their treatment of the subject of aging. The real value of this information source, central to reaching legislators, corporate personnel directors, and others in the decision-making community, appears likely to escape the attention of many advocates for some time to come.

In matters of information dissemination, it is important to decide what should be disseminated, to whom it should be disseminated, and finally how it should be disseminated. While dissemination of information usually focuses on legislators as the receiver of information, it is important to remember that the decision-making community is diverse with many people making decisions about programs and policies that will directly affect the lives of older people living in the community. Perhaps the best way to influence policy outcomes in ways favorable to the elderly is to maintain good working relations and open channels of communication with all segments of the decision-making community.

NOTES

1. See, for example, Thomas R. Dye, Understanding Public Policy, 2nd ed. (Englewood Cliffs, N.J.: Prentice-Hall, 1975);

A. Lee Fritschler, Smoking and Politics: Policymaking and the Federal Bureaucracy, 2nd ed. (Englewood Cliffs, N.J.: Prentice-Hall, 1975); Graham T. Allison, Essence of Decision: Explaining the Cuban Missile Crisis (Boston: Little, Brown, 1971); Harold Seidman, Politics, Position and Power: The Dynamics of Federal Organization (New York: Oxford University Press, 1970); Charles E. Lindblom, "The Science of Muddling Through," Public Administration Review 19, no. 2 (Spring 1959): 79-88; Martin Meyerson and Edward C. Banfield, Politics, Planning and the Public Interest (New York: Free Press, 1955).

2. Dye, Understanding Public Policy, p. 15.

3. Compare the perspectives of Alice M. Rivlin, Systematic Thinking for Social Action (Washington, D.C.: Brookings Institution, 1971) and Walter Williams, Social Policy Research and Analysis: The Experience in Federal Social Agencies (New York: American Elsevier, 1971).

4. Nathan Caplan, Andrea Morrison, and Russell J. Stambaugh, The Use of Social Science Knowledge in Policy Decisions at the National Level: A Report to Respondents (Ann Arbor: University of Michigan, Institute for Social Research, 1975).

5. Ibid., p. 47.

6. Ibid.

7. See Henry J. Pratt, "Old Age Associations in National Politics," Annals of the Academy of Political and Social Science 415 (September 1974): 106-19; Robert H. Binstock, "Aging and the Future of American Politics," Annals of the Academy of Political and Social Science 415 (September 1974): 199-212; Robert B. Hudson, "Rational Planning and Organizational Imperatives: Prospects for Area Planning in Aging," Annals of the Academy of Political and Social Science 415 (September 1974): 41-54.

8. Caplan, Morrison, and Stambaugh, The Use of Social Science Knowledge.

9

Decision-Makers Assess the Effect of "Senior Power" on Social Policy Outcomes

The past decade has brought growing speculation about the role of the aged as a cohesive interest-group force in U.S. politics. Americans endorse the role of interest-group activity in the political bargaining process, where decisions are made regarding who gets what. The common assumption is that in a pluralist democracy such as the United States, the public interest is probably best served and social justice probably best achieved through the competition, conflict, and accommodation that continually take place among organized groups, each seeking to fulfill their own interests within the policy process.[1] Accordingly, the measure of the democratic functioning of the system is the extent to which multiple, and ideally, all interests are represented in this political bargaining process. The recent awakening of minority group interests among ethnic minorities, women, homosexuals, and other identifiable subgroups in U.S. society, culminating as it often does in political group organization and activism, has been hailed as the essence of pluralist democracy in operation. Today many believe that in this same tradition the aged will assume a similarly assertive role in the policy processes.

Speculations about the enlarged role the aged may play in the political arena have been stimulated by the dramatic increase in both the absolute and relative size of the elderly population in U.S. society in past decades of the twentieth century and the projections for continued growth of the elderly population in the early decades of the not too distant next century. Because discussions of the impact of senior power on political processes are typically based on the assumption that large numbers mean potential power, if not power in fact, political analysts monitoring the possible emergence of senior power in U.S. politics have been concerned with studying the impact of the elderly on political decision-making in those areas where large numbers are theoretically most important: electoral outcomes and interest-group activity. The crucial inquiries concern whether "the aging vote" determines the outcomes of elections and whether mass membership aging organizations have significant power to influence outcomes in the processes of conflict and accommodation that characterize U.S. interest-group politics.[2]

This chapter examines the way a cross section of the decision-making community assesses the impact of senior power from its perspective as participants in some of these policy decision-making processes. After briefly considering how social and political analysts have assessed the impact of senior power in U.S. politics in past, present, and future decades, the remainder of the chapter will examine the decision-makers' own evaluations of the impact of senior power from their various positions within the policy process. The contrast in perspectives on senior power taken from inside versus outside the policy process is dramatic, as this chapter will illustrate. Implications of the decision-makers' perceptions of senior power for planning advocacy strategies on behalf of the elderly in the policy process are discussed.

THE SUBCULTURE OF THE AGING AND POLITICAL INTEREST-GROUP ACTIVITY

A generally accepted definition of an interest group is a "shared attitude group that makes certain claims upon other groups in the society"; it becomes a political interest group if and when it makes such a claim on any institution of government.[3] The words "senior" and "power" should thus not be tossed together casually, because age-based activism implies several very specific prerequisite conditions:

1. That chronologically old individuals in the society (for example, those in their 60s or older) identify themselves as the elderly citizens in the society.
2. That elderly people have certain life experiences in common in the last stage of the life cycle, experiences that are uniquely a function of their being old and therefore span the disparate experiences of being male or female, white or ethnic, and rich or poor. (Among the mutual concerns of the aged most frequently listed are shared health and money problems, similar leisure lifestyles and recreational pursuits, common life events including retirement and widowhood, and similar generational experiences such as the Depression and two world wars.)

3. That older people recognize that they share these problems occasioned by their being old with others who are their chronological age, while, at the same time, they realize that they share these same problems with no other individuals or groups in the society.
4. That the elderly believe the blame or responsibility for their abject life circumstances belongs not so much to themselves, individually or collectively, but rather to the operations of institutions and ordered relations in the social system as a whole.
5. That the elderly perceive that these unjust social arrangements in the system that are responsible for creating their disadvantaged position in society can and should be changed by a program of social and political action undertaken by the aged on behalf of the aged.
6. That the elderly then take collective action as a "shared-attitude" group to change the society and their position in it.

Only then can the elderly properly be considered an age-based interest group that is making concerted demands on other groups in society to redress the unfairly disadvantaged position of the aging in U.S. society.[4]

In the political arena, such age-group activism would typically translate into bloc voting on the basis of identifiable age-group interests in order to manage electoral outcomes in favor of the elderly as well as a more formal coalescence around age-group interests in the establishment of mass membership organizations of the elderly dedicated to effecting favorable outcomes to the elderly in the ongoing political bargaining process that constitutes the daily activity of government.[5] To speak of senior power necessarily infers that the elderly age group possesses sufficient power to effect outcomes favorable to their own age group in elections and/or interest-group politics. The assumption of gerontologists for some time has been that the elderly would develop the prerequisite age-group consciousness and inevitably emerge as a viable political interest group in the U.S. democratic tradition.[6]

More than a decade ago the observation was made that the "evidence of the growing group-identification among older people in the United States today is available to even the casual observer."[7] But the empirical evidence does not support the assertion. There is not in the recent past, the present, or the foreseeable future any indication of the elderly influencing the outcomes of elections by bloc voting. In fact, empirical investigations demonstrate precisely the opposite, that the political attitudes and behaviors of the aged population are as diverse and stable in character as those of middle-aged adults.[8] Although the elderly constitute about 15 percent of the electorate, a group theoretically large enough to swing the outcome of elections in its own favor through bloc voting, the elderly do not vote together as a group. Age-based interests are not now nor are they likely to be sufficiently cohesive to become a strong force in U.S. politics.

The reason is that the elderly lack a cohesive age-group identification. In spite of theoretical formulations that would predict the emergence of a subculture among the elderly, with the subsequent development of an age-group identification and the eventual appearance of age-based political interest groups as practically inevitable outcomes of the rapidly growing aged population in U.S. society, the coalescence of the elderly around age-group concerns never materialized. First, many elderly people refuse to identify themselves as old. Many individuals in their 60s and even early-to-mid-70s persist in identifying themselves as "middle-aged" or "late middle-aged."[9]

Second, elderly people do not all share the same problems in growing old. The well-to-do elderly share few problems in common with the impoverished aged; aging men typically confront different life experiences in old age than do aging women; health decrements tend to occur much later for whites than for ethnic minorities. The complex biological, social, and psychological experience of aging, rather than providing a common denominator among all aging individuals, instead builds upon and heightens the differences that have surfaced among adults in their earlier years deriving from, among other things, race, sex, and social class distinctions.[10]

Third, many aged simply do not define their most pressing problems (income, health, housing, and transportation) as aging problems.[11] Many elderly thus have some investment in disassociating themselves with the label of old age and the image of sharing problems in common with other people their age.[12] Such behavior obviously inhibits the emergence of the age-group identification that would be necessary to underwrite bloc voting by the elderly based on age-group interests. The prophesized emergence of senior power to affect outcomes in electoral politics not only has not emerged but it also seems unlikely to emerge at least in the foreseeable future of U.S. politics.

Conceptually distinguishable from the issue of electoral politics is the subject of interest-group politics, although both spheres of political activity are similarly affected by the level of age-group identification in the elderly population. The Townsend Plan and the Han-and-Eggs Movement, both aged-based movements organized in the 1930s to press for the enactment of an income-maintenance plan for retiring workers, were short-lived, dissolving soon after the enactment of the Social Security Act of 1935.[13] The demise of both movements has been attributed to the inability of the organizational leadership to develop cohesive political units due to the lack of a solid age-group identification among the elderly.[14] One study of the history of these age-based political movements concluded, "One of the necessary conditions for the formation and maintenance of interest groups is a homogeneity of characteristics among the membership. An effective interest group, then, should have more in common than just age. Other important shared characteristics may be ethnicity, nativity, educational background, occupational status, race and rural-urban residency. Lacking similarity beyond age (and perhaps the state of retirement), the old age political movements were handicapped from their very inception."[15]

If short-lived, perhaps at least these age-based interest groups were successful in their chosen goal to effect passage of an old-age insurance system. One social scientist thus posed the question: Were old age political organizations, as interest groups, responsible for the enactment of income-maintenance legislation, or was this legislation the product of broader concerns deriving from social movements that were not age-based?[16] His conclusion, based on a careful analysis of available records and historical accounts, was that income-maintenance legislation for the elderly was the result of pressures brought to bear by large social movements that were non-age-based rather than the effective pressure brought by the old-age political interest groups. Referring to the latter, he noted, "Memberships may have been large, but they were not financially solvent; they were not able to mobilize their membership into an effective voting bloc; and having a weak organizational structure, they were unable to bring pressure upon the state and federal polity."[17]

If not in the past, perhaps the age-based political interest-group organizations have become effective agents on behalf of the elderly in the political process in present times. In the mid-1970s, ten national organizations or associations purported to represent the interests of the elderly in the political bargaining process; three are mass membership organizations that draw members directly from the elderly population.[18] Political analysts seem somewhat divided in their assessment of the effect that lobbying efforts by these national organizations have had on improving the general well-being of the elderly population over the past years. Analysts agree that the aging interest-group organizations have been rather successful in pressing for new programs and expansion of existing programs to assist the elderly. Some believe that the elderly have been the direct beneficiaries of the escalation in funding of aging programs over recent decades.[19] Others maintain, however, that the political and economic gains have gone primarily to the aging organizations to expand their staff and lobbying activities, while the objective circumstances of the aged population have been relatively little affected by the political gains marshalled by these age-based interest groups in the politics of bargaining and accommodation in the policy process.[20] Thus it appears important to ask not only if age-based interest groups have sufficient power today to affect policy outcomes but also to ask for whom they affect policy outcomes. The age-based interest groups appear foremost capable in meeting their own organizational survival needs and thereafter attending to the needs of their aged constituencies.

As to the future role of these age-based organizations in interest-group politics, the present and sometimes fierce competition among different organizations serving diverse constituencies in the aging population suggests that unification in goals, objectives, and procedures is no more likely to occur among the leading age-based political interest groups in their political bargaining strategies than cohesive bloc voting is likely to occur among the diverse elderly in the population. Age alone appears too weak a variable in individual and collective identity upon which to organize mutual political interests and mobilize political action; and beyond age, the elderly are too diverse a population in all other matters to find sufficient common interest in even a limited platform of goals and objectives. On this score, most social and political analysts are in agreement today. The 316 decision-makers who were interviewed in this study are actors actually located in various positions in the social policy process, however, and they offer a very different perspective on the elderly's role and impact on program outcomes in the policy process.

DECISION-MAKERS' PERSPECTIVES ON POLITICAL AGE-GROUP CONSCIOUSNESS AMONG THE AGED

At a time when social gerontologists increasingly emphasize the heterogeneity in the life circumstances and philosophical outlook of elderly people, the cross section of the decision-making community interviewed in this study nearly unanimously (96 percent) agreed that older persons share similar problems regardless of race, class, or other differences. Thus, in contrast to social and political analysts who often offer their observations as spectators to the policy process, these decision-making participants do believe that the essential objective conditions exist to underwrite an age-based political interest-group movement among the elderly. That is, the aged do share common experiences, common interests, and common problems by virtue of their being old and, more important, that such common aging experiences span the differences created by sex, race, or social class distinctions. For these decision-makers, the foundation for an age-based interest group exists in the unavoidable realities of aging.

The logical follow-up question is whether the decision-makers believe that the elderly perceive these common problems and seek to act together on the basis of them. On this score, the decision-makers showed considerably less agreement. They were nearly evenly split on the question of whether older people are sufficiently aware of their common problems to form a political bloc. Slightly more than one half (52 percent) of the decision-makers believed that the elderly are sufficiently aware of shared problems to form a political bloc in contrast to four in ten who believed that the elderly are not aware of sharing common interests (see Table 9.1).

Legislators and advocates for the aged were the most likely of the six original subsamples to believe that elderly persons are sufficiently aware of the interests they share in common to form a political bloc. Should the elderly mobilize, their vote and political activism would logically have the greatest impact on these two groups in the decision-making community; not to recognize or to underestimate the elderly's potential to organize politically would undoubtedly be a far more serious tactical error for these decision-makers to make than would overestimating the political strength of this constituency.

Corporate directors of personnel were the least convinced that the elderly were sufficiently aware of their problems to form a cohesive political bloc. The personnel officer of a manufacturing company (I.D. 413) observed that the elderly are "shut up in their own area. They do not communicate so they do not realize that they all have the same problems. If they communicated more, they would become aware of the need to form a bloc." Another personnel officer (I.D. 402A) suggested, "They are aware but they don't do anything about it. Again, they are too complacent to care about anything." It would be interesting to know whether this and other personnel managers who view the elderly as politically apathetic also view the elderly as passive and apathetic consumers in the economic marketplace where the goods and services produced by their companies are sold. The observation has often been made that the business world overlooks the very profitable market of the aging consumer.[21]

Another interesting finding is that the personnel administering various income-maintenance systems were the least likely of any subgroup in the entire decision-making community to believe that the elderly age group was sufficiently aware of its common problems to form a political bloc. Ironically, four decades earlier, hundreds of thousands of elderly people across the country joined age-based political groups in order to lobby for an old-age social insurance system that would guarantee retiring workers a minimum monthly income once they no longer derived earnings from employment. But that was past and possibly forgotten history for this generation of pension plan administrators.

TABLE 9.1

"Are Older People Sufficiently Aware of Their Common Problems to Form a Political Bloc?"
(percent responding "yes")

Positional Characteristics of the Decision-Makers	
Position in the Policy Process	
Legislators (N = 71)	59
Agency administrators (N = 70)	53
Service delivery personnel (N = 70)	49
Corporate directors of personnel (N = 35)	40
Union local presidents (N = 35)	54
Advocates for the aged (N = 35)	57
Responsibility for Aging Programs	
Primary function (N = 85)	53
Important but not central function (N = 88)	52
Minor function (N = 143)	52
Area of Program Expertise	
Health (N = 37)	57
Mental health (N = 23)	48
Housing (N = 29)	52
Employment (N = 92)	47
Income maintenance (N = 26)	19
Recreation/leisure (N = 18)	39
Senior citizens affairs (N = 49)	51
Generalists (N = 42)	57
Personal Characteristics of the Decision-Makers	
Age of the Respondent	
Under 45 (N = 98)	50
45-54 (N = 98)	56
55-64 (N = 90)	48
65 and over (N = 30)	63
Sex of the Respondent	
Male (N = 230)	52
Female (N = 86)	53
Ethnicity of the Respondent	
White (N = 235)	52
Minority (N = 81)	54
Educational Level of the Respondent	
High school graduate or less (N = 42)	57
Some college (N = 64)	55
College graduate (N = 99)	49
Postcollege professional education (N = 111)	53
Total (N = 316)	52

Source: Compiled by the author.

The directors of senior citizens clubs and multipurpose senior citizens centers were also considerably less likely than most of the others in the decision-making community to believe that the elderly are politically aware of their common interests to the point of voting as a bloc. These are the very associations that many have predicted offer the road to grass-roots political involvement for the aged. One proponent of the concept of emerging age-group consciousness asserted that, "The elderly who are organized into recreational groups sometimes shift naturally into political pressure groups."[22] Such observations did not escape these decision-makers; one senior citizens affairs specialist (I.D. 266), for example, observed that "social action retirement clubs are becoming more active than serving merely as recreation clubs. The theme of most senior programs is strength in numbers." If, however, the directors of these senior centers and recreational groups cannot agree in the majority that the elderly are aware of their common problems to a degree sufficient to vote as a political bloc, then perhaps senior power is farther from reality than others, such as the advocates or legislators, anticipate.

The decision-makers cited many factors inhibiting the elderly's developing the sort of awareness of their common problems that would sustain the formation of an active age-based political bloc. A city councilman (I.D. 114) commented that the elderly are "too diverse--they're not unified." A local housing authority official (I.D. 226) recounted his own confrontation with divisive dimensions within the elderly population: "The impact is very limited. They become discouraged. Some senior citizens groups, upper or middle income, are interested only in their next trip or excursion--they are not interested in the needs of the poorer minority. We tried once to get upper- and middle-income senior citizens groups to help us get funds for more housing for seniors, for those who are really poor. Those contacted were really too busy with travel activities, and so on to give their time to help us. We received no encouragement or help from these seniors for their poorer peers. It's sad."

Other decision-makers observed that the problem was less one of diverse interests and competing alliances within the elderly population than one of the elderly failing to make any alliances at all based on their age-related problems: A union local president (I.D. 529) asserted, "From what I see, there is no interest in forming a political bloc." The personnel director in a media company concurred, "I doubt if the elderly would be that activist." The director of a state employment office (I.D. 251) elaborated on the problem, "This is part of the fear of being old. Old people recognize problems only when they are abused. It is hard for them to accept age-related problems. They no not unite collectively to form a political bloc." An advocate working with the elderly (I.D. 608) reported that he finds "the elderly are aware of the problem, but not enough to form a bloc or remedy the situation. Some won't even sign a petition."

The manager of a large retirement income system suggested a possible reason for the reluctance of the elderly to get politically involved: "Right now older people are aware of the problem and not aware of the system. They are distrustful of the system. But as more older ones get into the system they will form these political blocs for their own benefit." The personnel director of a retail store chain concurred in this assessment of the problem, "The elderly are aware of their problems but they are disenchanted. They feel, 'why fight city hall?'" A nursing supervisor (I.D. 329) also affirmed, "Those I've come in contact with feel that they are forgotten, that no one is going to listen to them."

Still other decision-makers located the problems of an ineffective political bloc with the existing leadership, not with the seniors themselves. A housing official critically observed, "The elderly are being organized now. I think it's being done in a simplistic way, however." A state legislator (I.D. 145A) believed to the contrary, "No one has taken time to organize them. The seniors are not aware enough to organize. Others groups will have to organize them, because the individual senior is not going to join in on his own." A local legislator (I.D. 101) maintained, "There has not been enough leadership or coalition. They need to unite together as an effective group to have more power." A national congressman (I.D. 169) insisted that the leadership would have to come from outside the ranks of the elderly, "The elderly have tried, but they were not effective. It's difficult. They are so close to death--they need a younger person to work reforms."

Many decision-makers who believed that the elderly were not yet aware of their mutual interests or not yet acting collectively on the basis of those shared interests nevertheless believed the elderly would be very active politically in the future. Typical of their comments was the observation made by a district health officer (I.D. 209), "The elderly today don't think about forming a political bloc. But the senior citizens of tomorrow will have the knowledge to put together a powerful bloc."

DECISION-MAKERS' PERSPECTIVES ON POLITICAL ACTIVISM BASED ON AGING GROUP INTERESTS

Five out of six of the decision-makers interviewed in this study reported seeing signs that the elderly are already beginning to organize politically in order to advocate programs that would benefit them personally and to oppose other programs they perceive to be against their best self-interests (see Table 9.2). The more closely involved a decision-maker was with aging programs, the more he reported feeling pressure on issues pro and con from his elderly constituents. As to be expected, the advocates for the aged nearly unanimously affirmed the political activism of their elderly constituency. In contrast, only two out of three of the corporate directors of personnel were persuaded about the elderly's political inclinations. The corporate directors of personnel were, however, the most skeptical in the entire decision-making community.

Seven out of eight of the decision-makers affirmed their belief that even more older persons would be organizing politically "in the very near future" (see Table 9.3).[23] The advocates were the only subgroup unanimous in this perception, but no fewer than eight out of ten in every subgroup concurred. Again, decision-makers more closely involved with aging programs and elderly people were more likely to believe in the future political force that this age group would have. It deserves highlighting in passing, however, that one in six legislators remained completely unpersuaded of the elderly amassing significant political clout at any time in the foreseeable future. The unconvinced were fairly evenly apportioned among the legislators elected to local, state, and national offices; state legislators, however, were somewhat less likely than local or national legislators to insist that the elderly would not become a major political force in the near future.

The decision-makers were asked to identify the issues they believed would be most likely to motivate the elderly to organize politically in order to influence social policies in their own favor. Nearly three out of four (72 percent) mentioned economic problems; one out of two (52 percent) health care issues; one out of three (36 percent) housing and environment concerns; and one out of four (26 percent) transportation needs (see Table 9.4). Only a small minority of the decision-makers mentioned crime, unemployment, and problems with age discrimination or leisure and recreation issues as inciting the elderly to organize politically to lobby for better programs and policies on their own behalf. The decision-makers thus tend to see the political activism of the aged restricted to the more traditional areas of policy assistance to the aged--income, health, and housing--as well as to the emerging transportation issue.

Union local presidents and advocates for the aged were the most likely of the subsamples to assert that the issue of retirement income levels and a decent standard of living in old age would be a rallying issue for political activism among the elderly. Union local presidents were the most likely to overestimate the extent of severe poverty in the elderly population. This perception plus the union

TABLE 9.2

"Do You See Signs That the Elderly Are Already Organizing Politically?"
(percent responding "yes")

Positional Characteristics of the Decision-Makers	
Position in the Policy Process	
Legislators (N = 71)	80
Agency administrators (N = 70)	83
Service delivery personnel (N = 70)	83
Corporate directors of personnel (N = 35)	69
Union local presidents (N = 35)	77
Advocates for the aged (N = 35)	97
Responsibility for Aging Programs	
Primary function (N = 85)	92
Important but not central function (N = 88)	81
Minor function (N = 143)	75
Area of Program Expertise	
Health (N = 37)	78
Mental health (N = 23)	83
Housing (N = 29)	79
Employment (N = 92)	74
Income maintenance (N = 26)	81
Recreation/leisure (N = 18)	94
Senior citizens affairs (N = 49)	92
Generalists (N = 42)	86
Personal Characteristics of the Decision-Makers	
Age of the Respondent	
Under 45 (N = 98)	85
45-54 (N = 98)	83
55-64 (N = 90)	77
65 and over (N = 30)	83
Sex of the Respondent	
Male (N = 230)	81
Female (N = 86)	84
Ethnicity of the Respondent	
White (N = 235)	79
Minority (N = 81)	90
Educational Level of the Respondent	
High school graduate or less (N = 42)	83
Some college (N = 64)	86
College graduate (N = 99)	79
Postcollege professional education (N = 111)	81
Total (N = 316)	82

Source: Compiled by the author.

TABLE 9.3

"In the Near Future, Do You Think More Older Persons Will Organize Politically to Advocate or Oppose Policies That Will Affect Them?"
(percent responding "yes")

Positional Characteristics of the Decision-Makers	
Position in the Policy Process	
Legislators (N = 71)	82
Agency administrators (N = 70)	89
Service delivery personnel (N = 70)	89
Corporate directors of personnel (N = 35)	80
Union local presidents (N = 35)	86
Advocates for the Aged (N = 35)	100
Responsibility for Aging Programs	
Primary function (N = 85)	95
Important but not central function (N = 88)	86
Minor function (N = 143)	83
Area of Program Expertise	
Health (N = 37)	84
Mental health (N = 23)	91
Housing (N = 29)	83
Employment (N = 92)	84
Income maintenance (N = 26)	81
Recreation/leisure (N = 18)	94
Senior citizens affairs (N = 49)	98
Generalists (N = 42)	86
Personal Characteristics of the Decision-Makers	
Age of the Respondent	
Under 45 (N = 98)	94
45-54 (N = 98)	86
55-64 (N = 90)	81
65 and over (N = 30)	87
Sex of the Respondent	
Male (N = 230)	86
Female (N = 86)	91
Ethnicity of the Respondent	
White (N = 235)	85
Minority (N = 81)	93
Educational Level of the Respondent	
High school graduate or less (N = 42)	90
Some college (N = 64)	88
College graduate (N = 99)	87
Postcollege professional education (N = 111)	86
Total (N = 316)	87

Source: Compiled by the author.

leaders' own role in negotiating better pensions for retiring workers surely contribute to their perception of the role that the issue of retirement finances is going to play in mobilizing the elderly for political action. The more central was the decision-makers' involvement with aging programs, the more often he stressed the incentive that inadequate income would give the elderly to organize politically for an improved standard of living.

Income-maintenance specialists were less likely than many other decision-makers, however, to suggest that income concerns would be a mobilizing factor in the elderly's political activism. Data presented in Chapter 3 documented considerably less concern for the elderly's disadvantaged income status among the personnel of various income-maintenance systems than in other sectors of the decision-making community; income-maintenance specialists, for example, were much less likely to overestimate the extent of severe poverty in the elderly population and they were also much less likely to believe that income alone would solve most of the elderly's pressing problems. Such perceptions explain why the income-maintenance specialists were not all agreed that more income and an improved standard of living would be a major rallying issue among the elderly.

Health as a potential political issue for the elderly has considerably greater selective visibility in the decision-making community. Whereas only one in three corporate directors of personnel (34 percent) proposed health as a political issue for the aged, more than two out of three advocates for the aged (69 percent) did. Surprisingly, only two out of five legislators (42 percent) identified health as a vocal concern of the elderly. Legislators could logically have been expected to be more sensitive to health as a political issue for the elderly in light of the considerable public debate over the inadequacy of medicare as a national health insurance plan for the aged, on the one hand, and the current debates over the need for a national health plan for the public in general, on the other. The medical allied health professions did not appear particularly sensitive to health care as a potential political issue in the elderly population, but these health professionals were also relatively more likely to overestimate how adequately medicare provided for the elderly's health care costs. In the health establishment, only the mental health personnel emphasized the importance of health and health care issues in the growing activism of the elderly.

Housing will be a major political issue according to the advocates for the aged and the service delivery personnel. Somewhat less than one out of two of these decision-makers identified housing as one of a number of potential issues that might lead the elderly to form political action groups. In contrast, only one in five corporate directors of personnel identified housing as a major political issue

TABLE 9.4

Policy Issues That Decision-Makers Believe Will Elicit an Age-Based Political Response among the Aged

Decision-Makers' Positional and Personal Characteristics	Financial (percent)	Health Care (percent)
Positional Characteristics of the Decision-Makers		
Position in the Policy Process		
Legislators (N = 71)	69	42
Agency administrators (N = 70)	70	50
Service delivery personnel (N = 70)	73	61
Corporate directors of personnel (N = 35)	63	34
Union local presidents (N = 35)	83	60
Advocates for the aged (N = 35)	83	69
Responsibility for Aging Programs		
Primary function (N = 85)	80	59
Important but not central function (N = 88)	72	45
Minor function (N = 113)	69	52
Area of Expertise		
Health (N = 37)	62	51
Mental health N = 23)	83	78
Housing (N = 29)	79	52
Employment (N = 92)	70	47
Income (N = 26)	69	54
Recreation/leisure (N = 18)	61	50
Senior citizens affairs (N = 49)	86	61
Generalists (N = 42)	69	40
Personal Characteristics of the Decision-Makers		
Age of the Respondent		
Under 45 (N = 98)	84	59
45-54 (N = 98)	68	48
55-64 (N = 90)	67	31
65 and over (N = 30)	67	47
Sex of the Respondent		
Male (N = 230)	72	52
Female (N = 86)	74	53
Ethnicity of the Respondent		
White (N = 235)	71	50
Minority (N = 81)	75	62
Educational Level of the Respondent		
High school graduate or less (N = 42)	69	62
Some college (N = 64)	75	53
College graduate (N = 99)	75	48
Postcollege professional education (N = 111)	70	52
Total (N = 316)	72	52

Source: Compiled by the author.

Issues Most Likely to Elicit Greater Political Organization among the Aged				
Housing (percent)	Transportation (percent)	Crime (percent)	Employment (percent)	Leisure (percent)
35	25	3	3	4
36	26	11	4	4
41	30	3	9	1
20	23	3	3	0
34	14	9	0	6
49	31	14	3	0
38	35	12	7	1
34	20	6	5	6
37	23	4	2	2
32	30	5	5	3
39	13	0	4	0
14	28	0	3	3
30	17	8	3	3
42	23	2	4	4
61	50	5	6	0
51	31	12	6	0
36	31	6	2	7
36	26	7	6	1
36	27	10	1	4
32	21	3	6	4
53	37	3	3	0
36	25	8	3	3
38	28	6	7	1
34	26	6	4	3
44	25	9	4	3
50	26	7	5	5
30	20	12	5	5
37	26	13	2	3
34	28	13	5	1
36	26	7	4	3

for the elderly; the personnel directors consistently downplayed housing as a major problem for many elderly people, however. Decision-makers who themselves were elderly emphasized housing as a viable political issue among the elderly. Younger decision-makers mentioned housing as a distant third behind income and health issues, while the oldest group of decision-makers identified housing as a more viable political issue than the elderly's concerns over health care. Recreation/leisure specialists also showed greater agreement on housing than health matters as a rallying issue for the elderly in the political arena. Senior affairs specialists tended as well to stress the importance of housing as a political issue for the elderly; though more than one out of two identified the housing issue, it still ranked third in order of visibility to this group of decision-makers behind income and health matters.

Housing planners in various government agencies, on the other hand, did not generally believe that housing would soon become an agenda item on the elderly's list of political action priorities. Moreover, the data in Chapter 6 suggest that these housing planners not infrequently held inaccurate impressions regarding the housing needs and preferences of elderly people. Without political pressure brought to bear on housing officials by the elderly residents in the community, federal and state housing assistance monies are likely to be channeled into more congregate age-segregated housing projects as opposed to being used to subsidize elderly people in their own homes in the community as most of the elderly personally prefer. Housing planners for the most part believe that housing, in the future as in the past, will not be among the elderly's more vocal concerns.

Transportation was typically the fourth most frequently mentioned political issue, but it was less selectively visible in the decision-making community than the other major issues. Those who say they work closely with the aged tended to emphasize transportation as a potential political issue more than those who work less closely with the aged. Recreation and leisure specialists were the only subgroup in the decision-making community who believed in the majority that transportation would be a major political issue for the elderly. Decision-makers who themselves belong to this older age group also tended to emphasize the transportation concerns of the elderly more than younger ones did. But even these elderly decision-makers listed transportation a distant fourth behind income, housing, and health care issues as the elderly's primary motivation to organize politically.

Although crime is a matter of great concern to many elderly persons (see Table 2.6) and is gaining some attention in the decision-making community as a special problem for the elderly, very few of the decision-makers believed crime would become a major political issue for the elderly. The advocates for the aged (one in seven) and the senior citizens affairs specialists (one in eight) were the most likely to view crime as a potential issue to elicit an age-based political response from the elderly. Similarly, despite all the public debate such issues as age discrimination and mandatory retirement practices have generated on the basis of their inherent unfairness to older workers (see Chapter 8), very few decision-makers believed that such employment concerns would achieve the status of a political issue among the elderly population as a whole. Finally, despite all the expressed concern about the elderly's use of leisure time in the retirement years (Chapter 8), only a very small percentage of this cross section of the decision-making community believed that such leisure and recreation concerns would become a major political issue among the ranks of the elderly.

The important point is that these decision-makers believe the elderly are or will soon be active on a range of issues that directly affect their age group. In the past, political activism on the part of the elderly has been confined to a specific legislative issue (for example, income maintenance) and as a result activism has subsided and old-age organizations dissolved after legislative enactment (social security). Today, the decision-makers appear to be saying that political activism in the elderly population is directed toward a sufficiently wide set of issues as to endure as a continuing force in U.S. politics. In this sense, political activism on the part of the elderly is a relatively new phenomenon in the political arena.

DECISION-MAKERS' EVALUATIONS OF THE ROLE OF ORGANIZATIONS FOR THE AGING IN INTEREST-GROUP POLITICS

A key to ensuring a more or less permanent and significant role in the policy decision-making process is the development of a formal organizational structure to facilitate advocacy on behalf of the elderly members of society. This formal structure for the articulation of the elderly's interests is ostensibly held by a group of ten organizations that purport to be more or less exclusively concerned with aging issues in the policy process at the national level--three mass membership organizations (the National Retired Teachers Association-American Association of Retired Persons, the National Council of Senior Citizens, and the National Association of Retired Federal Employees); four trade associations (the American Association of Homes for the Aging, the American Nursing Home Association, the National Council of Health Care Services, and the National Association of State Units on Aging); and three professional associations (the Gerontological Society, the National Council on the Aging, and the National Caucus of the Black Aged).[24]

Additionally, aging advocate organizations are frequently organized at the state and city or county levels. In Los Angeles County, for example, there is a network of local committees on aging in the county that has grown in number from 33 to 50 in the several years it has taken to complete this study. Though discussions of the impact of aging organizations on effecting policy outcomes favorable to the elderly typically focus on national organizations and national politics, state and local aging organizations in state and local politics are also a significant part of the total picture.

From their own perspective based on their respective positions in the policy process, the 316 decision-makers interviewed in this study were asked to evaluate how effective organizations lobbying on behalf of the elderly's interest in the political bargaining process were in comparison to the performance of those organizations lobbying on behalf of the interests of minorities, veterans, labor, youth, education, and welfare groups (see Table 9.5). In all comparisons but two, the majority of the decision-makers found the aging advocates significantly less effective than their competitors. The majority was agreed, however, that the aging lobbyists were competitively even or superior to the lobbyists for children and welfare recipients. It was in comparison with the labor lobbyists that the aging lobbyists fared worst. Nearly three out of four of this cross section of the decision-making community believed that the elderly's advocates were far less effective than the labor lobbyists.

These findings should not be viewed as critical of the aging lobbyists. More accurately, the data can be said to reflect the recent entry of the elderly's advocates into the political scene where domains of power and influence are bitterly contested and only slowly acquired because they are only very reluctantly redistributed. The elderly's advocates have spent several decades (only since the early 1960s) working to gain a more or less permanent foothold in the U.S. political arena, and their power has only recently begun to emerge as a consistent and effective political force. Examining the data from another perspective, then, the fact that nearly one in two decision-makers consider the aging lobby more or less competitively even with the lobbying organizations of minorities, veterans, youth, education, and welfare is really a remarkable record of achievement for the aging organizations, which have been in existence less than two decades. Nevertheless, the perceptions of the remaining half of the decision-maker sample suggest that there may be considerable room for improvement in the lobbying efforts of the aging organizations.

Not unexpectedly, decision-makers were likely to entertain different perspectives on the effectiveness of advocacy efforts on behalf of the elderly depending upon what position they occupied in the policy process. For example, advocates for the aged were relatively more likely than other subsamples to assert that aging lobbyists are at least as effective as the lobbyists for other constituencies. Only in comparison with the lobbying efforts of labor (by a wide margin) and of education (by a narrow margin) did the advocates for the aged in this sample collectively assess the strength of their efforts on behalf of the elderly as significantly less effective. In all other comparisons, the majority of the advocates evaluated the aging lobbyists as more or less equally effective.

The legislators, who make many crucial resource allocation decisions regarding programs and policies that could affect the elderly, were in close agreement with the advocates' reading of the success with which aging organizations lobby on behalf of the elderly. In only two comparisons--with labor and education--did the majority of legislators believe that the elderly's lobbyists were less effective. In competition with youth, welfare, minorities, and veterans, the majority of legislators maintained that the aging advocates managed as effective competitors for scarce dollars. The legislators viewed the aging lobbyists as particularly effective when compared to lobbies for youth and veterans. That the legislators in large numbers should have rated the aging organizations on a par with those of the more established minority and welfare groups would appear to be a considerable credit to the efforts of the aging organizations, particularly because most of the lobbying efforts of these aging organizations have been directed toward influencing the decisions of these very decision-makers in their resource-allocating function in the policy process.

The elderly's advocates may pay a price if they focus their lobbying efforts too exclusively on legislative decision-makers and do not seek as well to influence agency personnel or decision-makers in the private sector. The corporate directors of personnel and the union local presidents, for example, were far less favorably impressed with performance of the elderly's lobbyists than were the legislators. Similarly, the staff of various government social agencies were considerably less impressed with the record of the aging lobbyists than were the legislators. Aging programs are typically housed in the health, education, and welfare departments of government. The advantage the agency personnel in these departments accord to the elderly's lobbyists over those for youth, education, and welfare groups could prove to be an important influence on the allocation of dollars and personnel in the agency to aging programs as opposed to programs for these other constituencies. Advocates for the elderly need to remain alert to the allocation decisions that are made by agency administrators and service providers.

TABLE 9.5

Decision-Makers' Comparisons of the Effectiveness of the Aged's Lobbyists with Those Lobbying on Behalf of Selected Other Groups in the Political System

Decision-Makers' Positional and Personal Characteristics	Lobbyists for Minorities	Lobbyists for Veterans
Positional Characteristics of the Decision-Makers		
Position in the Policy Process		
Legislators (N = 71)	46	37
Agency administrators (N = 70)	51	60
Service delivery personnel (N = 70)	51	54
Corporate directors of personnel (N = 35)	69	51
Union local presidents (N = 35)	60	74
Advocates for the aged (N = 35)	40	40
Responsibility for Aging Programs		
Primary function (N = 85)	49	51
Important but not central function (N = 88)	41	45
Minor function (N = 43)	60	57
Area of Program Expertise		
Health (N = 37)	54	57
Mental health (N = 23)	52	65
Housing (N = 29)	45	45
Employment (N = 92)	62	63
Income (N = 26)	58	58
Recreation/leisure (N = 18)	44	39
Senior citizens affairs (N = 49)	43	43
Multiple expertise (N = 42)	43	33
Personal Characteristics of the Decision-Makers		
Age of the Respondent		
Under 45 (N = 98)	55	46
45-54 (N = 98)	51	53
55-64 (N = 90)	51	59
65 and over (N = 30)	40	40
Sex of the Respondent		
Male (N = 230)	52	50
Female (N = 86)	53	58
Ethnicity of the Respondent		
White (N = 235)	57	54
Minority (N = 81)	41	47
Educational Level of the Respondent		
High school graduate or less (N = 42)	57	53
Some college (N = 64)	53	56
College graduate (N = 99)	60	54
Postcollege professional education (N = 111)	42	47
Total (N = 316)	52	52

Source: Compiled by the author.

Percentage Who Believe the Aged's Lobbyists Are Significantly Less Effective			
Lobbyists for Labor	Lobbyists for Youth	Lobbyists for Education	Lobbyists for Welfare
70	14	55	46
71	30	47	36
73	39	51	46
66	43	43	57
63	43	49	46
77	40	51	40
74	33	51	44
73	31	49	43
73	33	50	45
81	35	57	46
83	35	57	39
72	31	52	48
65	42	48	48
85	23	50	42
72	28	50	39
77	35	49	43
69	12	45	40
80	35	53	45
72	30	50	43
71	33	47	44
54	30	50	47
70	28	49	44
88	44	53	45
74	31	50	46
72	35	49	38
64	38	43	40
70	33	48	44
78	35	55	49
75	27	50	41
73	32	50	44

The extent of a decision-maker's professional involvement with elderly persons in his job had no significant or consistent influence on his perceptions of the elderly advocates' success in lobbying for the elderly. His area of professional expertise had some influence, however. Both senior citizens affairs specialists and recreation/leisure program directors were significantly more likely to rate the elderly's advocates as fairly competitive with other advocate groups. Most other subgroups in the decision-making community were not nearly so generous in their evaluation of the effectiveness of the aging lobby.

Neither the age nor education seemed to influence the decision-maker's perception of the success of organized lobbying efforts on behalf of the elderly; the sex and ethnic background of the decision-maker, on the other hand, did appear to influence his perceptions. Women, for example, consistently rated the aging lobbyists as less effective than men did. Decision-makers of minority race or ethnic background tended to evaluate the organized aging lobby efforts more favorably than white decision-makers. Of particular interest is the significantly higher rating minority decision-makers gave aging advocates when compared with minority advocates and welfare lobbyists.

Effective lobbying on behalf of the elderly's best interests would ideally attempt to influence decision-making at all levels in the policy process. Local officials in legislative and agency positions who make many important allocation decisions, as well as advocates for the elderly, must be as concerned to have input in these decisions as in the decisions made by legislators and agency administrators in the nation's capital. Similarly, decisions made by those in the business community often impact rather directly on the welfare of the retired and elderly population. Advocates for the elderly should be dedicated to reaching these decision-makers in the private sector as well. In a world of scarce dollar resources, social problems compete for attention. This means that programs to assist the elderly must compete for scarce funding and personnel resources with programs providing assistance to minority groups or children or welfare groups. The comparative effectiveness of the aging lobby relative to the lobbying efforts of these other groups is important, for it may affect the resource allocation decisions of these decision-makers and others similarly situated. It is the old story of the squeaky wheel getting the grease.

DECISION-MAKERS' SUGGESTIONS FOR IMPROVING ADVOCACY ON THE AGED'S BEHALF

Keeping in mind that the elderly's advocates are relatively recent newcomers to the scene of local, state, and national politics, many decision-makers found the aging advocate organizations able to compete more or less on a par with other advocate groups. Nevertheless, a slim majority of the decision-makers believed that the elderly's advocates operated at a disadvantage and were clearly less effective than other advocate groups in influencing policy outcomes. Regardless of their measure of the aging advocates' success in the policy process to date, all of the decision-makers offered suggestions for improving the role played by aging organizations in interest-group politics.

These decision-makers most often recommended improving advocacy efforts on issues related to the elderly's interests by first increasing the grass-roots participation of the elderly themselves through the organization of more senior citizens centers and "golden age" clubs. The implicit hypothesis of these decision-makers was thus the same as that offered by many gerontologists--bring the elderly together in a single physical location and in face-to-face interaction. Thus structured by the situation, the elderly will begin to talk together and explore their mutual interests and problems, and eventually they will begin to seek recourse for their shared problems through social and political action. Nearly one third of the decision-makers (31 percent) believed that these senior clubs, even though primarily recreational in character, might someday be transformed into instruments for organized collective action in the political or social arena. These decision-makers seemed to believe that there exist no better advocates for the elderly's best interests than the elderly themselves and that to the extent the elderly are organized, they will be an effective force in political and social institutions.

Another one in five of the decision-makers suggested that elderly people need to get more politically involved as individuals in order to have a successful impact on policy outcome. This would entail urging other elderly people to vote, lobbying for votes on various political issues among their age peers, organizing letter-writing campaigns to elected officials, staging public protests and demonstrations, and the like. These decision-makers emphasized the importance of the tasks that the elderly's advocates face in educating the elderly about their political rights and duties and the even greater burden these advocates face in getting many of these elderly to assert their rights individually and collectively.

Some decision-makers (one in ten) focused on the roles of leadership and professional advocates in the aging organizations, urging that lobbying efforts on behalf of the elderly would be more successful if leaders were more responsive to the needs and desires of their elderly constituency. A state assemblyman (I.D. 147) commented, "Their representatives should be more varied by ethnic background, education, and income level so as to become a fully integrated system." There seemed to be a persistent feeling among some in the decision-making community that lay and professional leaders steering the major aging organizations may be out of touch with their aged constituency, and that they ought to narrow the gap either by encouraging more grass roots by the elderly and/or by opening up the ranks of leadership to more diverse input, thereby improving the elderly's position in the political and social arena. In this regard, a U.S. congressman (I.D. 167) observed that, "Self-serving groups are using the elderly--handmaidens of labor unions, for example. They do a great disservice to the elderly."

The decision-makers frequently underscored the importance of having professional and well-paid lobbyists to represent the elderly and their aging organizations at all levels, local, state, and national, in the political process. One advocate (I.D. 601) believed it was important "to have lobbyists that are age 65 or older--they would understand the needs." But a state senator (I.D. 141) objected to the contrary, "They have to get a younger man. It's a strenuous job to walk the halls of the legislature and you need a young energetic person." A hospital administrator (I.D. 208) wasn't concerned about the age of the lobbyists, but insisted on the need to "hire professionals." These decision-makers at least agreed that "the success of a lobbying effort for the elderly lies in having a full time lobbyist at all levels and fully paid by citizens, attending state, county, and federal sessions--full-time lobbies at all times, not just at election time" (director of a special services program to help the elderly, I.D. 334A).

Unfortunately, as more than one in seven of the decision-makers acknowledged, the aging organizations need improved financial backing in order to attract better lobbyists and field an effective campaign of education and influence. The president of a public employees union (I.D. 503) suggested, "If the lobbyists spoke for a large membership of dues-paying members, it means they would have money available. The mother's milk of politics--any group who wants to succeed has to have money." The head nurse in a retirement home (I.D. 343) agreed, "Money is the power behind lobbying." A state housing official (I.D. 229) also insisted, "It's all a matter of money and they don't have the money. . . . I say this having been a lobbyist."

By and large, even when these decision-makers discussed lobbying efforts to influence programs and policy outcomes in favor of the elderly, the primary target of influence was perceived to be the legislators, because they make the initial decisions to adopt new or expand old programs. But one state legislator (I.D. 154) cautioned, "They need to have more effective contact with the executive branch. Those of us close to people are more in touch and aging is like motherhood--we all vote in sympathy for it. The executive always vetos." Increasing the visibility of the elderly age group's needs and problems to decision-makers in business and labor union groups was rarely suggested by these decision-makers. Similarly, only a handful of the respondents recommended that the elderly's advocates seek greater visibility for the elderly's problems through the mass media. Data presented in the prior chapter, however, suggest that the mass media may be a very effective and very efficient way to reach a broad cross section of the decision-making community with information about the most pressing needs and problems confronting elderly people living in the community. One advocate (I.D. 602) cheered, "Senior power is becoming very active. It's beginning to be recognized by the media." But this is a far cry from advocates collectively and actively pressuring the media into providing more informative presentations on the elderly's life circumstances that could serve as a stimulus to alter the general climate of decision-making that fashions aging programs and policies.

Some decision-makers (one in nine) spoke of the need for advocates and organizations representing the elderly to unify behind a program of explicit goals and objectives. A senior citizens affairs official (I.D. 201B) asserted that, "If there were some unifying force to pull together a great variety of lobbyists and groups of the elderly, I think they'd be more effective." A state assemblyman (I.D. 150A) urged greater selectivity in their agenda for political action: "They have to begin to provide some of the things they would like to see happen. . . . They have had too many things on their list. . . . They need to get several pinpointed to begin with." Another state legislator (I.D. 140) linked unity in organization to developing a workable political agenda: "There should be one central organization. Now they are split too many ways. There are so many organizations. If these were just one voice, a total voice, they would be more consistent and more effective."

Positional or personal characteristics of the decision-makers generally had little influence on their perceptions regarding how to improve advocacy strategies on behalf of the elderly in the policy process. A few examples where the perceptions appeared to be particularly selective are worth noting in passing however. Agency administrators stressed the need for more grass-roots organizations of senior citizens; this is consistent with the trend toward the institutionalization of greater citizen participation in the development of program guidelines being structured within their own agencies through the implementation of citizen advisory panels and other administrative setups. Corporate directors of personnel were particularly sensitive to need for leadership in these aging organizations that would be more responsive to the needs of the elderly membership. Advocates for the aged, on the other hand, were more concerned about obtaining highly skilled professional lobbyists to project the elderly's cause in the public forums of debate. The veterans of advocacy and collective bargaining, the union local presidents, were the most likely to assert the need for unifying lobbying efforts on behalf of the elderly, articulating a common set of policy goals and program objectives and then monitoring program outcomes to see that they met stated intentions. And, as could be expected, the legislators were the most likely to recommend a program of political activities that the elderly as individuals could engage in regularly--voting their age-related interests, writing their elected representatives, asserting their rights to protest, and so forth.

The more central responsibility for aging programs was to the decision-maker's professional position, the more likely he was to express a need for professional advocates to campaign on behalf of the elderly; otherwise the centrality of work with the aging to the decision-maker's job was unrelated to the kind of recommendations he made for improving advocacy on behalf of the elderly in the policy process. Minority decision-makers, perhaps drawing upon their own experiences in advocating minorities' needs within the policy process, were more likely than white decision-makers to identify the need for greater grass-roots organization of the elderly in clubs and greater professionalism among the formal spokesmen or lobbyists for the elderly's advocacy campaign in the policy process.

The decision-makers' suggestions for improving advocacy efforts on behalf of the elderly were numerous. Few suggested that the elderly should form political coalitions with other groups (such as the blacks or the poor); in contrast, most of the decision-makers accepted the idea that an age-based program of political activism was both feasible and desirable. Most agreed that elderly individuals need to support the efforts of their advocates to lobby in their behalf through their greater involvement in age-based organizations, through programs of individual and collective political activity in their own communities, and through providing greater financial backing to their lobbyists than they have in the past. While decision-makers believed that better articulation of the elderly's interests in the policy process would come through more responsive leadership and more skilled lobbyists, these decision-makers also clearly urged greater social and political activism from the elderly individuals who in the past have chosen to ignore politics in general or age-based politics in particular. Ultimately, these decision-makers believed the elderly will need to speak out for themselves.

INTEREST-GROUP POLITICS AND PROGRAM OUTCOMES: THE NEED FOR ADVOCACY ON BEHALF OF THE AGED

A few in the sample of 316 decision-makers said in effect, "The elderly have no controversial issues. They need no lobbyists" (I.D. 151, a state senator). But the recent impact of revenue-sharing grants on expenditures for aging programs at the state and local levels of government provokes quite the contrary response. Revenue sharing was enacted to return program spending decisions from the federal agencies in Washington back to state and local jurisdictions, which theoretically should be more responsive to the local needs than Washington bureaucrats because of their closer contact with the people who are actually going to be served by the programs. As currently operative, revenue sharing consists of two types of grants--general revenue sharing (GRS) with eight spending categories and special revenue sharing.[25]

Although revenue sharing was intended to address the needs of the local population in a manner more responsive to their expressed needs, there is some question as to whether this has happened in fact. As for revenue sharing meeting the needs of the aging population in particular, there has been even greater concern expressed, precisely because of questions about whether aging lobbyists are sufficiently effective in state and local politics to garner funds for aging programs in the interest-group politics of resource-allocation decision-making.[26]

The available data suggest that the concern of aging professionals on this score is not unfounded. According to one study, 36 percent of all GRS funds have been expended for capital outlays, while 64 percent have been allocated to support program operations, with only some 25 percent of the programs newly created under the GRS grants. Of the $9.5 billion expended under GRS by June 30, 1974, only 4 percent had been allocated to social service programs serving the poor or aged.[27] It is also significant that the states seemed to have committed a larger percentage of GRS funds to this category than local jurisdictions (the available figures suggest 7 percent versus 2 percent), probably because the aging lobby in most states is better organized at the state than at the local level.

It is difficult to specify from existing records of GRS allocations precisely how much of the GRS funds allocated to programs for the poor or aged goes to programs serving primarily or exclusively the aged residents. An analysis of GRS expenditures prior to July 1, 1973 finds that of 218 government units, only 28 (12.8 percent) authorized the allocation of revenue-sharing funds to categoric aging programs, and the total monies allocated to those programs were .2 of 1 percent of the total revenue-sharing funds available to these 218 government units.[28] Based on these data, one researcher concluded, "For whatever reasons, when released from federal requirements, programs for the elderly may slip into oblivion in the U.S.A. under such a New Federalism strategy. This is especially probable in the case of unconditioned (General) revenue sharing, because support for aging programs has to be renegotiated with advocacy efforts in each of the more than 39,000 individual jurisdictions which receive revenue sharing funds."[29]

In this context, then, it is appropriate to inquire how the decision-makers interviewed in this study assign the priorities for revenue sharing in Los Angeles among the eight designated spending categories: public safety, environmental protection, recreation, libraries, public transportation, health, social services for the poor or aged, and financial administration. In order to delve behind the choice between social programs for the poor versus the aged in the seventh spending category, these two program categories were given split consideration in the interview, as in fact they would be in real-world deliberations over the allocation of monies within the single GRS spending category for social services.

There was a good deal of consistency in the priorities that this diverse sample of decision-makers assigned to various categories of spending under GRS for Los Angeles (see Table 9.6). Nearly all of the subgroups in the decision-making community collectively ranked health or public transportation as first or second priority. Public safety, social services for the poor, and social services for the aged were collectively arranged by the decision-maker groups in some order of third, fourth, and fifth spending priority. Recreation and environmental protection vied for spots of sixth and seventh priority, while libraries and administrative costs were located alternately in eighth or ninth priority.

Advocates for the aged, agency administrators, and service delivery personnel collectively assigned social services for the aged third priority for GRS funds. Legislators, on the other hand, assigned social services for the aged fifth priority, while according public safety (fire, police, and so on) third priority. Corporate directors of personnel and union local presidents also accorded aging programs lower priority than did the service-oriented agency personnel and advocates for the aged. The greatest concern must be reserved for the priorities that legislators assign to spending revenue-sharing funds for aging programs, because these legislators are the ones who make the initial decisions regarding the allocation of those monies. Thus, the point to underscore here is that the legislators among all segments of the decision-making community placed the lowest collective priority on social services for the aged. As to be expected, the more central work with the aging was to the decision-makers' jobs, the higher they collectively assigned rank to aging programs.

A quick look at the individual rankings these decision-makers assigned the single spending category of social services for the aged will confirm these trends in priority assignment offered by various groups in the decision-making community (see Table 9.7). Whereas one in three advocates (34 percent) gave programs for the aging first or second spending priority under the revenue-sharing program, less than one in five of the legislators (19 percent) concurred in that priority; and whereas only one advocate placed aging programs as low as sixth priority, eleven legislators (15 percent) placed aging programs sixth priority or lower. Senior citizens affairs specialists--in fact, all persons in categoric positions--were far more supportive of aging programs for top or second priority in spending than the rest of the decision-making community. The minority decision-makers also stressed top priority for funding aging programs. The fact remains, however, that all of these groups have failed to persuade the legislators of the high priority programs for the aging should be given under revenue sharing, at least according to these data.

Here, then, emerges a real and immediate task for groups seeking to promote advocating policy outcomes favorable to the elderly. The allocation of revenue-sharing funds to programs for the aging will not happen except as advocates and informal groups of the elderly can mount an extensive and persuasive campaign on the elderly's behalf.

STRATEGIES FOR ADVOCACY ON BEHALF OF THE AGED: THE IMPORT OF THESE DATA

Based on the data in this and the preceding chapter, it is clear that aging organizations have some degree of access to public officials in legislative and executive or agency positions, and with such access comes the opportunity to exert influence on policy outcomes. Taking effective advantage of available opportunities to advocate and influence policy actions on aging problems, however, has always been fraught with problems--inadequate financial backing, lack of unity and numbers, lack of sophisticated lobbying techniques. But in spite of these apparent barriers, the aging organizations are emerging ever stronger and more effective protagonists of aging programs in the politics of distribution and redistribution. In this study, as many as half of the decision-makers compared the elderly's aging advocates with the advocates of youth, education, welfare, minority, and veterans groups

TABLE 9.6

Decision-Makers' Expressed Priorities for Revenue-Sharing Allocations among Spending Categories

Decision-Makers' Positional and Personal Characteristics	First	Second	Third
Positional Characteristics of the Decision-Makers			
Position in the Policy Process			
Legislators (N = 71)	Transportation	Health	Public safety
Agency administrators (N = 70)	Health	Transportation	Services/aged
Service delivery personnel (N = 70)	Health	Transportation	Services/aged
Corporate directors of personnel (N = 35)	Health	Transportation	Public safety
Union local presidents (N = 35)	Transportation	Health	Services/poor
Advocates for the aged (N = 35)	Transportation	Health	Services/aged
Responsibility for Aging Programs			
Primary function (N = 85)	Transportation	Health	Services/aged
Important but not central function (N = 88)	Transportation	Health	Public safety
Minor function (N = 143)	Health	Transportation	Public safety
Area of Program Expertise			
Health (N = 37)	Health	Transportation	Public safety
Mental health (N = 23)	Services/poor	Health	Services/aged
Housing (N = 29)	Transportation	Health	Services/aged
Employment (N = 92)	Transportation	Health	Services/poor
Income maintenance (N = 26)	Health	Transportation	Services/aged
Recreation/leisure (N = 18)	Health	Transportation	Services/aged
Senior citizens affairs (N = 49)	Transportation	Health	Services/aged
Generalists (N = 42)	Transportation	Health	Public safety
Personal Characteristics of the Decision-Makers			
Age of the Respondent			
Under 45 (N = 98)	Transportation	Health	Services/aged
45-54 (N = 98)	Health	Transportation	Services/poor
55-64 (N = 90)	Health	Transportation	Services/aged
65 and over (N = 30)	Transportation	Health	Services/aged
Sex of the Respondent			
Male (N = 230)	Transportation	Health	Services/aged
Female (N = 86)	Health	Transportation	Services/aged
Ethnicity of the Respondent			
White (N = 235)	Transportation	Health	Services/aged
Minority (N = 81)	Health	Transportation	Services/aged
Educational Level of the Respondent			
High school graduate or less (N = 42)	Transportation	Health	Services/aged
Some college (N = 64)	Health	Transportation	Services/aged
College graduate (N = 99)	Health	Transportation	Services/poor
Postcollege professional education (N = 111)	Transportation	Health	Services/aged
Total (N = 316)	Transportation	Health	Services/aged

Source: Compiled by the author.

Allocation Priorities of Decision-Makers for Revenue Sharing Funds

Fourth	Fifth	Sixth	Seventh	Eighth	Ninth
Services/poor	Services/aged	Recreation	Environment	Library	Administration
Services/poor	Public safety	Environment	Recreation	Library	Administration
Services/poor	Public safety	Environment	Recreation	Administration	Library
Services/poor	Services/aged	Environment	Recreation	Administration	Library
Services/aged	Public safety	Environment	Recreation	Administration	Library
Services/poor	Public safety	Environment	Recreation	Administration	Library
Services/poor	Public safety	Environment	Recreation	Administration	Library
Services/aged	Services/poor	Environment	Recreation	Library	Administration
Services/poor	Services/aged	Environment	Recreation	Administration	Library
Services/aged	Services/poor	Environment	Recreation	Administration	Library
Transportation	Environment	Public safety	Recreation	Library	Administration
Public safety	Services/poor	Environment	Recreation	Administration	Library
Services/aged	Public safety	Environment	Recreation	Administration	Library
Environment	Public safety	Services/poor	Recreation	Library	Administration
Public safety	Services/poor	Environment	Recreation	Library	Administration
Services/poor	Public safety	Environment	Recreation	Administration	Library
Services/poor	Services/aged	Recreation	Environment	Library	Administration
Services/poor	Public safety	Environment	Recreation	Library	Administration
Public safety	Services/aged	Environment	Recreation	Library	Administration
Services/poor	Public safety	Environment	Recreation	Administration	Library
Services/poor	Public safety	Recreation	Environment	Administration	Library
Services/poor	Public safety	Environment	Recreation	Administration	Library
Services/poor	Public safety	Environment	Recreation	Library	Administration
Services/poor	Public safety	Environment	Recreation	Library	Administration
Services/poor	Public safety	Environment	Recreation	Administration	Library
Public safety	Services/poor	Recreation	Administration	Environment	Library
Services/poor	Public safety	Environment	Recreation	Library	Administration
Services/aged	Public safety	Environment	Recreation	Administration	Library
Services/poor	Public safety	Environment	Recreation	Library	Administration
Services/poor	Public safety	Environment	Recreation	Library	Administration

TABLE 9.7

Decision-Makers Rank Social Services for the Aged among the Priority Uses for Revenue-Sharing Funds in Los Angeles County

Decision-Makers' Positional and Personal Characteristics	First Priority	Second Priority
Positional Characteristics of the Decision-Makers		
Position in the Policy Process		
Legislators (N = 71)	8	11
Agency administrators (N = 70)	11	10
Service delivery personnel (N = 70)	16	13
Corporate directors of personnel (N = 35)	9	6
Union local presidents (N = 35)	9	17
Advocates for the aged (N = 35)	17	17
Responsibility for Aging Programs		
Primary function (N = 85)	24	15
Important but not central function (N = 88)	8	9
Minor function (N = 143)	7	12
Area of Expertise		
Health (N = 37)	8	5
Mental health (N = 23)	4	26
Housing (N = 29)	14	10
Employment (N = 92)	11	11
Income (N = 26)	15	8
Recreation/leisure (N = 18)	22	6
Senior citizens affairs (N = 49)	18	16
Generalists (N = 42)	5	14
Personal Characteristics of the Decision-Makers		
Age of the Respondent		
Under 45 (N = 98)	10	11
45-54 (N = 98)	10	12
55-64 (N = 90)	12	13
65 and over (N = 30)	20	10
Sex of the Respondent		
Male (N = 230)	10	12
Female (N = 86)	15	13
Ethnicity of the Respondent		
White (N = 235)	9	11
Minority (N = 81)	19	14
Educational Level of the Respondent		
High school graduate or less (N = 42)	19	14
Some college (N = 64)	20	12
College graduate (N = 99)	5	9
Postcollege professional education (N = 111)	10	14
Total (N = 316)	12	12

Source: Compiled by the author.

Rank Accorded Social Services for the Aged among Revenue-Sharing Priorities (percent)

Third Priority	Fourth Priority	Fifth Priority	Sixth Priority	Seventh Priority	Eighth Priority	Ninth Priority
14	18	22	7	6	1	1
24	18	20	16	4	1	0
19	23	10	13	0	0	4
11	14	26	20	3	3	0
17	31	9	11	3	0	3
26	17	20	3	0	0	0
23	18	14	5	1	0	1
22	18	25	9	2	2	1
15	20	15	17	4	1	3
16	30	21	14	0	0	3
30	17	9	9	0	0	4
24	14	21	3	3	0	3
16	18	15	17	4	1	1
8	23	27	12	0	4	0
11	28	11	17	0	0	6
24	12	22	4	2	0	0
19	17	14	12	7	2	0
23	19	13	13	3	2	3
12	15	20	16	4	1	1
20	24	18	7	1	0	1
20	13	20	7	4	0	0
18	17	19	13	3	1	1
20	24	13	8	1	0	2
20	18	20	11	3	1	1
16	21	11	14	2	0	4
17	21	17	10	2	0	0
19	22	14	6	3	0	1
21	19	17	16	1	2	3
17	16	21	12	5	1	1
19	19	18	12	3	1	2

and rated the aging lobby as competitively effective. Only in comparison with the veteran union lobbyists did the elderly's advocates fall far short of achieving comparable rating. These decision-makers evidently consider the aging lobbyists a permanent addition to the world of interest-group politics.

The decision-makers virtually unanimously believe the elderly share many age-related problems in common and thereby possess the basis on which to build a significant age-based movement. The majority of the decision-makers believes a rising age-group political consciousness is already underway in the elderly population; most of the other decision-makers foresee growing political activism in the elderly age group in the near future. These decision-makers anticipate their own greater accountability to a vocal elderly population across a range of issues, but focusing particularly on money, health, housing, and transportation issues that directly affect many elderly people.

The success of the elderly in interest-group politics is dependent on their achieving at least a modicum of coalescence around a set of specific issues. There simply is no substitute for a show of unity in numbers. Unfortunately, by the time the elderly population achieves overwhelming concurrence on a particular policy issue, the weight of general public opinion has mandated the same policy outcome, so that the elderly lobby or the elderly vote is not crucial to policy adoption.[30] On issues of considerably greater public debate, the elderly also appear unable to produce consensus, even though it is precisely in this situation that the elderly could provide the crucial swing vote or exert a determining influence on the outcome of policy deliberations. When the elderly age group can coalesce on otherwise controversial issues and swing the critical vote, even if it happens only occasionally, then the elderly will constitute a permanent and effective force in interest-group politics.

In the meantime, aging organizations can perhaps skillfully work off the capital they have accumulated by virtue of the decision-makers' own beliefs in the strength of the aging political bloc. The aging organizations purport to represent millions of older persons across the United States. In fact, the National Retired Teachers Association-American Association of Retired Persons, with a reported membership of 6.02 million older persons, is one of the largest of such membership associations in Washington, D.C., the seat of government power. To the extent that the leadership of NRTA-AARP and other aging organizations can purport to speak for their members and mobilize their constituency to action in support of their proposals when required, the aging organizations are in a position to develop progressively more effective positions of power and influence in the policy process. To the extent that the decision-makers anticipate political organization and activity among the elderly now or in the near future (as shown by these data), the aging organizations should have an easier task convincing them that the elderly are already organized, that these aging organizations are their duly appointed spokesmen, and that the elderly's articulated demands require due attention under the threat of alienating an entire constituency should the elderly's needs go unredressed.

Most decision-makers do not wish to anger the older population and give the elderly cause to mobilize with punitive intentions. The decision-makers would prefer to satisfy as many of the constituency's articulated needs as possible. To the extent that the aging organizations can establish themselves in the eyes of the decision-making community as the legitimate spokesmen for the aged population and their needs, they guarantee themselves a role in the political deliberations. The leadership in these aging organizations seems to understand that their survival in the world of interest-group politics depends on the legitimacy of their role as spokesmen for the elderly's interests. If they can convey a sense of unity of purpose in their elderly constituency, these data suggest that the decision-making community is prepared to listen, and where feasible, heed the articulated demands.

The decision-making community anticipates strong lobbying efforts to publicize the elderly's needs and it anticipates growing political activism in the elderly population. Now it is up to the aging organizations and others of the elderly's advocates to build a political agenda based on age-related concerns that will draw the support of many of the elderly in a display of unity the likes of which these decision-makers and others like them across the country have not seen to date. Decision-makers know it is only a matter of time before they will have to contend with a highly organized and articulate elderly constituency, and that time most see as not very far away.

NOTES

1. For a provocative challenge to these commonly held beliefs, see Theodore J. Lowi, The End of Liberalism (New York: Norton, 1969).

2. Robert H. Binstock, "Aging and the Future of American Politics," Annals of the American Academy of Political and Social Science 415 (September 1974): 199-212.

3. David B. Truman, The Governmental Process: Political Interests and Public Opinion (New York: Knopf, 1951), p. 37.

4. This step-by-step analysis of the emergence of age-group consciousness is derived from a very useful paradigm developed by

Richard T. Morris and Raymond J. Murphy, "A Paradigm for the Study of Class Consciousness," Sociology and Social Research 50, no. 3 (April 1966): 298-313.

5. Robert H. Binstock, "Interest-Group Liberalism and the Politics of Aging," Pt. I, Gerontologist 12, no. 2 (Autumn 1972): 265-80; Binstock, "Aging and the Future of American Politics."

6. The reader will develop an appreciation for the emergence and growing popularity of the age-group consciousness concept in the gerontological literature by perusing some of the following books and articles: Milton L. Barron, "Minority Group Characteristics of the Aged in American Society," Journal of Gerontology 8, no. 4 (October 1953): 477-82; Milton L. Barron, The Aging American: An Introduction to Social Gerontology and Geriatrics (New York: Crowell, 1961); Frank A. Pinner, Paul Jacobs, and Philip Selznick, Old Age and Political Behavior (Berkeley: University of California Press, 1959); Abraham Holtzman, The Townsend Movement (New York: Bookman Associates, 1963); Arnold M. Rose, "The Subculture of the Aging: A Framework for Research in Social Gerontology," in Older People and Their Social World, ed. Arnold M. Rose and Warren A. Peterson (Philadelphia: Davis, 1965), pp. 3-16; Arnold M. Rose, "Group Consciousness among the Aging," in Older People and Their Social World, ed. Arnold M. Rose and Warren A. Peterson (Philadelphia: Davis, 1965), pp. 19-36; Erdman B. Palmore and Frank Whittington, "Trends in the Relative Status of the Aged," Social Forces 50, no. 1 (September 1971): 84-90; Erdman B. Palmore and Kenneth Manton, "Ageism Compared to Racism and Sexism," Journal of Gerontology 28, no. 3 (July 1973): 363-69; Pauline K. Ragan and James J. Dowd, "The Emerging Political Consciousness of the Aged: A Generational Interpretation," Journal of Social Issues 30, no. 3 (December 1974): 137-58; Vern L. Bengtson and Neal E. Cutler, "Generational and Intergenerational Relations: Perspectives on Age Groups and Social Change," in Handbook of Aging and the Social Sciences, ed. Robert H. Binstock and Ethel Shanas (New York: Van Nostrand-Reinhold, 1976), pp. 130-59; Gordon F. Streib, "Social Stratification and Aging," in Handbook of Aging and the Social Sciences, ed. Robert H. Binstock and Ethel Shanas (New York: Van Nostrand-Reinhold, 1976), pp. 160-85; Robert B. Hudson and Robert H. Binstock, "Political Systems and Aging," in Handbook of Aging and the Social Sciences, ed. Robert H. Binstock and Ethel Shanas (New York: Van Nostrand-Reinhold, 1976), pp. 369-400.

7. Rose, "Group Consciousness among the Aged," p. 14.

8. See, for example, findings reported by Elizabeth B. Douglass, William P. Cleveland, and George L. Maddox, "Political Attitudes, Age, and Aging: A Cohort Analysis of Archival Data," Journal of Gerontology 29, no. 6 (November 1974): 666-75; and

Angus Campbell, "Politics through the Life Cycle," *Gerontologist* 11, no. 2 (Summer 1971): 112-17.

9. Matilda White Riley and Anne B. Foner, eds., *Aging and Society*, Vol. I, *An Inventory of Research Findings* (New York: Russell Sage Foundation, 1968), pp. 302-05; Bernice L. Neugarten and Joan W. Moore, "The Changing Age-Status System," in *Middle Age and Aging*, ed. Bernice L. Neugarten (Chicago: University of Chicago Press, 1968), pp. 5-21.

10. A concise summary of the literature describing ethnic, sex, and social class differences in patterns of aging is available in Vern L. Bengtson, Patricia L. Kasschau, and Pauline K. Ragan, "The Impact of Social Structure on Aging Individuals," in *The Handbook of the Psychology of Aging*, ed. James E. Birren and K. Warner Schaie (New York: Van Nostrand-Reinhold, 1976), pp. 327-53.

11. Eva Kahana et al., "Perspectives of Aged on Victimization, 'Ageism,' and Their Problems in Urban Society," *Gerontologist* 17, no. 2 (April 1977): 121-30; Riley and Foner, *Aging and Society*.

12. Elderly people commonly attribute problems to other people their age that they say do not affect them personally. Louis Harris and Associates, *The Myth and Reality of Aging in America* (Washington, D.C.: National Council on the Aging, 1975), pp. 29-39. These findings were also confirmed in the USC companion survey of community residents aged 45 to 74 when they were asked to identify their three most pressing problems and the three most pressing problems that commonly confront other people their age.

13. For an historical description of these age-based social movements, consult Pinner, Jacobs, and Selznick, *Old Age and Political Behavior*; and Holtzman, *The Townsend Movement*.

14. Gordon F. Streib, "Are the Aged a Minority Group?" in *Applied Sociology*, ed. Alvin W. Gouldner and Stephen M. Miller (New York: Free Press, 1965), pp. 311-28.

15. Michael Kaye Carlie, "The Politics of Age: Interest Group or Social Movement?" *Gerontologist* 9, no. 4 (Winter 1969): 261.

16. Ibid., p. 259.

17. Ibid., p. 261.

18. Henry J. Pratt, "Old Age Associations in National Politics," *Annals of the Academy of Political and Social Science* 415 (September 1974): 106-19.

19. Ibid.

20. Binstock, "Aging and the Future of American Politics"; Binstock, "Interest Group Liberalism"; Robert B. Hudson, "Rational Planning and Organizational Imperatives: Prospects for Area Planning in Aging," *Annals of the Academy of Political and Social Science* 415 (September 1974): 41-54.

21. A few years prior to the present study, a leading business magazine featured a rare special report on the aged consumer in the economic marketplace. The article reported that the 65 and older age group represented a $60 billion consumer market, and that as such, it was "far larger than the vaunted and highly amorphous youth market variously estimated at between $20 and $45 billion." In spite of the statistics, the article observed advertising was still for the most part directed at the under-25 age group. Except to promote the sale of laxatives and denture adhesives, advertising and business sales promotion almost totally overlooked the elderly consumer. "The Power of the Aging in the Marketplace," Business Week, November 20, 1971, pp. 52-58.

22. Rose, "The Subculture of the Aging," p. 14.

23. As an aside to examine the academicians' theoretical perspectives on the emerging age-group political consciousness, it is interesting to note that nearly one in three of the decision-makers (30 percent) perceived organized political activity among the elderly residents in the community, although those same decision-makers asserted that the elderly are not sufficiently aware of their own interests to form a political bloc. This conjunction of beliefs seems to suggest either that recognition of mutual age-based interests is not a necessary condition for the emergence of an age-based political interest group or that age-based political activism can be sustained by conditions or circumstances other than shared attitudes regarding mutual interests and goals. Such propositions contradict political theory dating back to Karl Marx's early formulations of the concept of "class consciousness" and the distinction between a "class in itself" and a "class for itself." The decision-makers' observations of age-based organized political activity without the predicted awareness of mutual needs may be entirely plausible, as empirical investigations of the cumulative dimensions of political group consciousness have been none too successful. See, for example, Patricia L. Kasschau, H. Edward Ransford, and Vern L. Bengtson, "Generational Consciousness and Youth Movement Participation: Contrasts in Blue Collar and White Collar Youth," Journal of Social Issues 30, no. 3 (December 1974): 69-74. Unfortunately this intriguing theoretical question cannot be explored further with the available data.

24. Pratt, "Old Age Associations in National Politics."

25. For a brief description of the revenue-sharing program in general outline, see Michael D. Reagan, The New Federalism (New York: Oxford University Press, 1972).

26. Robert B. Hudson and Martha B. Veley, "Federal Funding and State Planning: The Case of the State Units on Aging," Gerontologist 14, no. 2 (April 1974): 122-28; Jerome Kaplan, "Revenue Sharing: Myth or Reality for the Aged?" Pt. I, Gerontologist 13, no. 3 (Autumn 1973): 274.

27. C. L. Estes, "Revenue Sharing: Implications for Policy and Research in Aging," Gerontologist 16, no. 2 (April 1976): 141-47.

28. Ibid.

29. Ibid., p. 145.

30. Binstock, "Aging and the Future of American Politics."

10

The Climate of Decision-Making in the Field of Aging: Varied Perspectives on Aging as a Social Problem

THE DECISION-MAKING COMMUNITY: DIVERSE PERSPECTIVES ON THE PROBLEMS AND THE SOLUTIONS

The 316 decision-makers interviewed in this survey were intended to comprise a cross section of the decision-making community that would accurately reflect whatever diversity of opinion currently exists regarding the problems people typically encounter in growing old and the most appropriate social policies and programs that could assist older people in managing those problems. The interviews with these 316 decision-makers confirm that considerable diversity of opinion does exist in the decision-making community. Far from being monolithic in nature, the decision-making community reveals pockets of accurate perception and misperception of the elderly's problems as well as a patchwork of support and opposition for specific policy recommendations to assist elderly persons living in the community. The major task of this book has been to portray as accurately as possible the full richness in the diversity of opinions that does exist among decision-makers who are instrumental in fashioning programs and policies to assist the elderly, and then to look beyond the differences in perceptions and attitudes for possible patterns that might help to explain who is likely to hold what beliefs and why.

This final chapter is presumably to provide an overview of the climate of decision-making in the field of aging that will neatly summarize how various decision-makers view the aging problem in U.S. society. The assignment is impossible to fulfill, however, precisely because of the complexity of the policy-making environment. Policy-making is to a large extent situationally determined, and to that extent, it is fragmented. Policy outcomes depend on how the specific policy issue is framed for consideration and what specific actors are asked to make the final determination. Moreover, in the context of any single decision-making event, the outcome is not shaped singularly or even primarily by rational planning and implementation. Political forces, institutional imperatives, and budgetary constraints also affect the decision.

The context of decision-making is thus fragmented, and so, too, are decision-makers' planning orientations. The decision-makers interviewed in this study not infrequently seemed to hold incompatible beliefs and entertain discordant perceptions. For example, 29 percent of the sample suggested that the secret to successful old age was "to stay as active as ever" and, at the same time, "to relax and take life easy." It is difficult to interpret the two prescriptions as compatible with each other. Or to take another example, 40 percent of the sample maintained that "most older people are set in their ways and are unable to change," while insisting that "most older people can learn new things as well as younger ones." Again, the jointly held beliefs are difficult to explain. Many other examples could be drawn from the data.

There was yet another problem of attitude consistency. It rarely proved possible to identify central attitude clusters that organized a decision-maker's thinking about the aging problem. For example, decision-makers who distorted the prevalence of severe poverty in the elderly population were no more likely than decision-makers with accurate information about the elderly's income status to cite cost barriers to the elderly's obtaining adequate medical care or cost barriers to the elderly's continued mobility in the surrounding community or the financial motives for retirees desiring to return to work. Similarly, decision-makers who deplored the elderly's poor health status were no more likely than decision-makers who accorded the elderly good health status to suggest that poor health constitutes a serious barrier to continued employment past age 65 or that there is a need for housing specially designed to accommodate the elderly's declining functional capacity in the later years or that demand-response transportation systems are required to ensure that the frail elderly have transportation service in the community. Again, other examples are plentiful in the interview data.

The decision-makers in this sample seemed to hold inconsistent beliefs and attitudes without much concern for the lack of consistency reflected in their reasoning. Logical consistency is the linchpin in the ordering of human affairs. It enables man to understand, to predict, and finally to respond to the behavior of other beings and objects in his environment. Ordinarily, cognitive dissonance is so discomforting that the individual will rework the conflicting elements of thought or thought and behavior until they are reasonably consistent. Why should cognitive consistency not characterize as well the decision-makers' responses in these interviews? One plausible explanation is that these decision-makers usually contend with narrow aspects of the aging problem on any given occasion, but rarely, if ever, are required to think about the aging problem in its entirety, as they were asked to do in this interview. Whatever the explanation, it is important to premise the analysis of decision-makers' planning orientations on the fact that decision-makers' analyses of social problems are not characterized by cognitive consistency, and their social policy actions do not reflect attitude-behavior consistency.

If the reader can bring himself to accept these premises, he will begin to understand why it would be impossible to summarize neatly the climate of decision-making in the field of aging by describing who believes what and who is therefore likely to support or oppose which policy proposals. Nevertheless, the data presented in this volume afford the opportunity to sketch some broad outlines of the climate of decision-making underlying policy deliberations in the field of aging. This is the sole task of this concluding chapter.

The decision-making community is so diverse and the policy decision-making process is so complex that it is possible to examine only a part of the total picture at any one time. Individuals who study the policy process in order to understand and predict policy outcomes typically narrow their inquiry to particular issues and/or specific decision-making units in the policy process. Only in these more circumscribed contexts are generalizations about the climate of decision-making and the policy process meaningful and useful for understanding program outcomes. In recognition of the impossibility, or at least the impracticability, of analyzing decision-making in the field of aging as a single entity, the first chapter of this volume laid out five models of the policy process that focused on different, albeit sometimes overlapping, aspects of policy-making and program implementation. These models provide a meaningful context in which to highlight selected aspects of the climate of decision-making in the field of aging. Each of the models provides a useful way to examine some part of the climate of decision-making that fashions aging programs and policies, and though some models appear to have wider applicability and hence greater general utility, no single model adequately accounts for the diversity of opinions and program outcomes in the field of aging. This chapter is devoted to reviewing selected aspects of the decision-making environment in the field of aging from each of the five analytic perspectives.

OBSERVATIONS ON SOCIAL POLICY IN THE FIELD OF AGING FROM A RATIONAL PLANNING PERSPECTIVE

The rational planning model of the policy process stresses the development of social programs in response to well-documented needs in the target population. Rational decision-making depends upon having accurate information about the needs and problems in the target population and the relative effectiveness of alternative modes of social intervention. The data presented in the preceding chapters suggest that decision-makers lack the requisite information base for rationally planning and implementing programs to assist the elderly.

Only one third (34 percent) of the decision-makers interviewed in this study maintained that their information base detailing the elderly's needs and problems was sufficient for their decision-making responsibilities vis-a-vis the elderly and/or aging programs. Although decision-makers most closely involved with aging programs were relatively more likely than the rest of the decision-making community to express satisfaction with their present data base, well more than half (59 percent) of these categoric decision-makers complained that their information base was insufficient for their decision-making responsibilities.

Most of the decision-makers did not even possess basic demographic information about the elderly population. They typically stereotyped the elderly in welfare-dependent terms that would constitute a distortion of the status of even the oldest and most disadvantaged segments of the elderly population (those elderly over 85 years of age). Less than one third of the decision-makers (29 percent) estimated that fewer than one out of three elderly live in poverty (the correct figure is between 15 and 20 percent). On the other hand, nearly half of the decision-makers (43 percent) estimated that at least one out of every two elderly persons lived in poverty, and one seventh of the decision-makers asserted that as many as two out of three elderly persons or even more lived in dire poverty. Only one quarter of the decision-makers (28 percent) maintained that most elderly people enjoy good health.

More commonly, these decision-makers believed that substantial numbers of the elderly population were institutionalized because they could no longer manage their affairs at home and in the community with sufficient independence. Although less than 5 percent of the elderly population is institutionalized, only one in seven of the decision-makers estimated the institutionalized elderly to comprise less than 10 percent of the total elderly population; in contrast, more than one third of the decision-makers believed that as many as one in three of the elderly or more were institutionalized. Lacking basic information about the income and health characteristics of the elderly population, how can decision-makers plan programs that will adequately address the needs of all elderly?

Inaccurate information about the elderly's needs and problems has a visible impact on planning programs to assist the elderly. For example, because the decision-makers overemphasized the prevalence of dire poverty in the elderly population, they perceived excessive housing costs to constitute the major barrier to the elderly's obtaining adequate housing, and hence they emphasized solving the elderly's major housing problems by building more low-cost housing. At the same time, because these decision-makers believed that most elderly who have difficulty managing at home are institutionalized, the decision-makers did not place as high a priority on providing in-home support services or designing more barrier-free housing units for the open market. To illustrate the impact of misinformation on program planning with a second example, the decision-makers vastly overestimated the elderly's reliance on public transportation as their primary means of getting around in the community. But because of this misperception, many decision-makers seemed to feel that barrier-free mass transit is the primary solution to the elderly's mobility problems in the community. Although many elderly households still rely on their own automobiles for transportation, the problems confronting the elderly driver were substantially overlooked by the decision-makers.

Conceivably, the amount of misinformation a decision-maker possesses would be related to the nature of his primary information sources--specifically, whether he relied upon empirical data or depended mostly on nonempirical information about the elderly's problems and unmet needs. It seems reasonable to assume that decision-makers who rely on government reports packed with statistics and/or findings from social science research would possess more accurate information about the nature and the magnitude of problems afflicting elderly residents in the community than would decision-makers who rely for information primarily on personal contacts with old people and/or directly personal or vicarious experiences with aging in their own lives. Data from the interviews with these 316 decision-makers, however, revealed no such relationship between the decision-makers' primary information sources and the accuracy of their information base on the subject matter of aging. This empirical finding damages the prospects for more rational program planning in the field of aging.

Although rational decision-making appears to be an inappropriate way to characterize program development in the field of aging at the present time, it persists as a desirable goal for decision-makers in all sectors of the decision-making community.

Nearly nine out of ten of the decision-makers in this sample (89 percent) believed, for example, that social science research can play a useful role in decision-making and program planning for the elderly. Similarly, nearly two out of three of the decision-makers (63 percent) believed that the decennial White House Conferences on Aging result in better programs for the elderly. The function of both social science research and the White House Conferences was typically defined in terms of amassing data on the elderly's unmet needs to inform decision-makers who have instrumental roles in shaping policies and programs that directly affect the elderly.

The assumption persists in the thinking of these decision-makers that with accurate information about the elderly's problems and the relative effectiveness of alternative strategies of social intervention, rational problem-solving will guide program development. In the quest of greater rationality in program planning and implementation, two out of three of the decision-makers interviewed recommended specific ways to improve the existing data base in the field of aging. At the same time, nearly half of the decision-makers (47 percent) wished that they themselves had greater opportunities to provide feedback to decision-makers in other positions in the policy process about information they had acquired in working with the elderly that would improve the operation of existing programs and policies. These decision-makers frequently expressed the hope, and sometimes the confidence, that policy-making could be made more rational.

In the first chapter, it was suggested that rational decision-making may assume a greater role in times when the decision-makers perceive a crisis that requires direct and immediate social policy response. The data from the interviews with these 316 decision-makers reveal that they did identify some crises in making suitable provision for the nation's elderly and that, as anticipated, the decision-makers were prepared to take heretofore unimagined policy actions to redress the problems. One such instance concerns the fiscal crisis now confronting the income-maintenance system. As a result of extended life expectancy and the trend toward early retirement, more workers are living more years of their lives in retirement, and the majority of the decision-makers agreed that the swelling size of the retiree population creates serious problems for existing income-maintenance programs. This sense of crisis is one reason why the decision-makers overwhelmingly supported an overhaul of the private pension system to ensure solvency and fiscal responsibility for covered beneficiaries.

But the situation was viewed as most critical for the social security retirement program. As a result of the perceived fiscal crisis, the majority of the decision-makers interviewed in this survey (54 percent) supported a proposal to refinance the social security retirement program at least in part from general revenues. Since initiation of the public retirement program back in the 1930s, the system has been financed exclusively by payroll tax contributions from the currently employed and their employers. This payroll tax is an integral part of the social insurance image of the program that analogizes retirement benefits to deferred wages. The insurance image has been cultivated in order to distinguish the retirement program from welfare programs that dispense benefits according to need rather than on the basis of prior contributions. As recently as the 1965 amendments to the original Social Security Act, which added the medical insurance plan to cover the elderly's health care costs, the payroll tax method of financing the social security system was overwhelmingly supported.

In the early 1970s, however, studies projected fiscal shortages in the trust fund less than a decade off; hefty payroll taxes would be required to keep the system current on a pay-as-you-go basis. Although proposals to abandon the payroll tax method of financing the social security system had never enjoyed much support before the identification of the system's fiscal crisis, the data presented in Chapter 3 reveal that a majority of decision-makers now support a radical restructuring of the mechanisms for financing the retirement benefit program, away from singular reliance on the payroll tax to partial or total reliance on general revenues. Proposals for reform of the social security system presented to Congress by the Carter administration suggest that reform of the financing mechanism along these lines may not be too far off in the future.

The decision-makers were similarly united in the identification of mandatory retirement policies as a source of personal crises for innumerable workers making the transition from working to retired status. Although mandatory retirement policies have become an increasingly common employment practice throughout the twentieth century, the decision-makers in this sample voted overwhelmingly to reverse this common business practice. Nearly three quarters of the sample (74 percent) insisted that there should be no mandatory retirement policy, that conversely, older people should be allowed to work as long as they want to and are able to work. Steps have already been taken on federal legislation that would prohibit mandatory retirement at a specific chronological age in federal government positions and raise the mandatory retirement age in the private sector to age 70. The legislation marks the first serious effort by the federal government to mandate changes in the mandatory retirement practices of private business and industry. The decision-makers' perceptions of widespread retirement crises are responsible for making the climate of decision-making ripe for such public policy action.

Decision-makers are capable of rational problem-solving when appropriate information is available to guide decision-making and a virtual crisis of some sort has been identified that is in need of immediate and direct social policy action. In such circumstances, it does not take long to marshal the decision-makers' support in favor of logical public policy responses. As a general rule, however, the climate of decision-making is not conducive to rational problem-solving. Other perspectives on the policy process may be more useful for understanding program outcomes.

OBSERVATIONS ON SOCIAL POLICY IN THE FIELD OF AGING BASED ON AN INTEREST-GROUP MODEL

An interest-group model of the policy process stresses diverse constituencies in the population with diverse needs each seeking to influence decision-makers to allocate resources to programs that will provide assistance to them and others like them. Because public monies are finite but demands for their application are infinite, the various constituencies in the population are typically in competition with one another to impress decision-makers with the urgency of their unmet needs.

Utilizing an interest-group frame of reference on the policy process would raise questions about the nature of the perceptions of the elderly's problems and unmet needs that are entertained by advocates for the aged who purport to represent the elderly's best interests in the political bargaining process. Do the elderly's advocates accurately understand the elderly's most pressing problems? Have the advocates been able to convey successfully to legislators and other decision-makers the elderly's particular needs for public policy assistance? How effective are the elderly's advocates rated in comparison with the lobbyists for other interest groups that are organized to influence policy outcomes? The data gathered in the interviews with this sample of 316 decision-makers often fit with an interest-group perspective on the policy process.

The perceptions of the elderly's problems and needs entertained by the advocates for the aged often differed from the perceptions expressed by other subgroups in the decision-making community, and far more often than not, the advocates' perceptions more closely paralleled the expressed needs of elderly residents in the community. Advocates were nearly twice as likely as any of the other five subsamples to mention transportation among the elderly's three major problems, collectively giving transportation a rank second only to the elderly's financial problems. Interviews with Los Angeles County elderly residents confirmed that nearly half of them (49 percent) reported having major problems getting around in their neighborhoods or the larger surrounding community. Similarly, advocates for the aged were the most likely of the original six subsamples to cite housing as one of the elderly's three most pressing problems. Although elderly residents in the county did not often identify housing as one of their major problems, well more than half of these elderly respondents (58 percent) identified serious problems with their present housing arrangements when queried directly about potential problems.

On the subject of health care, the advocates were the only subsample that in the majority appreciated the limits of the health insurance coverage that medicare afforded the elderly. They were also the most critical of the health care services that elderly patients typically receive in the health services delivery system. Nearly three quarters of the advocates (71 percent), for example, maintained that many physicians are reluctant to treat elderly patients. In these and other areas, the advocates appeared to be particularly sensitive to the elderly's special needs and problems, and hence seemed to be well prepared to lobby on behalf of the elderly's interests in the political bargaining process.

The elderly's advocates typically received relatively good evaluation for their lobbying efforts on behalf of the elderly, although the legislators and advocates were generally more likely to give the elderly's advocates a higher rating than were other decision-makers in the sample. Only in comparison with labor and education lobbyists did a majority of the legislators and adgocates find the elderly's advocates at a severe competitive disadvantage. By way of contrast, only in comparison to youth and welfare lobbyists did the rest of the decision-making community accord the elderly's advocates competitive parity. The decision-makers overwhelmingly agreed that the elderly's advocates are at the greatest disadvantage when competing against the veteran labor lobbyists; curiously, however, business and union leaders gave the elderly advocates somewhat more favorable marks in comparison with their labor lobbyists than did the rest of the decision-making community. Another surprise is that the agency administrators gave the elderly's lobbyists a more favorable rating against the lobbyists for competing youth, welfare, and education constituencies than did other decision-makers.

In light of the fact that organized lobbying efforts on behalf of the elderly date back only 15 to 20 years, it must be considered a resounding success that a near majority or a clear majority of the decision-makers sampled from all sectors of the policy process perceived the elderly's lobbyists as reasonably competitive when compared to the lobbyists of more established constituencies like youth, welfare, minorities, veterans, and education.

Allocation decisions for revenue-sharing funds demonstrate the need for organized lobbying efforts on behalf of the elderly. Among the eight possible spending categories for general revenue-sharing monies, all sectors of the Los Angeles decision-making community agreed on transportation and health care services for the community as the top spending priorities. There was considerable diversity of opinion, however, concerning the priority that social services for the elderly should have. The elderly's advocates, of course, ranked social services for the elderly third, immediately behind community transportation and health services. In contrast, the legislators, who ultimately make the decisions regarding any allocations of general revenue-sharing funds, ranked social services for the aged fifth, lower in priority than social services for the poor and fire and police department needs subsumed under the rubric of public safety.

It would appear that the elderly's advocates face an uncompleted task. Given the prospects for the continuation of these revenue-sharing grants for the foreseeable future, advocates for the elderly will have to organize an assertive and persistent lobbying campaign in an effort to persuade local legislators of the need to fund special service programs to assist elderly residents living in the community. This situation prevails not only in Los Angeles County but in most other communities across the country. The elderly will not receive their fair share of these revenue-sharing funds unless their needs and demads are articulated clearly and persistently to local legislators who make the funding decisions.

Although formal organizations representing the elderly's interests in the policy process through the efforts of paid professional lobbyists are crucial to ensuring a fair representation of the elderly's needs in the political bargaining process, there can be no substitute for political awareness and activism in the entire elderly constituency. The decision-makers nearly unanimously believed that the basis for an age-based political activism exists in the realities of growing old. That is, older people share similar problems on account of their advanced age that span the differences created by race, social class, or other distinctions among them. Only half of the decision-makers (53 percent), however, maintained that the elderly are sufficiently aware of their common problems to coalesce in a political bloc. At the same time, decision-makers overwhelmingly agreed (87 percent) that older people will more and more in the future be organizing to advocate or oppose policies that affect them. Most of the decision-makers (82 percent) insisted that there are signs that elderly people are already becoming more politically aware and politically active on age-based issues.

The importance of a well-organized advocacy effort by and on behalf of the elderly in order to impress decision-makers with the urgency of the elderly's pressing problems and unmet needs is made all the more critical by the decision-makers' predominantly passive information-seeking behavior. The clear majority of the decision-makers interviewed in this study relied primarily on information about the problems of growing old they gleaned from reading newspapers and watching television, from their on-the-job contact with elderly people, and from their personal and vicarious experiences with aging in their own lives. Many of the decision-makers did not actively seek out information from professionals and experts in the field of aging or from aging organizations; neither did they regularly consult government reports or social science research findings.

The import of these findings is that the elderly and their advocates must approach the decision-makers with information about the elderly's needs and problems and recommendations for the best program solutions. Moreover, given the information-seeking behavior of most of the decision-makers, the mass media appear to offer the best way to reach the most decision-makers. Advocacy outreach efforts should thus be directed toward the mass media in order to improve not only the image of aging as it is presented in everyday entertainment programming but the quality of documentary, news, and other informational broadcasts as well.

The mass media represent but one way to broaden the outreach efforts of the elderly and their advocates. Advocacy on behalf of the elderly has focused heavily on the legislators at all levels of government. The policy process, however, is far broader than just the legislative component. Agency personnel at all levels in public and private social agencies make decisions regarding the allocation of program resources that could affect the delivery of services to the elderly population. They, too, are in need of education about the elderly's special problems. Similarly, business and union management policies have a direct impact on the lives of older workers and retirees as well as their dependents. Data presented in Chapter 8, however, suggest that approximately half of these corporate and labor officials never utilize information disseminated by aging organizations. The elderly's advocates have important lobbying work to do in private business and industry. For example, under persistent pressure from these aging organizations, corporate personnel officers and union local presidents might be persuaded to develop effective retirement preparation programs or to structure opportunities for continued involvement of retirees in corporate and union functions.

In less than two decades, aging organizations have mounted a visible lobbying effort on behalf of the elderly. They have impressed decision-makers with the potential of an aging political bloc, although they have not yet succeeded in coalescing support in the elderly population around a range of age-based policy issues. In order to become an effective force in interest-group politics, this kind of age-based political activism must extend to more than just a small minority of politically aware senior citizens. The responsibility ultimately rests with the elderly's advocates to stir and to organize political sentiment in the elderly constituency. Advocacy for the elderly can never substitute for advocacy by the elderly.

OBSERVATIONS ON SOCIAL POLICY IN THE FIELD OF AGING BASED ON A MODEL OF ELITE PREFERENCES

In many ways, the elite preference model of the policy process is the opposite of the interest-group model. In the latter, diverse constituencies actively seek to influence a diverse group of decision-makers about the urgency of their needs, and the decision-makers wait for various constituencies to bring their problems to them. In the elite preference model, the decision-makers are envisioned as a more or less unified elite group who agree upon identified problems and appropriate solutions. In contrast to the interest-group model, where policy preferences flow upward from constituents to decision-makers, policies and programs under the elite preference model are developed out of the consensus of opinion among the elite decision-makers and subsequently imposed on a more or less passive citizenry. The fit of the interview data from the present study with the interest-group model of the policy process described in the preceding section does not preclude application of the elite preference model to this same data set, although, as could be anticipated, the elite preference model seems to explain far fewer program outcomes in the field of aging.

More than consensus, diversity of opinion seems to characterize the decision-making community. The elite community does not emerge as monolithic but rather as fragmented and not well organized. On the issue of the consensus of elite opinion concerning the elderly's most pressing problems and the best way to redress those problems through social policy intervention, the model does not accurately describe the diversity of opinions expressed by the cross section of the decision-making community interviewed in this study.

The elite preference model still provides a valuable perspective on some areas of policy-making in the field of aging, however, if the focus is shifted from the search for a consensus of elite opinion to an examination of any tendency of the decision-making community to impose policies and programs on the elderly constituency without regard for the elderly's expressed needs or policy preferences. The major policy areas in the field of aging in which the elite preference model provides an enlightening perspective are housing and transportation.

Decision-makers in this study were concerned about the housing situation of many elderly. The image most frequently conveyed by these decision-makers was of impoverished elderly persons forced to find or stay in substandard housing in the cheaper and less desirable parts of town. The major problem, agreed the overwhelming majority of the decision-makers, is that the elderly are too poor to compete for decent housing on the open housing market. The solution, they agreed, is to construct more housing, particularly more low-cost housing for the elderly.

Most of the decision-makers maintained this view even though they acknowledged that most elderly people, given the choice, would prefer to have government monies made available to repair their present housing rather than to make new housing available to them. It is as if the decision-makers had decided that it would be better for elderly persons living in substandard housing to move into new living environments regardless of the elderly's personal desires to remain in their present housing units. Some of the decision-makers contrasted cheery new living environments with the dirty, old, and shabby environments of the elderly's present living arrangements in order to justify their position in favor of constructing new housing for the elderly. Other decision-makers maintained that extensive home repair and home maintenance programs to allow the elderly to continue living in their own homes would be prohibitively expensive and, in the oldest parts of the city, counterproductive. They, too, favored razing and rebuilding the inner cities in order to create planned living environments that would better accommodate the needs of elderly and other residents in the locale.

Similarly, nearly all the new housing construction for the elderly has been in the form of age-congregate living environments. Although the clear majority of the decision-makers interviewed here acknowledged that most elderly would prefer to live in age-integrated rather than age-segregated living environments, the decision-makers still generally believed that age-congregate housing arrangements facilitate the delivery of services to the elderly. Hence, many decision-makers favored relocating ill-housed elderly into new planned communities that provide a full range of life-support services in the immediate environments, in spite of the elderly's own expressed preferences to remain in their own communities in their present neighborhoods. Moreover, it is likely that housing construction policies in the foreseeable future will continue to reflect the elites' rather than the elderly's preferences.

The decision-makers' predominant focus on the plight of the poorest elderly living in substandard housing and their attendant emphasis on constructing more low-cost housing seemed to draw the elites' attention away from the plight of elderly homeowners, who comprise nearly four fifths of the elderly population. Elderly people who own their own homes are not likely to sell and move into new age-congregate public housing communities; they will do so only after they have exhausted all possibilities for remaining in their own homes. Skyrocketing property taxes and the rising cost of home maintenance and home repairs, however, have driven increasing numbers of elderly poeple from their homes in recent years. For many of these elderly, relocation is into less desirable, cheaper housing arrangements; many may have to rent because they are unable to purchase another home in the inflated housing market.

To date, public housing programs for the elderly have slighted the elderly homeowners' needs for assistance. In the long run, however, it may be more economical and more desirable to find ways to subsidize the elderly in their own homes rather than to encourage their relocation into new housing. In-home support services and home repair assistance programs are viable modes of public housing assistance that would enable the elderly to remain in their homes longer in the years of advanced old age. The reluctance to develop those avenues of public housing assistance for elderly residents living in the community represents an elite decision, not the choice of most elderly residents, who have repeatedly expressed desires to remain in their own homes rather than relocate to new living environments.

Transportation policies also reflect this element of decision-making based on elite perceptions and elite preferences. The decision-makers in this study collectively defined the substantial majority of the elderly residents relying on public transportation to get around in the community, and they thought almost exclusively in public transportation terms when they evaluated ways to improve the elderly's mobility within the community. The decision-making community believed that the primary way to solve the elderly's transportation problems is to provide barrier-free mass transit. Few of these decision-making elite questioned whether a mass transit system designed to serve an entire metropolitan region can provide adequate service within and between small neighboring communities inside the larger service area. Most elderly, however, require transportation service to destinations within a few miles of their home, not across town or downtown. Even if the central public system is constructed barrier free to accommodate elderly and handicapped passengers, it is questionable whether the system will adequately service destinations where the elderly will want to go.

Like in-home support services, door-to-door transportation service for the handicapped and frail elderly provided by some kind of demand-response transit program appears to be challenged by the decision-making community as a legitimate expense, and hence such programs have failed to develop beyond the experimental stage. Many elderly residents will use demand-response transportation services for short distance trips when such service is available to them, but local decision-makers balk at the cost of subsidizing such service for the elderly residents in the community. Hence, experimental programs typically fold after federal seed monies run out. It is again an elite decision that reflects elite preferences rather than the expressed needs or preferences of the local elderly residents.

The decision-making community appeared to be nearly exclusively concerned with the problems of the transit-dependent elderly; the problems of the elderly car owner and the elderly driver were virtually ignored in the decision-makers' deliberations over the elderly's transportation problems. The elderly car owner, who is confronted with high insurance rates, rising gasoline prices, and increasing vehicle maintenance costs, receives no special assistance. Only when he is forced to give up his car and join the ranks of the transit-dependent does the elderly individual's transportation problem become of some concern to the decision-makers. In not encouraging transit independence by subsidizing the elderly car owner as necessary, the decision-making community may be encouraging transit dependence in the elderly population. It is possible that the decision-making elite want to encourage transit dependence in the elderly population, that is, they would like to see older drivers relinquish their private vehicles and rely more on public transportation to get around in the community. But whether the elites are consciously or unconsciously encouraging transit dependence in the older population is not clear. From the standpoint of those interested in fostering transportation services that will adequately serve the needs of elderly residents, the answer should be clarified.

Although there seem to be only infrequent occasions of overwhelming consensus in the decision-making community concerning the identification of problems and the proposals of appropriate remedies, the elite preference model still has considerable validity for highlighting instances in which policies appear to be imposed by groups of the decision-making elite on a more or less passive citizenry. It is true that there are times when the decision-making community will need to respond to latent needs in the elderly population, and policies may justifiably reflect elite preferences. When elite policies, however, run counter to expressed needs or manifest policy preferences of elderly residents, they deserve closer scrutiny by those working on behalf of the elderly's interests.

OBSERVATIONS ON SOCIAL POLICY IN THE FIELD OF AGING BASED ON A MODEL OF INSTITUTIONAL ACTIVITY

One reason that policies and programs endure in the face of contrary preferences expressed in the elderly population or the lack of other ostensibly rational justifications for their existence is that institutional entities inside and outside government support these programs or policies as a further justification for their own existence, that is, for their own, not the elderly's, survival needs. Programs mean financial and staff resources for the administering agency; added resources and expanded clientele constituencies mean more power and more prestige in the government bureaucracy that can be parlayed into more programs, more budget, and more personnel. Programs, departments, and agencies all have institutional survival needs that are nurtured by expanding existing programs and adding new programs. Adopting an institutional perspective on the policy process raises such questions as whether categoric decision-makers currently employed in various aging programs urge the expansion of those and other categoric programs, as well as how specialists in other program areas define the needs of elderly clients.

As to be expected, categoric decision-makers showed a special concern for the plight of the elderly and often showed greater support for the development of additional categoric programs to deal with the elderly's special needs. Categoric decision-makers, especially senior citizens affairs officials in the government, were significantly less likely than the rest of the decision-making community to believe that money alone could resolve most of the pressing problems that people typically face as they grow old. Categoric decision-makers were more than twice as concerned as generic decision-makers about the lack of medical personnel with geriatric specialization and the lack of special medical programs designed to provide elderly patients with health care services designed to treat their particular health needs. They were also significantly more concerned than generic decision-makers about the apparent reluctance of many physicians to treat elderly patients. Categoric decision-makers were nearly twice as likely as generic officials to support the expanded development of in-home support services to assist the frail elderly in their own homes. Similarly, the categoric decision-makers were more supportive of demand-response programs to provide the handicapped and frail elderly with transportation services in their surrounding community.

The categoric decision-makers understandably lobbied hard for the expenditure of revenue-sharing funds on social programs for the elderly. Not only would the additional resources for the aging programs mean more service benefits for the elderly but the additional program resources might secure their jobs for another year or two. Nearly one out of four of the categoric decision-makers interviewed in this study believed that social services for the aged deserved the top spending priority for general revenue-sharing funds. In contrast, less than one in twelve of the generic decision-makers accorded social services for the aged that top priority. Five out of every eight of the categoric decision-makers ranked social services for the aged among the top three spending category priorities, whereas only half that many generic decision-makers accorded such emphasis to aging programs.

Specialists in other program areas also offer perspectives on existing policies and programs that could be interpreted as reflecting institutional imperatives. For example, income-maintenance specialists were significantly less in favor of refinancing the fiscally troubled social security retirement benefit program out of general revenues from the U.S. Treasury. They similarly were less supportive than the rest of the decision-making community of many pension plan reforms, most notably, the portability provision, which would mean considerably more bureaucratic red tape and paperwork for these retirement program administrators. Many corporate directors of personnel, who administer their companies' private pension plans, similarly opposed outside regulation of these plans, particularly mandatory portability provisions and investment standards for the plans.

In the health care field, health care providers were more likely to stress the generally poor health status of the elderly population, and they were considerably more likely to overestimate the proportion of the elderly population currently institutionalized. Naturally, then, the health providers were nearly twice as likely as the rest of the decision-making community to stress health as one of the elderly's three most pressing problems. In terms of the elderly's access to available medical care, health providers tended to look at the quality of the psychosocial context in which medical services are delivered to the elderly patient, while outside observers of the health services delivery system tended to focus more exclusively on the high costs of medical care and the barriers those costs could erect to the elderly's utilization of available health care services.

Housing planners' assessments of the elderly's housing problems similarly differed from those of the larger decision-making community. They were twice as likely as the rest of the decision-making community to blame some of the elderly's housing problems on the lack of housing designed especially to accommodate the changing functional capacities of individuals in advancing old age. The housing planners were also nearly twice as likely to observe that elderly residents were isolated from needed life-support services in their communities.

To solve these and other housing problems confronting many elderly residents, the housing planners were particularly supportive of constructing more housing for the elderly. They specifically favored housing that would be specially designed to accommodate the elderly's declining health status in the later years and housing that would be built close to necessary services. They were fond of thinking about age-segregated planned housing environments that would greatly facilitate the delivery of needed services to the elderly population. Housing planners, in contrast to the rest of the decision-making community, seemed to believe that the frail elderly would be better off living in these service-support, age-congregate living environments than in the homes of their adult children. The housing planners were more likely to believe that it usually doesn't work out too well for the elderly to live with their adult children, while, at the same time, they were less likely to accept the proposition that it is better for the elderly to live with their family than in a home for the aged. The housing planners' perspectives on this issue stood out as relatively distinct.

Hence, it is not unusual for those closely involved in a particular program area to have distinctive perspectives on the elderly constituency's most pressing problems in that area, and they not infrequently proposed intervention measures that would add to the range of programs in their general jurisdiction. While concern for the elderly's well-being is doubtless one of their motivations, it is equally likely that program expansion and institutional survival are others. That programs and policies can sometimes persist in the face of contrary manifest demands in the elderly population suggests the strength of programs' and agencies' survival needs. Policies and programs that otherwise seem irrational may be perfectly rational formulations when viewed in the context of institutional imperatives.

OBSERVATIONS ON SOCIAL POLICY IN THE FIELD OF AGING BASED ON A MODEL OF INCREMENTAL CHANGE

Incremental changes in policies and programs from year to year are the rule rather than the exception in the democratic policy process. Incremental expansions satisfy the survival needs of social agencies and other organizations providing services to the elderly, while ensuring continued benefits to elderly recipients who have come to rely on the program assistance. Tried and found to be reasonably successful, increasing existing program benefits is a safer political decision than initiating new programs that might prove to be less successful. For these reasons, incremental expansions of programs and policies tend to continue until more radical decisions are required by unusual circumstances in the climate of decision-making.

Thus it is in the vein of routine decision-making that the 316 decision-makers interviewed in this study typically recommended construction of more low-cost housing units to solve the elderly's most pressing housing problems or that they proposed the installation of barrier-free equipment on existing and planned mass transit systems to ease the elderly's mobility problems. More radical restructuring of existing policies and programs is simply unlikely to occur in the absence of the identification of a problem of crisis proportions requiring immediate action. The lack of adequate information about needs in the elderly population and the relative effectiveness of alternative strategies for social intervention lead decision-makers to prefer to stick with present programs rather than experiment with new programs.

The decision-making community perceive a fiscal crisis confronting the social security system, and they have ample information about the dimensions of the problem. Confronted with the data and projections of the impending demise of the social security trust funds sometime in the early- to mid-1980s, the decision-makers interviewed in this study seemed to accept the need for radical restructuring of the financing mechanism for the retirement benefit program, which is the mainstay of retirement income support for the overwhelming majority of the elderly population. The prospect of reducing benefits to elderly beneficiaries was not seriously considered; the decision-makers' attention focused almost exclusively on refinancing the retirement benefit program so that it can accommodate the increased demands from an expanding retiree population. Only one in four of the decision-makers proposed to deal with the social security crisis by raising payroll taxes by whatever is required to cover current beneficiary obligations. Rather, perceptions of the impending fiscal crisis primed the majority of the decision-makers interviewed in this study to favor refinancing the social security retirement program at least in part from general revenues. Only a few years ago, such an idea would have been considered a breach of the cherished social insurance concept that underlies the payroll tax method of financing the benefit program.

Despite the bold, iconoclastic thinking reflected in this sample of decision-makers when confronted with planning for the financial security of future generations of older Americans, the politics of incrementalism prevailed in the last major piece of social security legislation. The fiscal crisis was solved, for the time being at any rate, by once again raising payroll taxes as necessary to cover the increasing beneficiary obligations. This program outcome in the face of decision-makers' planning orientations favoring a more drastic reorganization of the retirement program is convincing documentation that it is easier for legislators to agree on making minor modifications in the existing program than it is for them to agree on radically restructuring the concept and design of the program.

In contrast to the perceived critical state of affairs in providing income maintenance for elderly people, the decision-makers interviewed in this study perceived numerous deficiencies in the existing medicare program, but they did not appear to identify a crisis in the level of medical care that the program currently provides for elderly beneficiaries. The predictable result is that only a small minority of the decision-makers urged turning medicare into a comprehensive national health insurance plan to cover all the health care costs of the elderly. More commonly, the decision-makers supported a limited expansion to cover some of the elderly's more common health care costs that are not presently covered by the health insurance program--outpatient drug prescription costs, eye and dental care, and preventive health care costs.

The value of the incremental model of policy-making is to highlight program areas where the status quo is being challenged, and program outcomes are likely to be radically restructured because of unusual circumstances in the climate of decision-making. Typically, the incremental mode of decision-making is abandoned when decision-makers are confronted with a crisis, and they have a reasonably sound data base on which to design an effective alternative strategy of social intervention. In these situations, the decision-makers are able not only to identify and accurately survey the problem but also to identify what appears to be the best way to solve the problem; in these situations, the decision-makers want to respond to what they perceive to be the demands of the "public interest."

PERSONAL CHARACTERISTICS OF THE DECISION-MAKERS AND THEIR PERSPECTIVES ON SOCIAL POLICY FOR THE AGING

Apart from the decision-makers' position in the policy process, it was speculated that the decision-makers' personal characteristics--

specifically, age, sex, ethnicity, and educational background--might influence their "perspective map" on issues in aging and social policy. Analyses in the preceding chapters focused only secondarily on the impact of the decision-makers' personal characteristics on their perceptions and attitudes because the analyses were sufficiently complicated tracing the possible influence of the decision-makers' position in the policy process on their assessment of various issues in aging social policy. A brief overview of possible relationships between the decision-makers' personal characteristics and their perspectives on aging policy issues nevertheless offers some interesting findings. A few of the more interesting ones will be highlighted here.

The Decision-Maker's Age

A local legislator (I.D. 112A), age 58, summarized his observations on program developments in the field of aging this way: "I feel I don't know as much as I should. Maybe the biggest problem is that no one knows the blight until we are there ourselves." These data confirm that decision-makers who are elderly themselves frequently do entertain different perspectives on the problems confronting elderly people and likewise often prefer different strategies for social intervention in comparison to younger decision-makers. The difference between the old and the young decision-makers is that the former have personally experienced some of the problems of growing old, and according to many of these elderly decision-makers they draw heavily on their personal experiences to understand the nature of the problems that people frequently encounter as they grow old in U.S. culture.

The elderly decision-makers particularly emphasized the seriousness of the elderly's housing and transportation problems far more than did younger decision-makers. They further believed that these shared housing and transportation problems would be primary rallying issues that would ultimately spur the elderly into political activism on their own behalf. These elderly decision-makers were considerably more confident than younger members of the decision-making community that senior citizens already are sufficiently aware of their common problems, such as housing and transportation, to form a political bloc and collectively support or oppose policies that directly affect them. At the same time, however, these elderly decision-makers tended to overestimate the percentage of elderly who are actively involved in neighborhood senior citizens centers and other age-based organizations. Perhaps age-based political activism is further off in the future than these elderly decision-makers currently project.

The elderly decision-makers are the most vocal about the need to structure more opportunities for the elderly's continued involvement both in employment roles in the private sector and in community service roles in the public sector. The elderly decision-makers' perceptions are no doubt influenced by their own continued involvement in socially productive roles in the public and private sectors. The elderly decision-makers strongly supported elimination of mandatory retirement policies based on the belief that the elderly can perform as well as younger workers in most jobs. They stressed both the financial and the social psychological factors that caused the vast majority of elderly to want to continue working in the labor force at least part time after their initial retirement.

Like the rest of the decision-making community, the elderly decision-makers overwhelmingly perceived retirement as forced on the worker by the employer's mandatory retirement policy, and they believed that as a result of these forced retirements, many older workers experience financial and social psychological crises attendant to making the transition from working to retired status. The elderly decision-makers were strongly supportive of all the pension reforms discussed in the interview; they perceived private pension plans to offer an important means of income security for retirees. At the same time, however, these elderly decision-makers believed that multiple efforts would be required to lift most retirees out of their present financially troubled position. More than younger decision-makers, the elderly ones lobbied for more job opportunities for seniors willing and able to work and more subsidized government services for those elderly without alternatives to supplement their retirement income.

The elderly decision-makers' perceptions of the nature and the magnitude of the elderly's problems were not always more accurate than the younger decision-makers', although many times they were. Similarly, their perceptions of the elderly's own policy preferences were not always more accurate than the younger decision-makers', but many times they were. These elderly decision-makers often seemed to exhibit a special sensitivity to many of the elderly's problems, and they were the only subgroup in the entire decision-making community who in the majority felt comfortable about advising senior citizens that "the key to successful old age is to relax and take life easy." They strongly believed that old age should be the harvest years for the seeds of hard work sown years earlier.

The Decision-Maker's Sex

Although there were differences recorded in the perceptions of male versus female decision-makers, most of the differences were small and did not seem to conform to any particular pattern. Only a few observations have much substantive interest.

Women decision-makers were considerably more likely than their male counterparts to stereotype the elderly in welfare-dependent terms. The majority of the women, for example, maintained that the majority of the elderly population lived in dire poverty. The women were also substantially more likely than the men to insist that one out of every three elderly or even more are currently institutionalized because they can no longer manage independently on their own in the community. Finally, and consistent with the other dependent imagery, the women decision-makers far more than the men stressed transit dependence in the elderly population.

Certain of the women's policy preferences accorded with their perceptions of the elderly's dependence and generally disadvantaged status. Women decision-makers, for example, were substantially more supportive than men of demand-response transportation programs to improve the elderly's mobility in the neighboring community. Similarly, women more often lobbied for the construction of housing units specially designed to accommodate health decrements in the later years, as well as advocated the expansion of in-home support services to assist the frail elderly to remain in their own homes as long as possible.

The women stressed independence in old age in spite of the elderly's disadvantaged status. The women tended to believe more strongly than their male counterparts that elderly people ought to be more independent of their families. The women's emphasis on restructuring housing and community environments to be as barrier free as possible and their emphasis on expanding in-home support services to assist the most frail of the elderly residents represent an effort to construct living environments in which even the frail elderly can manage without becoming dependent on their families. Conversely, the male decision-makers were significantly more likely than the females to insist that adult children have an obligation to care for their aged parent(s). The women's perspectives on the role of familial obligations versus the staunchly independent lifestyle in the later years is all the more interesting in light of the fact that actuarial tables confirm that they will probably be the surviving parent and someday these may be personal decisions for them.

The women felt far less able to influence policy outcomes with their feedback than did male decision-makers. In no small way, their frustration at not being able to make greater inputs into the process of policy formulation and program implementation is probably attributable to their concentration in service-provider positions at relatively lower levels in the government hierarchy. Their role in the policy process is thus usually defined in terms of carrying out the program directives formulated by agency officials higher up in the bureaucracy and not in terms of helping to fashion program guidelines. Women's liberation has not yet brought full equality to women in the realm of employment.

The Decision-Maker's Ethnic Background

Like the women decision-makers, the minority decision-makers also characterize the elderly population in overly pessimistic welfare-dependent terms. Minority decision-makers were nearly twice as likely as their white counterparts to project the majority of elderly living in dire poverty. Compared to whites, the minority respondents consistently rated the elderly's health status as more inferior, so much so, in fact, that nearly half of the minority group (41 percent) maintained that one out of every three elderly or even more are presently institutionalized because they are unable to manage independently. Minority decision-makers also emphasized transit dependence in the elderly population significantly more than did the white decision-makers.

The concept of familial responsibility for dependent aging parents is a norm currently undergoing revision, in the society generally and in ethnic communities in particular. The tension created by the changing norm is evident in the decision-making community as well. Ethnic communities have long been characterized as having extended family networks that would typically incorporate and take care of an aging parent who was left alone in the later years. But, in the interviews with this sample of 316 decision-makers, it was the white significantly more than the minority decision-makers who maintained that it is the obligation of adult children to care for their aged parents. At the same time, however, these white decision-makers were far more likely to suggest that it usually does not work out too well for aging parents to live with their adult children, and they were twice as likely as the minority decision-makers to insist staunchly that older people ought to be more independent of their families. In the final analysis, then, minority decision-makers were still more strongly committed to the proposition that it is better for the elderly to live with their families than in a home for the aged.

Minority decision-makers lobbied in significantly greater numbers than did white decision-makers for more senior citizens housing, for comprehensive national health insurance to cover the elderly's health care costs, for free transit provided to all senior citizens, and for demand-response transportation services to provide increased mobility for the frail elderly in their neighboring community. Although minority decision-makers, like the women, were disproportionately clustered in the service-provider roles within the policy process, the majority of these ethnic decision-makers maintained that they had ample opportunity to offer input in the formulation and implementation of programs in their area.

Recent affirmative action policies represent conscious efforts by the decision-making community to recruit minorities into their ranks. Although these minority individuals are still clustered disproportionately in lower level positions in the policy process, it seems that their opinions are sought, particularly within programs and agencies seeking to improve services to the ethnic elderly. Many of the ethnic decision-makers held positions in neighborhood clinics and branch offices located in communities heavily populated by their own ethnic group. Many agencies have made deliberate efforts to recruit minority personnel to staff offices located in the minority communities on the assumption that the minority decision-makers would be better able to understand and administer to the needs of the ethnic elderly.

Data from the interviews with this diverse group of decision-makers confirm that the minority decision-makers do hold differing perspectives on aging problems and the desirable modes of social policy intervention. In particular, the minority decision-makers seemed more closely in touch with the special problems confronting the ethnic elderly living in their respective minority communities. The perspectives of the minority decision-makers thus constitute a valued contribution to the climate of decision-making in the field of aging. They represent an assurance that programs and policies in the future will address more of the needs evident in the diverse elderly population.

The Decision-Maker's Educational Level

Of the four personal characteristics of the decision-makers examined with these data, the decision-maker's educational level appeared to have the least effect, or the least consistent effect, on the decision-maker's perspectives on aging and social policy. The major difference in perceptions, as might be expected, occurred between those decision-makers who had never attended college and those who had attended at least some college.

Decision-makers having no more than a high school education focused consistently on the plight of the most disadvantaged segments of the elderly population. They emphasized the elderly's problems with chronic illnesses to the point of grossly overestimating the percentage of elderly who are institutionalized. They also stressed transit dependence in the elderly population considerably more than did the college-educated decision-makers. The lesser educated decision-makers stressed the elderly's housing problems, showing greater sensitivity to the problems of low-income renters and the problems of living in high-crime areas. The high school educated decision-makers, however, were the most optimistic in the entire decision-making community that the elderly's most pressing problems could be solved by providing the elderly with an adequate retirement income.

CONCLUDING OBSERVATIONS ON THE CLIMATE OF DECISION-MAKING IN THE FIELD OF AGING

The reader may feel many questions remain unanswered at this point and the author would be the first to agree. But this has been intended as an exploratory investigation designed to raise more questions than it could answer. It is but one piece of research in an area heretofore little explored--the decision-makers' perceptions on a range of issues in aging and social policy. Decision-makers' planning orientations are an important part of the climate of decision-making in the field of aging, but only a part of the environment that fashions aging policies and programs. This research has made a special effort to portray accurately the complexity of the decision-making environment in the field of aging, but much more research and analysis are required before the many intricacies of the decision-making environment will be properly understood by those seeking to participate in shaping policy outcomes on behalf of the elderly. This book will have accomplished some of its goals if it stimulates others to field research investigations aimed at improving gerontologists' understanding of the climate of decision-making that fashions aging programs and policies.

But the major goal of this book has been to provide information on the perspectives of various subgroups in the decision-making community that could inform the lobbying efforts of the aging organizations and lay and professional advocates seeking to influence policy outcomes in favor of the elderly. It is hoped that they will find information contained in this volume that will aid their advocacy efforts, that will enable them to build bridges where support for their efforts is strong and to lobby effectively where opposition to their goals seems most vigorous. It is in the hands of these protagonists that these data may ultimately have their greatest utility in influencing the existing climate of decision-making in the field of aging. For the ultimate goal of this research has always been to contribute to improving the quality of life for older Americans through the development of more effective strategies of social intervention.

APPENDIX
Research Design and Methodology

AN OVERVIEW OF THE ENTIRE RESEARCH PROJECT

This survey of decision-makers was but one component of a much broader research investigation into aging and social policy. A second phase of the research was a companion survey of middle-aged and older community residents living in metropolitan Los Angeles County. In-depth interviews were conducted with a stratified probability sample of 1,269 county residents in order to discover how growing old was similar or different for men and women, for well-to-do versus impoverished individuals, and for white as opposed to minority persons--all living in the same locale.

A third and somewhat more independent component of the research project involved a number of anthropological investigations of aging within a wide variety of cultural contexts. Mexican Americans living in an East Los Angeles barrio and Mexicans living in the valley surrounding Mexico City were studied by two Mexican American anthropologists. A colony of Yugoslav immigrants and descendants living in the San Francisco area was studied by an anthropologist of similar ancestry, who traveled as well to Yugoslavia to observe the rituals of aging in the native country. Additional anthropological investigations of aging were conducted in peasant villages in Tanzania, Africa, and in a rundown suburban neighborhood of Los Angeles (Venice), where several subcultures coexist in poverty, including one of aged East European Jews. The anthropologists' research findings are described in two books: *Life's Career--Aging: Cross-Cultural Studies in Growing Old*, edited by Barbara G. Myerhoff and Andrei Simic; and *The Divided Cloak: Growing Old in an Urban Jewish Community* by Barbara G. Myerhoff. The community survey responses similarly have been analyzed independently and are reported in a separate monograph entitled *Black, Brown, White, Old: Styles of Aging* by Pauline K. Ragan (available from the National Science Foundation, grant no. APR 21178).

A particularly close relationship existed between the decision-maker and community resident surveys in both design and implementation. To appreciate fully the comparisons to be made between the decision-makers' and the community residents' responses to queries about the problems of growing old and the adequacy of social programs to redress those problems, the reader should understand something about the explicit interdigitation of these two studies, and in particular, how that interdigitation affected the design of the decision-maker survey.

DESIGNING THE DECISION-MAKER SAMPLE: RATIONALE FOR THE STRUCTURE

Theme of Perceptual Congruence

This study of decision-makers was originally designed to complement the survey of Los Angeles County residents aged 45 to 74 who were queried about the problems of growing old. The purpose of conducting the two surveys as companions was to analyze the congruence of the decision-makers' perspectives on the problems of aging and appropriate program interventions with the perceptions of community residents who may be or may become at some point in their later years a recipient of one or more of the various social services available to assist them. The theme of congruence between the two surveys was implemented by restricting sampling of decision-makers to those who had formal jurisdiction over programs and policies affecting older persons who lived in Los Angeles County.

Apart from the effort to achieve some congruence with the companion community survey, the restriction of sampling to decision-makers who had formal jurisdiction over programs operating within the county was necessary to give the study a manageable and coherent framework. Studies of decision-making are typically conducted within a single locale or in some other narrowly defined context. Elite surveys are far more difficult and costly to field than are community or public surveys, and hence the former are often constructed of considerably more limited proportions. An even more critical problem inherent in the design of elite surveys, however, is that the context of decision-making changes character from one locale to another, and even from one issue to the next, and meaningful interpretation or generalization of the findings of the study is precluded if the context of decision-making selected for analysis has been too broadly defined. Similar to most studies of decision-making, then, this study was limited to a group of decision-makers operating in a single locale and concerned with a cluster of overlapping policy issues.

Each of the six subsamples in the decision-maker study reflects this emphasis on interviewing persons who have some official responsibility for developing or implementing programs and policies that impact directly on the lives of middle-aged and older residents of Los Angeles County. In the legislative subsample, either the individual legislator was an elected representative to local, state, or national office who counted aging persons in Los Angeles County among his represented constituency, or the legislator had formal policy-making responsibilities such as committee assignments or chair positions in substantive policy areas where programs impinged rather directly on the well-being of the aged (for example, the aging committees or committees overseeing health care systems or employment/retirement practices).

Within the administrative agency heads and service delivery personnel subsamples, the individuals had to have substantial responsibilities in the management or actual operation of social programs providing assistance to the aging residents of Los Angeles County. In the corporate and union subsamples, only management officials based in Los Angeles County were interviewed. Selecting the largest corporations headquartered in Los Angeles and the largest union locals based in the county ensured that the organizations' employment, retirement, and pension policies had a measurable impact on many employees residing in the county. Finally, in the advocate subsample, the ranking officer was interviewed from each organization that over a two-year period had been identified as lobbying extensively or exclusively in state or local politics on behalf of elderly residents in Los Angeles County.

Channels of Decision-Making Authority

This study was not, however, limited to interviewing local decision-makers. Every effort was made to sample multiply within the channels of formal decision-making authority stretching from local agencies providing important generic or categoric assistance to the elderly up through line state agencies to the initiating federal agencies. Similarly, the role of the legislative body at each level of government--local, state, and national--was represented in the sample.

At the same time, it was important to ensure that the state and federal decision-makers were familiar with the Los Angeles area, because it was the context of decision-making in aging and social policy that had been selected for the study. At the state and federal levels, therefore, decision-makers were selected on the basis of their relatively direct responsibility for and/or involvement in Los Angeles County programs affecting the aged. To illustrate the import of this sampling restriction, the appropriate regional administrators from state and federal agencies who were located in or in close proximity to the Los Angeles area were selected for inclusion in the sample in lieu of the bureaucrat with potentially broader decision-making authority who was positioned in Sacramento or Washington but who was familiar with the Los Angeles context only through reading reports sent forward by the lower level regional administrators who were actually in contact with the programs at the local level.

The final sample of 316 decision-makers was thus distributed as follows: 253, or 80 percent, held positions at the local level; 42, or 13 percent, held positions at the state level; and 21, or 7 percent, held them at the federal level. With emphasis in sample selection on local-level decision-makers and focus in substance on the applicability of social policy for aging residents in the more or less typical urban locale represented by Los Angeles County, this study must be considered timely in light of the probable continuation of revenue sharing. The innovative revenue-sharing grants were instituted by President Nixon in an effort to return greater decision-making power regarding social programs to local-level decision-makers on the premise that they would be in a better position than decision-makers in the state or national capital to identify local needs and to make rational decisions on the funding of social programs to address those needs.

At the same time, however, revenue sharing was initially considered a fad that would end when the Nixon administration vacated Washington, because nearly all assumed that local-level decision-makers would prove too corrupt or irresponsible to make rational decisions about funding social programs for the community's needy. A change in administration was thus expected to signal the end of revenue sharing. Instead, President Ford elected to renew and extend revenue sharing. The power of local decision-makers to decide the fate of social programs at the local level is guaranteed well into the 1980s, and by that time revenue sharing should be fairly well institutionalized in the political process. A study of decision-makers and decision-making in the local context thus appears to have considerable relevance in these historical circumstances.

Formal Position versus Reputational Sampling

Yet another major decision was encountered in designing the sample of decision-makers for this study: whether to select decision-makers on the basis of their formal position or their informal reputation for exercising influence in the decision-making process. The decision-makers were selected for inclusion in this sample on the basis of their formal position of authority in the decision-making process; that is, their position was identified as involved in fashioning social policy for the aging. This decision was founded on a number of reasons. It is the people in these visible, formal positions of authority who are officially charged with the responsibility, and hence are ultimately accountable, for providing social services to elderly residents in the community. Moreover, it is the occupants of these positions of formal authority with whom aging persons in the community would be most likely to have personal contact in the course of applying for or receiving assistance from any of the various social programs.

Many observers of the policy process have argued that the most influential participants in the policy-making process are not necessarily those in such formal positions of decision-making authority; but rather they may be, and often are, persons who operate outside the formal authority structure. Such influential elites, it is argued, can only be identified by informal reputation. Identification of relevant decision-makers on the basis of reputation alone, however, is also open to challenge on grounds of reliability and validity.[1] For example, the list of decision-makers generated on the basis of reputation is likely to differ depending on the specific "knowledgeables" asked to generate the list of reputedly influential decision-makers (different knowledgeables would identify different decision-makers) and on the specific policy issue under consideration (different elites may emerge influential on different issues).

The time and cost of doing a solid reputational study of power and decision-making in Los Angeles County, with its 78 independent municipalities, not to mention in the state and national capitals, as a prelude to selecting the sample of influential decision-makers to be interviewed in this study of aging and social policy were, of course, prohibitive. No such reputational-design studies were even available from earlier research to use for reference. For the sake of budget and convenience, then, the decision was ultimately made to sample decision-makers on the basis of their formal position in the policy process.

The research staff was very satisfied that the representativeness of the decision-making community that fashions aging social programs was reflected in the final sample design. Statistical representativeness of the entire population of decision-makers whose decisions impact on the myriad social programs affecting middle-aged and older persons is not implied here; such a study would undoubtedly be impossible to design and perform. Nevertheless, the staff is confident that the sample of 316 decision-makers captures much of the diversity of the policy-making climate that shapes aging programs that are currently operative in metropolitan Los Angeles County.

The final sample of 316 closely matched the specifications of the original sample design. Response rates for the six subsamples ranged from 56.8 percent in the legislative group to nearly 90 percent in the advocate sample (see Table A.1). Table A.2 details the interview completions in the legislative subsample, where the completion rates were the lowest. The reader can thus see how under even the most unfavorable circumstances encountered during conduct of the research, the final sample still reflects the specifications of the initial sample design.

CONSTRUCTION OF THE INTERVIEW SCHEDULE

A debate waged over whether the items in the interview should be open or closed-ended. Closed-ended items might prevent the decision-maker from adequately expressing his own point of view; on the other hand, a largely open-ended interview would prove difficult to analyze and would endanger comparability of responses to specific items across the various subsamples of decision-makers. In the end, a compromise was effected. The majority of items (67 percent) in the interview schedule was closed-ended in format to allow for comparison of responses across the subsamples, but decision-makers were periodically encouraged to elaborate on their responses. Interviewers were further instructed to record verbatim all comments offered by the respondent during the course of the interview, and ample space was left on the interview schedule to note all of the respondent's spontaneous comments and elaborations.

That the average length of the completed interviews was 1 hour and 40 minutes, one third longer than the projected length, suggests the decision-makers were eager to expound on their answers. Although the initial intent of the researchers was to incorporate carefully the verbatim comments into data analysis, most often the decision-maker's additional remarks did not clarify or elaborate, but merely repeated or reaffirmed his short answer. The verbatim comments thus added little information to the subsequent analysis of the data, but they did function usefully in permitting the decision-maker to answer the question fully to his own personal satisfaction. In this way, the procedure of eliciting elaboration on responses prevented the respondents from feeling constrained and ultimately alienated by questions that they believed allowed them too little freedom to respond as they desired.

TABLE A.1

Interview Response Rates

Reason for Incompleted Interview	Decision-makers' Position in the Policy Process						
	Legislators	Administrative Agency Heads	Service Delivery Personnel	Corporate Directors of Personnel	Union Local Presidents	Advocates for the Aged	Total
Refusal--no reason given	23	6	3	5	8	--	45
Refusal--too busy	6	--	--	3	--	--	9
"Runaround"--no refusal but unable to set up appointment	6	--	--	--	--	--	6
No longer in office position	4	4	4	--	2	3	17
Unable to locate	4	--	--	--	--	1	5
Failed to keep appointments	3	--	--	--	--	--	3
Unavailable--out of the county	3	--	1	--	1	--	5
Unavailable--due to illness	1	--	--	--	1	--	2
Too busy--give only restricted time for interview (for example, 15 to 30 minutes)	1	--	--	--	--	--	1
Terminated	2	1	--	1	--	--	4
Ineligible according to sampling criterion	1	1	1	--	--	--	3
A. Refusals and incompletions	54	12	9	9	12	4	100
B. Completed sample size	71	70	70	35	35	35	316
C. Response rate (A/A+B) (percent)	56.8	85.4	88.6	79.5	74.5	89.7	80.0

Source: Compiled by the author.

TABLE A.2

Decision-Makers Identified as Eligible and Actually Interviewed in the Decision-Maker Survey

Subsample	Formal Position	Number Identified as Eligible	Number Originally to Be Interviewed	Number Actually Interviewed
Elected officials/local level	Los Angeles County Board of Supervisors	5	4	3
	Mayors and city councilmen of the five largest cities in Los Angeles County:			
	Los Angeles	16	8	8
	Long Beach	9	5	5
	Torrance	7	3	3
	Glendale	5	3	4
	Pasadena	7	3	4
Elected officials/state level	State assembly representatives from Los Angeles County (four overlap with the list of eligible committee chairmen in the state legislature listed below)	28	14	16

	State senate representatives from Los Angeles County (two overlap with the list of eligible committee chairmen in the state legislature listed below)	13	6	5
	Joint Committee on Aging in the State Legislature	6	6	3
	Chairmen of selected committees in the state legislature (four overlap with the list of state assembly representatives and two overlap with the list of state senate representatives)	22	10	12
Elected officials/national level	U.S. senators elected from Los Angeles County	2	1	0
	U.S. representatives elected from Los Angeles County	16	8	8

Source: Compiled by the author.

DATA REDUCTION: INTERCODER RELIABILITY

The UCLA Institute for Social Research was responsible for data collection (conducting the interviews using specially trained elite interviewers) and data reduction (coding the interview responses and preparing a clean computer tape containing the data). Because much of the interview consisted of fixed-alternative items, much of the coding consisted merely of transcribing the code number of the responses on the questionnaires to the computer tape. Approximately one third of the questionnaire, however, consisted of open-ended items that elicited unstructured responses from the decision-makers. The ultimate test of the quality of the open-ended data analyzed from these decision-maker interviews depends upon the coder reliability or intercoder consistency in applying coding schemes to the open-ended responses in the interviews.

The UCLA Institute for Social Research provided estimates of the coder reliability in this study based on an adaptation of a measure of intercoder consistency for categorical data developed by Kathleen S. Crittenden and Richard J. Hill.[2] The measure reports the percent agreement among coders on their choice of a code category for any given item. The general formula for coder reliability (R) is:

$$R = \frac{Dmax - Do}{Dmax} = 1 - \frac{Do}{Dmax}$$

where Dmax is the maximum number of coder disagreements possible on any one question and Do is the observed to actual coder disagreements on the question. When all coders are perfectly consistent in choosing a code category for a particular item, R has a value of 1.0; when there is maximum inconsistency among the coders, R has a value of 0.0. Reliability scores computed by this method are to be interpreted as the percent agreement among the coders rather than as traditional intercorrelation coefficients, which would not be appropriate for categoric data. Thus R = .66 would mean the coders agreed in their choice of a code category about 66 percent of the time.

UCLA conducted a reliability study based on 25 open-ended questions containing 71 different responses or items in a sample of 35 interviews. Four trained coders participated in the reliability study. The coder reliability in the decision-maker study ranged from .50 to 1.00 with an overall reliability computed across all 71 items for all 35 cases of .73. In other words, the four coders agreed in their choice of a code category about 73 percent of the time. The coder reliability scores for separate questions are presented in Table A.3.

TABLE A.3

Coder Reliability Scores for Individual Questions in the Decision-Maker Interview

Question in the Survey	Coder Reliability
What are the three major problems facing people living in Los Angeles County who are 65 years of age or older?	.77
What are the three major problems older people face in getting the medical care they need?	.73
Why do you think physicians are reluctant to treat the elderly?	.85
If medicare coverage were expanded, what kinds of coverage do you think it would be most important to add?	.66
If a medical breakthrough came in 30 years to extend average life expectancy, what problems do you think this might create for American society?	.67
What are the three major obstacles preventing older people from getting around Los Angeles as they might like to?	.74
Considering the problems older people have getting around Los Angeles, what do you see as the most practical solution?	.66
What are the three most pressing housing problems faced by older persons living in Los Angeles County?	.82
Considering the housing problems facing older persons, what do you see as the most practical solution?	.69

TABLE A.3 (Continued)

Question in the Survey	Coder Reliability
How might the negative attitudes toward old age be changed?	.68
What obstacles do you see to employing more older persons?	.73
What can be done to change the obstacles to hiring older people?	.72
Many people are poor for the first time in their lives when they retire on inadequate incomes. How can this situation be changed for future retirees?	.63
Why don't more companies offer retirement preparation programs?	.79
What kinds of issues do you think would make older persons organize politically?	.82
Why do you feel that White House Conferences on Aging do/do not result in better programs for older people?	.65
How could lobbyists for the elderly become more effective?	.71

Source: Compiled by the author.

The complex task of coding open-ended responses in a survey of elites is reflected in the wide range of reliability estimates that were obtained across the 71 separate items. Coding frames were unusually long in order to retain subtleties in the decision-makers' responses to the questions; but the greater the number of categories in the coding frame, the greater the number of disagreements among the coders in this reliability study ($r = .66$, $p < .01$). Additionally, a problem typical of elite studies such as this one is that many responses often involve a level of conceptual technicality that can be difficult for coders inexperienced with the complex concepts to interpret. In the briefing sessions, for example, the USC researchers often had to instruct the UCLA coders on the operation of private pensions, social security, or medicare so that the coders could interpret decision-makers' comments about the operation of these systems.

Despite these problems, the coder reliabilities obtained in the decision-maker survey are sufficiently high (more than 42 of 71 items, or 60 percent, had a reliability score of .70 or above) to warrant a reasonable degree of confidence in the findings presented from the survey.

NOTES

1. Now classic discussions of the issues in reputation versus position sampling in studies of decision-making can be found in the following books and articles: John Walton, "Discipline, Method and Community Power: A Note on the Sociology of Knowledge," American Sociological Review 31, no. 5 (October 1966): 684-89; Robert A. Dahl, Who Governs? Democracy and Power in an American City (New Haven, Conn.: Yale University Press, 1961); Nelson W. Polsby, "How to Study Community Power: The Pluralist Alternative," Journal of Politics 22, no. 3 (August 1960): 474-84; Robert O. Schulze and Leonard Blumberg, "The Determination of Local Power Elites," American Journal of Sociology 63, no. 3 (November 1957): 290-96; Charles Bonjean and David M. Olson, "Community Leadership: Directions of Research," Administrative Science Quarterly 9, no. 4 (December 1964): 278-300; Thomas J. Anton, "Power Pluralism and Local Politics," Administrative Science Quarterly 7, no. 1 (March 1963): 425-57; Floyd Hunter, Community Power Structure (Chapel Hill: University of North Carolina Press, 1953).

2. Kathleen S. Crittenden and Richard J. Hill, "Coding Reliability and Validity of Interview Data," American Sociological Review 36, no. 6 (December 1971): 1073-80.

ABOUT THE AUTHOR

PATRICIA L. KASSCHAU was Project Director for this study of Aging and Social Policy while at the Gerontology Center, University of Southern California. Previously, she was a Resident in Law and Social Science, Russel Sage Foundation, a Senior Fulbright Lecturer at the Instituto Sedes Sapientiae, Brazil, and consultant to the RAND corporation.

Dr. Kasschau has contributed to several books and journals in sociology and gerontology, and received a Ph. D in Sociology from the University of Southern California in 1972. She is currently completing work for a J. D degree.

RELATED TITLES

Published by Praeger Special Studies

*THE AGED IN THE COMMUNITY: Managing Senility and Deviance

Dwight Frankfather

HOUSING AND SOCIAL SERVICES FOR THE ELDERLY: Social Policy Trends

Elizabeth D. Huttman

COORDINATING SOCIAL SERVICES: An Analysis of Community, Organizational, and Staff Characteristics

Neil Gilbert and Harry Specht

PUBLIC POLICY TOWARD DISABILITY

Monroe Berkowitz, William G. Johnson, and Edward H. Murphy

THE CYCLE OF VIOLENCE: Assertive, Aggressive, and Abusive Family Interaction

Suzanne K. Steinmetz

*Also available in paperback.